THE CASE FOR PENAL ABOLITION

Edited by
W. Gordon West
and
Ruth Morris

Canadian Scholars' Press Inc.   Toronto   2000

THE CASE FOR PENAL ABOLITION
edited by W. Gordon West and Ruth Morris

First published in 2000 by
Canadian Scholars' Press Inc.
180 Bloor Street West, Suite 1202
Toronto, Ontario
M5S 2V6

CSPI acknowledges the financial support of the Government of Canada through the Book Publishing Industry Development Programme for our publishing activities.

CANADIAN CATALOGUING IN PUBLICATION DATA

Main entry under title:

The case for penal abolition

Includes bibliographical references.
ISBN 1-55130-147-4

1. Criminal justice, Administration of. 2. Punishment – Philosophy. 3. Imprisonment. 4. Alternatives to imprisonment. I. West, W. Gordon, 1945- . II. Morris, Ruth, 1933- .

HV8665.C37 2000   364.6   C00-930935-7

Managing Editor: Ruth Bradley-St-Cyr
Marketing Manager: Susan Cuk
Copy Editor: Gerry Biederman
Production Editors: Linda Bissinger, Trish O'Reilly
Page layout: Brad Horning
Cover image and design: Amy Seagram

00   01   02   03   04   05   06   6   5   4   3   2   1

Printed and bound in Canada by AGMV Marquis

Contents

PART 1

INTRODUCTION: ABOLITION AS A HOPEFUL CRITIQUE OF PENALITY

1

Introduction to the Case for Penal Abolition

W. Gordon West and Ruth Morris

The degree of civilization in a society can be judged by entering its prisons.
—Dostoevski

Our introduction to this collection of powerful and informative papers intends to provide an orientation both to those readers new to issues of penal abolition, and those scholars working in the area.

The contemporary movement to abolish prisons is as old as modern prisons themselves. In the 19ᵗʰ century, voices like Thomas Buxton of the British Parliament and Victor Hugo of France condemned the prison system and retributive justice. In 1976 Gilbert Cantor, a former editor of the Philadelphia Bar magazine, wrote in that prestigious magazine: "If our entire criminal justice apparatus were simply closed down... there would probably be a decrease in the amount of behaviour now labeled "criminal." The time has come to abolish the game of crime and punishment, and to substitute a paradigm of restitution and responsibility. The goal is the civilization of our treatment of offenders (Morris, 1997).

ICOPA (The International Conference On Penal Abolition) is a worldwide movement to challenge existing revenge approaches to criminal justice, and to

3

seek healing for all: victims, offenders, their families and wider communities. ICOPA was founded in 1983 by the Quaker Committee on Jails and Justice, a Toronto group dedicated to prison abolition.

In 1987 ICOPA broadened its goal to *penal* abolition, because if prisons alone are abolished but revenge remains the central goal, equally unacceptable and offensive results will result. So, initially, we want to note that we are concerned with *penal* abolition, not simply "prison" abolition. By the term *"penal* abolition," we signal not only our concern with abolishing prisons as physical environments for caging human beings as we cage animals, but we also signal our commitment to transforming our societies' notions and approaches to human conflicts and wrong-doings, questioning their bases on "legalized" vengeance. Instead we advocate the possibilities of healing justice.

ICOPA challenges the roots of a revenge-oriented system that pretends to deal with crime while in reality reinforcing the barriers between social classes, races, genders, and ages. We believe that "restorative" justice alone can easily become a trap within the present penal system: attempting to balance wrongs and rights on an imaginary scale of justice, often seeking to provide a "restoration" to a pre-existing justice which never actually existed. Instead, we seek a *transformative* or *healing justice*, which will take crime as an opportunity to get to root causes and transform them, bringing power to the community and healing to victims and offenders alike.

Contemporary penal abolition movements such as ICOPA have many deep roots: some based primarily on religious or faith convictions, some based on searing historical experiences, others based on pragmatic social science-research, and some arise from radical critiques of our conceptions of *penality* itself!

ᴍ SOME FAITH FOUNDATIONS

Many of our notions of crime, criminality, punishment and penality go back to Greek and Biblical texts which gave us the language of our societies' legal foundations. For instance, Plato's depiction of Socrates indicates that this greatest of philosophers was centrally concerned with seeking the meaning of "justice," a search profoundly human and spiritual as well as logical. We will return to this partly spiritual tradition in the next section.

More self-evidently spiritual, there are the stern indictments of the Ten Commandments and the many rules constructed to implement them. There is also much evidence in the Old Testament of the frequent savage punishments wrought by a sometimes vengeful God. In contrast, there are also roots of liberation theology in the Old Testament shared by Jews, Muslims, and Christians alike. Regular years of Jubilee were to be celebrated by forgiveness of debts and by freeing prisoners: "proclaiming liberty throughout the land" (Leviticus 25:10). The outrage of the later prophets against social injustices and official or "corporate exploitation" also indicates a concern for a truer justice than that operating under the existing legal system:

> *The LORD says to them, "The truth is that at the same time as you fast, you pursue your own interests and oppress your workers.... The kind of fasting I want is this: Remove the chains of oppression and the yoke of injustice, and let the oppressed go free.... If you put an end to oppression, to every gesture of contempt, and to every evil word; if you give food to the hungry and satisfy those who are in need, then the darkness around you will turn to the brightness of noon (Isaiah, 58: 3, 6, 9-10).*

And, of course, there are numerous very straightforward texts in the New Testament, for instance:

> *I was hungry but you would not feed me, thirsty, but you would not give me a drink; I was a stranger but you would not welcome me in your homes, naked but you would not clothe me; I was sick and in prison but you would not take care of me. Then they will answer him, "When Lord, did we ever see you hungry or thirsty or a stranger or naked or sick or in prison, and would not help you?" The King will reply, "I tell you, whenever you refused to help one of these least important ones, you refused to help me (Matthew 25:42-45).*

Every Christian community or movement has at various historical times raised serious questions about existing revenge-based penality, having often directly experienced imprisonment with petty street criminals! The Society of Friends ("Quakers") not only are universally credited with inventing the "Pennsylvania system" of isolated contemplation, at the birth of the modern prison system, but have been very active in criticizing it ever since! Indeed the contemporary penal abolition movement in the United States and Canada has evolved from these faith roots.

More recently, revival of indigenous traditions, not only politically and socially, but also linguistically and spiritually, has provided another spiritual basis for questioning penality. An interesting discussion has appeared lately on the internet under the title: "Return of the Heart, We the Coltaywanej: Justice and Community Reconciliation in the Indigenous Tradition" (see http://www.interlog.com/~ritten/icopa/news.htm). The consideration and occasional incorporation of indigenous healing justice traditions has occurred not only in North America (e.g., justice healing circles), but also in many other historically colonized areas (e.g., New Zealand's Maori-inspired family conferencing).

It is clear also that ordinary citizens throughout the world have an increasing concern and a sense of moral unease (if not outright disdain) for contemporary penal systems in their failure to address issues of morality and meaning. This is manifested weekly if not daily in riots and uprisings against formally legal penal decisions, some protests contained, some leading to revolutions. It is impossible to list all those wrongfully convicted and imprisoned, but names such as Gandi, King, Ortega, Walesa, Havel, and Mandela are indicative of many later vindicated by history as 20th century heroes of justice struggles.

The wider population has developed both an inordinate and unrealistic fear of crime, and a sense of moral unease. While some of this is, without a doubt, connected to sensationalist mass media over-portrayals of danger, often manipulated for political purposes, some major concerns arise from the cold legal formality of *penality* failing to address concerns of very real human victims of wrongdoing.

Unfortunately, other than in a few demonstration projects, imprisonment and penality have remained unanswerable to moral, ethical and faith concerns, remaining under the control of state and professional powers lacking effective community control, or moral resolution. These practices have been systematically utilized by the rich and powerful to oppress the poor and weak on a global scale, developing continuing outrage about injustices!

⋔ SOCIAL SCIENCE RESEARCH: THE BANKRUPTCY OF WESTERN PENOLOGY

A second strand of penal abolition comes from within a major aspect of professional penology itself: professional social research clearly has demonstrated that penality is a failure in its own terms, for each of its professed goals!

The classic Greek heritage of seeking "the just" has been repeatedly mined and re-mined throughout western philosophical thought, from Boethius through Augustine, St. Thomas, and later through Hobbes, Locke, Hume, Mill, Russell and Wittgenstein among "empiricists," and Descartes, Rousseau, Voltaire, Compte, and Sartre among "rationalists." Such formal logic, combined with inspiration from, the success of scientific discovery and technological achievements in the physical sciences has birthed an enormous institutionalized effort in the social sciences. Basically, if we can engineer successful bridges, should we not be able to engineer crime-free societies, by scientifically identifying, treating and correcting all criminals?

Unfortunately, from its inception, penology has accepted state policies and subsidies, compromised its claim to intellectual objectivity throughout its history, and remains a beggared, regularly violated handmaiden to the state. Penalization, and especially imprisonment, continues to be justified on some five "principles" or "objectives":

1. **Justice**: meaning vengeance and retribution based on Old Testament notions of "an eye for an eye," etc.
2. **Protection of Society/Detainment of the Truly Harmful**
3. **General Deterrence:** severe punishment will deter others who are tempted.
4. **Individual Deterrence**: Severe punishment will deter the individual offender.
5. **Rehabilitation**: Penalization and imprisonment will provide an opportunity to "correct" offenders by, for instance, providing job training, or anger management courses.

Unfortunately, contemporary penalization practices *fail* on every point! The penological literature (summarized for instance in Knopp et al., 1976; Cohen, 1992) demonstrates this failure. In reverse order:

5. Imprisonment and contact with the penal justice system *impairs* inmates in ever becoming "productive members of society"; rather, it locks them into a cycle of re-offending. Penalization and imprisonment do not *re*-habilitate, they *dis*-habilitate!
4. Attempting to deter individual adults by state inflicted violence works no better than does familial use of violence with children:

7

offenders themselves become victims, angry and vengeful. That is why Corrections Services Canada now spends so much effort in "anger management programs": it has to undo the anger that *it itself has created*—of course, without acknowledging its own guilt!

3. For most crimes, the chances of even being caught, even for the most serious crimes are so low as to be negligible, so notions of general deterrence have very weak empirical and rational support. Crime is not controlled by some magisterial display of vengeful authority, nor by augmented police force, but by a coherent community of social control, which makes available healthy non-criminal activities. Morally, how can one justify harsh treatment for those unlucky enough to be caught as a "pre-emptive punishment" for others?

2. Admittedly, there are a few very dangerous persons in all societies but they are much under 10% of those presently incarcerated. It's irrational—*and insanely expensive*—to treat the other ninety per cent as equally dangerous! Most of this ninety per cent are incarcerated for property or drug crimes. In these cases, other solutions, such as treating the roots of their problems of poverty and addiction, would be much more sensible and cost effective than incarceration. Furthermore, almost all those incarcerated will be released back into society—but probably *more* dangerous than when they were first incarcerated—unless serious targeted treatment programs are inaugurated, in settings less damaging.

1. Serious interpersonal harm has *not* been successfully "reconciled" by *vengeful* state penal intervention. The murder of a loved one cannot miraculously be granted "closure" by a conviction. These are moral issues beyond human capacities in a formal sense. Relying upon Old Testament authorized state vengeance has not satisfied anyone— no more in 2000 than it did in 32 AD when the carpenter from Nazareth questioned its inadequacy (Crossan, 1995).

Quite simply, penality (not only in the practice of penalization, but also penal research, penal theory, and penal philosophy) is revealed by its own research both to be a failure—and a *sham*! Restated, our present system of penal justice is not only NOT working, it is systematically achieving the direct opposite of its stated goals. It is a house of cards, an emperor without clothes, maintained only by its own injustices and cover-ups. It has become a gargantuan machine, composed of media clips, police departments, law schools, professional associations, our judiciary, our criminological research efforts, and our penal systems, treatment cages and state death chambers. This machine, once set in motion, exists primarily to feed itself, growing hungrier by the year. Most amazingly, it is *we* who have institutionalized this irrational system of internal state terrorism, directed at all citizens—and at ourselves!

Unfortunately, other than in a few "demonstration projects," while remaining under control of state powers without effective community control, imprisonment and penality have remained systematically utilized by the rich and powerful to oppress the poor and weak on a global scale. On their own terms and goals, penal policies and practices are a dismal universal failure without realistic hope of redemption through additional social research or "corrections"!

🏛 TWENTIETH CENTURY EXPERIENCES OF PENALITY: TOTALITARIANISM, HOLOCAUST, GENOCIDE—AND BEYOND

Our "classic heritage" of Greek and Roman thought centres upon a search for "Justice," "The Good," and "The True." Plato's dialogues and especially his *Republic* centre on constructing a "rational-legal" just society—a quest which remains as vibrant today as then. Unfortunately, historically, this grand intellectual rational-legal quest for justice has spawned rationalisations for totalitarianism as often as for democratic justice!

It is crucial to note that the incorporation of strict Greek logic into Roman law provided a tradition that has dominated Western jurisprudence from ancient times to the present. The genius of the Roman legal empire was its provision of "Pax Romana": a stable "universal" administrative and tax structure, a common language, and—crucially—a standard legal code, which allowed for an empire-wide administrative structure. Yet this penal-justice model which we still admire so much was based on slave labour, an often brutally efficient military dictatorship, and grounded in engineering advancements financed by an efficient administrative exploitation of colonial resources of the empire!

This Roman "legal genius" has inspired contemporary Western legal systems to develop legal codes that are logical and rational, but also open to evolution to meet changing circumstances and needs. (There are certainly major differences between "continental" and "common law" systems, but they need not concern our general argument here.) If such a legal administration worked so well for the Romans in establishing an exploitative empire, why not for the later Spanish, French, German, British, and American empires? While the exploitative and unjust aspects of such legal regimes continuously plagued various succeeding European empires and repeated colonial revolts, excuses concerning inadequate development, trained personnel, resources, *et cetera* have always been made.

From the perspective of Western European civilization, the major military/ political events of the past century certainly have been a major influence on the movement for abolishing penality. This has been a century of uninterrupted military struggle between contending nation states and economic blocks seeking imperial domination of the globe. Two horrendous world wars, and a half century of unofficial "cold war" between superpowers (sustained via very hot wars throughout the rest of the world) leaving millions of people dead, maimed, homeless, destitute and displaced. Throughout these struggles, the state apparatus of penality has been used as a means of control and domination. In other words, the supposed "neutrality" of legality has systematically been undermined to further state and private corporate interests.

The most horrendous and flagrant examples, of course, have been the Soviet and especially the Nazi twisting of legality into the service of state needs, whereby *anyone* could be detained without adequate protections as a state security risk. Nils Christie once remarked that the Nazi occupiers of Norway didn't need to change anything in the existing criminal law (other than invoking a "war measures act" which all "we" Western liberal democracies had also). They simply arrested anyone they didn't like, and then successfully found some basis in law for imprisonment. Since everyone commits some legal infraction at some point, everyone is liable to prosecution. So much for humane justice under strict Greek logic and Roman codes.

But the so-called Western democracies fell prey to very similar aggressive extensions of state power, from the deportations and imprisonment of East European-derived union organizers during the First World War, to the horrendous racist treatment of Japanese-, German-, and Italian-descended citizens in Canada during the Second.

The experience of the Western European judicial, academic, and cultural elites under Nazi occupation lead to a strong revulsion to arbitrary imprisonment for the half century following the Holocaust. In Western European Nazi-occupied countries imprisonment rates have been consistently a third to a half of those in non-occupied Western liberal democracies. That experience has at least until lately been a primary motivator to restrict the use of penality and especially imprisonment to contain only the most obviously dangerous, and to use short sentences with a rehabilitative approach. Western European scholars such Louk Holsman, Thomas Mathiesen, Nils Christie, and Herman Bianchi (all themselves personal victims of the shortcomings of the Western legal tradition) have documented these issues and struggles concerning legalization of penality, and are inspirations to many of the papers in this volume.

Coincident with these searing historical experiences, which revealed the brittle artificiality of relying simply upon logical legal codes without a political and social culture to realize their claims of administering humane justice, an international movement for human rights has arisen. The need for such universal claims to establish an international legal system arose not only to provide a framework for relations between nation states, but also to provide some legitimacy for the immediate need to exact revenge on Nazi mass murders who had acted within the law of Germany. The initial UN Human Rights declaration, largely drafted by a Canadian, included not only civil and political rights, but also economic and social ones.

Unfortunately, after the Nuremberg trials of Nazis and Nazi collaborators, during the entire half-century of the Cold War, the International Declaration ceased to be further used, in large part because the contending empires were its major violators. The agonies of Central America, the Balkans, and the Caucasus region continue to haunt us. Logically sound, Greek and Roman inspired law statutes and human rights codes remain vacuous without a social context, and the effective power of enforcement. While the revived International Court in the Hague has taken some actions to prosecute individual perpetrators of horrendous human rights violations, it remains totally uninspired, unfunded, and unwilling to consider seriously prosecuting war crimes committed by the victors! *That* would amount to biting the hands that feed it: *Western capitalist* powers!

It is in these senses that issues of *penality* and *penal abolition* not only reflect but are centrally implicated in the crises of contemporary civilization throughout our globe: crises which are not only spiritual and personal, but also intellectual and institutional, historical and political.

Unfortunately, other than in a few show trials, imprisonment and penality have remained under the control of state powers without implementation of human rights, nor effective community control. Penality has been systematically utilized by the rich and powerful nations to oppress the poor and weak on a global scale.

🏛 NEW QUESTIONS, NEW ANSWERS! THE NEED FOR A TRANSFORMATIVE JUSTICE

While recognizing these abolitionist roots in faith communities, social research, and historical experiences, the contemporary movement for penal abolition embodied in the biannual ICOPA conferences and this particular collection strive to move beyond traditional issues that focus on the inadequacies of individual state penal sanctions concerning particular individuals.

We do indeed acknowledge our roots, and need to continue addressing "traditional" penal abolition issues raised in contemporary societies by so-called "street-crime." And new questions have arisen in this area, with the identification of various systemic injustices perpetrated by the powerful against women, children, minorities, etc. Often these systemic injustices are intertwined (e.g., regarding child abuse in government run church schools for First Nations Canadians). They remain as complicated issues needing serious attention by those who advocate penal abolition.

But it is increasingly clear that *harm* is inflicted upon people much more by *corporations* and *nation states* rather than by *individuals*. Most of these corporate entities are based in the wealthy north/western countries, most are highly tied into the political system and have systemically avoided being penalized for their activities, even when murderous.

Given the failure of penality in addressing individual (traditional, "street") crime, how should penal abolitionists respond to corporate (new, "suite") crime? Abolitionists have traditionally opposed increased control. Should they now consider increased control for these new kinds of criminality?

These are new questions, which require new answers. It is in this sense that we in ICOPA call for a *transformative justice*, not simply a restorative justice, nor simply a healing justice.

ṁ THIS COLLECTION

The papers in this collection are a mix of recent previously published and unpublished essays. While the authors come from all of the abolitionist perspectives outlined above, and may have considerable respect for each other, they do not always agree. Abolition of penality remains a debate even within the community of penal abolitionists. Nonetheless, we have managed to group the papers into a few major themes, which reflect contemporary abolition debates.

In this introductory section, Viviane Saleh-Hanna provides a much broader introduction to concepts, research, and politics of penal abolition. Ruth Morris follows that with a short history of ICOPA as a specific penal abolition movement, and Gordon West provides a more academic penological *problematique* of conceptual terms useful for not only understanding and identifying issues in the remaining papers, but also a set of terms useful for further inquiry

Following this, our authors seek to identify and address "traditional" abolition issues regarding penality. How could penalization of "street criminality" be abolished? A discussion of such traditional issues is essential not only to remind us of our roots, but also to introduce others to the shocking facts of penality and its injustices. John Clarke's paper "Serve the Rich and Punish the Poor" makes the centuries-old case about class oppression by penality. While he provides information on the medieval origins of contemporary prisons, he centres his discussion on a contemporary context: Toronto, declared by various UN studies to be one of the desirable places in the world to live. Marc Mauer, in "The Race to Incarcerate" expands this argument about class oppression into race, revealing the incorporation of racism into American imprisonment. Ruth Morris follows this with a classic abolition paper, addressing a key issue: "But What About the Dangerous Few?" Finally, Laureen Snider, in "Towards Safer Societies: Punishment, Masculinities, and Violence Against Women" raises crucial abolition issues in regard to the call from some seemingly progressive groups such as feminists concerned with spousal assault, who call for more incarceration and penality. These papers not only cover the traditional gamut of issues regarding penal abolition for street crime, they raise new issues, and provide new suggestions for questions.

In our next major section, the authors turn the focus from traditional penal abolition issues from "street crime" to "suite crime." With the increasing recognition of corporate crime being far more dangerous and harmful than traditional street crime, under what circumstances *could* penalization of "suite criminality" be abolished? Philosopher John McMurtry meticulously dissects traditional defences of penality, and formally introduces issues of corporate criminality calling for increased sanctioning. Laureen Snider comments that we have already "abolished corporate crime" by not enforcing regulations! Frank Pearce and Steve Tombs, from an international perspective, follow this with a detailed consideration of issues regarding the possibilities of increased regulation of corporations, arguing that at least some to the traditional goals of penality might be more likely realized in regard to corporate crime. Morris follows this with a faith-based call for reconciliation.

Our final substantive section on "Critique and Hope: New Questions, New Directions" tries to address issues arising from the previous sections. Lisa Finateri and Viviane Saleh-Hanna not only provide a reflective recounting of efforts towards abolition by such organizations as ICOPA, but also offer a number of criticisms regarding our past efforts, and suggestions for future directions. From the USA, Hal Pepinsky suggests some new directions (spiritual, political, and practical) in his paper. Father Jim Consedine, from New Zealand, in "Towards a Theology of Transformative Justice," revives spiritual issues with a listing of practical alternatives. David Moore, Australia, describes the principles and operations of their "Community Conferencing" programs as a "supply side contribution to prison abolition." Finally, we end with some inspirational words from Thomas Mathiesen, from Norway, "Towards the 21st Century: Abolition — An Impossible Dream?"

In the short Afterword, Ruth Morris and Gord West make reference again to spiritual roots as providing guidance.

In addition to continuing the rich discussions on issues of penal abolition regarding traditional street crime, this volume seeks to introduce some aspects of key connections between the penal system and the "new" corporate agendas; between corporate crime and incarceration rates pathologically growing around the world, locking up more and more of the unemployed, unhoused, uncared for, and marginalized. No previous collection has focused so explicitly on how the *penal system* and this *corporate agenda* serve each other, while violating community, justice, and reconciliation. In so doing, we hope to widen the reach of ICOPA and strengthen alliances between those interested in both issues, in the on-going struggle against various forces which are threatening the future of our lives, our communities, and our world.

It is in these senses that issues of *penality* and *penal abolition* not only reflect but are centrally implicated in the crises of contemporary civilization: crises

14

which are not only spiritual and personal, but also intellectual and institutional, historical and political. Only through addressing issues towards a *transformative justice* addressing contemporary crises in progressive directions will "crime problems" be resolved to produce a more just society.

REFERENCES

S. Cohen, *Against Criminology,* Englewood Cliffs, New Jersey: Transaction, 1992.

J. D. Crossan, *Jesus: A Revolutionary Biography*, New York: HarperCollins, 1994.

F.H. Knopp, and others, *Instead of Prisons: A Handbook for Abolitionists.* Syracuse, NY, USA: Prison Research Education Project, 1976.

R. Morris, "But What About the Dangerous Few?" Toronto: Rittenhouse, 1994.

2

Critiquing The Globalization of Penality and Imprisonment: Conceptualizing Penal Abolition Globally

W. Gordon West

In this introduction to theoretical roots of abolition, I seek to identify and outline a *problematique* (a set of concepts, identifying and relating issues) which are useful for abolitionists—and used (often unstated) throughout this volume. This is needed for abolitionists to conceptually challenge penologists. (Unfortunately, penologists presently dominate public, policy and research discussion concerning crime and social reconciliation.)

I can illustrate the importance of how a conceptual *problematique* relates to our research, political, and practical activities very quickly: The latest annual conference of The American Society of Criminology was thematically entitled: "Explaining and Preventing Crime: The Globalization of Knowledge." In one paper, Jock Young once again effectively trashed the still dominant yet intellectually indefensible notions of positivist (American) criminology, which argues that we can simply "explain" in a natural science sense, the "causes" of "crime." Such a penological *problematique* assumes that "crime" and its "causes" are akin to physical objects, easily identifiable, able to be isolated, and manipulated, like stresses and strains on bridges. Other papers (e.g., West, 1999) questioned any easy acceptance of "globalization" as a glib term averting attention

Revised from "Towards a Global Criminal Justice Problematic" in *The Journal of Human Justice*, Vol. 1, No. 1 (1989), pp. 99-112.

from the Americanization of mass media, including internet social science transmissions (which rely upon programs ninety percent of which are US developed). The danger of such presumed globalization of knowledge is that corporate imperialist technology will be used to convey American solutions concerning crime and justice to the entire world.

There might be some claim to the appropriateness of such communication and emulation if one were talking of business success, or technological invention: America has clearly lead the world in the past century. But in the area of crime, criminality, criminal justice, etc.—the United States is universally acknowledged as the world's leading failure with the highest imprisonment rate in the world. It is a society which seemingly not only fails to prevent crime, it somehow actually promotes criminality and criminalization. And, given its geographical and cultural egocentricity, criminological research in the United States has taken as its own *problematique* an intellectual wrestling match with its own extremely criminalizing culture to "explain and prevent crime." How could the ASC fail to recognize that globalizing its own society's conceptualization of criminality, and responses to such issues, amount to a global theoretical imperialism of criminological failure through its policies of imprisonment and penality—matching its military and economic hegemony? It must be the blinders of imperial cultural hubris.

This chapter seeks to define a set of alternative concepts which are critical of the conceptual framework of the horrifically and tragically failed American positivist *problematique* in penality—and its criminology. This has been a failed *problematique* not only relying upon imprisonment as the specific icon of societal response to wrong-doing, but the more general notion of penality: that penal revenge is the appropriate response to social conflict.

I will begin by offering a brief overview of critical criminology, and then argue that a global perspective is demanded by methodological considerations, pointing out that traditional comparative criminology has been seriously flawed in its assumptions and preconceptions. Instead, a critical comparative criminology must be based on a world system and/or dependency model, coupled with human rights concerns. The second section of the paper will identify what I believe are crucial concerns identified by critical criminology (embedded in a problematic of the concepts: "reproduction," "production," "the state," and "transformation"), in hopes of identifying how these concerns are taken up by various papers in this collection regarding penal abolition. The concluding section will explicitly draw out some implications, and many questions, for penal abolition.

🏛 INTRODUCTION

Much of the inspiration and intellectual underpining for penal abolition in the English-speaking western world (the "north/west") has relied on the contribution of critical theory. The initial basic premise of class determination of legality and the legal system in the first world has been elaborated in expositions of corporate crime (e.g., Snider, 1978; Goff and Reasons, 1978) , delinquency (e.g., West, 1984a), state operations, policing and the ideological nature of media (e.g., Hall, et al., 1978). Progressive major critiques have been launched by feminists (e.g., Smart, 1976) in creating what may be called a neo-Marxist feminist synthesis (e.g., Gavigan, 1983; Messerschmidt, 1986). Young (1999) has again elaborated these into a major synthesis of cultural and economic issues. Although one cannot claim a single unified critical criminological theory, for the sake of brevity, however, this paper will be forced to collapse many internal disputes, in presenting what I paradigmatically take to be the main features and issues along the central path of development of this theory.

Critical theories (e.g., Taylor, Walton, and Young, 1973; Quinney, 1977; Chambliss, 1977, Young, 1999) argue that societies are maintained by force and ideological mystification (in part supported by mainline social research), with continuous conflict between groups with opposing goals and values. In capitalism, the fundamental conflict occurs between labour and capital, grounded in contradictory, historically specific relations of production. Marxists have seen this fundamental conflict crucially revealed in the increasingly social and public organization of labour, contrasting with increasing private concentration of profit and wealth. Feminists have rightly pointed out that such relations of production need not be limited only to those regarding material goods, but also of labour power itself (primarily through gender relations based in patriarchy), and of culture, social institutions, etc. The central questions in such critical theories would seem to be how is deviance defined, legally proscribed and controlled, and in whose interest (Snider and West, 1979). In claiming that crime is an intrinsically political activity, such critical theorists argue that crime is behaviour which is deemed by state officials to be contrary to the interests of the powerful.

I would like to argue (admittedly somewhat provocatively) that in *Capital*, Marx does not simply *do* political economy, but rather offers a *critique* of political economy (e.g., Marx, 1858/1975; Sayer, 1979; West, 1984b). He proposes a methodology needed for examining the concrete empirical social relations necessary for such political economy concepts as "commodity" to have validity in understanding a particular mode of production dominant within a particular social formation. Following this, what is needed is not so much a *political economy* of crime nor of justice, but rather a *critique* of criminology as a *problematique*. (This would obviously need to include an analysis of specific local political economies, but also needs to include an analysis of the relations of reproduction, politics and law, etc.)

Such a critique necessitates revealing the limits of the applicability of contemporary conceptualizations, in other words demands a comparative analysis, using historical and contemporary "cross-cultural" material. For instance, in what circumstances might imprisonment make "sense" socially? Perhaps in defending the revolution during the 1980's in tiny, poverty-stricken Nicaragua, attempting to defend itself against contra terrorism sponsored by the United States. The desperation of the counterrevolutionary war situation certainly made implementing "penal alternatives" developed in the prosperous and secure north/west extremely difficult organizationally and financially, and unlikely politically and morally. Such a grounded comparative analysis is needed not only to understand the justice-relevant behaviours of the majority of people on this planet (living in the third world), but also to better begin to understand the ethnocentrism of our definitions of criminology in our wealthy west "first world" societies. Furthermore, as critical criminologists are committed to progressive social transformation towards a more fully human justice, Horton and Platt (1986) have advocated the necessity of doing concrete studies on justice in existing "transitional" socialist societies, many of which, of course, are also "third world" or "underdeveloped" societies.

A critical *problematique* implies in its very terms an advance beyond traditional comparative criminology (e.g., Shelley, 1981; Clinard and Abbott, 1973), because the latter has accepted, uncritically, the salience of nation state boundaries in providing units of analysis, generally limiting itself to analyses of conventional crime, and tended not to take seriously problems of measurement (hence the explanation of criminal justice reactions to crime). Neo-positivist criminology has too easily assumed that the social world is composed of distinct units, self-evidently comparable across time, in different cultural locations, etc., by means of assumedly durable data (usually official statistics); it has forgotten the necessity of sensitivity to indigenous social definition. The "objectively" same behaviours in different contexts are differently defined, and a self-critical methodology demands recognition of this. Furthermore, we need more attention directed to the formulation of concepts and theory which can guide us. Theories about what? Why? For whom? The "proof" of a theory is not only its correspondence with the facts, which in the present world are the reflection of the institutionalization of an oppressive system, but also its utility in furthering justice, in offering an understanding useful for social change. Only recently, however, have such analyses been tentatively extended towards understanding law and crime in the third world (e.g., Sumner, 1982; del Olmo, 1975; Cohen, 1982).

Perhaps most importantly, traditional comparative criminology has naively assumed that the less developed countries were simply a few years behind, but catching up with the more developed west, which we have ideologically viewed (at least until post-modernism) as on an endlessly upwardly inclined plane of increasing justice as well as economic production. Recognition of the fallacy of steady progress and development, of course, has been anticipated by a couple of decades within development research itself, with the critiques of traditional development theory by world-systems and dependency theories (see Brewer, 1980; Horton and Platt, 1986). The recurring crises of third world debt within the international monetary system, and western government deficits provide graphic empirical support. Comparative criminology has been the reconstitution of the results of and reaction to imperial exploitation as legal dereliction of duty, of right: it has reconceived race, age, gender, class, and imperial differences as reasons for extended social control (del Olmo, 1981). Ironically, this "development-is-good" framework fails to address satisfactorily how and why the "most-developed" country, the United States, has the highest official crime rate.

An "underdevelopment" perspective, of course, is most theoretically compatible with critical perspectives on crime and justice. "Dependency" or "underdevelopment" theory argues that the third world has not been and is not independent of the first and former second (former Soviet bloc) worlds but intimately linked; indeed the "retardation" of its crime and justice problems are dialectically related to first world development through imperialist exploitation (see Sumner, 1982). Zaffaroni specifically argues that social control cannot be understood as cross-culturally equivalent (i.e., official statistics reflect local cultures and cannot be internationally compared as indicators of criminal behaviour), that "development" and "modernization" are not simply linear processes or concepts, that Latin American economic history has not followed a parallel course to first world countries, but is dependent, and that hence criminalization there is "adjusted to the conditions imposed by the socioeconomic structures of periferal capitalism, and ... highly sensitive to the dangerous defects of the same." (Zaffaroni, 1982:36; see also Aniyar de Castro, 1979-80:7-15; Del Olmo, 1981; 1986; Riera and del Olmo, 1981; 1985; Sandoval, 1985; Sepulveda A., 1984; Marco del Pont, 1983; Borrero Navia, 1983; Asociacion Colombiana de Criminología, 1988)

Although early in the development of critical criminology in the west, Schwendinger and Schwendinger (1973) suggested the need for a broader human rights definition of criminal justice issues. This has been little developed in the industrialized countries, but rather has evolved as a central issue in Latin America. Such issues suggest the advisability of founding criminological conceptualizations of human justice upon formulations of universal human rights (see, e.g., Schwendinger and Schwendinger, 1975; Aniyar de Castro, 1987; Barratta, 1985; White, 1989). In 1948, forty-eight countries of the United Nations approved the Universal Declaration of Human Rights, including both civil and political rights (in articles 3 to 21) and economic and social rights (in articles 22 to 27). Basic human rights (such as those guaranteeing life, physical integrity, freedom from arbitrary detention, and adequate access to food, clothing, medical care, and shelter) address fundamental human needs. Subsidiary rights include freedom of electoral franchise, expression, peaceful assembly, movement, employment, and participation in cultural life. While offering a legalistic framework, it should be noted that such a human rights foundation for human justice research extends our concerns well beyond formal criminal codes. The following notes raise more questions than they answer in attempting to extend narrow legality towards a search for more fundamental and global human justice.

▥ ISSUES FROM CRITICAL THEORY

I suggest the various contributions to critical theory offered by developments in western criminological research schematically indicate a basic problematique of conceptual concerns: those of gender and patriarchy or Reproduction; those of class and political economy, or Production; those of justice and legitimacy, or State and Law; and those of Transformation. On a theoretical level, elucidation of these key concepts and the issues embedded in them would seem a prerequisite in directing critical human justice studies. In part to offset the traditional economistic focus on the political economy of crime, or Production, and in part because it seems to me to be arguably and actually more fundamental, I have placed Reproduction in the primary position.

Reproduction

Global Patriarchy: Gender, Race, and Age Relations

Critical feminists have convincingly argued that continuation of human life (including criminal and justice behaviours) requires the biological development and reproduction of the species, which is socially organized along gender, racial, and age dimensions as well as class. In almost all contemporary social formations, patriarchy predominates: males occupy dominant positions in almost all social institutions, ranging from the family, through education, the economy, religion, the media, and politics—and such relations are reinforced by law as well as more informal customs. Specifically in regard to criminology, sex crimes and the universally inordinately high occurrence of males in criminal justice statistics (especially regarding violent activities) indicate that narrowly economistic explanations are inadequate, and require other perspectives, such as feminist ones. What would "penal abolition" mean to such victims of male abuse?

Exactly how feminist and neo-Marxist theories can be integrated remains a problem despite many recent attempts (e.g., McIntosh and Barrett, 1982; Gavigan, 1983; Lacombe, 1988; Brock, 1984). Early work focussing upon differential socialization and gender roles has been extended in a number of much more sophisticated and thoroughly feminist directions.

But basic world demographic facts should at least make us reconsider western issues regarding reproduction and justice. For the vast, disproportionate majority of the world's children are being reared by women in countries least able to adequately provide for them.

> *In 1975, 1.44 billion children were under 15 years of age. This represents 36 percent of the world population, an increase of nearly 50 percent in the population of children within two decades. Eighty percent of all children live in Africa, Asia, and Latin America, where they comprise nearly half of the total population and where 50 percent of all deaths are accounted for by children under five (OISE, 1981).*

The burdensome tasks of combining primary responsibility for children plus basic food production and household work tend to devolve upon women, whereas the males are more likely to participate in the growing cash economy. This leaves third world women in an extremely exploited position (see, e.g., CIERA, 1985; Mies, 1986), with different immediate concerns regarding criminality and human justice. Many third world social formations have radically different gender and age relationships, wherein the western nuclear family is neither traditional nor predominant; sexual relations may be much more polygamous and serial, with children raised by extended family relations or entire communities (e.g., throughout Africa). Some Nicaraguan research, for instance (INSSBI, 1982), indicates nearly half of Managuan households are female headed, half the population is under age 16, and half the children are born out of formal wedlock. Concepts such as "broken home," "prostitution," "patriarchy," and "control over one's body" take on radically different meanings, as do our western governments' trade and aid policies. While inter-governmental negotiations are typically between "bands of armed men," it is women and children who suffer the consequences. How do our politics (and criminal justice research in Canada) maintain such a global patriarchy?

But again: is some simplistic imprisonment of (the usually male) miscreants productive or helpful for the women and children left behind? Obviously not, in most cases. Penality fails to address the wrong or provide a righting of the situation.

We also cannot ignore the media hype around *age* as a component of criminality and penalization. On the one hand, various western governments (such as the current Ontario Tory government) want to criminalize and penalize all "violent" young offenders, while denying the same people their rights as citizens. For instance, young people under 18 are denied the vote, while being considered as adults for various offences if aged 14.

Consciousness, Ideology, and Global Reproduction

Although it is also often linked within discussions of the state, I wish to suggest here how ideology can be considered a crucial part of social reproduction. The ruling class must amalgamate widespread support within a power bloc in order to control mass democratic struggle. The securing of consent through the unquestioned rule of authority (hegemony) is a far cheaper and more effective mode of domination than outright coercion (Anderson, 1977; Gramsci, 1971; Weber, 1964). "Democracy," "the franchise," "citizenship," "nationalism," "law and order," "crime," "deviance," and "bad boys" are all seen as key terms which claim to guarantee formal political equality while deflecting attention from substantive inequality. Various kinds of centralized negotiations between government, industry, and labour (via social democratic contracts, corporatism, the national security state, or fascism) maintain legitimacy while reconciling crises.

Undoubtedly the ordinary person's conceptual framework has developed initially within families (and later within peer groups and schools) (Dorn and South, 1983/89), and is crucial in such ideological reproduction. For it is in such settings that language is first learned, where human relations first develop, and where individuals continue to orient themselves throughout their lives (Rowbotham, 1972). In regard to education, within most conceptions of social development, we have unthinkingly assumed that more and better schooling would automatically mean development and cultural transmission (but see Dale, 1982). But globally, "of the school-aged group (5-14 years) nearly 35 percent are not in school" (OISE, 1981).

Clearly, we need to re-evaluate such influences. The mass media attraction for spectacular crime news, the demand of deadlines, the reliance on authoritative (and authoritarian) sources, etc., set up distinct media cultures separate from the state, and reflect the interaction of classes rather than simple upperclass domination through ownership (cf. Clement, 1975; Ng, 1981). The influence of the four or five world-dominant, western-controlled news agencies (United Press International, Associated Press, Reuters, and Agence France) cannot be underestimated regarding their defining of world events: "terrorism" is committed by Arabs, not Israelis or Americans bombing Libya; "innocent civilians die" in North Ireland not in mountainous hills of Nicaragua; "drugs" are a problem because of Colombian warlords and black ghetto youths, not because of Central Intelligence Agency needs for "off-the-record" funds (see Cockburn, 1987).

Under such circumstances, how is ideological hegemony maintained? Upon what kind of normative regulation do the extant notions of human justice rely? Not infrequently, it would seem that western colonial models of criminal law, which conflict with many traditional indigenous notions of rights, have been imposed by colonial powers in concert with local comprador elites (e.g., Kanyuka, 1989). How have progressive third world revolutionary movements been so successful in substituting progressive ideological commitments for repressive ones? Understanding such issues comparatively is crucial in understanding moral order and justice, not only globally, but in the west.

Production

Relating Class and Crime at the Centre and the Periphery

There are serious ambiguities within the definition of crime in class analyses (see Scraton and South, 1984): Frequent reference to the large disproportion of working class criminals represented in the official statistics is sometimes used to argue that oppressive class conditions actually generate more criminal behaviour, and sometimes to argue that the officials are singling out such people in a biased manner. On the other hand, self-report statistics, which indicate few if any class differences in rates, are often criticized as recording only juvenile offences, and as relying upon the biased formulation of capitalist legal categories. Besides the definitional/methodological problems, much more specification is needed regarding how class relations are linked to both crime and crime control, perhaps in probabilistic terms. The claim that behaviour that is labelled delinquent is that which is deemed by officials to be contrary to the interests of the powerful (Quinney, 1977; Chambliss, 1977) is not always fully accurate: surely prohibiting murder is in everone's interest, not just that of the rich. Perhaps such a conflict definition is not so much a definition of crime, as it is an orienting hypothesis, albeit one which needs careful examination.

Critical theories within the industrialized liberal democratic states of the capitalist western "first world" have been developed particularly in regard to relatively discrete problem populations (Spitzer, 1975). In contrast to Latin American, Asian, or African countries, western "problem" populations are now generally regularized, well regulated or sufficiently contained so that they can be addressed as involving only "delinquency," or only "prostitution," or only "false advertising"—as relatively isolated and taken-for-granted issues. They are generally no longer seen as problems involving entire communities and populations that are "marginalized" (see, e.g., Pahl, 1984; Walker Larrain, 1983; West, 1986b; 1988b; Tefel, 1972). The implied difference between "deviance" and "marginalization" remains, then, to be explored: why are similar behavioural and legal phenomena conceptualized so differently in first and third world social research? When a majority of a country's population survives by the nefarious "marginal economy," are they really "deviant," or are they quite "normal"? (See West, 1988, and the other papers in *Social Justice* , vol. 15, nos. 3-4, 1988.)

Aside from questions of poverty's relation to crime being salient and problems with the validity of official statistics, most third world countries present some unusual questions for critical theory. The relatively gross and brutal exploitation in many dictatorships (for instance, the Somozas in Nicaragua) make ordinary street crime pale as an issue (del Olmo, 1980), and forces confrontation with some old definitional difficulties: How violent and murderous does legal repression need to be before we are forced to consider it as criminal? How blatantly exploitative and oppressive does transnational extraction of surplus value need to be before it becomes theft or usury (see Vega Vega, 1987) (despite even Marx's own caution in this definition)? What limitations do such realities place upon our use of comparative data? And how are we to conceive of Canadian government relations with such regimes (see White, 1989) or the relationships of our "progessive groups" (e.g., unions) with third world workers?

Class Imperially Extended: Debt Means Dependency, Not Development

The Schwendingers' stimulating paper (1975) arguing that definitions of crime should include evils of exploitation, imperialism, sexism, and racism has certainly encouraged much debate, although it has not resulted in consensus as to an appropriate definition. Only recently, and in a few countries, has explicit attention been paid to the evolution of criminal law and activities through history, relating them to changing dominant modes of production within specific historical formation as a world system (e.g., Thompson, 1976). We need to begin to suggest how the peculiarities of particular societies and laws might inform criminological analyses. What effects, for example, do world market price fluctuations in staples and commodities (wheat, oil, minerals, pulpwood, coffee, cotton, sugar, beef, etc.) have upon particular countries' crime rates? If comparative criminology is reconceived as periphery-metropolis differences, can higher American arrest rates for crime be seen as resulting from more surplus value available for theft (from profits amassed in the metropolis on the basis of extraction from the hinterland) or more being spent on control efforts (viz, Mcdonald, 1976), or simply usuriously extracted (Vega Vega, 1987)? Much remains to be explored, of course, as to exactly how social control is variously maintained in poorer hinterland areas (see Gaucher, 1983), which may experience more material pressures toward crime as a consequence of economic exploitation, but have fewer resources for enforcement. The initial work in utilizing dependency theory looks most promising (Sumner, 1982; del Olmo, 1975; Reira Encinoza, 1979).

But to what extent can revolution and political will be effective? New leaders may want to implement the best for their people, but are left with many of the same old "capitalist" problems—where best to invest to stimulate growth, etc. There are some real differences if basic needs are met for more people, and decisions are in some ways made collectively and democratically rather than autocratically. But what rather darker structural implications lie in the continuing third world debt crisis for crime and criminology? And how do first world countries such as Canada participate in this (e.g., via their voting power at the World Bank or the International Monetary Fund)? Only recently have any social democrats in the developed countries begun to address the problems of the world economy (see, e.g., Brandt, 1980).

State and Law

No Criminal Justice Without a (Liberal-Democratic) State?

Since the publication of *Policing the Crisis* (Hall et al., 1978), the coercive and ideological securing of capitalist order must be seen centrally as state tasks that are of major interest to critical criminology. Miliband (1969), Poulantzas (1973) and others have extended the definition of the state going beyond "government," and attempted to identify its relations to social classes. These theories claim that there is a state guarantee of the pre-conditions of capitalism through assuring social order, capital accumulation, and legitimacy. Earlier versions of critical theory have tended to adopt earlier state theories' superfunctionalist assumptions: Certain policies must be adopted to preserve the capitalist relation of production (Clarke, 1977). Such crude rationalistic and instrumentalist arguments run aground at the first policy which contravenes capitalist interests. It is necessary that structuralist arguments be entertained here, that conflict be recognized as occurring internal to the state apparatus, and that contradictions be explored in studies of concrete historically specific politically organized conjunctures (Laclau, 1977; Gramsci, 1971; Jessop, 1977; 1982). Further, Lea (1979) and Cohen (1979), among others, have suggested a much more radical notion of dispersed micro-political power. In this conception, multifold panoptic atomized relations of power are the basis of institutional power, not vice versa. That is, widely dispersed, fragmented, multidimensional power relations (for instance, within family units, between neighbours, among peers, and other small groups differing in age, gender, race, and class) become aggregated in varied ways to produce more traditionally recognized "political" power (for instance, between parties, classes, etc.) Power is not exercised to repress as much as to discipline and generate more power (Foucault, 1977).

But how do these notions apply to most countries, where the majority of third world states seldom embody the liberal-democratic assumptions of the above theories? Again, how have our central liberal-democratic states supported such non-liberal-democratic regimes, and what does such support imply regarding a critical theory of justice in Canada? Surely, at least, our foreign policy becomes a topic for criminological investigation.

No Crime Without Law

The legal system would seem to be the most obvious instance of the coercive and legitimating aspects of modern states. The justice system in all its branches performs a key mediating function. The police (and also the military, especially in their role as aids to the civil power) remain ready and alert to exercise coercive force when predominant interests are threatened. Although liberal democratic ideology regards law as impartial, given the hegemony of the economic elites in other institutional sectors of our society, it surely strains belief to suggest that these same forces refrain from exercising their sway in the legal system. Picciotto (1979) invokes Pashukanis' (1981) analysis of the intertwining of legal form and content, with emphasis on either being prone to the danger of fetishization: formal legal equality can mask underlying susbstantive inequalitities; yet the form of law must be analyzed in its peculiarities to avoid mesmerization by particular content. The law is contradictory.

The colonial imposition of "modern" formal criminal codes in most third world states indicates the inadequacy of simply a formal legal analysis towards understanding law, justice, and crime. What is clearly needed is regard for the different underlying social relations, the substantive inequalities versus the formal legal equalities. What issues remain, e.g., in the implementation of localized, substantive and humane justice, with needs for efficiency, equity, perhaps central control and accountability? Internationally, how are we to understand the implications of the "Iran-Contra" scandal, and the U.S. refusal to acknowledge the World Court's jurisdiction regarding its mining of Nicaraguan harbours? (West, 1986c/1987a; 1988b/c; Cockburn, 1987; Brophy, 1986)

Progressive Transformation

Transformation

Critical approaches have often been short on useful suggestions (Mungham, 1980), although most criminologists reject Hirst's (1975) argument that criminology is a peripheral topic, about which little can be done "until after the revolution." A further problem is that many critical analyses have too often casually assumed that deviant or delinquent behaviour is interpersonally benign, or somehow part of the pre-revolutionary vanguard (Cohen, 1979b). If some control is necessary in any society, questions must address which reforms can be regarded as progressive, which repressive, and what social control and social justice should be in a truly just and progressive society (Fine, 1979: 38, 44; Birkbeck and Martinez-Rincones, 1989).

Can the Nicaraguan block committees be seen as quite progressive moves to avoid some serious problems entailed in simply following a western model? What treatment procedures have been instituted since the revolution? In what sense are they progressive, and in what sense do they simply replicate the "best of liberalism" (e.g., psychiatry?—as suggested in del Olmo, 1983)? What can we in the west learn from such experiments under progressive regimes?

A Progressive Criminological Praxis

Crude conflict theorists have either espoused a positivistic rejection of value commitments, or blithely adopted the traditional leftist line that the working class at its most contradictory point will become appropriately class conscious and morally self-interested (Lukacs,1921). Increasingly, there is the recognition on the progessive left that researchers must become involved in the active rational formulation of humane and progessive policies through public debate regarding values and ethics (Cohen, 1979b). The claim of value-free social science is no longer possible (Oquist, 1976). Theories must be related to the daily practice and experience of our potential allies. Our concerns must be expressed in understandable language and concrete, viable, alternative strategies must be developed and implemented that make sense to ordinary people.

But such involvement has been seen (especially by traditional economistic or structuralist Marxists) as threatening the scientificity of the analysis. Critical theory has retained an interest in causation or, perhaps better, determination (see West, 1984b). Besides a defensible rigour in traditional methodological issues, however, critical theorists must proceed beyond the narrow demands of neo-positivism, even those unthinkingly wedded to economistic orthodox Marxism. What is required is not so much a political economy of crime but rather a critique of criminology, one which would replicate Marx's critique of political economy (West, 1984b). Only historically and comparatively grounded research will allow us to develop such a critique.

A variety of methodological approaches is required even to begin to answer many of these questions. Some are relatively standard: legal scholarship to specify the evolution and impact of legislation: historical research on the background to the present revolutionary events and organization; compilation of whatever official data are available (as much to chart official activities as their presumed recording of crime); interviews and observations regarding key traditional and innovative institutions.

But there are opportunities to develop more innovative and progressive methodologies. Rather than simply correlating surface appearances, one could ground the explanation of phenomena in the underlying conditions that make marginal activities and collective social control uniquely possible within the third world social formations. Within the west we must assist our "subjects" to develop their own analytic capabilties and utilization of whatever research we collectively produce *together* with them to enable the progressive realization a critical criminal justice. For instance, exploration and development of alternative research strategies and methodologies such as participatory research with the subjects of the investigations (e.g., see Walker Larrain and West, 1984; Arnold, Barndt, and Burk, 1986) draw upon critical pedagogies (e.g., Freire, 1970) and liberation theology within a "popular church" (Baum, 1986) in developing critical theory (Aniyar de Castro, et al., 1986).

ᛦ SOME IMPLICATIONS

The preceding sections have attempted to outline a conceptual problematic for critical human justice studies (based on "Reproduction," "Production," "State/Law," and "Transformation"), indicating central issues within western critical criminological research over the last decades. Fundamental human rights issues (regarding rights to life, physical integrity, food, clothing, shelter, and medical care) have been invoked as prior to our western championed rights regarding civil liberties: freedom to exercise the franchise, expression, assembly, movement, employment, and cultural participation. I have tried to indicate how we need to understand criminal justice issues in the third world (which encompasses most of us humans) in order better to understand even our first world issues. But I have also argued that the crucial element in critical human justice studies relies not so much upon specific substantive claims (e.g., that the working class is exploited, or working class women are particularly exploited—both of which are true), but upon critique—the ephemeral but quintesential human quality of denying and challenging the taken-for-granted, whether in intellectual discourse, or in lived reality. Hence a critical human justice is centrally distinguished by its methodology and by its critique of concepts and presumptions which define and delimit valid application and understanding.

In part through cultural imperialism and lack of local resources, in many third world countries such as Nicaragua, there doesn't presently exist an indigenous criminology (a specific theory, or even much written from a criminological perspective), but there certainly exist experiences relevant to crime and justice that need explication and explanation, raising comparative questions. These criminological practices demand a critical comparative criminology capable of revealing the theory implicit in such practices, and their necessary preconditions, which is historically and cross-culturally grounded, yet with expanded topics and perspectives in our investigations.

This conclusion will indicate further relevancies for criminology in first world justice research. We must go beyond simply applying western concepts and theories—even the best ones—not only to more fully understand the richness of experiences elsewhere in the world, but to challenge criminology itself. Only through such challenges based on comparative historical and cross-cultural research can we begin to specify the relevance of our analyses in particular social formations, and to understand the social pre-conditions required for such analyses to be valid, true, or useful in constructing a more just human society.

Some Substantive Implications

Global Reproduction, Gender, and Justice.

Crude demography insists that we acknowledge that the majority of the world's population is deprived of basic human rights and justice—and most of these people are women and children. They have been born into circumstances not of their own choosing, but condemned to lives of oppression, poverty, and violent assault.

We in the prosperous west must somehow acknowledge this, conceptually come to terms with it, and move beyond in admitting the provincial nature of many of our favourite issues (whether the "right to choose" regarding abortion, or "fathers' rights" regarding access after separation). Substantively, we must begin to reconceptualize issues such as refugees and immigration in terms of the Canadian government policies regarding free trade: in capital—but what about labour?

But it is precisely such third world educational, social and health programmes which the International Monetary Fund and the World Bank (with Canadian government support) has demanded be cut to obtain their support for further international loans required to maintain payments on foreign debts (typically contracted in Latin America by military dictatorships), so we in the north can continue clipping our bank coupons. Quite literally, in Latin America, millions of children today are starving and uneducated because the international banking system demands that they pay for the sins of the thugs who stole democracy from their parents, with the clear direct collusion of northern bankers and governments. Simply put, almost all the social development programmes acknowledged as instrumental in crime-prevention in the west are precisely those which our banks, our Canadian government (both directly and through international agencies), and our companies in which we hold stocks are demanding be cut.

What Might Just Economic Development (and Class Relations) Mean in a World of Underdevelopment?

We must consider the global economic context. Precisely in regard to Nicaragua, the American boycott and war of attrition criminally violated not only international law (e.g., in regard to the General Agreement on Trade and Tariffs—GATT), but also directly threatened one of the most hopeful and sustained efforts at social development in the underdeveloped world. Policies here have effects there.

In looking at the above, one is forced to specify some underlying patterns. The grand programs for development of the third world espoused by countries such as Canada since the Second World War through international aid agencies have often not resulted in development for the majority of the target population, but rather have resulted in worsening underdevelopment). Cashcrop development for agroexport economies, for instance, often results in peasants being increasingly forced off their small subsistence plots, with a real decline in the nutrition of the majority (Barry, Wood, and Preusch, 1983). This demands seriously reevaluating our policies regarding global social development, basic human rights, and human justice.

With more difficulty, how do we understand how do our favoured labour unions and farmers relate to such exploitation of labour in the third world? And for us—as criminologists—what are the implications of (basically economic) marginality for conceptualizing deviance?

Perhaps the International State Organization of Legality Is *the* Crime?

Traditional comparative criminology has assumed that most serious crime is committed by young adolescent males who are socially disadvantaged: these are indeed those who most come to the attention of northern and southern social control agencies (i.e., those persons most arrested).

In contrast, McIntosh (1975) has argued that crime had evolved from bandit to racket to project and into business organization. But all too often, in Latin America, it has further developed to become government itself, the total corruption of the state apparatus in the service of criminal groups (e.g., Wheelock Roman,1974/79; del Olmo,1980), often oriented towards first world markets (e.g., in drugs). Our notions of state power and legitimacy are narrowly grounded upon western liberal democratic criminology, and state theory, automatically discounting other types of rule—those dominant throughout the globe.

Third World Challenges

It has also indicated how third world experiences challenge many of our assumptions embodied in such concepts, demanding that we be more specific and globally relevant in our claims. Finally it has suggested how such a comparative perspective is crucial to articulate a critical global criminology. In an era of mass media communications and the international transference of culture and technologies, I believe it is absolutely essential that we take a comparative perspective of human justice. Immigration and cultural transference bring new populations and behaviours to our shores; international terrorism specifically transcends national boundaries; we increasingly define our national political priorities in such global terms; and our society's development is increasingly tied to the development of other countries.

As Howard S. Becker so eloquently and cogently expressed a few decades ago: "Whose Side Are We On?" (Becker, 1963).

𝕞 ENDNOTES

My personal thanks to Dr. Ruth Morris and Giselle Dias of Rittenhouse; ICOPA IX supporters; Dra. Vilma Nunez de Escorcia of La Comision Nacional Para la Promocion y Proteccion de los Derechos Humanos; Judy Butler and Carlos Vilas of El Centro de Investigaciones y Documentaciones de la Costa Atlantica; Beth Woroniuk of El Instituto de Investigaciones Economico-Sociales; Jose Garcia and Joe Gunn of El Fondo Canadiense Para la Ninez; and students in classes at both the Centre of Criminology and the Ontario Institute for Studies in Education, especially Stephen Piper, Larry White, Jorge Moraga, Horacio Walker Larrain, Marianne Kelly, and John Maine. The Canada Council, the Solicitor-General of Canada, the Centre of Criminology, and the Ontario Institute for Studies in Education, Correctional Services Canada, the Ontario Solicitor General, and the Ontario Ministry of Social Services; and especially Liz Flanagan, Greg Dunham, Thorsten Laue, and Dave Kirby have all financially supported the basic research drawn upon in this paper, although the analyses expressed herein are my own.

𝕞 BIBLIOGRAPHY

Aniyar de Castro, L., "Notas Sobre el Poder y El Abuso del Poder, Para el Topico: Delitos y Delincuentes Fuera del Alcance de la Ley," *Capitulo Criminologico*, 7/8, 1979-80: 8-13.

Aniyar de Castro, L., "Derechos Humanos Como Fundamentacion Teorica de los Delitos Internacionales: El Caso de America Latina," *Memorias*. La Habana, Cuba: Ministerio de Justicia, 1987: 40-9.

Arnold, R., Barndt, D., and Burke, B., *A New Weave: Popular Education in Central America and Canada*, Toronto: OISE/CUSO, 1986.

Asociacion Colombiana de Criminologia (eds), *Lecciones de Criminologia*. Bogota, Colombia: Edit. Temis, 1988.

Barry, T., Wood B., and Preusch, D., *Dollars & Dictators*, New York: Grove Press, 1986.

Birkbeck, C., and Martinez Rincones, J.-F. (eds), *Criminologia Latinoamericana: Balance y Perpspectivas*, Merida, Venezuela: CENIPEC, Universidad de los Andes, 1989

Borrero Navia, J.M., *Modelos de Desarrollo y Criminalidad*, Cali, Colombia/San Jose, Costa Rica: Fundacion para la Investigacion y Proteccion del Medio Ambiente (FIRMA /ILANUD), 1983.

Brewer, A., *Marxist Theories of Imperialism*, London: Routledge, 1980.

Brock, D., *A Feminist Perspective on Prostitution*. unpub. MA thesis, Carleton University, Ottawa. 1984.

Brophy, R., *Contra Terror in Nicaragua*, Boston: South End Press, 1985.

Chambliss, W.J., "Functional and Conflict Theories of Crime' in W. Chambliss and R. Seidman, eds., *Whose Law? What Order?* New York: John Wiley, 1977.

CIERA (El Cento Para el Estudio de la Reforma Agricola), *Tough Row to Hoe: Women in Nicaragua's Agricultural Co-Operatives*, Managua: CIERA, 1985.

Clarke, S., "Marxism, Sociology, and Poulantzas' Theory of the State," *Capital and Class*, 1977, 2: 1-23.

Clement, W., *The Canadian Corporate Elite*, Toronto: McClelland and Stewart, 1975.

Clinard M., and Abbott, D.J., *Crime in Developing Countries*, New York: Wiley, 1973.

Cockburn, L., *Out of Control: Reagan, Nicaragua, Arms, and the Contra Drug Connection*, New York: Atlantic Monthly Press, 1987.

Cohen, S., "The Punitive City," *Contemporary Crises*, 1979.

Cohen, S., "Introduction," *Folk Devils and Moral Panics*, London: Martin Robertson, (second edition), 1979.

Cohen, S., "Western Crime Control Models in the Third World: Benign or Malignant," *Research in Law, Deviance, and Social Control*, JAL Press, 1982.

Dale, R., "Learning to Be... What?" in T. Shanin, ed., *The Sociology of Underdevelopment*, New York: Monthly Review, 1982.

Deighton, J. et al., *Sweet Ramparts: Women in Revolutionary Nicaragua*, London: War on Want and the Nicaraguan Solidarity Campaign. Trade Distribution: Third World Publications, 151 Stratford Road, Birmingham, 1983.

del Olmo, R., "Violence in Latin America," *Crime and Social Justice*, 10, 1975.

del Olmo, R., *Los Chiguines de Somoza*, Caracas: Edit: Ateneo, 1980.

del Olmo, R., *America Latina y su Criminologia*, Mexico: Siglo XXI, 1981.

del Olmo, R., "Remaking Criminal Justice in Revolutionary Nicaragua," *Crime and Social Justice*, 1983: 18.

del Olmo, R., "Aerobiologia y Drogas: Delito Internacional," *Memorias*, La Habana, Cuba: Ministerio de Justicia, 1987.

Dorn, N. and South, N., *Of Males and Markets: A Critical Review of Youth Subculture Theory*, Research Paper #1, Centre of Occupational and Community Research, Middlesex Polytechnic, Enfield, England. Reprinted in Spanish in M. Cerri, L.E. Gonzales, and W.G. West, eds., *La Modernizacion: Un Desafio para la Educacion*, Santiago de Chile: CIDE/PIIE/UNESCO, 1989.

Fine, B., "Law and Class," in CSE/NDC, Fine, Kinsey, Lea, Picciotto, and Young, eds., *Capitalism and The Rule Of Law*, London: Hutchinson, 1979.

Fitz, J., "The Child as a Legal Subject," in R. Dale, G. Esland, R. Fergusson, and M. MacDonald, eds., *Education and The State: Politics, Patriarchy and Practice*, vol II. Milton Keynes: Open University Press, 1981.

Gaffield, C. and West, W.G., "Children's Rights in the Canadian Context," in H. Berkeley, C. Gaffield and W. G. West (eds.), *Children's Rights: Legal And Educational Issues,* Toronto: OISE Press, 1978: 1-4.

Gaucher, R., *Origins of the Canadian Penitentiary*, unpub PhD Thesis, University of Sheffield. 1983.

Gavigan, S., "Women's Crime and Feminist Critiques," *Canadian Criminology Forum*, 1983, 6 (1) : 75-90.

Globe And Mail, Toronto, 1986, June 11, June 12.

Goff, C. and Reasons, C.E., *Corporate Crime in Canada: A Critical Analysis of Anti-Combines Legislation*, Scarborough, Ontario: Prentice-Hall, 1978.

Gramsci, A., *Selections from the Prison Notebooks*, (ed. and trans. Q. Hoare) London: Lawrence and Wishart, 1971.

Hall, S., Clarke, J., Critcher, C., Jefferson, T., and Roberts, B., *Policing the Crisis: Mugging, the State, and Law and Order*, London: Macmillan, 1978.

Hirst, P.Q., "Marx and Engels on Law, Crime and Morality," in I. Taylor, P. Walton, and J. Young, eds., *Critical Criminology*, London: Routledge and Kegan Paul, 1975.

Horton, J. and Platt, T., "Crime and Criminal Justice Under Capitalism and Socialism: Towards a Marxist Perspective," *Crime And Social Justice* 25, 1986.

INSSBI (Instituto Nicaraguense de Seguridad Social y Bienestar), *La Prostitucion en Nicaragua*, Managua: INNSBI, 1982.

Jessop, B., "Recent Theories of the Capitalist State," *Cambridge Journal of Economics*, 1977, 1: 353-73.

Jessop, B., *The Capitalist State*, London: Macmillan, 1982.

Kanyuka, M., "Moral Regulation Of Young Offenders In Malawi: A Study of the Chilwa Approved School," Unpub Ph.D. Thesis, University of Toronto/OISE, 1989.

Laclau, E., *Politics and Ideology in Marxist Theory*, London: New Left Books, 1977.

Lacombe, D., *Ideology and Public Policy: The Case against Pornography*, Toronto: Garamond, 1988.

Lea, J., "Discipline and Capitalist Development," in B. Fine et al., (CSE/NDC) (eds.) *Capitalism and the Rule of Law*, London: Hutchinson, 1979.

Lukacs, G., *History and Class Consciousness*, London: Merlin, 1921/1979.

Marco del Pont, L., *Crimologica LatinAmericana*, San Jose, Costa Rica: ILANUD, 1983.

Marx, K., "Introduction to the Grundrisse," in *Karl Marx: Texts on Method*, ed. T. Carver, Oxford: Basil Blackwell, 1857/1975.

McDonald, L., *The Sociology of Law and Order*, Montreal: Book Centre 1979, Toronto: Methuen.

McIntosh, M., *The Organization of Crime*, London: Macmillan, 1975.

McIntosh, M., and Barrett, M., *The Anti-Social Family*, London: New Left, 1982.

Messerschmidt, J., *Capitalism, Patriarchy, and Crime: Toward a Socialist Feminist Criminology*, Totowa, NJ: Rowman and Littlefield, 1986.

Mies, M., *Patriarchy and Capital Accumulation on a World Scale*, London: Zed, 1986.

Miliband, R., *The State in Capitalist Society*, London: Quartet, 1969.

Ministerio de Estranjero, *Informe sobre la agresion*, Managua, Nicaragua, 1985.

Mungham,G., "The Career of a Confusion: Radical Criminology in Britain," in J. Incardi, ed., *Radical Criminology*, Beverley Hills: Sage, 1980.

Ng, Y., *Ideology Media, and Moral Panics: An Analysis of the Jaques Murder*, Toronto: Centre of Criminology, University of Toronto, Unpub. MA thesis, 1981.

OISE (Ontario Institute for Studies in Education), *IE: International Education Newletter* 1981 # 2, March, Toronto: OISE.

Oquist, P., "The Epistemology of Action Research," in *Critica y politca en ciencias sociales*, Bogota: edit Paula de Lanza, Simposio Mundial de Cartagena, Vol. I, 1977.

Pashukanis, E., *Law and Marxism*, London: Ink Links, 1981.

Pearce, F., "Putting Foucault and Althusser to Work: The Legal Subject," Paper presented the the Annual Meetings of the Canadian Sociology and Anthropology Association, 1981.

Pearce, F., and Tombs, S., "The Control of Hazardous Products in the Chemical Industry Bhopal," paper presented to Annual Meetings of Canadian Law and Society Association, McMaster University, Hamilton, 1987.

Picciotto, S., "The Theory of the State, Class Struggle and the Rule of Law," in B. Fine, et al. (CSE/NDC) eds., *Capitalism and the Rule of Law*, London: Hutchinson, 1979.

Poulantzas, N., *Political Power and Social Classes*, London: Verso, 1973.

Quinney, R., *Class, State, and Crime*, New York: David MacKay, 1977.

Ramirez Mercado, S., "Countering American Propaganda," *This Magazine*, Toronto, 1983: 11-13.

Riera Encinoza, A., "Latin American Radical Criminology," *Crime and Social Justice*, 1979: 71-76.

Riera Encinoza, A., and del Olmo, R., "The View from Latin America: Against Transnational Criminology," *Crime and Social Justice*, 1981, 15: 61-70.

Riera Encinoza, A., and del Olmo, R., *Hacia una criminologia de las contradicciones: El caso Latinoamericano*, Caracas: Talleres de Italgrafica, 1985.

Sandoval Huertas, E., *Sistema penal y criminologia critica*, Bogota: Edit. Temis, 1985.

Sayer, D., *Marx's Method*, London: Harvestor, 1979.

Schwendinger, H., and Schwendinger, J., "Defenders of Order or Guardians of Human Rights," in I. Taylor, P. Walton, and J. Young (eds.), *Critical Criminology*, London: Routledge, 1975.

Scraton, P., and South, N., "The Ideological Construction of the Hidden Economy: Private Justice and Work Related Crime," *Contemporary Crises*, 1984, 8 (1): 1-19.

Sepulveda A., J.G. *Criminologia critica: I seminario*, Medellin, Colombia: Universidad de Medellin, 1984.

Shelley, L., *Crime and Modernization: The Impact of Industrialization and Urbanization on Crime*, Carbondale, Ill: Southern Illinois University Press, 1981.

Smart, C., *Women, Crime and Criminology: A Feminist Critique*, London: Routledge and Kegan Paul, 1976.

Snider, D.L., "Corporate Crime in Canada: A Preliminary Analysis," *Canadian Journal of Criminology*, 1978, 20: 2.

Snider, D.L., and West, W.G., "A Critical Perspective on Law in the Canadian State: Delinquency and Corporate Crime," in R. J. Ossenberg, ed., *Power and Change in Canada*, Toronto: McClelland and Stewart, 1980. (Reprinted in T. Fleming, ed., *The New Criminologies in Canada*, Toronto: Oxford, 1985).

Spitzer, S., "Toward Marxian Theory of Deviance," *Social Problems*, 1975, 22, June: 638-651.

Star, *The Toronto Star*, 1986, June 1.

Sumner, C., "Crime, Justice and Underdevelopment: Beyond Modernization Theory," in his ed. *Crime, Justice and Underdevelopment*, London: Heinemann, 1982.

Taylor, I., Walton, P., and Young, J., *The New Criminology: For a Social Theory of Deviance*, London: Routledge and Kegan Paul, 1973.

Thompson, E.P., *Whigs and Hunters: The Origins of the Black Act*, London: Pantheon, 1976.

Vega Vega, J., "El Delito Internacional de Usura," *Memorias*, La Habana, Cuba: Ministerio de Justicia, 1987: 30-9; English trans. "The International Crime of Usury: the Foreign Debt of the Third World," *Social Justice*, no. 30, 1988.

Walker Larrain, H., "Marginal Youth in Chile: Deviance Within a Context of Social Reproduction," *Canadian Criminology Forum*, 1983, 6 (1) : 19-34.

Walker Larrain, H., and West, W.G., "Estrategias de Participacion Popular: Fundmentando Investigacion Participativa en Observacion Participante y Etnografia Critica," *Cuadernos De Formacion*, 1984, #2. Santiago, Chile: la Red Latinoamericana de Investigaciones Cualitativas de la Realidad Escolar.

Weber, M., *The Theory of Social and Economic Organization*, Glencoe, Ill.: Free Press, 1964.

West, W.G., "Phenomenon and Form in Interactionist and New-Marxist Qualitative Educational Research," in L. Barton and S. Walker, (eds.), *Educational Research, Social Policy, and Social Crisis*, London: Croom Helm, 1984b.

West, W.G., "Trust Among Serious Thieves," in R. Silverman and J.J. Teevan, (eds.), *Crime in Canadian Society* (3rd ed.), 1986a, Toronto: Butterworths. Reprinted from *Crime et/and Justice*, Vol 7/8 (3-4), 1979: 239-48.

West, W.G., "The Marginalization of Latin American Youth in the Crisis: The Reproduction of Race, Gender, Class, and Imperialism Through Age, With Some Implications for Education, Work, and Political Community," Paper presented to the the Conference on The Present Conjunctural Crisis: Effects of Technology,

Implications for Education, Santiago, Chile, 1986b. Trans and revised version published as "Marginalidad, Inmoralidad, Desviacion, y la Juventud del Tercer Mundo" and "Nicaruagua Es Una Escuela," in *Modernizacion: Un Desafío para la Educacion* (ed. M. Cerri, L.-E. Gonzales, and W.G. West) Santiago: CIDE/PIIE/ UNESCO, pp. 31, 1989.

West, W.G., "El Terrorismo Internacional en Nicaragua," *Capitulo Criminologico*, Maracaibo, Venezuela: Universidad de Zulia, 1986c; Reprinted in *Poder y Control*, Barcelona, vol. 1, 1987.

West, W.G., "La Retorica del Sr Reagan: La Decadencia del Imperio, El Terrorismo Norteamericano, y La Presentacion Ideologica de la Tortura de Nicaragua," *Memorias*: IV Encuentro Latinoamericano de Criminologia Critica/II Seminario Sobre Control Social En America Latina) La Habana, Cuba, Septiembre de1986. Ministerio de Justicia, La Habana, Cuba. 1987b: 91-97. Translated and revised as West, W.G. "Courts, Congresses and (Media) Cajoleries: Reagan's Rhetoric and American State Terrorism in Nicaragua," presented to annual meetings of Canadian Law and Society Association, McMaster University, Hamilton, Ont. (Proceedings) of the 1987 Conference of the Canadian Law and Society Association. York University/ YULL Publications Microfiche, pp. 34, 1987c.

West, W.G., "Vigilancia Revolucionaria: A Nicaraguan Policing Resolution to the Contradiction between Public and Private," in C.D. Shearing and P.C. Stenning (eds.), *Private Policing*, Beverley Hills, Cal: Sage, 1987d.

West, W.G., "Developing Democratic Education in Central America Means Revolution: the Nicaraguan Case," in J. Kirk and G. Schuyler (eds.), *Central America: Democracy, Development and Change*, New York: Praeger, 1988a.

West, W.G., "Destabilizing Nicaragua: The Growth of Second Economy Crime is Not an Internal Flaw of Sandinista Social Justice," *Social Justice*, 1988b, 15 (3-4): 114-134. Revised and reprinted as West, W.G., "The Second Economy in Nicaragua is the Second Front: Washington's Efforts to Destabilize Any Succeeding American Revolution," in M. Los (ed.), *The Second Economy in Marxist States*, London: Macmillan/New York: St. Martin's, 1989a: 26.

West, W.G., "Una Practica Critica: Algunas Implicaciones de la Revolucion Nicaraguense para la Criminologia Latinoamericana," in C. Birkbeck and J-F. Martinez Rincones (eds.), *Criminologia Latinoamericana: Balance y perspectivas*, Merida, Venezuela: Universidad de Los Andes, CENIPEC, 1989b.

West, W.G., "Khaki-Collared Crime: 'Los Contra' and the Internationalization of Imperialist State Death Squads in Nicaragua," unpub. paper. 1990.

Wheelock Roman, J., *Nicaragua: Imperialismo y dictadura*. Havana: Ciencias Sociales, 1974/79.

White, L., *Low Intensity Warfare: American Political Crime in Nicaragua and El Salvador during the Reagan Years*, M.A. Thesis, Centre of Criminology, University of Toronto, 1989.

Wolf, L., "Feverish Overthrow Plan Builds Toward Climax," *Covert Activities Information Bulletin*, 1984, 22: 25-29.

Young, Jock (W.S.), *The Exclusive Society: Social Exclusion, Crime and Difference in Late Modernity*, Thousand Oaks, CA: Sage, 1999.

Zaffaroni, E.R., "Criminalidad y Desarrollo en Latinoamerica (ensayo critico motivado en *Crime and Modernization* de Louise Shelley) *Revista de Ilanud*, 1982: no. 13 y 14.

3

Taking Too Much for Granted: Studying the Movement and Re-Assessing the Terms

Viviane Saleh-Hanna

Penal Abolition is a framework that encompasses action and defines a specific goal. Dissatisfaction with penology and its failure to create a safe and balanced society has resulted in a movement that focuses on structures which enforce this failure, while working constructively to change the elements which justify its existence. To comprehend penal abolition, one needs to place it within its proper historical context while understanding it in relation to the field of criminology and the theoretical dispositions that exist around it.

It is important to recognize that the penal abolition movement is extremely diverse and complex in nature. The essential element that binds it together is the desire to abolish the brutalities that are inflicted and perpetuated by penal institutions, policies and modes of thought. Some aspects of the movement focus on specific institutions and the structures in which they function, while others focus on the ideology that maintains that existence and legitimacy.

🏛 PENAL ABOLITION: AN OUTLINE OF MAJOR CONCEPTS

Penal abolition is a concept that embraces three domains. First, it is a social movement that fits within a larger historical context and functions in association with the futuristic goal of abolishing the penal structures. It stems from dissatisfaction with the processes, experiences (for victims, offenders and the community) and outcomes of penal processes. Second, it is a theoretical perspective; its framework is critical in its assessment of social/power structures and it is quite focused on the conceptualization of oppression (of victims, offenders and the community) and resistance. Third, it is a political strategy dedicated to the promotion of human rights and the creation of a safe society that provides equal opportunities to all its citizens (De Haan, 1991). These three domains cannot exist independently of each other and often, they serve as functions of one other. In order to fully comprehend penal abolition, it is important to acknowledge all aspects of the movement and to recognize that it is quite complex in nature and diverse in strategy. Some of the major assumptions within penal abolitionist ideology are that "the relationship between criminal justice and punishment needs to be re-examined. Punishment is the deliberate inflicting of suffering: it is legal violence… punishment is counter-productive and needs fresh examination, as does the system that perpetuates it. This system is revealed as an emperor with no clothes. The idea that it can be reformed is a myth. That it is the only or best way of dealing with offenders is not true" (Consedine, 1995: 19).

Often viewed as an idealistic mission and a naïve goal, penal abolition is frequently brushed aside and discredited as a radical, unobtainable "dream." Generally, this is due to a lack of understanding of penal abolitionist ideology. In addition, a certain degree of uncertainty and anxiety is directed towards this framework because it questions and puts into disrepute some of the essential elements that support the structures which shape integral elements of our everyday lives. The concepts of "crime," "community," "harm," "victimization," and "punishment" are questioned, deconstructed and reassessed within abolitionist literature. To deal with the apprehension that emerges because of this line of questioning, penal abolitionist literature and activism need to make clear its intentions, assumptions and goals.

One of the main assumptions of penal abolitionist work is that "social life should not and, in fact, cannot be regulated effectively by criminal law and that therefore, the role of the criminal justice system should be drastically reduced while other ways of dealing with problematic situations, behaviors and events are being developed and put into practice. Abolitionists regard crime primarily as the result of the social order and are convinced that punishment is not the appropriate reaction" (De Haan, 1991: 355). In this conviction, it is crucial to note that penal abolition is *not* a short-term goal. It is a *movement* that works toward building a society that will function cohesively and, as a result, will have no use for penal sanctions. While many critics of penal abolition feel that it is a concept that promotes anarchy and fails to consider safety, it is important to assert that penal abolitionists claim the creation of a safe society is their *top* priority. Ruth Morris appropriately summarizes this priority in her statement that abolitionists "can play a major part in bringing in a new order of transformation, where the needs of victims, offenders and the community take priority over the dead hand of retribution" (Morris, 1995: 121).

₥ THE PRISON, A SELF-SUSTAINING AND SELF-PERPETUATING STRUCTURE: THE WIN-WIN SITUATION

The penitentiary is the ultimate penal structure, as society would know it today. Supposedly, the prison functions to punish, to protect, to rehabilitate and to transform, among other things. In terms of the everyday functions of the prison, ironically enough, the same people whom it oppresses maintain it. In the American prisons, "inmates have produced all of the work that supports the prison system, such as making the clothes, washing the clothes, and building the cell equipment, day room furniture, lockers, and mess hall tables" (Browne, 1996: 66). Aside from the building and maintenance of the prison's physical structure, prisoners have also made "shoes, bedding, clothing, detergents, stationery products, license plates and furniture for all state agencies. In addition, convict laborers have provided 'special services' such as dental lab work, micro graphics, and printing" (Browne, 1996: 66). All of the above mentioned tasks generally fall within the realm of the male prisons.

Consistent with gender stereotypes, "the women's prison industries have generally been in the areas of re-upholstery, fabric production, laundry, and data entry. In men's prisons all of this type of work is done, as well as metal production, wood production, and the operation of farms, dairies, and slaughterhouses" (Browne, 1996: 1966). The above-mentioned processes and tasks add up to a multi-million dollar industry. Not only are prisons saving money when convicts build, maintain and clean the prisons, but the prisons also make money when labour outside the realm of prisons brought into the oppressive, unequal power dynamics of the penitentiary. It has been said that "this enormous, multi-million dollar industry was purportedly created to address the problem of 'inmate idleness'… by helping in rehabilitation, building effective work habits, and providing job training. Yet a prisoner who spends a ten-year sentence processing stationary products on an assembly line or washing laundry has not learned any highly employable skill [outside the prison industry], nor has he been mentally or emotionally challenged through this service to the state" (Browne, 1996: 66). In essence, the prisoners are taught skills that will provide them with experience to work in the prison, for the prison, and only within the conditions that are prescribed and enforced by the prison.

﬘ ACADEMIC PROFIT

The power dynamics involved in defining and applying criminal justice, and the profit that results from those decisions have become a central focus within the penal abolitionist discourse. This argument emphasizes both the financial and the academic profit which is involved with penology. Academically, criminological discourse is highly dependant upon the existence of crime and crime definitions. Within that discourse, division, competition, politics and profit play a major role. "In the same way that our courts, prisons, probation officers, and police 'need' crime, so does the criminologist" (Cohen, 1992: 46). The *crim*inologist's academic identity is central to the concept of crime. Publications, diplomas, conference presentations, paid teaching positions and research grants are a few of the achievements which can be accomplished in the context of studying "crime."

A more concrete example of profit-making in criminology lies within the "study of violence" which is presented forth in the name of safety. The culture of "violence research" is both very costly and highly professionalized. "There are huge materials, hardware and labor needs, as well as some statistical expertise [which requires expensive training]" (Fekete, 1994: 37). Some of the financial figures involved in this type of training are huge. In 1993, the Violence Against Women Survey conducted by Statistics Canada cost about $2 million, while the CanPan (hearings plus organizing data) cost $10 million. The academics who contracted for this study were each paid "$50,000 for a mere summary of their findings" (Fekete, 1994: 37). It is interesting to note that all this money was spent in light of the knowledge that "it is virtually impossible to understand the complexities of human interactions using survey instruments" (Fekete, 1994: 37). Ironically enough, an academic who is currently involved with this type of research and profit made this comment. The most productive reason for statistical research that she cited was that big a survey "puts a problem on the map" and gives it exposure. The fact that the Canadian government needs to spend an average of $12 million to "make a problem known" is highly problematic. These figures say a lot about the type of concerns which will be brought forth and the type of "victims" and "offenders" they will identify.

🏛 PENAL? WITHIN THE FIELD OF CRIMINOLOGY

This analysis of the field of criminology is not meant to undermine the importance of the study of crime; its purpose is to contextualize the criminological field within the context of "crime" and the academic/financial profits which come forth due to the existence of "crime." Keeping in mind that the rise of the prison played a major role in the creation of "criminology" as a recognized discipline, one also must recognize that the role of penal abolition within the field of criminology can seem contradictory.

Garland explains that "the operation of the disciplinary prison gave rise to a new body of information and knowledge about the criminal which was not previously available" because it provided a setting in which offenders could be "studied" and in that the individualization of "the delinquent" took rise (Garland, 1993: 148). These changes from public to private, and then from physical torture to physical and mind control, did not eliminate the brutality of punishment; it simply displaced it. This has resulted in the expansion of crime control at many levels. One such expansion occurred within the "criminological" field. These changes and shifts have blurred boundaries and created some confusion within academic definitions of control but "luckily for us all, criminologists have got this matter well in hand and are spending a great deal of time and money on such questions. They have devised quantitative measures of internal control, degree of community linkage, normalization… standardized scales… and scores" (Cohen, 1985: 58). Cohen's cynicism towards the criminological field stems from his belief that it is too narrow and its involvement with accepted social/power structures is too intimate thus rendering it insufficient for appropriately dealing with issues related to human rights violations. He states that while "it would be ludicrous to claim that Western criminology over the past decades has completely ignored the subject of state crime or the broader discourse of human rights…the subject has often been raised and then its implications conveniently repressed" (Cohen, 1993: 489).

In studying *crim*inology, it is almost impossible to adequately criticize "crime" and the broader implications of that phenomenon. In the same way, *penal* abolitionists may be too closely connected to the "penal" system in their critique of the responses to and definitions of problematic behavior. At the same time, such a focus is necessary for the creation of a specialized field that will focus all its resources on this issue. In order to avoid the trap of being too close to see the larger picture, penal abolition must function within the specific goal of abolition. Only negative reforms (eg. a prison-building moratorium) can be supported along with the exposure of penal brutality in resistance to the culture of denial. The sociology of denial, which Cohen describes in the academic discourse of human rights, can be paralleled to the denial that has occurred through the evolution of punishment and the creation of the "invisible" walls (i.e. electric monitoring) and the remote-controlled prisons.

In placing the discipline of criminology within the broader historical, academic and political context, one can see that penality lies within the roots of its conception. If penal abolition was to achieve its goal of abolishing penality, one must keep in mind the possibility of abolishing the discipline of criminology in the process. It is important to note that the "abolition of criminology" can be categorized as a consequence of penal abolition and not necessarily as a tool for the abolition of penality. In the meantime, the role of "criminology" within the penal abolition movement needs to be well established and better defined. One of the challenges which criminology faces lies in the analysis of the social conditions that give unwanted acts their particular meaning (Christie, 1998: 130). In carrying out this analysis, criminology might take a more productive approach in offering advice for preserving and nurturing the "social conditions which work against recent trends of seeing so many unwanted acts as crime in need of penal action. Instead, we can open the way for alternative forms of perception and alternative ways of control. Doing this, criminology might come to play an important role in the defense of civil society" (Christie, 1998: 130).

🏛 ALTERNATIVE FORMS OF PERCEPTION: QUESTIONING AND REDEFINING THE TERMS

Penological definitions and assumptions are so engrained in so many aspects of the social structure and at so many different levels, that the mere questioning of them tends to create great anxiety for the community while presenting a minor threat to the power structures which profit from them. To properly deconstruct penality within the overwhelmingly strong structure in which it is encompassed, some basic concepts, terms and assumptions need to be addressed. Terms like "crime," "victim," "harm," "community" and "suffering" are central to penality, criminology and the media; also, they are frequently used in everyday conversation. Radical criminology and critical modes of thought have academically debated, deconstructed and reconstructed those terms into numerous shapes, forms and definitions. Within the penal abolitionist discourse, a basic concept necessary in studying crime is the Hippocratic principle: "First, do no harm." With that as a core value, penal abolitionism asserts that the field of criminology can begin to challenge the social conditions which give "unwanted acts" their particular penal meanings (Christie, 1998: 130). In doing so, "criminology might be able to give advice on how to find, preserve and nurture those social conditions which work against recent trends of seeing so many unwanted acts as crime in need of penal action" (Christie, 1998: 130). Within this analysis, criminology can also examine the use of viable alternatives and in doing this "criminology might come to play an important role in the defense of civil society" (Christie, 1998: 130).

🏛 OVER-PROFESSIONALIZATION VS. UNDER-PROFESSIONIALIZATION

Penal abolitionism arose from discontent with penal policies, practices and outcomes. Theoretically, penal abolition evolved out of prison abolition and within the roots of prison abolition was the rejection of population segregation and the imposed brutalities of exclusion. Cohen points out that "the destructuring and abolitionist movements... represent the moment when the inclusionary impulse dominated social control rhetoric. The structures of knowledge that allow for exclusion should now be weakened, bypassed, or eliminated altogether" (Cohen, 1992: 216). It was clear that exclusion causes stigma and that this penal stigma had proven itself counter-productive within the context of community safety. In this realization, it became evident that the problem of crime within the community needed to be dealt with *in* the community. Standing in the way of such reforms were the professional enterprises of law and order, crime control, and convoluted academic explanations of those phenomenons. Keeping these concerns in mind, it is also necessary to make sure that this community which needs to deal with violence and intentional harm, also needs to have a representative, holistic and contextualized understanding of its problems.

A need to find a balance between over-professionalizing and under-professionalizing has arisen. In an era where the "information highway" is taking over the dissemination of events and the distribution of knowledge, this task is not necessarily impossible. A positive aspect of this era's methods for the distribution of information is that there are new venues for critical thought to be expressed to larger numbers whereas, in the past, access to such venues was quite limited. A negative aspect of this venue is that there is also more opportunity for propaganda and vigilante rhetoric to be distributed; because this type of information is more familiar to the general population, it will be more popular (i.e. in terms of support and "hit sites" on the Internet). In addition to the Internet, the media still plays an extremely influential and political role in defining crimes and in prioritizing harm.

We live in an era where the world is more accessible than ever. Technology has increased both speed and the amount of international knowledge which we can access from the privacy of our homes. This "mass communication allows for knowledge to be generated not only in scholarly disciplinary forms, but also in popular extra-disciplinary forms… the production of criminological knowledge, which was primarily confined to the writings and research findings of the professionally trained experts or disciplinaries, today, by contrast includes widely disseminated information propagated by non-expert criminological sources" (Barak, 1998: 10). The fine balance between over-professionalization and under-professionalization lies in the differentiation between such references to "expert" vs. "non-expert" sources. In the end, a critical outlook upon inaccurate assumptions along with a realistic recognition of harm and suffering needs to be established. A call for community awareness now resounds. The right-wing, conservative definitions and assumptions have been vocalized. It is time for the leftist radical to be heard outside the realm of academia and "informed" activism.

Once this is accomplished, the general population will be better equipped in deciding its path for dealing with crime, violence and suffering within the community. One of the penal abolitionist goals should be community education and an increased awareness of critical thought in the general population. A move beyond criminological audiences needs to be better established and pursued; after all, crime and human suffering/oppression is a topic and reality which affects more than just the members of criminological audiences.

ᛘ WHAT IS COMMUNITY?

Aside from the academic, industrial, economic and political barriers, there are also some conceptual walls which obstruct the path to penal abolition. A key notion which needs clarification is the concept of "community." A major assumption within penology is that the community is an entity which *can* be broken up and separated. The prison, for example, is based on the assumption that by building a highly controlled setting and placing individuals within it for long periods of time, a separation from the community has been created. This form of reasoning seems analogous to that of an ostrich. By sticking its head in the sand, this bird assumes that its surroundings have disappeared. By putting up the walls (whether they be concrete prison walls or stigmatizing, exclusionary social walls), penology assumes that a segment of the population has been *removed*. In essence, these walls do not prevent the people behind them from affecting society. In their mere existence, these walls hold a huge role in the economic (as stated above), political and moral convictions of the society which built them. Out of sight for penology certainly does not mean out of mind for the community, for if the ostrich leaves its head in the sand for too long, it will inevitably suffocate. Penal abolition ideology places the solutions for community victimization within the context of that community. In doing so, it is much more likely to succeed at creating a safe and balanced society.

ᛘ A DEFINITION OF "CRIME" AND "VICTIMIZATION"

The term "crime" is used to describe a wide array of actions and events. Louk Hulsman asserts that the only binding thread among such a diverse set of actions and events is that "the c.j.s. [criminal justice system] is authorized to take action against them" (Hulsman, 1986: 27). He also addresses the "harm" created by crime and states that some crimes "cause considerable suffering to those involved, quite often affecting both perpetrator and victim" (Hulsman, 1986: 27). Placing "crime" within the proper historical and social contexts shows that "the concepts of 'crime' are not eternal. The very nature of crime... is social, and is defined by time and by place" (Virgo, 1996: 47). In addition to the political, cultural and historic complexities involved in defining "crimes," there is also complexity in the vast categories and the immense assumptions, actions and implications of "crime." "Banditry, resistance, protest, and rebellion are all terms that can be defined by social science and in terms of behavior alone.... Crime, on the other hand, is one of many possible definitions... that can be attached to certain behaviors or events, but only by a legitimate authority (usually the state). Crime is an infraction and not just an action" (Cohen, 1992: 281).

Hulsman does not refer to illegal acts as "crimes." He prefers to speak of "criminalizable events." The purpose of this use of language is to emphasize the fact that a conscious choice was made in dealing with a human act as a "crime." "Crime could be almost infinite. An enormous number of human acts could be so described.... The modern tendency is to... introduce the criminal law into many areas of life... to criminalize more people, and to do so at a younger age" (Stern, 1998: 340).

Richard Quinney's theory of the social reality of crime asserts that "...the reality of crime is *created* and... it is created in a way that promotes a particular *image* of crime: *The image that serious crime—and therefore the greatest danger to society—is the work of the poor*" (Reiman, 1990: 46, italics in original). Like Hulsman (1986), Quinney denies the ontological reality of crime. These types of arguments and philosophizing need to proceed cautiously to avoid denial of harm for victims of crime and a removal of responsibility for the offenders. Academically and theoretically, in light of the historical context and the constant changes in the law, it makes sense that we question the ontological reality of crime. An obstacle to overcome here is the conceptual tendency of dependence on the state/authorities to define harm. If an action that harms someone else is not defined as a crime by the state, does this mean that the harm has not occurred? No, of course not. The harm *has* occurred and that reality is *not* being denied by a theorist who claims that ontological reality of "crime" needs critical assessment. The state's definitions, authorities and responses are the issues which are being questioned, and not necessarily the victim's experience of harm/suffering; but, a cautionary note is still needed as problems can arise if academic research becomes a tool for the denial of harm and re-victimization.

Another common fallacy within the criminological field is that harm needs to be defined by the proper authorities in order to elicit appropriate reactions and encompass legitimate claims of suffering. There is the belief that if an act is not a defined "crime," then it is not necessarily a "bad" or harmful thing to engage in. This fallacy is dangerous because it aids in the denial of harm and perpetuates the disempowerment of the community's ability to define and deal with its own problems. In contemporary times, "images of victims of natural disasters, political conflict, forced migration, famine, substance abuse, the HIV pandemic, chronic illnesses of dozens of kinds, crime, domestic abuse, and the deep privations of destitution are everywhere. Video cameras take us into the intimate details of pain and misfortune" (Kleinman and Kleinman, 1997: 1). The media is constantly and systematically bombarding us with detailed images of violence and human suffering. Such exposure can lead to desensitization for the viewers and the result in a hardened, inhumane response, or, if presented in a different light, such exposure can raise awareness and elicit wider support for social activism and resistance. For now, the general "outlook has been tainted by propaganda and demagogues" and thus there is a need to "rethink" approaches to human rights atrocities and the implications of the media's role (Johnson, 1995: 72-73).

In studying the media as a powerful tool of political manipulation and the formulation of public opinion, it is important to look at instances where the media has been used in a positive manner to advance social change and to challenge the government's political agenda. It has been well documented that mainstream journalism in America has been greatly controlled by the government. In analyzing the American mass media institutions, Chomsky and Herman state that they constitute highly "effective and powerful" establishments which achieve a "system-supportive propaganda function by reliance on market forces, internalized assumptions, and self-censorship… This propaganda system has been even more efficient in recent decades with the rise of the national television networks, greater mass-media concentration, right-wing pressures on public radio and television, and the growth in scope and sophistication of public relations and news management" (Chomsky and Herman, 1988: 306). In light of this "power," Chomsky and Herman declare that "this system is not all-powerful…. Government and elite domination of the media have not succeeded in overcoming the Vietnam syndrome and public hostility to direct U.S.

involvement in the destabilization and overthrow of foreign governments" (Chomsky and Herman, 1988: 306).

Many examples of success in this area do exist (Iraq, Yugoslavia, Central America, etc.) but in studying the failure in relation to the Vietnam situation, abolitionist literature can better articulate effective policies and approaches to destructuring political control over the mass media. For activism in this area to be effective, it needs to function at the level of the community and routines of daily life. "The organization and self-education of groups in the community and workplace, and their networking and activism, continue to be the fundamental elements in steps towards... any meaningful social change. Only to the extent that such developments succeed can we hope to see media that are free and independent" (Chomsky and Herman, 1988: 307). In working to achieve such developments, the road to abolition will be made smoother in terms of destructuring myths about crime and suffering while questioning the effectiveness and the need for penology and criminal justice. In popular, mainstream culture, suffering is routinely distorted and globalized. This "globalization of suffering is one of the more troubling signs of the cultural transformations of the current era: troubling because experience is being used as a commodity, through this cultural representation of suffering, experience is being remade, thinned out, and distorted" (Kleinman and Kleinman, 1997: 2). This remaking and distortion of experiences is instrumental in the presentation of an extremely inaccurate image of victimization and suffering.

A common assumption about victims of crime (as represented in the media, this only includes people who have experienced street level crime) is that their victimization can only be dealt with in the realm of imposing victimization in the form of state regulated punishment or revenge. Ironically enough, this assumption is not only highly problematic in the academic, theoretical, radical context of "victimization" but it also misrepresentats the reactions of many victims of violent street crime. This is exhibited in the following account of a victim's experience of the murder of his brother:

> *In a classroom at Indiana University, a young man, Mike, whose sixteen-year old brother was murdered, is explaining his opposition to the death penalty: "When someone in your family is killed, you have this great rage. But you have to stop and ask yourself—do you want to be responsible for an execution? I did not want to have someone killed in my brother's name." Mike is a member of Murder Victims' Families for Reconciliation, a modest, grass-roots organization,*

composed of people who have lost family members to murder, dedicated to abolishing the death penalty" (Kaminer, 1995: 67).

This image of the "victim" and the needs of a "victim" is seldom presented to mainstream audiences. In fact, "since the 1970s, victims' rights has nearly displaced 'law and order' as a rallying cry for people who believe that crime is largely the consequence of an excessively lenient criminal justice system" (Kaminer, 1995: 74). One of the main re-enforcers of public opinion in relation to crime and criminal justice policies in North America is the media. Much research has been dedicated to this area and it has been shown in a number of studies that there is a consistent positive correlation between the amount of media one consumes and the support held for punitive policies and ideology for criminal justice issues (Surette, 1998: 196). Because public opinion is greatly influential in the formulation of policies and the enactment of laws, it is relevant to examine the effects of the media on public opinion, and in turn the outcome of policies based on those opinions. It has been noted that the "single most significant social effect of media content is not its generation of crime but its effect on our criminal justice policies. The fear and loathing we feel toward criminals is tied to our media-generated image of criminality. The media portray criminals as typically animalistic, vicious predators" (Surette, 1998: 236).

In conjunction with this portrayal is the image of the "victim" within the context of the media. The definition of "victimization" is often portrayed in an extremely narrow and politically conservative context. These definitions have been used in many "moral crusades" and have often been politically motivated to enforce policies and attend to political agendas. "When the government launches its periodic crime campaigns, the media dutifully serve as its publicist, even though officials often promulgate distorted conceptions of the crime problem and predictably counter-productive solutions... Increasingly, [these campaigns] have been launched in the name of victims: we have get tough (as if we had not been before) to help victims" (Elias, 1993: 13). In addition to helping the victims, "people must be willing to forego their rights to secure greater security against victimization" and in that must adhere to the policies presented as necessary for such protection (Elias, 1993: 13).

These concepts of victimization are well complemented by the "animalistic" images of the criminal. It is essential within abolitionist ideology to recognize the politicized nature of "victimization" and "offending" and the roles which these definitions play in further reinforcing penal ideology and the its solution to "crime" (Elias, 1993). The victims' movement is largely "dominated by politically conservative organizations or groups that have been moved to support conservative policies.... Victim advocates holding feminist, antiracist, human rights, or anticorporate perspectives have been largely blocked from access to government programs. Instead, groups narrowly toeing the conservative crime-control line have emerged as dominant" (Elias, 1993: 55).

A major consequence of the images presented in the media and the policies which have been enacted is the dichotomization of rights. This dichotomy implies that the offenders receive rights at the victims' expense. Based on this assumption, policies to take rights away from offenders are legitimized and justified in the name of "victims rights." Usually, these policies do little for the empowerment of the victim and even less in terms of creating security within the community. These dichotomies, along with the narrow definitions and stereotyped images which are presented in the media, are quite effective in reinforcing "myths" of crime and in building barriers along the path towards penal abolition. In fighting this, penal abolitionists need to work harder in broadening the general definitions of "victims" and "offenders" and in that negating, the illusion of dichotomy.

In the penal context, these dichotomies create boundaries between victims and offenders which often perpetuate a simplified and stereotyped image of victimization. A good example of the inaccurateness of the simplified notions of victimization and victims' needs is presented in the following account of a prisoner's experience in an American prison: "David was gang raped not once, but twice. Now in his late twenties, he has served close to half his life in institutions and has made most of the important decisions of his life based on experience interacting with inmates" (Hassine, 1996: 72). David has obviously committed a criminal offense (hence his incarceration) so he definitely falls within the "offender" category. The above-mentioned account also places him within two more categories: victimization at the hands of the individuals who raped him and double victimization at the hands of the state that has institutionalized him *and* placed him in a position where he is vulnerable to physical, sexual and psychological attacks. In the presentation of David's victimizations, Hassine expands the categories of harm beyond solitary individual notions into the broader realm of punishment and state-imposed victimization (Reyna, 1975: 141).

Another prisoner gives a different account of victimization. He states that his experiences in Soledad prison and the overall use of imprisonment as punishment against human beings has proven itself "inevitable in leaving some kind of traumatic scars within one's mind. Prisoners upon their return back to the world are never the same.... It's not knowledge they lack, what they lack is courage to liberate themselves from the fear driven into them by prisons" (Reyna, 1975: 141).

🏛 VICTIMS, OFFENDERS AND COMMUNITY: AN ILLUSION OF THE "US AND THEM" ANALOGY

The penal system is a power structure with explicit instruction to one segment of the population to oppress and control another specified segment of the population. It is a structure which creates dichotomy through conflict in the realm of power relations. "Much like soldiers in combat, inmates and prison staff have little overview of the arena where their conflicts play out. They can only glean a narrow glimpse of it from the small plots of turf they happen to occupy at any given moment. Consequently, inmates and guards alike can never afford themselves a complete view of the prison in which they live, work and struggle" (Hassine, 1996: 48). This enforcement of an "us and them" analogy in penal institutions is dangerous because it is dehumanizing and can justify great violence and harm inflicted upon all those involved. The prison is an ultimate presentation of this dichotomized analogy because the "us and them" analogy is an essential element of the prison's everyday functions. "The modern prison has tried, with very mixed results, to break down the time-entrenched barriers between "us" and "them," the guards and the guarded. Everyone in prison is on guard—this much at least the two groups have in common" (Murphy and Murphy, 1998: 49).

This type of dichotomizing also exists in other aspects of the penal structure. In the context of American courtrooms and the advocacy of the use of the death penalty, a prosecutor explains his position and thinking process. The following clearly portrays the dangers of "othering" and the brutalities (state executed murders) which are justified within the realm of the "us and them" analogy. "Instead of focusing on what 'we'—law-abiding citizens—do to 'them'—convicted murderers—you focus on what they have done to us... their savage, senseless crimes... terror of their victims and the lifelong pain.... More than bad luck—a brutal childhood, a mental or emotional disorder, an incompetent attorney—put them on death row…; they were put there as well by their acts…" (Kaminer, 1995: 154). This line of reasoning plays victims' pain against revenge towards the offender. This leads to a justification of imposing more harm in order to deal with an already harmful situation. The prosecutor went as far as to suggest that "you are likely to assert that the people we execute are bad enough and the reasons for executions are good enough" (Kaminer, 1995: 154). This implication of "good" in relation to the imposition of state-justified violence/death is a perfect example of the extremely dangerous elements of the "us and them" analogy.

🏛 COMMUNITY EMPOWERMENT

Dominant academic and political discourse often works within an elitist, exclusionary mindset where knowledge is produced and then disseminated downward. It has been said that "the intelligent few must recognize the 'ignorance and stupidity of the masses'…. The masses must be controlled for their own good, and in more democratic societies, where force is unavailable, social managers must turn to 'a whole new technique of control, largely through propaganda'" (Chomsky, 1999: 55). The Criminal Justice System and the penal paradigm largely operate within this mindset. The processes and policies are too complex for the common lay person and thus can only be performed and controlled by those who have the proper (expensive) training. In addition, the community is often bombarded with propaganda while continually being excluded from the decision-making processes and agendas. In essence, criminal justice procedures are in place to respond to human, interpersonal conflicts. Unfortunately, criminal justice policies attempt to deal with these conflicts outside the realm of human, interpersonal communication and interaction, thus setting itself up for failure and dissatisfaction.

Penal abolitionist discourse should aim to de-professionalize the study of crime and the reactions to harm. The community needs to empower itself with the right to deal with its problems, in its own terms. This path to empowerment will cover many issues and face diverse concerns. Past attempts have erected many obstacles, despite the academic foundations for critical thought and radical movement. "So when we talk about empowerment, about injustice, a generation after William Ryan's *Blaming the Victim* (1971), this is part of what's going on.

Disparities in empowerment and in social justice are at least as profound as they were twenty years ago. And personal connectedness to the problem seems at least as hard to find" (Lykes, 1996: 296). An important element which needs to be embraced is one that works to create and represent social solidarity in the struggle to defend human rights. In the penal context, it needs to be made clear that "you can't solve powerlessness by frightening or treating it, but only by being willing to share your power with it" (Morris, 1993: 15).

ᾔ A CRITICAL ASSESSMENT OF CRITICAL DEFINITIONS

Romanticizing crime and deviance

In addressing the political concerns of oppressed populations and in highlighting the racism, classism and inequality of penal processes and definitions of crime, a cautionary note needs to put forth. Theoretically, crime has been defined and explained in countless forms. One of the more problematic issues in theorizing about crime and criminals arose in the "romanticizing" of deviance. In understanding this romanticism, it is necessary to recognize that different types of romanticizing theories did arise. Aside from the individualized notions of "street crime," "bad boys" romanticized theories, there have also been developments in the romanticization of "militant and politicized" resistance movements. "With the rise of militant and aggressive deviant groups, some of the new theories... started (and some have never stopped) celebrating such deviance and claiming it as evidence of a newfound political consciousness. Virtually any antisocial activity became elevated in this way" (Cohen, 1992: 103). Statements like "deviants of the world unite. You have nothing to lose but your stigma" provide an "excessively romantic" view of deviants as helpless victims of stigma and leaves little room for practical, productive social activism (Cohen, 1992: 104).

In the face of oppression, the human spirit can revolt without mercy. In the U.S. this happened but the romanticization of crime and violence served to undermine the power of such resistance. This destructive romanticism of violence is exemplified in popular writings such as this poem which Nikki Giovanni wrote:

Nigger
Can you kill
Can you kill
Can a nigger kill
Can a nigger kill a honkie…
Can you splatter their brains in the street
Can you kill them…
Learn to kill niggers
Learn to be Black men.

In response to such statements, Cummins states that "to today's reader, Giovanni's poem may seem indiscriminate in its praise of criminal terror, but by the beginning of the 1970s any crime, including homicide, regardless of motive, might become justified as a revolutionary act" (Cummins, 1994: 141).

In defense of radical thought and its justification of such romanticism, it is important to state that "it has been quite some time since radical criminologists portrayed law-breakers as 'romantic' victims or proto-revolutionaries. Even during the early years of radical criminology… this image of the criminal represented only one part of the emergent critical paradigm, a part that was associated with the 'tear down the walls' movement centered around a group of high profile revolutionaries' such as George Jackson, Angela Davis, Eldridge Cleaver, and Huey Newton (Platt 1988)" (Michalowski, 1991: 32). Radical criminology in the late 1970s is better represented in a mode of thought which viewed street crime as a "serious, structurally induced threat to social order, rather than acts of romantic self-liberation by victims of proto-revolutionaries" (Michalowski, 1991: 32). These acts of romanticism and violent justifications were a valuable lesson for critical theorists. It became clear that "despite the obvious injustices and horrible conditions of life in the ghettos… and in other pockets of racism and poverty… it is just plain dangerous to call street crime political crime, making street criminals automatically antistate revolutionaries…" (Cummins, 1994: 278).

It is also inaccurate and unfair to place so much emphasis on social/ revolutionary structures while completely eliminating the individual responsibility of harm exerted by one person upon another. Unfortunately, the lessons of the past do not always get proper recognition and value. The romanticism of violence continues to exist in some pockets of radical thought. As a warning against repeating past mistakes, Cummins states that "convicts of the 1990s will only be too easily convinced to see themselves as guerilla heroes. Sadly, if it comes to that, these... prisoners will likely become ideological pawns in another cultural crossfire, this time perhaps in a race and class war of which they will be the first victims" (Cummins, 1994: 278).

In avoiding further romanticization, a precise understanding of the concepts which define "political prisoners" needs to be established. "In one sense, most prisoners are political prisoners insofar as their incarceration is directly related to oppressive conditions within our society. However, to say this is to leave no room for distinctions among people who are arrested for murder, rape, or burglary on the one hand, and expropriations, bombing US installations, attending demonstrations, or disabling nuclear weapons, on the other" (Lopez, 1996: 261). In addition to this, Lopez points out that prisoners who have engaged in right-wing political activity against the government do not fall within the realm of his definition of a "political prisoner" "since the right wing is fighting to reinforce the system that commits these [very] crimes" which the above defined political prisoners are opposing (Lopez, 1996: 262).

How do we define the "Dangerous few"?

A major theoretical- and policy-oriented problem within the penal abolitionist literature and mindset is the issue of the "dangerous few." Research and evidence has shown that most prisoners are poor, they come from minority populations and have faced great discrimination and racism/classism in the community both before they committed their crimes and during the criminal justice process. Some are women who have responded violently to the violence in their lives, others have committed horrible, violent acts, even murder, "but the violent act was an isolated event prompted by extreme circumstances... they spend the rest of their lives consumed with guilt and a wish to atone. Their long sentence reflects the appalling nature of their crime rather than the need to protect people from them" (Stern, 1998: 171). While few prisoners in most parts of the world will fall within the above categories, a minority of them will. These are the people for whom "it could be said, prison has been designed. Some of them will be cruel and conscienceless. Some will have committed crimes that are beyond imagination in their heinousness. A few are so dangerous that they are likely to be a threat to others, including those who guard them [and those who are forced to live around them], for most of their natural lives" (Stern, 1998: 171-172). In response to the question of dealing with "those people"

Morris responds that it is "idiotic to treat 99 percent of prisoners in the way we do on the basis of the one to two percent who make up the dangerous few" and she adds that "the present system responds very poorly to the challenge of the dangerous few and our need for protection from them" (Morris, 1994: 1). Issues of definitions are yet to be sufficiently addressed. How do we draw the line between the dangerous and the non-dangerous and in the process of defining that line, how do we avoid the minimizing (which tends to lead to denial) of harm which may occur through categorizing it into subtitles which differentiate in such a quantitative, positivistic approach? In light of such problems, penal abolition needs to work harder at refining its stance in relation to the dangerous few and in figuring out what can be done in response to this matter.

Academia vs. Activism

Another problematic concern within penal abolitionist discourses is the dichotomy between academia and activism. Surely academic contributions which change perceptions and contextualize things are a form of activism; but another aspect of penal abolitionist academia is highly critical of social activist attempts and often make references to issues of co-optation and net widening. "One thing that is often said of us 'radical' criminologists is that we are free with our criticism but short on constructive alternatives" and in response to that criticism there has been an increased focus within the left on concepts of Restorative Justice and Peacemaking criminology (Pepinsky, 1991: 317). "Peace*making*" criminology, like penal *abolition* is a term that encompasses motion and defines a specific goal: to *make* peace, to *abolish* penality. In these perspectives, alternatives to penality are viewed as the future.

A Crime Free vs. A Penal Free Society: Understanding Punishment's Place in Society

In his book *Anti-Criminology* Cohen discusses one of the biggest critiques against radical and critical criminology. He states that "one of the more remarkable claims in the new criminologies, one that is now sometimes played down for being utopian, was that it is possible to envisage and work toward a crime-free society" (Cohen, 1992: 136). Cohen goes on to explain that this view places too much criminal emphasis on the capitalist social structure and not enough on the individual. He makes references to the abolishment of social control in crime-free societies and he questions whether such a society can ever come to exist.

This sort of critique is often directed at penal abolitionism and thus, clarification seems necessary. Penal abolitionists do not seek the creation of a crime-free society. As an ideal, society should constantly strive towards it, but as Mathiesen has explained "any attempt to change the existing order into something completely finished, a fully formed entity, is destined to fail: in the process of finishing lies a return to the by-gone" (Mathiesen, 1974: 95). This sort of ideology encompasses the constant motion and change which defines the state of existence for any social setting. Concrete goals (such as the possible creation of a crime-free society) will never exist within this constant evolution and movement. What penal abolitionists seek to abolish is penality and this need for punishment. The response to crime is the target, not necessarily crime itself.

Such a goal stems from the repeated failure and inhumanities imposed within this penal-oriented punishing mindset. Garland (1993) claims that neither the prison, nor any of the penal institutions which operate in contemporary and in historic societies have ever achieved successful, instrumental ends. "Despite recurring Utopian hopes and the exaggerated claims of some reformers, the simple fact is that no method of punishment has ever achieved high rates of reform or of crime control—and no method ever will. All punishments regularly fail in this respect because... it is only the mainstream processes of socialization... which are able to promote proper conduct on a consistent and regular basis" (Garland, 1993: 288-289).

Garland (1993) explains that a proper evaluation and understanding of penal institutions needs to encompass a multi-disciplinary, integrated approach. He states that the complexity of the penal institutions needs to be recognized within the wide array of its penal and social functions. He also states that in presenting viable, humane, community-based alternatives, one can challenge the penal mindset/institutions but the base of these alternatives first needs to reject exclusion while de-demonizing the offenders and reducing fear towards them. This can be accomplished if the "unknown" aspect of "criminals" is addressed since much of the fear which exists in the community is based in a "fear of the unknown" in relation to a few highly publicized, unrepresentative cases (the dangerous few).

Garland also suggests that the exposure of "the real psychological violence which exists behind the scenes of the best prisons" will support the argument that such violence is unnecessary within the realm of a civilized society and does little to improve the conditions which were imposed in the times of corporal and capital punishments (Garland, 1993: 290-291). Also, in challenging the outrageous cost of the penal system, one could challenge its existence as a means of expressing punitive sentiments and thus call for a redistribution of funds towards victim compensation, community building, education and empowerment. Garland concludes that "thinking of punishment as a social institution should change... our mode of understanding penality... it should lead us to judge punishment according to a wider range of criteria... to question the narrow, instrumental self-description that the modern penal institutions generally adopt and... suggest a more socially conscious and morally charged perception of penal affairs" (Garland, 1993: 290-291). Penal abolition takes this process one step further in advocating for a change in perceptions from "penal affairs" to "community affairs" and thus challenging on a greater level, the definitions of harm and crime while redirecting power into the hands of victims, the community members, and those who have "offended" them.

ṁ CONCLUSION: A JOURNEY INTO THE UNKNOWN

A move towards an individualized focus on crime within the context of the greater social structure seems to be approaching. "If the social and global sufferings ever are to be ended, we must deal with the suffering of personal existence. What is involved, finally, is no less than the transformation of our human being. Political and economic solutions without this transformation inevitably fail... there is no shortcut to the ending of suffering" (Quinney, 1991: 4). The power to change and cause positive social transformations is not far from reach. In the critical analysis of "crime" one can begin to reject the common assumptions related to harm. In general, "most of us accept the images and the definitions that we have been taught as true, neutral, self-evident, and eternal; so the power to paint the picture—to define what is right and wrong, what is lawful and what is criminal—is really the power to win the battle of our minds. And to win it without ever having to fight it" (Virgo, 1996: 48).

Penal abolition is a concept which brings forth hostile information in relation to the power structures of society and the functions of the criminal justice system. It is a movement which faces many obstacles and barriers. A main factor of resistance to penal abolition is a fear of both the known and the unknown. Most people *know* that the penal system is not effectively functioning to reduce crime and violence in the community. What is *unknown* is the outcome: what will happen to our society if penal abolition was to be achieved? The answer to this question is essential to the notion of penal abolition; unfortunately, the answer cannot be formulated *prior* to the abolition of penality. This "unknown" aspect of penal abolition presents a certain risk factor which presents an obstacle along the path of the movement. A fear of this "unknown" results in misconceptions and passive acceptance of the present failing system.

The penal abolitionist movement needs to make more effort in educating the public about the history of penality. In that, a study of societies that existed without the oppressive, brutalizing structures which dominate the present system may dispel some of the fears and deconstruct the myths which surround them. It is not possible to look into the future and predict whether or not penal abolition will ever occur. In the instance that it does, one cannot predict the outcomes of that achievement or the new challenges which will arise within it. What *is* evident is that the existing situation is unacceptable. In this unacceptability, one searches for instability and in finding that instability, one may begin to build resistance. In doing this, society begins to venture into the "unknown," risking outcomes that are unexpected and potentially non-definable within the traditional criminological domain. *This* venturing away from the known failures and into the unknown potential for success should be the driving force for the resistance movements.

In resistance to the power structures which dominate penality and in defiance of a system which oppresses and destroys too many lives, I find that it is most appropriate to end a paper on penal abolition with the words of a political prisoner. These words were written during his confinement within one of the most dehumanizing, controlling, industrialized prisons in the world. Mumia Abu-Jamal's words provide strength for the penal abolitionist vision and in resistance to his confinement and the overall manipulation of the social structures that maintain the penal system, he writes:

> *People say they don't care about politics; they're not involved or don't want to get involved, but they are. Their involvement just masquerades as indifference or inattention. It is the silent acquiescence of the millions that supports the system. When you don't oppose a system, your silence becomes approval, for it does nothing to interrupt the system… look at the system, look at the present social "order" of society… Do you see law and order? There is nothing but disorder,*

and instead of law, there is only the illusion of security. It is an illusion because it is built on a long history of injustices: racism, criminality, and the enslavement and genocide of millions. Many people say that it is insane to resist the system, but actually, it is insane not to." (Abu-Jamal, 1997: 11).

ﬁ Bibliography

Abu-Jamal, Mumia, *Death Blossoms: Reflections from a Prisoner of Conscience.* Farmington: Plough Publishing House, 1997.

Johnson, Donald, "On Media Manipulation" in *Extracts from Pelican Bay* edited by Arguelles, Marilla. Berkeley: Pantograph Press, 1995.

Barak, Gregg, *Integrating Criminologies.* Boston: Allyn and Bacon, 1998.

Browne, Julie, "The Labor of Doing Time" in *Criminal Injustice: Confronting the Prison Crisis* edited by Rosenblatt, Elihu. Boston: South End Press, 1996.

Cohen, Stanley, *Visions of Social Control.* Cambridge: Polity Press, 1985.

Cohen, Stanley, *Against Criminology.* New Jersey: Transaction Publishers, 1992.

Cohen, Stanley, "Human Rights and Crimes of the State: The Culture of Denial" in *Australia and New Zealand Journal of Criminology* 26: 97-115, 1993.

Consedine, Jim, *Restoring Justice: Healing the Effects of Crime.* Lyttelton: Ploughshares Publications, 1995.

Christie, Nils, *Crime Control as Industry: Towards Gulags Western Style.* Oslo: Scandinavian University Press, 1993.

Cummins, Eric, *The Rise and Fall of California's Radical Prison Movement.* Stanford: Stanford University Press, 1994.

De Haan, Willem, "Abolitionism and Crime Control" in *Criminological Perspectives* edited by Muncie McLaughlin and Langan. London: Sage Publications, 1991.

Elias, Robert, *Victims Still: The Political Manipulation of Crime Victims.* London: Sage Publications, 1993.

Fekete, John, *Moral Panic: Biopolitics Rising.* Montreal: Robert Davies Publishing, 1994.

Garland, David, *Punishment and Modern Society: A Study in Social Theory.* Chicago: The University of Chicago Press, 1993.

Gibran, Khalil, *The Prophet.* New York: Alfred A. Knopf, 1923.

Hassine, Victor, *Life without Parole: Living in Prison Today.* Los Angeles: Roxbury Publishing Company, 1996.

Herman, Edward and Chomsky, Noam, *Manufacturing Consent: The Political Economy of the Mass Media.* New York: Pantheon Books, 1988.

Hulsman, Louk, "Critical Criminology and the Concept of Crime" in *Abolitionism: Towards a Non-repressive Approach to Crime* edited by Bianchi, H. and Swaanigen, R. Amsterdam: Amsterdam Free Press, 1986.

Kaminer, Wendy, *It's all the Rage: Crime and Culture*. Massachusetts: Addison-Wesley Publishing Company, 1995.

Kleinman, A. and Kleinman, J., "The Appeal of Experience; Dismay of Images: Cultural Appropriateness of Suffering in Our Times" in *Social Suffering* edited by Kleinman, Das and Lock, Berkeley: University of California Press, 1997.

Lopez, Jose, "Prisons as Concentration Camps: It Can't Happen Here—Or Can It?" in *Criminal Injustice: Confronting the Prison Crisis* edited by Rosenblatt, Elihu. Boston: South End Press, 1996.

Lykes, Banuazizi, Liem, Morris, *Myths Contesting Social Inequalities About the Powerless*. Philadelphia: Temple University Press, 1996.

Michalowski, Raymond, " 'Niggers, Welfare Scum and Homeless Assholes:' The Problems of Idealism, Consciousness and Context in Left Realism" in *New Directions in Critical Criminology* edited by MacLean, Brian and Milovanovic, Dragan. Vancouver: The Collective Press, 1991.

Mathiesen, Thomas, *The Politics of Abolition*. New York: Wiley Press, 1974.

Morris, Ruth, *Penal Abolition: The Practical Choice*. Toronto: Canadian Scholars' Press Inc., 1995.

Morris, Ruth, "Just Give Us the Facts: Statistics and Facts on Criminal Justice." Toronto: Rittenhouse, 1994.

Murphy, P.J., and Murphy, Jennifer, *Sentences and Paroles: A Prison Reader*. Vancouver: New Star Books, 1998.

Pepinsky, Harold and Quinney, Richard, *Criminology as Peacemaking*. Bloomington: Indiana University Press, 1991.

Reiman, Jeffrey, *The Rich Get Richer and the Poor Get Prison: Ideology, Class and Criminal Justice*. New York: Macmillan Publishing Company, 1990.

Reyna, Ruben, "University of the Poor" in *Soledad Prison University of the Poor* edited by Faith, Karlene. Palo Alto: Science and Behavior Books Inc., 1975.

Stern, Vivien, *A Sin Against the Future: Imprisonment in the World*. Boston: Northeastern University Press, 1998.

Surette, Ray, *Media, Crime and Criminal Justice: Images and Realities*. West Wadsworth: An International Thompson Publishing Company, 1998.

Virgo, Sabina, "The Criminalization of Poverty" in *Criminal Injustice: Confronting the Prison Crisis* edited by Rosenblatt, Elihu. Boston: South End Press, 1996.

4

History of ICOPA

Ruth Morris

international conference on penal Abolition

🏛 A Short History Of Conferences

In 1981, the Canadian Quaker Committee on Jails and Justice planted the seed that grew to become ICOPA. Since 1982, eight international conferences have been held in all regions of the world.

1. TORONTO, CANADA, 1983: Founding conference: "How To Include All The Most Difficult Prison Groups In The Community."
2. AMSTERDAM, NETHERLANDS, 1985: "Theoretical Directions in Abolitionism."
3. MONTREAL, CANADA, 1987: "From Prison Abolition to Penal Abolition."
4. KAZIMIERZ DOLNY, POLAND, 1989: "Abolitionism In Eastern Europe."
5. BLOOMINGTON, INDIANA, USA, 1991: "Aboriginal Roots and Radical Empowerment."
6. SAN JOSE, COSTA RICA, 1993: "Challenging Third World Governments To Adopt Abolitionitionist Steps."
7. BARCELONA, SPAIN, 1995: "Penal Abolition, A Real Utopia."

8. AUCKLAND, NEW ZEALAND/AOTEAROA, 1997: "Pathways To Penal Abolition."
9. TORONTO, CANADA, 2000: "Transformative Justice: New Questions, New Answers."

🏛 A FULLER ICOPA HISTORY: CONFERENCES ONE TO EIGHT

The movement to abolish prisons is as old as prisons themselves. In the nineteenth century, voices like Thomas Buxton of the British Parliament and Victor Hugo of France condemned the prison system and retributive justice. In 1976 Gilbert Cantor, a former editor of the prestigious *Philadelphia Bar* magazine, wrote in that prestigious magazine: "If our entire criminal justice apparentus were simply closed down... there would probably be a decrease in the amount of behaviour now labeled 'criminal.' The time has come to abolish the game of crime and punishment, and to substitute a paradigm of resitutition and responsibility. The goal is the civilization of our treatment of offenders."

The modern abolition movement has roots in European criminologists promoting abolition, and American (mostly Quaker) abolitionists. Fay Honey Knopp's group in the USA produced a landmark book called *Instead of Prisons*. This group and this book helped infect Canadians with the abolition "bug." The Quaker Committee on Jails and Justice, of the Canadian Friends Service Committee, worked for years to educate Canadian Quakers. As a result, in 1981, Canadian Quakers came to complete agreement on prison abolition with a statement which read in part:

> *The prison stystem is both a cause and a result of violence and social injustice. Throughout history, the majority of prisoners have been the powerless and the oppressed. We are increasingly clear that the imprisonment of human beings, like their enslavement, is inherently immoral, and is as destructive to the cagers as to the caged.*

Humbly grateful for this mountaintop revelation, Quaker Committee on Jails and Justice dared to dream in 1982 of the First

International Conference on Prison Abolition in Toronto, for 1983. Bob Melcombe, Ruth Morris, Jake Friesen, and Jonathan Ruden were the leaders of a band of six or eight who, with God's help, made the miracle happen. ICOPA I in Toronto attracted 400 people from fifteen countries in North America, Europe, and Australia. With the vital input of Frank Dunbaugh, a structure was put in place for an interim committee, and a newsletter (run by Ruth in those early years), with input from nine different countries. It was agreed that Conferences would take place every two years, that the International Steering Committee would have policy responsibility to keep the abolition goal and plan sites and general broad themes for each conference, and that once a site was decided, local committees would arrange all the immediate details. ICOPA Conferences would not be like others talking about alternatives within the system, and providing a platform for governmental people to defend the indefensible. They would provide the only opportunity for those who knew this system was terminally ill to offer strategies of the future.

It was also agreed that, in general, Conferences would alternate between North America and Europe, although it was recognized that as soon as we could get participation from other continents, it would be good to include Latin America, Africa and other places as ICOPA sites. Herman Bianchi of the Netherlands offered to host ICOPA II in 1985. ICOPA always brings together activists, ex-prisoners and their families, academics, visionary workers in the system and some politicians. ICOPA I included more activists and exprisoners, and Native people. ICOPA II included many European academics and had a strong base of academic presentations.

ICOPA III in Montreal in 1987 brought a major change, carefully decided by the International Planning Committee. We moved from PRISON abolition to PENAL abolition. The seriousness and the correctness of this change has become increasingly clear. A court and policing system based on revenge would need something just like prisons or even worse, if we got rid of prisons. So it was logical to move to penal abolition—getting rid of revenge as the purpose of the whole system.

ICOPA IV was held in Poland, organized by Monica Platek, and was historic because of its location in Eastern Europe in the days when that was very daring. ICOPA V dared again: it was held in Indiana, USA in 1991 when the USA had become the imprisoning capital of the world. Hal Pepinsky brought both academic excellence but also radical commitment, and the voice of Native people was heard there very strongly.

ICOPA VI in 1993 was another first. A meeting with Ruth Morris introduced Elias Carranza to ICOPA V. Elias was Deputy Director of ILANUD, the UN research institute on crime in Latin America, and he agreed to host ICOPA VI in Costa Rica. This brought increased respectability to ICOPA, as high-level justice and prison officials from many Latin American countries played an active and lively part in the Conference. There was a memorable opening day when Louk Hulsman, Monica Platek and Ruth Morris presented abolition and answered questions about it all day from these assembled participants, mostly from Latin America.

At about this time the Morris family established the International Foundation for a Prisonless Society, a small foundation located in Toronto, Canada, dedicated to supporting the conferences.

The momentum in the Spanish-speaking world continued when the first regional ICOPA was held in 1994 in Argentina, with about 160 people there, mostly Latin Americans, but several from Europe and North America. ICOPA VII was held in 1995 in Barcelona, Spain, organized by Maria Theresa Sanchez Concheira and her committee. Attracting Spanish officials and advocates from many parts of Europe, it brought the issue of abolition to formerly Franco Spain.

Another major move forward came in 1997 when ICOPA VIII came to Auckland, New Zealand. The lively Movement for Alternatives to Prisons, led by Jean Stewart, Jim Consedine, and others, has been a voice in the winderness during New Zealand's years of travail with "Rogernomics." Now it brought penal abolition experts from around the world to New Zealand and challenged its own officials to expand the youth Community Group Conferencing system to the spirit of the whole system. It also thrilled the participants with a wonderful day at the Marae, hosted by Maori.

The travels and work of Prof. Hulsman and a small group of committed people from many countries have built a movement out of a vision, and the movement continues to grow. At present Ruth Morris' visits in Costa Rica and

ILANUD's work there under the guidance of Elias Carranza have led to the proposal to hold a Regional ICOPA in El Salvador in April 1998. But the next full ICOPA, ICOPA IX, will come home to Canada: Toronto in 2000, at Ryerson Polytechnic University and Metropolitan United Church (with generous help from the University of Ottawa's strongly activist Criminology Department, with Bob Gaucher, Lisa Finateri, Viviane Saleh-Hanna and others.)

Adapted from "The International Conference on Penal Abolition" by Ruth Morris, Rittenhouse, 1997.

PART 2

TRADITIONAL ISSUES: HOW COULD PENALIZATION OF "STREET CRIMINALITY" BE ABOLISHED?

5

Serve the Rich and Punish the Poor: Law as the Enforcer of Inequality

John Clarke

A couple of years ago, as I stood with a group of homeless people outside a Toronto drop-in centre, a tow-truck happened to pass by, pulling behind it an immobilized police cruiser. The entire group broke into a rousing and spontaneous cheer at the sight of their enemy's misfortune. In an affluent neighbourhood, such a response would be unthinkable. No such gut-level hostility would present itself for the very obvious reason that the frontline enforcers of the Law play very different roles in the lives of rich and poor. For the rich, the police protect property and turn a blind eye to their private vices. For those who may produce wealth but live in poverty, the police function very differently. They patrol their neighbourhoods and intervene in their lives with an overt intention to keep them in line and punish them for any infraction of a legal code that has been designed as a weapon against them.

That prisons constitute the ultimate sanction of this legal code and that these institutions are de facto warehouses for poor and homeless people is an assertion that no one can credibly deny. A well-known former judge once told me that "the justice system is a class-based system and the police are its gatekeepers." That the poor, rather than the rich, end up on the receiving-end of that system is quite understandable. Largely, it is a question of how crime is defined. Acts of survival that the poor may engage in are deemed to be the most evil acts known to humanity. The much more damaging antics of polluters, corporate tax evaders, et cetera, are, on the other hand, dealt with outside the Criminal Code, if they are not totally ignored, or deemed to be perfectly legal.

Even on those rare occasions where a rich person falls afoul of the law and is charged with a criminal act, money and social position offer important protections. There will be no hurried conversations with some distracted duty counsel but the best lawyer money can buy. Should it come down to sentencing, all pretence at "blind justice" goes out the window. Anyone who has sat in on any criminal court proceedings will know that punishment increases the lower the convicted person stands on the social ladder. A business person or upscale professional will have his or her "useful role" in the community taken into account, while a welfare recipient will be assumed to have no redeeming qualities whatsoever. If it is a question of making bail, being homeless is, in and of itself, a reason to remain locked up. Put simply, if you are poor you are more scrutinized by the Law, your actions are more likely to be viewed as criminal and, if you do end up in court, your poverty will massively undermine your prospects of acquittal or any hope of lenient treatment. This is an obvious injustice but it has to be viewed as part of the broader question I alluded to at the outset of how the state and legal structure deal with both rich and poor.

The Law is not set up to punish the rich but, on the contrary, plays the role of protector and facilitator of wealth making. It confronts the poor, however, as a repressive agent. When the rich think of lawyers and courts, they are not even likely to be thinking about the criminal justice system at all. Lawyers are people who fix it so they can legally defer their taxes. Courts are places where they take business rivals over issues like breech of contract, or where they stall people who have been injured by their products to avoid having to compensate them. When, on the other hand, a poor person thinks about lawyers and courts, it centres on things like pleading guilty and hoping for reduced time in a triple-bunked prison cell.

Even where the Law is forced to constrain the rich, it certainly doesn't deal out criminal penalties. I was once asked to meet with officials from the Human Rights Commission in London, Ontario. They informed me that they had done a survey of local landlords who, in large numbers, had cheerfully told them that they did not rent to people on welfare. However, the landlords had also told them that they would be amenable to changing this behaviour if they could be assured that the rent would be paid directly to them by the local welfare office. Because this is not the normal way for benefits to be allocated, the Human

Rights office was considering petitioning the Province to give the landlords what they wanted. They wanted to know if the London Union of Unemployed Workers (with which I was then involved) would support them in this. I replied that people on welfare should have as much right to control their finances (such as they are) as anyone else. However, since a refusal to rent to people based on source of income is a violation of the Human Rights Code, I suggested that going after landlords who broke the Law in this regard would be a better approach. In fact, I suggested, that if anyone was going to be petitioned, it would be better to tell the Federal Government that denying shelter to a person because they are on welfare is a serious enough matter to have it placed under the Criminal Code. Needless to say, this was the last time we were consulted by the local defenders of human rights.

The incident I describe is really quite instructive when it comes to viewing how the legal system defines crime and deals out punishment for the rich as opposed to the poor. In order to restrain the most rapacious elements within the ranks of the employers, landlords and other moneybags, and to prevent too much indignation at their excesses, it has been necessary to pass some laws that place restrictions on them. However, such restrictions are never too serious, always weakly enforced and rarely place the guilty party before the criminal courts. An even more illustrative incident took place few weeks ago in the work of the Ontario Coalition Against Poverty (OCAP). We were contacted by a man who had worked for a Toronto gas station for a week before being told his services were no longer needed. When he asked for his back pay, he was told that he was not entitled to any money because he had not, in fact, been working during this time but had been receiving "training" from the employer.

The conduct I describe is, of course, totally illegal. He had an iron-clad claim to the week's wages but what actual remedy was available to him? To go to the Labour Board would mean months and months of delay before he MIGHT eventually see his money. And, after this delay, all that the employer would face, after knowingly and illegally cheating this man out of his wages, would be a judgement ordering him to pay up. The same legislators and enforcers who see so much value in deterrents for the poor have no time for even the tamest sanctions for those at the other end of the social scale. OCAP's method of securing redress for this man brought this curious double standard out in a very clear and ironic fashion. Rather than waiting for a toothless government agency to stall this matter to death, we went the much simpler route of picketing the gas station to get the money. Had this man gone to the cops about the employer's theft of his wages, he would have been told it was "not a police matter." As soon, however, as this employer found a picket line outside his place of business, he was able to immediately bring in police officers to protect his operations. They even obliged him by arresting one of our members. Next time you see a police cruiser with "serve and protect" written on it, be sure to read the fine print! (As an aside, the attempt to intimidate us failed and the man got his money.)

It might, at this point, be worthwhile to stress something that emerges in the above incident. By this I mean the degree to which the Law functions as a private army to protect the amassing of wealth and the exploitative means by which this is performed. Historically, this has been by far the most important function of the State and its laws. If we look at how the present, capitalist, form of society came into being then we are immediately struck by the huge role of legalized terror in laying this foundation. This is true both in terms of the clearing of the old, feudal landholdings and in the way in which a modern workforce was created and disciplined. Speaking of the enclosure acts of late sixteenth-century England, A.L. Morton states:

> *Feudal agriculture had been largely collective, based on... joint cultivation of the common lands.... The peasantry had to be atomized, broken up into solitary and defenceless units, before they could be reintegrated into a mass of wage labourers....*[1]

To remove any doubts as to the means employed to create these "defenceless units" out of the peasant population, it is worth quoting from a description of an episode during the later Highland Clearances in Scotland:

> *Thirteen days before the May term the burners came like an army – Factor and Fiscal, Sheriff Officers and constables.... [T]he warrants for the eviction had been granted by Captain Kenneth MacKay of Torboll, an officer of Volunteers and an extensive sheep farmer, who was acting for the Sheriff's office.... The destruction was begun in the west at Grummore as the party approached it... and messages were sent ahead to all the other townships warning the people that they had an hour to evacuate their homes and take away what furniture they could. "I saw the townships set on fire," recalled Roderick MacLeod, who was a boy at the time, "Grummore with sixteen houses and Archmilidh with four. All the houses were burnt with the exception of one barn. Few if any of the families knew where to turn their heads or from where to get their next meal. It was sad, the driving away of these people.*[2]

In North America, of course, capitalism was directly imported from Europe and the dispossession of a peasantry was not required. However, the existing Native population was robbed of its land and nationhood. Here too, it was the agents of the Law who carried out this work as is shown by an example of legalized violence dealt out by the Canadian State against the Mohawk Nation. The following passage was written by Michael Mitchell of Akwesasne:

> *At 4.00 AM on May 1, 1899, Colonel Sherwood... came to Akwesasne, leading a contingent of police across the St. Lawrence River. They occupied the Council Hall, where they sent a message to the chiefs to attend a special meeting regarding the buying of stone [to rebuild a bridge].... As the chiefs walked into the council office, they were thrown to the floor and handcuffed. One of the women notified the Head Chief, Jake Fire, and as he came through the door demanding the release of his fellow chiefs he was shot twice, the second shot being fatal. The police marched their prisoners to the tugboat and left the village. Jake Fire was shot down in cold blood while fighting for Mohawk Indian government.... The seven chiefs were imprisoned. Five of them were kept in jail for more than a year.... Immediately after this affair, the representatives of the government took fifteen Indians over to Cornwall and provided them with alcohol. The Indian agents told them each to nominate one of the others present. This is how the elective government under the Indian Act system was implemented at Akwesasne. This is the way Canada introduced our people to the principles of their democracy.*[3]

The last two passages that I have quoted deal with how the Law was employed to take land and atomize existing ways of life. Once this had been effected, however, the use of legalized violence and coercion by no means came to an end. A.L. Morton, continues his examination of sixteenth-century England by looking at how the dispossessed peasantry was instilled with an appropriate respect for the "work ethic." Unemployment was made a crime and "sturdy vagabonds" (known as "single employables" today) were punished, as of 1536, by having their ears cut off. This leniency was shown only to first offenders. After you were caught without a job for the third time, they hanged you. Whipping and branding were also introduced for the jobless in 1547.[4]

As an effect, in part of the "normalization" of the new form of work relations and, on the other hand, under pressure from the unemployed themselves, who rebelled against such treatment, it became necessary to supplement direct repression with measures of limited provision. This led to the introduction of the Poor Laws at the end of the sixteenth and early seventeenth centuries. Under this system, unemployed people could receive relief but only under the most punitive, degrading and stigmatized conditions possible. This workhouse relief system, its practices and assumptions, laid the basis for modern social assistance regimes. The basic thrust has remained the same: that provision for the needs of the poor and unemployed must not be allowed to create resistance to taking low paying jobs. If such provision is reluctantly granted, then its recipients must be kept in poverty and branded as social pariahs. To the extent that the poor cannot be kept in line with the billy club, the miserable welfare payments that the lawmakers apportion to them will delivered by an intrusive bureaucracy that is well practiced in the "rituals of degradation." The "handouts" that the State permits the poor are delivered on a very different basis to the "incentives" that are showered on the rich in the form of tax breaks and direct giveaways.

The period we are now living in now is one in which this balance between reluctant social provision and repression is being tilted towards the latter direction. Social regulation of the poor means, less and less, income and housing programs and, more and more, takes the form of police patrols, courtrooms and prison cells. The fact is that social cutbacks in Canada, as elsewhere, are creating circumstances where the situation of those who are unemployed or totally excluded from the labour market is becoming measured in terms of vastly increased hardship and, often, outright destitution. The homeless population in major cities is mushrooming. More and more people are forced to sleep in parks and beg on the streets. This starts to become highly problematic for those that the Law serves. Widespread and visible homelessness starts to interfere with commercial development, tourism, upscale residential redevelopment, et cetera. "Resident" and business groups start to clamour for measures to "solve" the problem, which to them means removing it from their sight. They start to put pressure on politicians and police to act and have the social position and training to make that pressure effective. The drive against homeless people is often, falsely, presented as an "anti-crime" initiative. Acts of survival like petty drug dealing or prostitution are focused on but the real agenda is the "social cleansing" of the homeless. Moreover, as the social balance starts to shift and housing is built or renovated to cater to more affluent residents, then the push against the homeless extends to the removal of low-income housing stock and the blocking of social housing initiatives in the contested areas. At every turn, the demonization and criminalization of the existing poor and homeless population is an integral part of the procedure.

The return to an emphasis on repression as opposed to limited provision has produced an atmosphere of shock and crisis in Canadian cities, as homelessness explodes. That it is a return to earlier methods is beyond dispute. Writing at the start of the last century, Jack London describes the situation of the homeless in London, England. One incident he witnessed impressed him so much that he indicated that the passage should be emphasized in the text of his book. He writes:

> *From the slimy sidewalk, they [two homeless men] were picking up bits of orange peel, apple skin and grape stems, and they were eating them. The pits of green gage plums they cracked between their teeth for the kernels inside. They picked up stray crumbs of bread the size of peas, apple cores so black and dirty one would not take them to be apple cores, and these things these two men took into their mouths, and chewed them, and swallowed them; and this, between six and seven o'clock in the evening of August 20, year of our Lord 1902, in the heart of the greatest, wealthiest, and most powerful empire the world has ever seen.[5]*

A century later, it is far from uncommon in cities like Toronto to see human beings eating food from the streets and out of garbage cans and, indeed, only a hastily assembled and overworked network of private charity prevents such sights from being pervasive. London describes in the same work that homeless people in the East End of the City would sleep in the day time and walk about at night because they would face police persecution if they tried to sleep in public places during the night hours.[6] This, too, is an experience that the homeless of present day Toronto can attest to. Indeed, the drive to push out homeless people, by way of legalized brutality, is reaching new and unheard of levels. Through their so-called "Safe Streets" legislation, the Provincial Tories are preparing a huge crackdown on panhandlers, squeegeers and the homeless in general. Toronto's City Government has developed an initiative known as "Community Action Policing" that gives police a green light to target and persecute homeless people and the visibly poor. Local politicians are talking admiringly of the example of social cleansing that has been provided by New York City. They look to the day when it will be a crime to sleep on the streets and it will be possible to lock people away in hostels that have become de facto prisons. Toronto, in common with other major urban centres, refines its plans to hide away those homeless it is not able to drive out altogether through police terror.

While the attack is already well underway, the scope for its intensification was brought home to me by a conversation I had recently with a homeless man from New York. He told me that compared to those in his city, the Toronto cops are "ambs" who usually just "threaten you or rough you up a bit and tell you to move on." In his hometown, he told me, there are whole areas where, if the police see a homeless person, they will immediately pull out their billy clubs and use them. If you try to say that you didn't know you weren't allowed in the area, they will tell you that "this is so you'll know next time." Those of us who see up close the massive abuses against the homeless in Toronto by the police are justifiably outraged by what is going on. However, the expert testimony of this man and his matter-of-fact manner of delivering it, convinced me that there is ample room for things to get much worse

It's long been said that "there's one law for the rich and another for the poor." This is now being reworked so that the law for the poor is more straightforward and the very fact of being poor and destitute becomes a crime. Tory judges in the early 1800s applied the principle that "justice dares array herself in terrors when it is deemed necessary."[7] Ontario Premier Mike Harris, by his own admission, doesn't read books, but, if he did, this would be one of his favourite quotations. Obviously, a vital aspect of this political direction is to increase massively the use of incarceration of the poor. "Super jails" and boot camps are the shape of the future in Ontario. Again, it is to the United States that we can look to for the road ahead.

From a recently issued US Government report, we learn just where the mad drive to lock away poor people leads to. In 1998, nearly two million people in the US were serving sentences of one year or more. That is 461 inmates per 100,000 residents of the country. At the start of the decade only 292 per 100,000 were locked up for more than a year. In the State of Louisiana, an astounding 736 per 100,000 are serving major time in prison. The rate of incarceration has gone up in the 1990s by 65 percent in the state and 106 percent in the Federal prison systems. In Texas, the rate has shot up in this period by 155 percent. Male incarceration is up by 67 percent and female by 92 percent. Among black males in their late 20s, the 1997 rate of imprisonment was a truly shocking 8,630 per 100,000 and, even among black men of between 45 and 54, the rate was still 2,775 per 100,000.

As to the conditions that are produced by such a policy, the state prisons are at 13 percent to 22 percent over capacity and the federal institutions are 27 percent over their limit. The State of California is actually cramming into its prisons double the numbers they are designed to hold.[8] Amnesty International, commenting on the situation in womens' prisons in the United States, observes that sexual abuse by guards and the neglect of basic and medical needs are so pervasive as to be a routine part of life for women inmates.[9]

The Law and its repressive agencies confront the poor in a couple of ways. There are, on the one hand, the ongoing measures of punishment and regulation that we have seen employed over centuries. At different times and places the focus of this may change. In this essay, we have seen the dispossession of the peasantry and the terrorizing of the unemployed of Tudor England into accepting new forms of employment. In our times, we have looked at the driving of homeless people out of the core areas of major Canadian cities and the mass imprisonment of poor people in the US as a means of suppressing the acts of survival that they engage in. We must also consider, however, the use of legal repression against the poor when their resistance takes conscious forms and goes down the road of organized challenge to economic attack and oppressive authority.

During the Great Depression of the 1930s, when the resistance of the unemployed reached the level of a powerful social movement, the use of the State and its laws to crush such resistance reached the most shocking levels. Section 98 of the Criminal Code, allowed for organizations to be banned as subversive and for membership in them to be made retroactively a crime. Moreover, anyone who allowed gatherings of banned organizations to be held on their premises, faced imprisonment under this section. Tom McEwan, who was active in trade union and unemployed struggles during the 30s, provides us with an account of police attempts in Toronto at the time to stifle unemployed resistance. He quotes from a brief presented to a Royal Commission by the Canadian Labour Defence League:

> *1929: To all Hall-keepers and owners in the City of Toronto: "You are hereby notified that if any communist or bolshevist [as defined by the police] public meeting is held in a public hall, theatre, music hall, exhibition, show or other place of public amusement, proceedings or addresses or any of them are carried on in a foreign language, the licence for such public hall, etc., shall immediately be cancelled. By order of the Board of Police Commissioners."*

85

1929: During July and August there were almost daily occurrences of meetings being smashed up and people being beaten.

1931-32: Members of the famous Red Squad accompanied by police inspectors paid daily visits to the Workers Unity League and Unemployed Association offices, sometimes as often as three and four times a day. People on the premises were intimidated and roughly handled. Membership cards and relief cards found in their possession were promptly confiscated.

1932: The manager of the Workers Co-operative Restaurant [fined for operating without a license]. This restaurant was repeatedly refused [a license] on the grounds "that communists were eating there."

1930: [Following an arrest of McEwan himself]. Outside the station yard McEwan was pulled from the auto by Officer Lundy and another policeman and dealt a savage blow in the face which felled him to the ground. Officer Lundy leapt upon McEwan... pinning his knees on McEwan's chest and punched his face until it was suffused in blood. McEwan was then dragged into the police station, stood up against the wall and again attacked with blows to the face and savage kicks to the body. With blood streaming down his face and semi-conscious, McEwan was thrown into a cell. There Oscar Ryan and other prisoners tried to stop the flow of blood, and when unable to do so, raised the alarm. The police came and hurriedly removed McEwan to the General Hospital for emergency treatment.[10]

The resistance of the unemployed and homeless in present day Toronto has not yet reached the level of the 1930s. Nor, it must be said, is the State quite as free, at the moment, to trample on rights of assembly and expression. Still, the experiences of the Ontario Coalition Against Poverty in the recent period lead us to conclude that those who stand in the way of social cutbacks and repressive "solutions" to the problems of poverty and homelessness can expect their share of attacks. We have had undercover police officers at our actions and meetings. "Anti Terrorist" and Intelligence officers have visited our office and come to the homes of activists to intimidate their families. We have faced clubs, pepper spray, police dogs and police horses. Our members have sustained injuries when our marches have been blocked or attacked by the police or, in a number of cases, when subjected to assault while in custody. Since the coming to power of the Harris Regime and the sharpening of the struggle we find ourselves in, over one hundred and twenty arrests of OCAP members have taken place. Despite an almost total lack of successful convictions, the police continue to lay charges against us, many of them very serious ones. The list includes trespass, littering(!), mischief, assault, assault causing bodily harm, assault police, obstruct police, conspiracy to commit theft, forcible entry, counselling to commit an indictable offence, intimidation and unlawful assembly.

Those who live in poverty or who act to challenge its existence must soon come to the stark realization that the Law has nothing to do with justice but, to the contrary, serves as a weapon in the promotion and extension of inequality. It is, of course, vital that we push back against all attempts to extend the power of the Law and its agents. We must challenge reactionary new laws like the Safe Streets Act and oppose police "clean ups" of the poor and homeless. We should fight all their moves to cram the poor into prisons and to make the regimes in these places even more vile and inhuman than they already are. Where we can win concessions and reforms, we should press vigorously for such things. We should, however, keep sight of just who the Law and its many institutions serve. The rules and regulations that govern a society will always ultimately reflect the interests of those who control it. When society is just, its laws will be just. Until that day, the Law serves the rich and punishes the poor.

🏛 ENDNOTES

1   A.L. Morton, *A People's History of England*, p. 138, Lawrence and Wishart.

2   John Prebble, *The Highland Clearances*, pp. 95, 96, Penguin.

3   Ronald Wright, *Stolen Continents*, p. 319, Penguin.

4   Morton, p. 141.

5   Jack London, *The People of the Abyss*, p. 78, Lawrence Hill Books.

6   London, p. 76.

7   Bryan Palmer, *Working Class Experience*, p. 63, McClelland and Stewart.

8   *Prisoners in 1998* (NCJ-175687) Bureau of Justice Statistics.

9   *Not Part of My Sentence*, Amnesty International, 1999.

10   Tom McEwan, *The Forge Glows Red*, pp. 179-183, Progress Books.

6

The Race to Incarcerate

Marc Mauer

We're on a new higher plateau of crime, which means a new, higher and, I think, permanent prison population. It is very hard for a free society to figure out how to deal effectively with crime rates other than by imprisonment.[1] What an interesting populace we have. Nobody seems at all worried by the fact that we have the largest prison population and that it consists preponderantly of young blacks, a whole generation in jail.[2]

In January 1998, the Justice Department issued its semi-annual report on prison populations in the United States, noting that there had been a five-percent rise in the previous twelve months. Newspapers dutifully reported the story; just as they had similar rises the year before and the year before that. In fact, by now the story was a quarter century old, with the national prison population having risen nearly 500 percent since 1972, far greater than the 28 percent rise in the national population during that time. In the ten-year period beginning in 1985, federal and state governments had opened one new prison a week to cope with the flood of prisoners. The nearly 1.2 million inmates in the nation's prisons was almost six times more than before the inception of the prison-building boom and represented a societal use of incarceration that was virtually unique by world standards. The scale of imprisonment had come a long way since the birth of the institution.

Two hundred years ago, Quakers and other reformers in Pennsylvania had developed the institution of the penitentiary, an experiment in molding human behavior that befitted other innovations in the new democracy of the United States. Derived from the concept of "penitence," the new institution emphasized having sinners engage in hard labor and reflect upon the errors of their ways.

Prior to this, the preferred methods of responding to criminal behavior in both the European nations of the old world and in the American colonies did not include institutions. The jails that existed in Europe and the U.S. served primarily to detain defendants who were awaiting trial and debtors who had not fulfilled their obligations; they were not places of punishment for felons.

After a defendant was convicted of an offense, various measures were employed with the goal of deterring the individual from engaging in such antisocial behavior in the future. Deviant behavior was viewed not as reflecting a flaw in society but, rather, as sinful and pervasive in society. Those who had offended were generally subjected to relatively swift and severe sanctions, which often varied depending on one's status in the community. For persons of some means who had committed relatively minor offenses, fines were frequently imposed as punishment. Lower-status persons convicted of offenses—servants, apprentices, slaves, and laborers—were usually subjected to the stocks or public whippings. The death penalty was an option in serious cases, such as murder, but also for lesser offenses, such as third-time thievery. The use of capital punishment, however, was far less frequent in the colonies than in England. Offenders in the colonies who were not from the immediate community, and sometimes repeat offenders, were generally subject to banishment.

Much of the rationale for these various punishments can be found in the nature of the colonial society. In an environment where communities were relatively small and their inhabitants well known to each other, public approbation and embarrassment was seen as capable of shaming the offender into desisting from continued illegal activities. Wandering rogues who went from town to town committing crimes were usually banished. Moreover, in a society where labor was in short supply, benefits to the community were derived from swift and certain punishments, which did not unduly affect the laboring capacity of the community.

After the Revolution, however, new ways of thinking about crime and punishment began to emerge. In 1787, influential Quakers and others in Pennsylvania, led by Dr. Benjamin Rush, organized the Philadelphia Society for Alleviating the Miseries of Public Prisons.[3] A growing sentiment that the death penalty and other corporal punishments were barbaric eventually led to restrictions or elimination of capital punishment in the new states.

But if the death penalty was to be eliminated, or its use greatly reduced, how would serious offenders be punished? These and other issues were considered by the nation's leaders. Out of these deliberations came the notion of the prison as a new form of punishment and deterrence for both capital and non-capital offenders.

The initial experiment in confining convicted offenders took place in 1790: it involved converting sixteen cells at Philadelphia's Walnut Street Jail into housing for felons. This was later replaced and expanded upon at the Eastern State Penitentiary in 1829, which remained in use until 1970. The Pennsylvania penitentiary model was based on imprisoning offenders in solitary confinement and occupying them with labor and Bible study in their cells; those who were unable to read were aided by outside volunteers.

Ironically, and in retrospect quite tellingly, the first inmate admitted to the Eastern State Penitentiary was a "light skinned Negro in excellent health," described by an observer as "one who was born of a degraded and depressed race, and had never experienced anything but indifference and harshness."[4] Two centuries later, the confluence of issues of race and class with the prison system have become a fundamental feature of the national landscape.

Variations on the penitentiary model used the basic format of confining offenders to solitary cells, but exposing them to a congregate work environment. This approach was pioneered in the 1820s by the "Auburn model" in New York State, which required inmates to engage in work during the day; prisoners were prohibited from talking or even exchanging glances. Fierce debates raged at the time regarding the efficacy of the competing Pennsylvania and New York models in controlling crime. However, common to both systems was the belief that the less communication offenders had with each other, the less opportunity there would be to engage in criminal plotting or to reinforce each other's negative orientation.

By the mid-1800s, changes in the makeup of American society—no longer a relatively sparsely populated collection of small towns and cities—led to a new consensus regarding how best to respond to criminal behavior. The demographic and economic growth of the nation had spawned increasing concern about antisocial behavior and ways of maintaining order in an increasingly fluid society. Out of this came a growing consensus among leaders of the day regarding the need for an institutional response to potential disorder.

It is unsettling to speak of "caging" human beings, since we normally prefer to use this term for animals and to conjure up fond feelings for our favorite zoo (although our common feelings about the constraints placed on animals in cages have also changed markedly in recent years). But whether we call them "cells," or "housing units," or any other new name, it is difficult to deny that the basic reality of the system is that of the cage.

Looking back on two centuries of the prison in America, what is particularly remarkable is how little the institutional model has changed since the nineteenth century. While the philosophical orientation and stated goals of the prison have varied, the basic concept of imprisoning people in cages remains the central feature of the system.

To place the permanence of the model in perspective, we need only consider how other institutions and professions have evolved over these past two hundred years. In transportation, we have moved from the horse and buggy to the steam engine, the automobile, and now, ventures deep into the solar system. In medicine, healing methods based on limited scientific expertise have been eclipsed by such remarkably sophisticated measures as open-heart surgery and even the possibility of cloning human beings. Understandings of human behavior likewise have been dramatically altered by the advances of psychotherapy, along with a host of twentieth-century theories. Yet the prison cell endures after two centuries.

This is not to say that prison systems are necessarily operated in an eighteenth-century fashion, or that change is never instituted. Despite the re-introduction of chain gangs, old-styled convict uniforms, and other methods of humiliation, there still remain many corrections administrators who take pride in their work and are earnest advocates for humane conditions of confinement. Indeed, in some newer prisons, the cage itself has been replaced by locked rooms in a dormitory-like setting. Nevertheless, the themes of confinement and isolation remain central to the model of the prison.

The way a society deals with offending behavior is first conditioned on how that behavior is defined, a value that evolves over time and across cultures. Within the United States, alcohol production was prohibited in the 1930s, but has been permitted for the most part during all other periods. Even among more serious offenses, both cultural and situational relevance determine societal responses. Killing a person, for example, is clearly outlawed in daily life, but permitted by all nations in times of war. State-sanctioned killings in the form of the death penalty are permitted in such nations as the United States, China, and

Iran, but prohibited in most industrialized nations and many developing nations as well.

Prisons and the entire apparatus of a criminal justice system represent a response to offending behaviors. The system is viewed as a means of retribution and problem-solving, that of responding to persons and behaviors we find unacceptable. But, most critically, the system itself is premised on being a *reactive* model and a *punitive* system—that is, the criminal justice system comes into play only after a crime has been committed. At that point, the victim may call 911, the police will investigate, the prosecutor brings charges, and a judge imposes a sentence if there is a conviction. Each of these actions is appropriate in and of themselves, but our familiarity with them tends to mask any consideration of the underlying approach suggested by this model.

By identifying certain persons or groups of people as "criminals," a punitive model of responding to social problems is made to appear almost inevitable. However, this model of problem solving is hardly preordained. Families and communities regularly employ a host of services and resources to encourage what are believed to be appropriate behaviors and to discourage antisocial behaviors. In the vast majority of cases, these approaches are pro-active ones. Thus, we establish schools to educate our children, we form religious bodies to communicate values, and we act as parents to transmit styles of behavior that we regard as ethical or beneficial.

In many communities, applying these approaches results in an environment with well-functioning members that, in crime terms, is considered "safe." But when we think of a community that is "safe," is it one with the most police or the most frequent use of the death penalty? Of course not. Rather, it is one with clean, well-lit streets, open businesses, and little fear. These often happen to be communities with high income levels, strong families and community resources, and ones that both value their members and have the means by which to assure that most of them will do well in society.

In contrast, other communities become defined as "bad" or "unsafe," and are ones that contain inordinate numbers of "criminals." At this point, a rational society would be challenged to develop an approach to ensure more safety for these communities. One approach might be to provide the community with more resources, or to facilitate the ability of its members to assert more control over the offending behaviors. Increasingly, though, the model of choice has been the use of the criminal justice system and its punitive orientation. Whether intended or not, this approach is intimately connected with perceptions of race and class. So, while public support may be forthcoming for "tough" penalties and the politicians who propose them, when it is one of our own who gets into trouble, we seem to view the problem very differently.

In recent years, we have seen this distinction played out most directly in the national approach to drug abuse. Millions of middle-class families have experienced the pain of seeing a loved one succumb to drug abuse or addiction. Their response, by and large, is one that recognizes this as a social problem for which social interventions are necessary. Identifying a high-quality treatment program, with the aid of private insurance, becomes the preferred response to the problem.

In contrast, for nearly two decades the nation has been engaged in a very different "war on drugs" to respond to drug abuse and its associated ills among low-income and minority families. Treatment programs are likely to be in short supply, so the problem of abuse is much more likely to fester and eventually result in actions that will define it as a criminal justice problem.

None of this should suggest, of course, that crime is not a problem of serious concern, or that minority communities are not particularly affected by dramatically high rates of violence. In fact, for many years minority communities have bemoaned the lack of police attention to their concerns as well as complained of police harassment. A complex set of factors, though, fueled in large part by a haze of media images and political sound bites, has almost inured us to any approaches to these problems other than through punitive criminal justice models. And, while we continue to suffer from crime rates that are higher than the 1950s, a quarter century of "tough" policies has failed to provide sufficient safety or to substantially reduce the fear of crime.

Some observers of these developments have concluded that the crime and criminal justice policies of the present era represent a conspiratorial assault on minority communities. To believe this, though, negates the actual progress that has been made in securing minority representation in leadership positions within the justice system. Progress in this regard is still relatively modest in many jurisdictions, but the past twenty years have indeed witnessed a substantial increase in the number of black and Hispanic police chiefs, judges, corrections officials, and others in positions of authority.

It is more productive to examine the stated and unstated assumptions that have guided criminal justice policy, as well as the choices not presented or chosen. A black judge confronted with indigent drug addicts and inadequate treatment resources is in as difficult a position at sentencing as a white judge: both are daily confronted with the consequences of broader policy decisions that have disinvested in communities and implicitly chosen a reactive and punitive response to broad social problems, rather than a pro-active and constructive one.

The essentially reactive nature of the criminal justice model has been of concern to many, both in terms of its efficacy in responding to the problem of crime and in terms of establishing a two-tiered system of community problem solving. Indeed, throughout the history of the use of imprisonment in the United States, there have been critiques of the model, organized efforts at reform, and challenges to the prevailing wisdom. As early as the 1840s, Charles Dickens bemoaned the model he witnessed in Philadelphia: "Those who devised this system and those benevolent gentlemen who carry it into execution do not know what they are doing." On the nature of the institution, he concluded, "I hold this slow and daily tampering with the mysteries of the brain, to be immeasurably worse than any torture of the body."[5] In recent times, the social upheavals of the 1960s produced a prison reform movement both within the prisons and among outside supporters. Often led or influenced by black Muslims within the institutions, the movement raised a broad critique of the prison system itself, the definition of crime, and the coercive power of the state. While elements of this critique have always been present, events of the past quarter century have now elevated its significance in profound ways. During this period, public policy in the United States has resulted in what can only be termed a second wave of the great "experiment" in the use of incarceration as a means of controlling crime. As we shall see, a complex set of social and political developments have produced a wave of building and filling prisons virtually unprecedented in human history. Beginning with a prison population of just under 200,000 in 1972, the number of inmates in U.S. prisons has increased by nearly one million, rising to almost 1.2 million by 1997. Along with the more than one half million inmates in local jails either awaiting trial or serving short sentences, a remarkable total of 1.7 million Americans are now behind bars.

These figures take on more meaning in comparison with other nations in the industrialized world. The U.S. rate of incarceration per capita now dwarfs that of almost all such nations: our nation locks up offenders at a rate six to ten times that of most comparable countries. Ironically, the United States now competes only with Russia for the dubious distinction of maintaining the world lead in the rate at which its citizens are locked up. Although the Cold War has ended and the arms race is essentially over, these two nations with vastly different economies and social conditions now are engaged in a race to incarcerate.

Like the arms race, the race to incarcerate has a set of consequences for society that have generally been examined only in the most shallow of ways. Moreover, as we approach the new millennium, the nature and meaning of incarceration in the United States has changed in a variety of profound ways with far-reaching implications.

First among these is the virtual institutionalization of a societal commitment to the use of a massive prison system. More than half of the prisons in use today have been constructed in the last twenty years. These prisons can be expected to endure and imprison for at least fifty years, virtually guaranteeing a national commitment to a high rate of incarceration. The growth of the system itself serves to create a set of institutionalized lobbying forces that perpetuate a societal commitment to imprisonment through the expansion of vested economic interests. The more than 600,000 prison and jail guards, administrators, service workers, and other personnel represent a potentially powerful political opposition to any scaling-down of the system. One need only recall the fierce opposition to the closing of military bases in recent years to see how these forces will function over time.

Prisons as sources of economic growth have also become vital to the development strategy of many small rural communities that have lost jobs in recent years but hold the lure of cheap land and a ready workforce. Communities that once organized against the siting of new prisons now beg state officials to construct new institutions in their backyards. Add to this the rapidly expanding prison privatization movement focused on the "bottom line" of profiting from imprisonment. In the words of one industry call to potential investors, "While arrests and convictions are steadily on the rise, profits are to be made—*profits from crime.* Get in on the ground floor of this booming industry now."[6]

Nevertheless, it is not as if there are no models to guide us in making the transition toward less use of incarceration. The de-institutionalization of the mental health system, which began in the 1960s, was hardly an unqualified success, as a function, primarily, of the failure to enhance sufficiently community-based services; yet, it remains a model that demonstrates the possibility of embracing new approaches that challenge conventional wisdom.

Prison reformers of the 1960s and 1970s often maintained a cautious optimism that a de-institutionalization movement in corrections would follow that of the mental health system. Their reasoning was that similar critiques could be made of both types of systems, but that greater public empathy for mental patients than criminal offenders inevitably would result in an easier transition for the mental health model. With the benefit of hindsight, we can now see that this faith was quite misplaced.

The near-permanent status of the massive state of imprisonment is obvious despite the expressed concern over the "crisis" of prison overcrowding accompanying public policy discussion and media accounts of these issues. Pleas have been made that funding for an expanded prison system will divert resources from other public spending, and that prison capacity cannot be expanded quickly enough to accommodate a steadily growing number of inmates.

After a quarter century of prison growth, however, it is now apparent that while some corrections officials may feel the impact of an expanding system and overcrowding, in fact, there is really no longer a "crisis" mentality in many regards. Rather, vastly expanded expenditures on corrections system are now considered the norm, and in fact, represent the largest growth area of state budgets. Virtually every state has engaged in a significant, if not massive, prison construction program over the past two decades, financed through general funds, bonds, and more recently, public/private venture arrangements. While prisons in most states still remain overcrowded, the level of overcrowding has not changed appreciably since 1990, which demonstrates that state and the federal governments have been quite willing to construct new institutions in response to growing demand. Finally, while there still remains some discussion regarding the need to refrain from unlimited growth in the system, any consideration of an actual reduction in the absolute size of the prison population is virtually absent from public policy discussion.

Contributing to the establishment of this permanent state of mass incarceration is the impact of falling crime rates of the 1990s. For proponents of expanded imprisonment, a falling rate of crime is virtually all the proof needed to justify an expensive and inherently coercive institution: if imprisonment goes up and crime rates go down, they argue, the correlation between these two must be obvious. As we shall see later, this "relationship" is far from clear and certainly not one that should justify such a commitment of resources. Nonetheless, at a time when political leaders can boast of their "success" in reducing crime rates, any criticism of the prison state has difficulty gaining attention.

It is hard to imagine that this complacency would exist if the more than a million and a half prisoners were the sons and daughters of the white middle class. However, as the image of the criminal as an urban black male has hardened into public consciousness, so too, has support for punitive approaches to social problems been enhanced. Little talk is heard of the feasibility of expanded employment or educational opportunities as a means of crime prevention: welfare "reform" gains a bipartisan political consensus, despite dire predictions of large increases in child poverty, and policymaker acceptance of a "permanent underclass" proceeds apace. In a changed economy with less demand for the labor of many unskilled workers, imprisonment begins to be seen as an appropriate, if unfortunate, outcome.

While the impact of incarceration on individuals can be quantified to a certain extent, the wide-ranging effects of the race to incarcerate on African American communities in particular is a phenomenon that is only beginning to be investigated. What does it mean to a community, for example, to know that three out of ten boys growing up will spend time in prison? What does it do to the fabric of the family and community to have such a substantial proportion of its young men enmeshed in the criminal justice system? What images and values are communicated to young people who see the prisoner as the most prominent or pervasive role model in the community? What is the effect on a community's political influence when one quarter of the black men in some states cannot vote as a result of a felony conviction? Surely these are not healthy developments.

We have entered an era of technology and communications in which developments in crime policy in the United States take on an increasingly global influence. While the U.S. hegemony over world economies and culture has long been observed and often decried, there are now ominous signs that the incarceration models and mentality so pervasive in this country are affecting social policy abroad as well.

This trend is probably most obvious in England, where Michael Howard, the former Home Secretary of John Major's Conservative government in the mid-1990s, embraced many of the "get tough" policies developed in the United States. Breaking with a historic British tradition of granting broad discretion and independence to the judiciary, Howard proposed the adoption of mandatory sentences, boot camps, "supermax" high control prisons, and other U.S. innovations. This was accompanied by U.S. "photo-op" visits by Howard to such institutions as the Florence, Colorado, federal "supermax" prison, considered the ultimate form of institutional control, a high-tech operation with almost complete isolation of inmates from each other and the outside world.

The government's initiatives might have been dismissed as merely pandering to a conservative constituency had they not represented such a sharp break with the recent past of the Conservative government. Under the previous leadership of Margaret Thatcher, the government had instituted the 1991 Criminal Justice Act, which essentially recognized the limited impact of incarceration on crime and called for a halt in the growth of the prison system. Developed from a cost-efficiency standpoint, the policy had been promoted as fiscally conservative and responsible.

These developments are not confined to England, however. With worldwide access to media ranging from CNN to the internet, policymakers and the public are now virtually instantaneously exposed to social changes in the United States. In recent years, we have therefore seen such legislative proposals as a "three strikes and you're out" policy in the Czech Republic based on televised reports from California. More sinister is the broad reach of the American prison privatization movement; U.S. private prison companies are winning contracts from Australia to eastern Europe. Policies that imprison ever-larger numbers of young African American males in the United States are also likely to result, at least indirectly, in greater incarceration of immigrants in Norway or minority populations in France.

Thus, there is now an even greater obligation on the part of policymakers and the public in the United States to consider their actions and impact not only on the domestic "underclass" but also on democratic rights and traditions internationally.

🏛 ENDNOTES

1   James Q. Wilson, interview in *Criminal Justice Matters* (Autumn 1996), p. 4.

2   Murray Kempton, quoted in Alfred Kazin, "Missing Murray Kempton," *New York Times Book Review*, 30 Nov. 1997, p. 35.

3   Although prisons as institutions of punishment had not yet emerged in the new nation, jails for debtors and defendants awaiting trial had previously existed.

4   Negley K. Teeters and John D. Shearer, *The Prison at Philadelphia, Cherry Hill; The Separate System of Prison Discipline, 1829-1913* (New York: Columbia University Press, 1957), p. 84.

5   Charles Dickens, *American Notes* (1842; Penguin ed., 1972), p. 146, as cited in Lawrence M. Friedman, *Crime and Punishment in American History* (New York: Basic Books, 1993), p. 80.

6   Jennifer L. Berk, World Research Group, conference invitation letter, December 1996.

7

But What About The Dangerous Few?

Ruth Morris

🏛 INTRODUCTION

Whenever I talk about healing justice, one of the first questions I am asked is, "But what about the serial killer? What would you do with them?" That is a very important question, and a very reasonable one. The greatest fraud perpetrated by our retributive justice system is that it exists to protect us from the dangerous few.

First of all, it is idiotic to treat the 99 percent of prisoners in the way we do on the basis of the one to two percent who make up the dangerous few. Secondly, the present system responds very poorly to the challenge of the dangerous few, and our need for protection from them.

Nevertheless, fear of the dangerous few fuels many of our inappropriate responses to crime. The responses are unjustified, but fear of the homicidal maniac is wholly understandable. This essay is a brief response to the very real challenge of this question, "What would you do with the dangerous few?"

The first step is to accept the hard fact that there are no magic answers or perfect solutions for the dangerous few, any more than we have found solutions to traffic accidents, industrial accidents, family breakup, and many other terrible hazards of modern life. The potential for violence exists in people, and many social factors continue to create a few violent, dangerous people. Much more frequently, these same factors cause people not generally dangerous to break out into a once-in-a-lifetime act of serious violence. The once-in-a-lifetime stress murderer who kills in his/her own family is the most common type of killer, outside of the military.

But although there are no magic answers, there are positive directions. We are learning how to reduce traffic accidents and respond more effectively to them when they do happen; in the same way we can find ways to reduce serial killers, and respond more appropriately to them when they appear in our midst. Positive directions can reduce the number of truly dangerous people we produce, as well as the number of isolated acts of violence.

To find those better directions, we need to take the following steps:

Understanding of our fears
Prevention of the causes of violence
Separation and treatment of the dangerous few
Intensive Supervision in the community, if they are ever released
Research
Victim Support

ᛥ UNDERSTANDING OF OUR FEARS

It is entirely natural to fear the insane serial killer; it is a feeling shared by every thinking, feeling person. Yet we need to understand this problem in context. Our society projects many of our fears onto these people when in reality the majority of murders are within the circle of our friends and families — the outcome of domestic or ingroup stresses.

In fact, the dangerous few constitute no more than one to two percent of the prison population. They are not what our courts and prisons are about, and it is vital NOT to let our entire criminal justice system treat the vast majority of nonviolent property offenders on the basis of our fears of the violent few. University of Toronto criminologists Doob and Roberts found in 1983 that Canadians believe the violent crime rate is seven times higher than it actually is (Canadian Sentencing Commission 1986: 99).

Campaigns for the safety of women often focus on street lighting, more police, and longer sentences for street violence. Yet every study we have shows that the great majority of violence toward women occurs in the home: from their lovers, spouses, fathers, relatives, dates, and close friends.

Another way of setting our understandable fears in context is to consider the likelihood of suffering violent death from an industrial accident, from a drunk driver, and from homicide. Chances of violent death from these sources are as follows (Scott and McDonald, 1986):

> *6 times as likely from an industrial accident than from homicide*
> *2.5 times as likely from a drunk driver than from homicide*

Even within homicide risks, we are far more in danger from "family and friends" than from any stranger (CCJS, 1991):

> *8 times as many homicide victims die from family and friends as from strangers*

Finally, even among those tragic homicides by strangers, many are not committed by serial killers, but are isolated actions by a person driven to extremity on one occasion. This may not console the bereaved very much, but it is still important to recognize that the majority of stranger homicides are not by serial killers. The dangerous few represent a tiny proportion of our social hazards, as the attached graph illustrates. Their violence, although terrifying, is a tiny tip of the iceberg of violent death in our society; and they are a very small proportion of our prison population.

So our first challenge is to look at the violent few in a realistic context. Their actions are terrible and terrifying, but they are not a major source of violence in our society.

ᐧ PREVENTION OF THE CAUSES OF VIOLENCE

The violent few are the tip of the iceberg of our social violence. As with any other problem, it is much easier to *prevent* their growth into violence, than to *cure* their behaviour, once it is out of control. Differences in rates of violence from society to society demonstrate that we define how acceptable violence is by the way we socialize our children. Recently I saw a TV special on South Africa, in which a white mother in a strongly racist family proudly watched her nine-year-old son practising shooting at things with a pellet gun. Such attitudes beget a conviction that violence is normal, acceptable, and even desirable. War toys and violent television shows both give the same message. When society teaches that violence is acceptable, or even glamourous, the most disturbed among us are more likely to express this in ways beyond those socially sanctioned.

To prevent the growth of the dangerous few from today's toddlers, we need to seek the seeds of violence in our culture, and renounce them. We will examine just four important cultural seeds of violence here:

Sex Role Training

The high proportion of families where women and children are physically and/or sexually abused indicates we have a long way to go in establishing clear social norms against family violence. Research indicates that the dangerous few are almost always victims of childhood violence themselves, though by no means all victims of childhood violence join the select ranks of the dangerous few. For whatever reasons, the dangerous few pass on the violence they have received in even more extreme forms, to others beyond their family circles. Perhaps the fact that tens of thousands of socially acceptable families of all social classes live with abusive patterns for years weaves the fabric of a society in which truly disturbed individuals are more likely to become violent.

Even mental illness and social pathology follow socially patterned forms of expression. In a society where abuse of women and children is tragically as normal as it is in ours, pathology by the emotionally disturbed is more likely to take on extremely violent forms.

Family Crisis Intervention

Many of the future clientele of justice agencies could easily be identified by second or third grade. Nearly all are having reading and behaviour problems. Even the mildest inquiries show they are living in very difficult home environments. It does not take much intelligence to realize that an ounce of aggressive, preventive social work on an intensive basis at this point could save many pounds of punitive and treatment later on.

More important, such early intervention could save untold suffering in human lives, and at the community level. After a deep involvement with a high-profile offender, I asked myself: at what age does a person cease to be a vulnerable child, and become a monster in the eyes of society? Whatever the answer, we owe it to ourselves as well as to that person, to intervene before we define a human being as a social monster.

Reduction of Overt Media Violence

The National Coalition on Violent Entertainment estimates that this generation of TV viewers will see 500 times more assaults, 500 times more rapes, and 300 times more murders than their predecessors. This media diet increases our fears of violence, and also the belief by many that violence is acceptable, normal behaviour. A study by Dr. Gerbner of Annenberg School of Communications has shown that heavy TV viewers are more punitive in their philosophy and values, because of this distorted view of reality.

Thus television violence increases both the predisposition to crime and violence and the predisposition to punish, contributing to a violently divided, thoroughly unhealthy society. Steady middle class adult viewers of TV violence become locked in their own suburban picket-fence prisons with ultra-safe security systems, but with no freedom. Their younger counterparts take violence as play-acting fun, and the steady diet of exciting two-dimensional violence by actors who reappear whole and well gives the more vulnerable of our young an appetite for it.

Over 2000 separate studies link media violence to negative effects on children. Some of these have linked national rises in homicide to the coming of age of the first generations raised on television violence (Maude Barlow in Scott and McDonald 1986: 36).

Gun Control

While it is true that it takes a human hand to pull a trigger, the ready access to firearms is a demonstrable factor in countless suicides, accidental family deaths, and numerous family homicides. In addition, guns are like a lighted fuse in the hands of the dangerous few. Tight gun controls prevent deaths most of all from family fights, where a gun and explosive anger leave a lifetime of grief and sorrow for some, and death for others. Moreover, tight gun controls are part of a society which gives cues that violence is unacceptable, and the tools of violence are not to be generally available. Such messages are essential, if we are to create a society which produces fewer serial killers.

These four suggestions are just a few of the most obvious ideas for social prevention of the dangerous few. We must remember that *the dangerous few grow up as part of our society.* They do not drop full-grown from Mars; they are an integral part of our socialization processes. We are not helpless to modify those processes in constructive new ways.

ṁ SEPARATION AND TREATMENT

Persons who have committed a series of dangerous, violent acts need to be protected from their own impulses as much as we need to be protected from them. Such a separation must be in an environment completely different from our prisons, which are incubators of violence. Several obvious principles should be followed in the separation of the dangerous few:

1. They should not be mixed with nonviolent, young offenders, as they are at present in all our prisons. Even if they do not perpetrate more violence, their influence on such young offenders can only be negative, and the pressure of the young offenders on them will usually be destructive as well.
2. The environment for the dangerous few must be both humane and secure. Its focus, besides containment as long as necessary, must be treatment or re-education, and it should follow the best methods research on the dangerous few suggests.
3. To avoid further institutionalization (many of the dangerous few are already institutionalized) and to provide a family-like environment, it is vital that the environment be small and personalized. Only in such a setting is there any hope of undoing the damage of childhood and providing the kind of environment in which change may take place.

As simple and obvious as these three statements seem, they are rarely followed at present. The dangerous few are mixed all too often with other prison inmates, most of whom are young and nonviolent. They are put in environments which are usually inhumane, and vary in security. Because our retributive justice system takes property crime most seriously, it is slow to identify repeated violent rape as a serious crime, although feminists have made much progress on this issue. Finally, the dangerous few are usually incarcerated either in solitary confinement, which is crazy-making even for the well, or in massive institutions which are anything but small and caring and in whose violent environments any treatment programs get lost.

INTENSIVE SUPERVISION

Persons with a very violent past and with every indication of continued predisposition to violence, should not be released to the community as walking time bombs, straight from maximum security, 24-hour lockup situations. Our so-called "Special Handling Units" in both Canada and the USA could not be better designed for making a human being violent. The Pelican Bay Project has exposed evidence of so much widespread guard violence in American prisons that they have asked Amnesty International to look at the issue of torture. Caged, degraded, tormented and isolated, these men emerge straight into the street in a condition so enraged and desocialized that the miracle is that many of them do NOT commit violent crimes.

Parker Rossman in a searching book called *After Punishment, What?* (1980) which deals with very violent juvenile offenders, describes success by one judge who follows three steps:

1. Intensive supervision
2. Confrontation with victims
3. Restitution

Newer responses of crime are going back more and more to aboriginal community healing circle approaches, which involve the whole community in confronting the offender, expressing condemnation of the offence, but acceptance of the human being who did it, and faith that he or she can do better. Such positive confrontation results in an agreement for restitution, restitution which is not just a dollars and cents deal, but a true expression of contrition and an effort to rebuild a community of trust.

How does all this apply to the dangerous few? Their victims are even more entitled to the healing of a healing process, and the opportunity to express their grief to the person responsible for it, than those with lighter suffering. And while such sessions are not sufficient to treat deep psychiatric pathology, they may well be an important contribution towards healing.

But the key here is *intensive* supervision. Supervision programs make far too little distinction between the most trivial offender and the most dangerous one. Some years ago, I met a young man in Winnipeg who was one of two people paid full-time by Community Services to live with a severely retarded, emotionally disturbed, chronically institutionalized young man. It was cheaper and rightly considered better to pay two people full-time to give him daily, hourly support to enable him to live in the community, than to perpetuate his lifetime institutionalization. Why do we not hire such intensive help to give the community the safety it deserves, if it is decided it is time to release any of those formerly identified as the dangerous few?

If we continue to insist on caging our fellow human beings, we owe ourselves as well as them to provide gradual phasing down of security and gradual reintegration into the community. Such reintegration must include very intensive, continuing supervision, friendly but a protection for both offender and community against renewed violence.

ͫ RESEARCH

Some of the above presumes we can identify those who are the dangerous few. In fact, one of the most baffling problems is the inability of modern psychiatry to make such predictions accurately. But while we wait for improvement in this art, we can at least identify who are the *scary few*. Persons who have committed a series of homicides at different times are clearly part of the scary few, although it is interesting that we define soldiers who fit this description as heroes.

Fay Honey Knopp (1984) has researched the wide scattering of experimental programs around the USA attempting to treat sexual offenders. Her research also touches on the dangerous few. There are a few others who do research in this area, but in general we have far more lurid stories about their crimes than serious research into how to prevent and treat their pathology.

We need to ask our governments, now devoting so many counterproductive dollars to retributive justice approaches, to prioritize research on prevention and treatment of the dangerous few. Surely this is a significant problem! Its fear inspires so many measures that drain our resources from constructive uses. We seem mesmerized, content to let the fear they inspire drive us down paths which are destructive for every one of us.

ᛤ VICTIM SUPPORT

Despite all the lip service given to victim needs today, victims of violent crime and their families are not responded to in a healing way by our society. We need universal victim support services and self-help groups, preferably linked with agencies working with offenders. Ultimately, the answers victims and offenders seek are bound up in one another. At present, the five healthy core needs of all victims are met by the direct opposite of each need:

VICTIM NEED	SOCIETAL RESPONSE
1) Answers	1) Court process irrelevant to deep answers needed
2) Recognition of wrong	2) Blaming of the victim
3) Safety	3) Retributive justice process more important than safety
4) Restitution	4) Power and revenge more important than restitution; any restitution is money, not restoration of community
5) Significance	5) Revictimization by whole experience; disempowerment.

If we can create a society in which most people provide support for these five needs of all victims, healing will be all around us, and we will build a community in which the seeds of violence for future serial killers have little nourishment.

ᛤ CONCLUSION

The dangerous few are a symptom of the pathology of violence in our society. Our present response to them, using their existence as a reason for expanding a retributive justice system which embodies and creates violence, is completely counterproductive. Fear of the dangerous few is entirely normal and healthy. Let us use that fear to mobilize ourselves to root out the causes of violence in our society, and build a caring community which nurtures and includes all.

⅏ BIBLIOGRAPHY

CCJS, 1992, *Homicide in Canada, 1991,* Ottawa: Canadian Centre for Justice Statistics.

Canadian Sentencing Commission, 1986, *Report* (Archambault Report), Ottawa: Canadian Government Publishing Centre.

Daubney Committee, 1988, *Taking Responsibility* (Daubney Report), Ottawa: Canadian Government Publishing Centre.

Knopp, Fay Honey, 1984, *Retraining Adult Sex Offenders: Methods and Models*, Orwell, VT: Safer Society Press.

Prison Discipline Study, 1989, *Shattering the Myth of Humane Imprisonment in the U.S.* Sacramento, CA: Prison Discipline Study.

Rossman, Parker, 1980, *After Punishment, What? Discipline and Reconciliation,* Cleveland: Wm. Collins.

Scott, James and McDonald, Eleanor, 1986, *Why Kill People Who Kill People to Show that Killing People is Wrong?* Ottawa: Church Council on Justice and Corrections.

8

Towards Safer Societies: Punishment, Masculinities and Violence Against Women

Laureen Snider

This paper seeks to look beyond criminalization models to examine what is known about building less violent societies, at the macro, middle and micro levels. It argues that criminalization is a flawed strategy for dealing with male violence against women caused by a failure to theorize social control adequately, a failure that has led feminists and other progressive social movements to mis-identify penality as synonymous with social control. The first part examines the realities of agendas of criminalization and increased punitiveness through incarceration rates. The second part seeks to explain the dependence on criminal law and institutions of criminal justice by feminists and new social movements. Focusing on wife assault and battery, it points out that strategies of criminalization have benefited privileged white women at the expense of women of colour, aboriginal and immigrant women, and points out problems with the failure to engender concepts of social control. The third part looks at what we know about policies, strategies and identities with the potential to transcend criminalization and facilitate social transformation, paying special attention to the construction, roots and maintenance of hegemonic masculinity. Overall it

Reprinted with permission from *The British Journal of Criminology* 38, no. 1 (Winter 1998).

is argued that effective social control of aberrant behaviour must be sought outside criminal justice institutions, and that the feminist and progressive focus should shift towards examining how to create less violent people (particularly men), families, communities and societies.

> *The single minded pursuit of criminalization as the index of achievement for progressive social movements seems to me misconceived. (Cohen 1994: 105)*

> *... the moral sentiments which are internalized by individuals do change over time, as new normative codes are legislated and new generations are socialized in accordance with them. (Garland 1990: 54)*

> *Our [women's] status as a group relative to men has almost never, if ever, been changed from what it is. (MacKinnon 1992: 456)*

This paper is about praxis, domestic assault and the need to construct safer, more humane social orders. It is written, in part, to counteract the distressing tendency of progressive groups[1] such as feminism to embrace agendas of punishment, thereby reinforcing and legitimizing policies of coercive control which dominate the western world in the late twentieth century. This emphasis on punishment rather than amelioration has been noted by critics before, but few alternative models have been put forth,[2] in part, I suspect, because academics share the modernist predilection for cynicism over idealism, and for naming and blaming over strategizing on prevention. Criticism is so much easier—no one can prove negativism is misplaced, but it is easy to demonstrate that ameliorative social policies have not lived up to the expectations of those who originated them—contradictory and unrealistic as such expectations must be to survive the political process in modern democratic states. The rush to identify and punish bad guys is appealing as praxis because the politics of moral indignation, combined with the saleability of finger-pointing in sensation-seeking media, generates instant publicity, making this form of consciousness-raising comparatively simple. To effectively challenge beliefs that criminalization is *the* answer to problematic behaviour, and to develop and popularize strategies to change the policies, institutions and attitudes that reinforce violent responses in the first place, is an overwhelming task. The irony is that progressive academics, particularly feminists working in fields of criminology and law, have long acknowledged that deep-seated social problems such as domestic assault can only be ameliorated by ideological and structural change, the very time-consuming laborious process now being pushed into the background by policies of criminalization (Mandell 1994; Smart 1989; Mathiesen 1990). Decades of social science research, empirical and theoretical, critical and conservative, document the failure of criminal justice systems to improve the safety, life-conditions or life-chances of victims, or to transform offenders (Box 1983; Gottfredsen and Hirschi 1990; Rothman 1971, 1980; Ratner and McMullan 1987; Silberman 1980; Martinson 1974; McBarnet 1981; Garland 1990; Ericson and Baranek 1982).

In the area of domestic assault, such tendencies are particularly troublesome. With the supply of public monies getting smaller by the day, policies increasing criminalization virtually guarantee that money will be diverted from feminist shelters, consciousness-raising or empowerment programmes (Elias 1989; Matthews 1994) and channelled into criminal justice systems to finance compulsory arrest and/or charge policies. Counter-charging—the practice of laying charges against the complainant if there is *any* evidence of retaliatory violence or self defence—is endemic in many locales; it must now be counted a major deterrent to reporting offences. Worst of all, as we shall see, there is no persuasive evidence that reliance on criminal justice has made the female complainant safer or the male offender less violent, even in the short term (Sherman 1992; Marsh *et al.* 1982; Dobash and Dobash 1992; Dutton 1984; Caringella-MacDonald 1985, 1987, 1988). And, in the long term, the legacy of such policies is the creation of more misogynous men, more dependent women and more vulnerable family units, and the reinforcement of the impression, in media and public discourse, that the problem of domestic assault revolves around figuring out how to punish better, deeper and more. Surely, as feminists and academics, we have better suggestions to offer. Surely, even if the public demand for punitiveness is as overwhelming as right wing media and politicians insist (a dubious assertion, see Immarigeon 1991; Braithwaite and Mugford 1994), we should be challenging consensuses that reinforce law and order lobbies, laying the intellectual groundwork for counter-hegemonic battles and positing alternatives. Surely, as a minimum, we should be asking how to make the creation of safer societies a primary goal of social policy and progressive struggle.

That is the purpose of this paper. The first part examines the realities of agendas of criminalization through incarceration rates and increased punitiveness. The second part seeks to explain the dependence on criminal law and institutions of criminal justice by progressive groups and new social movements, particularly feminism. Focusing on wife assault and battery, it points out that strategies of criminalization have benefited privileged white women at the expense of women of colour, aboriginal and immigrant women, and examines our failure to theorize and engender concepts of social control. The third part offers preliminary thoughts on strategies with more potential to transcend criminalization and nurture transformative, counter-hegemonic change. Two questions are addressed here: how do macro level factors reinforce violence in social orders, and how can communities be restructured and dominant maculinities and identities changed? In other words, what steps are required for people to *feel* safer, *become* less vulnerable, and *prevent* intergenerational cycles of recurring violence?

Before delving into the arguments, several points must be made about language and the use of categories, because this paper employs essentializing categories such as women, class, visible minorities and people of colour, and attempts generalizations beyond the particularities imposed by individual situations. In addition, data (empirical "knowledge")[3] are used to develop arguments for and against certain theoretical perspectives. This is done despite the epistemological, ontological and practical limitations of statistics, on the one hand, and the risk, even the arrogance, of understating difference within the artificial, theoretically constructed collectivities employed on the other.[4] It is done because theory requires, at least initially, a willingness to "essentialise certain relationships as objects of knowledge which are not reducible to each other" (Carlen 1991: 14). This violates some postmodern canons (e.g. Winter 1992), but the value of this theoretical position—and others—must be judged by the validity and persuasiveness of the analyses produced (Garland 1995: 182), not by *a priori* and dogmatic prescriptions claiming, for example, that fragmentation and incoherence are all there is.[5] Such claims must be scrutinized just as severely as the positions they critique. Indeed, criminologists should be particularly wary of importing postmodern critiques in an uncritical fashion because they may have the unintended consequence of silencing progressive voices, thereby reinforcing hegemonic interests and agendas. Movement politics is hard work, it often requires a temporary suspension of disbelief, a sense of vision, of involvement in something bigger than oneself. "Speaking for the other," with all its risks, embodies this claim and this need. Given the perilous state of western economies with record levels of inequality within and between nation states, ideologies celebrating greed in the guise of free market economic theory dominating the "marketplace" of ideas, and spiralling rates of unemployment, progressive voices and alternative positions are desperately needed. When postmodernists deride such voices in the name of theoretical purity, they—we—risk weakening and destabilizing progressive movements. With mass media quick to publicize any evidence of dissent among leftist groups, the result is that hegemonic right-wing forces, unconcerned with the arrogance of appropriation of voice, monopolize public debate. Thus we see gun lobbies and law and order advocates skewing the definitions of right and left so violently that to be "progressive" in the United States in the late twentieth century means favouring electronic monitoring and urinalysis instead of caning and chain gangs. Constantly interrogating strategies is essential, but progressives must balance the risks of sometimes speaking for others (an essentializing and arrogant thing to do) against the very real need to get counter-hegemonic positions *heard*.

This does not mean that the categories employed in this paper are to be understood as conveying Truth. Macro-level structures such as capitalism and patriarchy are not meant to be seen as having one universal "meaning" or one inevitable behavioural, institutional or ideological consequence. But the events that result from the social relations of production or reproduction cannot be interpreted as purely random occurrences. To talk about capitalist economic systems or patriarchal relations means that certain gender identities, roles, languages, ideologies, ways of knowing and types of knowledge are reinforced, welcomed and otherwise *more likely to occur*. In any diverse collectivity, other ways of thinking, seeing and acting will be found, but they will usually be marginalized, derided, typically less common and certainly less influential, with fewer political, social or ideological "coat-tails" (Smart 1992; Howe 1994; Butler 1990). Concepts and structures, be they criminal justice systems or patriarchal families, are neither monolithic entities that "cause" behaviour (a determinist interpretation), nor constellations of actors whose interests and construction of reality have purely idiosyncratic implications (a pluralist/ postmodern interpretation).

On the micro level, this understanding of structural forces is consistent with a long-accepted sociological truism commonly credited to Mead: "everything is an interpreted thing and not a thing in itself" (Winter 1992: 793). Structures are real in the sense that they provide individuals with resources and meanings, and people construct identities from the structures that surround them (Giddens 1981). Ethnicity, class and gender direct—but none of them determine—the meanings individuals give to the structures. The selves people construct out of these meanings are mediated by social interaction and language.

"Genuine subjectivity is alienated from itself by the reified structures and collective myths of our society," as Boyle has said, but there remains "a necessary dialectic between personal phenomenologies and structural theories of ideology" (Boyle 1985: 757). In the end, of an infinite variety of possible selves that could be constructed, those that are publicly validated in that social system are *most likely* to occur. Thus, if a given society differentiates among its members using categories based on age, skin colour, sex, class, language, religion and sexual orientation (or uses eye colour, mathematical skill or the ability to communicate with extrasensory beings), the identities most commonly adopted will reflect (but not mirror) these categories. The range of publicly validated selves, infinite in theory, varies in practice with the social and cultural resources available. People both act, and are acted upon, they are subject and object, oppressor and oppressed. The social context of the individual provides discursive, semiotic and linguistic reference points to allow identities to be formed, while cultural and structural resources provide the building blocks (Oyserman and Saltz 1993). This conceptualization of structure and agency accounts for—in fact it predicts— a wide range of differences among people occupying identical social categories (such as race, gender and class).

iTi CRIMINALIZATION AS A GROWTH INDUSTRY

Rather than concentrating on building less violent social orders, the focus in western societies in recent years has been on discovering new ways to punish, and on delivering punishment more effectively. This section examines why punishment, through systems of criminal justice, has become the dominant guarantor of social order.[6]

Increasing penality through criminalizing behaviours that were formerly tolerated, abolishing parole and statutory remission, lengthening prison sentences, and replacing police and judicial discretion with mandatory charges and minimum sentences has become both symptom and symbol of the modern state. Penality, and the businesses and sciences that support it, is a growth industry (Christie 1993). The politics of law and order guarantees a steady supply of politicians promising to get "tough on crime"; arguing that these policies are futile, cruel or racist is electoral suicide. It is deeply ironic that the United States, one of the most violent and disordered countries in the developed world, and certainly among the least successful in controlling criminal behaviour, has become the world model for penal policy.[7] In the United Kingdom, the (then) shadow Home Secretary of the Labour Party copies the mandatory curfew policies adopted in Memphis, Tennessee to curb youth crime (*Sunday Times,* London, 2 June 1996: A6). In Australia, politicians in the 1995 elections in Queensland and New South Wales call for laws allowing householders to shoot intruders on sight and mandatory life sentences for repeat offenders, emulating California's "Three Strikes" legislation. And yet, in New South Wales armed robbery fell by 19 per cent between 1983 and 1993, and those claiming victimization from assault fell from 3.4 per cent in 1983 to 2.5 per cent in 1993 (Australian Bureau of Statistics 1994; Wynhausen 1995).

Crime rates, whether measured by police statistics or victimization rates, are falling in Anglo-American democracies. Crimes of violence, for example, fell by 4 per cent in the United States in 1994 (Appleby 1995), with urban crime down most dramatically—1994 homicide numbers were at a 25-year low, and they dropped a further 33 per cent during the first six months of 1995. Murder rates dropped by 8 per cent in 1995: "21,597 murders were recorded in 1995, 13 per cent fewer than in 1991"; and "property crime fell by 1 per cent to 12 million offences, the lowest number since 1987" (Thomas, *Guardian Weekly,* 20 October 1996: 15). Even crack cocaine use is slowing: statistics from the National Assessment of Educational Progress report the percentage of US blacks from 18 to 25 admitting use declined from 3.1 per cent in 1991 to 0.7 per cent in 1993 (Appleby 1995). In Canada, homicide in 1994 dropped by 8 per cent, making the 1994 rate 2.04/100,000, the lowest in 25 years. Violent crime overall— premeditated murder, sexual assault, robbery and verbal threats—dropped by 3 per cent and even the number of incidents reported to police declined by 5 per cent (Hess 1995: A5).

Three caveats are in order. First, many violent crimes go unreported, particularly in poor or minority areas where inhabitants know that calling the police doubles the oppression, and households where women take regular abuse from violent partners in the privacy of the family are not uncommon (Rodgers 1994; Dutton 1984; Ontario 1982). Secondly, every country has enclaves where crime rates are simply irrelevant to people's daily experiences—aboriginal towns in Australia, for example, where 90 per cent of the women (females over 15) and 84 per cent of girls (under 15) have been sexually assaulted (Greer 1994: 65–6); similar conditions characterize some First Nations reserves in Canada (LaPrairie 1993: 240–1). And third, stranger homicides, in the United States, have increased. Because these are random and unpredictable, they generate more public fear than the possible violence of acquaintances.[8] But this is *not* the reality elsewhere. There is no evidence that stranger homicides are rising in Canada, for example, where 13 per cent of all homicides in 1994 involved strangers, a statistic that has remained constant for the past decade (Hess 1995a). Indeed, in virtually every country except the United States (where young men are most at risk), infants under the age of one—hardly a group targeted by strangers—have the highest victimization rates (Hess 1995b, citing Statistics Canada). But the fact that American trends and fear levels are at epidemic levels shapes perceptions of danger and influences social policy everywhere else.

And in the United States the punitive movement goes from strength to strength: in 1995 alone bills allowing caning for minor offences and laws to bring back whipping were announced in New York, California and Mississippi (Dettmer 1995).[9] The Omnibus Crime Bill passed by the US Congress in 1994 calls for 100,000 new police officers by the year 2000 and authorizes state spending of $7.9 billion for prison construction and boot camps. Corrections budgets are the fastest growing sector in state governments (Thomas 1994); prison spending totalled $25 billion in 1990, two and a half times more than in 1971. Rates of incarceration have risen from 230 per 100,000 in 1979 to 504 in 1991 (Christie 1993: 90). In Canada they rose from 100/100,000 to 111/100,000 in one decade, 1979 to 1989, and jumped to 130 per 100,000 by 1995, with average offender caseloads up 29 per cent (Brodeur 1996). European countries are catching up fast, with Northern Ireland at 109/100,000, the United Kingdom at 92, Germany at 82, and France holding the line at 78 per 100,000 (these are 1990 figures, and the Netherlands and Scandinavian countries remain comparatively low) (Christie 1993: 91–93).

The United States continues to outpace the rest, however, with an incarceration rate for black males of 2,678/100,000, rising to 7,210/100,000 for those 25 to 29 years of age (all 1992 figures) (Walinsky 1995: 47). On any given day in the District of Columbia in 1991, 15 per cent of all black men aged 18 to 34 were in prison, 21 per cent were on probation or parole, and 6 per cent were awaiting trial or at large. Only 15 per cent of all black men living in Washington, it is estimated, would *not* be arrested at some point in their lives (Walinsky 1995: 47). One of every 193 adults in the United States was incarcerated in the summer of 1994, with state prisons holding 919,143 men and women, and federal prisons holding 93,708 (Thomas 1994). Women still constitute a tiny percentage of prison populations in most countries (5.7 per cent in United States in 1989), but female rates of imprisonment are going up even faster than male rates. In US jails, rates rose by 95.3 per cent from 1984 to 1989 (male rates rose by 51 per cent); in federal and state prisons they increased 24.4 per cent (while men rose "only" 12.5 per cent). The number of women incarcerated rose from 12,331 in 1980 to 40,566 in 1989, an increase of 229 per cent; men went from 303,643 to 669,489, up 120 per cent (Immarigeon and Chesney-Lind 1992: 2–4). This trend too is copied elsewhere—women's incarceration rates in the Australian state of Victoria more than tripled from 1979 to 1989 (Howe 1990a); similar increases took place in Canada (Johnson and Rodgers 1993).

Incarceration rates are but one component of a widespread weakening of civil liberties and an allied increase in state coercive powers. In the United Kingdom police powers have been enhanced and practices once seen as abuse have been normalized (Reiner 1992). In Canada maximum sentences have been lengthened, parole has become harder to get, and provinces are passing laws to allow the indefinite detention of repeat offenders. In Alberta and Ontario chain gangs have been proposed (Feschuk 1995). Over the last year the government of Alberta, citing public pressure to make inmates suffer,[10] has removed pool tables and colour televisions from provincial prisons, abolished pay for institutional chores, and cancelled conjugal visiting programmes (Feschuk 1995).[11] Several provinces as well as the federal government plan to ban (tobacco) smoking in prisons, a measure disguised as a health regulation which will have widespread punitive effects given the high percentage of inmates addicted to nicotine (Feschuk 1995: A7). In North America women guilty of "substance abuse" are increasingly likely to be incarcerated, to safeguard the "rights" of the foetus, a predicted collusion of medical and legal discourses that situates punitiveness even more deeply in the (female) body (Smart 1989; Edgley and Brissett 1990; Bagley and Merlo 1995). In the United States progressive lawyers, unable to argue for rights to shelter, welfare or health care for the destitute (all vitiated by Supreme Court decisions in the 1980s), are reduced to arguing for the constitutionally protected right to beg (Fudge and Glasbeek 1992: 59). (Surely the right to be homeless is next.) Protections against self-incrimination, laws disallowing evidence seized by pumping defendants' stomachs, laws banning the hiring of replacement workers or guaranteeing hard-won rights to organize collectively, to strike, or to minimum standards of education and health care, have been continuously eroded throughout Europe and North America (Bartholomew and Hunt 1990; Fudge and Glasbeek 1992).

119

ᛰ UNDERSTANDING FEMINIST AND PROGRESSIVE SUPPORT

This section examines the process by which left-wing progressive groups have come to support agendas of punishment and the consequences and implications of this. In particular it asks why feminism, a transformative social movement with "antimaterialist, antistatist, antibureaucratic" aims and "humanistic, interpersonal and communitarian values" (Handler 1992: 697), has come to see penality as both a primary objective of struggle and a criterion of its success. The key to this question lies, it is argued, in a mis-identification of penality with social control. The result has been that all the instrumental and symbolic anti-violence messages which are more properly and effectively conveyed by processes of socialization, conscience-building, ostracism and shaming (components of social control), have been vested into penality, where they cannot be achieved and should not be sought.

Right-wing support for agendas of law and order is theoretically and historically consistent (Thompson 1963, 1975). On the left, protracted ideological struggles in seventeenth and eighteenth century Britain forged a "respectable" working class whose identity depended, in part, on their sense of superiority to and difference from the despised "rabble" in the criminal classes beneath them; Marx himself vilified criminals as the reactionary, bribable tools of the bourgeoisie (Garland 1985; Melossi 1980; Melossi and Pavarini 1981). However most social democratic parties in the 1960s and 70s advocated mildly progressive policies such as prison reform or even abolition, and campaigned to improve prison conditions and end capital punishment (Lea and Young 1984; Kinsey et al. 1985). Early second-wave feminism opposed all forms of state punishment.[12] But not a decade later, criminalization and incarceration had become key goals of conservatives and progressives alike. For feminists this was, in part, a response to research revealing the full and horrendous extent of male attacks on women (Brownmiller 1975; Dobash and Dobash 1975); in part it reflected the extension of state funding as feminists in the 1970s and 80s reached the limits of volunteerism and turned to government for long-term funding of hot-lines, crisis centres and shelters. Control over hiring and policy passed to state agencies, resulting in mandatory record-keeping and reporting to police, individualistic and therapeutic approaches to women now constructed as "clients," an end to political action and consciousness-raising, and the creation of constituencies of therapists, social workers and lawyers with vested interests in criminalization (Matthews 1994; Michaud 1992; Dobash and Dobash 1992; Ursel 1992; Dekeseredy and Hinch 1991). Though oppositional voices remained, calls for greater punitiveness were more easily heard than others, and coercive policies were eagerly adopted by governments seeking to legitimate agendas tightening control over underclass populations (Snider 1985).

Thus Anglo-American democracies over the 1970s and 80s revised laws and policies on sexual and domestic assault, increased sanctions and introduced mandatory response, arrest and charging policies (Roberts 1991; Caringella-MacDonald 1987; Marsh *et al.* 1982). Such policies led, as they always do, to greater surveillance and criminalization of those who fit hegemonic definitions of "the criminal," those whose lives are easiest to scrutinize and those least able to resist intrusions. One result has been intensified immiseration of lower class women, visible minorities, native and aboriginal women. These are the women most vulnerable to contempt of court charges and to counter-charging practices, and least able to resist state action or find the resources to leave violent partners (Macleod 1995). Compulsory criminalization of native men has accelerated cultural genocide, legitimizing the placement of native children into (white) foster families and spotlighting the "inadequacies" of the native family (Monture-Okanee 1992). Arrest of the family breadwinner often deprives immigrant women and children of landed immigrant status and may lead to deportation, since dependence on the state (should welfare be sought) and criminal conviction (of the "head" of the family) are both grounds for deportation (Martin and Mosher 1995; Pratt 1995). Immigrants with any irregularities in their papers are quickly declared unfit for citizenship and the entire family unit is shipped back to its country of origin. For women of colour in Britain, Canada and the United States, increased surveillance and criminalization means increased vulnerability to the actions of racist police and judicial authorities. They have reinforced already powerful stereotypes of black men as violent and black families as pathological, and threaten both family and community—the two bulwarks people of colour have had against an alien and hostile white world (Carby 1982; Williams 1987). And the ultimate irony is that poor and minority women are most deeply affected by the cuts in English language courses, welfare, day care, health care and education deemed necessary to pay for the higher criminal justice costs that policies of mandatory criminalization require (Elias 1989; Michaud 1992; LaRocque 1995). The $9.5 billion Canada spent on criminal justice in 1992 (up 23 per cent from 1989 to 1991), for example, would have built 1,900 state of the art elementary schools (Tripp 1996).

There is little evidence that increased criminalization has empowered women or made them safer in or outside the home. Indeed, the empirical debate over the success of mandatory arrest policies for batterers (Sherman 1992) revolves around whether arrested men are more or less likely to be reported for offences again.[13] Surely the better criterion of success is whether criminal justice intervention was the solution desired by the putative victim, and whether it made her life or that of her children better, subjectively or objectively. The high levels of contempt of court charges (laid against women who refuse to testify against the alleged batterer) and of counter-charges (laid against women deemed to have retaliated or defended themselves with physical force) can be read as evidence that this is not the case. Women in such situations who call police are usually seeking help to put an end to the violence and, despite a century of feminist activism, police are still the only 24-hour state-funded service with this mandate. This, not the failure of police and judges to respond punitively enough, or the undeniable misogyny that underlies much discretionary decision making, is the most tragic consequence of feminist reliance on criminalization. (See, in general, Braithwaite and Daly 1994; Tifft and Markham 1991; Caringella-Macdonald and Humphries 1991; Andrews et al. 1990; Ekland-Olson et al. 1984; Snider, 1990, 1994).

But it is not the only tragic consequence. Continued feminist support for criminalization is also fed by anger and fear. Whatever official crime statistics say about the chances of victimization, high female levels of fear and vulnerability are both real and rational, given the circumstances of many women's lives (Canada 1988; Rodgers 1994; Lea and Young 1984; Hanmer and Stanko 1985; Stanko 1990). But the conceptual leap from acknowledging fear to promoting incarceration is neither rational nor automatic. Feelings of vulnerability are not ameliorated by higher imprisonment rates—and anyway these rates are already much higher than commonsense perceptions (Roberts 1994; Sacco and Johnson 1990). Such feelings can be tackled, on the other hand, by social and structural changes which give people greater control over their surroundings. Graffiti, empty public spaces, the erosion of inner-city urban environments, the disappearance of professionals, local services and beat cops from neighbourhoods, the absence of recreational facilities, the erosion of public transit and the decline of employment opportunities (which produces fear-producing groups of young men hanging out in public places) all promote fear and, in some cases, increased criminal opportunities as well (Skogan 1990; Jackson 1989; Wilson and Kelling 1982). So does the richly deserved loss of faith in the integrity and accountability of economic, political and religious elites (Calavita and Pontell 1995; Calavita 1986, 1983; Levi 1993, 1987, 1984). Opportunities for counter-hegemonic struggle abound, but groups caught up in agendas of legalism and criminalization tend not to see them.

Indeed, criminal justice systems are probably the least effective institutions to look for transformative change. Even the staunchest advocates of incarceration do not argue that prisons are successful institutions, only that they punish well. The failure of correctional institutions to deter or rehabilitate has been repeatedly documented in studies ranging from the asylum in the sixteenth century to the penitentiary in the nineteenth to the modernist, management-oriented institutions of today (Rothman 1971, 1980; Garland 1990; Ignatieff 1978; Mathiesen 1990; Walker 1993; Feeley and Simon 1992, 1994). That prisons increase recidivism, nourish criminal subcultures, create "schools for crime," impoverish prisoners' families and brutalize the keepers as thoroughly as the kept was recognized as early as 1820 (Foucault 1979).[14] Criminal justice systems appropriate personal problems, empowering states and court systems, not victims (Christie 1977; Braithwaite 1991). Prisons cannot provide jobs, someone to love you when you are depressed, to praise you when you do good things and administer the very real sanction of disapproval when you do not. Time inside makes those defined as offenders (disproportionately poor, native, minority men) more bitter, unemployable, and typically more misogynist as well. Prisons are most successful at delivering pain—people suffer inside prisons, before and after them as well (as Feeley (1979) pointed out, the process is the punishment).

Recognizing the horrific human cost of violence against women, and seeking to focus public attention on this in the face of massive resistance, feminism sought the material and ideological resources (i.e., media attention and state monies) that criminalization provides, forgetting that symbolic denunciation is not the same as providing solutions. Naming problems (Spender 1980) and heaping moral opprobrium on offenders is no substitute for attacking causes,[15] and meaningful, transformative social change can only be achieved by transforming identities, groups and structures. Ultimately penality fails because "the conditions which do most to induce conformity—or to promote crime and deviance—lie outside the jurisdiction of penal institutions" (Garland 1990: 289). Changing subcultures of belief and life-long patterns of behaviour is brutally difficult whether the target is crack users or City fraudsters. To do it humanely while respecting democratic norms of freedom of choice and action is almost impossible.[16]

For progressive groups with goals of amelioration and empowerment to embrace agendas of penality is significant. How we punish reveals much about dominant conceptions of social order, of gender, class, ethnic identity, and even of "civilization" (Elias 1982, 1978). Focusing exclusively on monsters or folk devils, the "otherness" of law-breakers and the futility of redemption speaks to manichean beliefs about the nature of people, about societies out of control where vengeance, the purposive infliction of pain, becomes the only response to nonconformity (Garland 1990: 276). Labelling every person who aggresses against another a "criminal" is epistemologically absurd; locking them all up is fiscally impossible. Focusing massive amounts of time, resources and attention on creating instrumental knowledge and seeking technical fixes to problems without technical solutions has chilling socio-cultural ramifications. Such a quest marginalizes and silences those seeking emancipatory or critical knowledge or pursuing counter-hegemonic strategies (Habermas 1968/1971). Policies of criminalization, as fact and discourse, speak volumes about hierarchy and dominance, about "proper" relations between the propertied and non-propertied, men and women, black and white and brown peoples. Entire subsets of laws—vagrancy, disorderly conduct, obstructing police and resisting arrest, prohibitions against disabling electronic shackles or "cheating" on urinalysis tests—celebrate the politics of authority (Schrecker 1990).[17]

One of the most serious consequences of the mis-identification of penality with social control, however, has been the paucity of theoretical attention paid to theorizing and engendering concepts of control. Social control, the discouraging of antisocial acts, is a prerequisite of social order. And while the acts deemed antisocial, the methods employed, the actors employing them and their effectiveness vary widely, all human collectivities attempt to control the practices and beliefs of those designated as members. Individual or self discipline is prescribed through the rewards and punishments of socialization; at the community level, social control is sought through processes ranging from verbal disapproval to ostracism and banishment. Punishment is an important component of social control, a shaming and socializing device with symbolic as well as instrumental functions (Garland 1990: 277–90; Polk 1994). But penality—institutions devoted to punishment through formal systems of criminal justice—is not the same thing, it has never been shown to be necessary to achieve social control and may well be counterproductive (Braithwaite 1989; Christie 1993).

The role and necessity of penality has seldom been explicitly debated, particularly by progressive groups (Pitch 1995). Professional literatures on penality abound; essentially non-reflexive, they calibrate with Foucauldian precision the exact amount of pain correlated with deterrence (rehabilitation having dropped out of fashion this decade) (Feeley and Simon 1992, 1994; Garland 1995). Public and political media, meanwhile, focus exclusively on denunciation and vengeance. To find arguments prescribing penality as an essential component of social control one must look to social theory, to the arguments of earlier scholars such as Durkheim and Freud. Durkheim saw penality as a prerequisite for social solidarity; he predicted that the need to punish would diminish as societies moved from mechanical to organic solidarity (Durkheim 1893, 1900). While this prediction has been shown to be incorrect (Grabosky 1984; Sorokin 1937), Durkheim's work is still being mined to great effect (Pearce 1989; Garland 1990), as it underlines the symbolic importance of penality as well as the individual and collective need to hold people/groups *accountable* for their deeds (not necessarily through criminalization).

Freudian arguments are less persuasive, as they rest on the assumption that the degree of repression required by modern industrialized societies is so great that creating a population of closet sadists must be considered a price of civilization. Because people in "civilized" societies have to discipline themselves most of the time, they need assurance that those who do not do so suffer for their failure. Evidence that the price of non-repression is high is necessary to strengthen the psychic defences of the conforming majority against the ever-present temptation to misbehave (Garland 1990; Elias 1978, 1982). Such arguments, however, assume that criminality is undisciplined behaviour, that criminal acts are impulsive, pleasurable, aggressive and uninhibited. At a time when everything from complex corporate fraud to sleeping in the streets has been declared criminal, this is simply incorrect.[18] And, while it is possible that the levels of discipline demanded in industrialized societies do have a psychic cost, jumping on the bandwagon of psychological determinism to justify high levels of incarceration is unwarranted at this time. Dozens of competing explanations for modern infatuations with penality are available and many, such as the politics of law and order and its resonance with agendas of hegemonic control, are more parsimonious and persuasive.

But the most important problem with arguments that vengeful state action is psychologically or biologically necessary is their failure to theorize gender, their assumption that humans all have similar responses to the suppression of aggression, and identical propensities to act out aggressive urges. And yet, since the development of the modern state, women, particularly privileged white women, have consistently sought and benefited from higher levels of state control.[19] As the physically weaker sex, women have the most to lose when formal control breaks down, as rapes in Bosnia and assault levels in urban ghettos attest. First-wave feminist movements sought laws to criminalize alcohol and drug use, abolish prostitution, sterilize the "feeble-minded," and create special reformatories for women and juveniles (Rafter 1983, 1985; Heidensohn 1992; Garland 1985; Ursel 1986; Chunn 1992). Nineteenth-century women were so enthusiastic about the potential of state control that they even took unwaged positions as social workers and police officers (Heidensohn 1992). Such roles were seen, and justified in rhetoric, as "natural" extensions in the public sphere of women's main private role, that of socializing the young. Mothering is (among other things) a controlling role, whereby children learn to conform, restrain antisocial impulses, and accommodate the discipline demanded of contributing adults in that society. Historically, then, insofar as generalizations across race and class are possible, women in western societies over the last 100-odd years have resisted the idea that state or social control is necessarily a bad thing. Feminism in particular has sought to harness state power as a counterbalance to patriarchal power in the private sphere. Being assigned the primary responsibility for children in most cultures has made it essential for women to find ways to control the labour and actions of adult males, since patriarchal cultures make women dependent on men for sustenance and protection. The ability of women to be financially—and therefore materially—independent of men is a new and still fragile phenomenon.[20]

The susceptibility of progressive groups to agendas of criminalization, then, and the allied failure to separate processes of control from institutions of penality, has had serious social consequences. Communities simply cannot be transformed into sane and civil places by installing cops on every corner or, for that matter, welfare workers in every home. Criminalization does not solve problems created by racism, de-industrialization or immiseration. It does provide satisfying outlets for much legitimate rage, but at the cost of leaving dominant groups unthreatened and dominant relations, of capital and patriarchy, unchallenged. The next section of the paper attempts to go beyond criminalization and examine the kinds of changes that might be sought, cultural and structural prospects with more potential to create truly safer societies.

🏛 PRELIMINARY THOUGHTS ON AMELIORATIVE STRATEGIES

Macro-Level Issues

If criminalization is not a solution to misogyny and violence, what is? This section of the paper examines what we know about building less violent societies, institutions and individuals. Ultimately such a goal requires change in the macro-level structures that maintain capitalism and patriarchy. But we have certainly learned by now that structural change does not guarantee that anything transformative will happen at micro levels. Conversely, the absence of macro-level change does not mean the absence of resistance or of significant counter-hegemonic victories at micro levels. Structures affect the chances and direction of change, they do not make it inevitable. However the present period of upheaval offers unique opportunities for transformative change due to the destabilization of institutions of governance, the ferment of opposing voices, the many groups vying to get "their" solutions adopted. And much has been achieved over the last century, through mechanisms of struggle and resistance, the skilful deployment of mass media and electoral politics and the process Braithwaite calls "model-mongering" (1994). Although much of this progress has been confined to the developed world, attitudes and behaviour, public opinion and law in a range of important areas have undergone radical change. There is less tolerance of corporate crime (Rossi *et al.* 1974; Cullen *et al.* 1982; Goff and Mason-Clark 1989), drunk driving, environmental pollution and interpersonal violence in general, particularly against women and children. Prejudice against visible minorities, homophobia and discrimination against women are now considered unacceptable by sizeable proportions of the population (which is not to say they have ceased to exist). The 1970s and 80s saw considerable progress (as well as extensive backlash) in the centuries-old process of redefining the behaviour, attitudes, manners and sensibilities required of "civilized" peoples (Spierenberg 1984; Elias 1978, 1982). Note, however, that many recent changes have been "net-widening"—they created new behaviours to be abhorred and controlled, not new choices to be celebrated.[21]

Let us start at the macro level, examining what we know about building less violent social orders. Anthropological studies of non-western societies show that many, though certainly not all, nomadic small-scale hunting and gathering communities achieved high levels of gender equality and low levels of in-group interpersonal violence. Take the seventeenth-century Huron, who lived on Georgian Bay in what is now the province of Ontario, for example. Each sex had a series of "locations" in a complex kin structure with matrilineal nuclear families in a matrilocal longhouse tradition. There were distinct, but separate and equal tasks for men and women in agriculture, politics and marriage, with both sexes enjoying a relatively free choice of marital partner, provided clan and exogamy rules were respected. Divorce was common, but sexual and physical aggression were rare (Anderson 1991). Rape-prone societies, on the other hand, more frequently feature non-egalitarian relations in language, culture and in the distribution of resources. The absolute level of material affluence is not significant provided a certain minimum is maintained, but the distribution of goods is, particularly whether they are shared or monopolized by male elites. In rape-prone societies force becomes a means of achieving goods and status, and both competition and violence are keys to manhood. Gender differences between men and women are exaggerated, highly valued tasks are reserved for men and "women's work" is denigrated. Socialization emphasizes roughness and cruelty, particularly towards boys who, it is believed, have to be toughened to survive. Women in rape-prone societies have few power bases of their own—few economic, political or spiritual arenas that confer status or power. Lacking personal or institutional power, trained to be compliant and submissive, females become easy and legitimate targets for male aggression (Harris 1991; Buchwald *et al.* 1993; Caringella-MacDonald and Humphries 1991; Knopp 1991; Archer and Gartner 1984).

Anthropological findings from tiny nomadic societies with minimal surplus or differentiation cannot be directly applied to industrialized capitalist states, highly stratified and specialized in every sense. And generalizing about patterns of crime and violence from such "evidence" is even more difficult. However modernist obsessions with record-keeping mean that, while it is difficult to infer causality from the data, considerable information about individual and illegal violence in developed societies can be found in official statistics and victimization surveys. And, while statistics on official or state violence are harder to come by (because much of this violence is normative), incarceration rates provide a rough approximation for it as well. While most crime indicators are so dependent on levels of public education, public reporting and police priorities that they are virtually useless for international purposes, homicide statistics are the great exception, and relatively reliable comparisons can be made.

Thus we know, as discussed above, that English-speaking Anglo-American countries, particularly the United States, have the highest rates of both official and criminal violence. The least violent industrialized societies by the data are Japan, several countries in north-west Europe, and the Scandinavian countries. The latter all have comparatively homogeneous populations, and low levels of economic inequality. Comparing after-tax incomes for the top and bottom 10 per cent in 13 different nations, the United States has the most unequal distribution of income with a ratio of 5.94, Canada stands at 4.03, Australia at 4.01 and Britain at 3.8. The least unequal countries are Finland at 2.59, Sweden at 2.73, the Netherlands at 2.84, Austria at 2.88 and Norway at 2.93 (Kesterton 1995: A16). The ratio of the pay of a typical worker to that of a typical corporate Chief Executive Officer (CEO) is 1:16 in Japan, 1:21 in Germany, 1:33 in the United Kingdom, and a whopping 1:120 in the United States (*Harper's* 1996: 46). While industrialized societies in general have wider gaps between rich and poor than hunting and gathering societies do, the clustering of less violent societies at the egalitarian ends of the scale is, to say the least, suggestive.

Less violent developed societies have superior social safety nets as well. The quality of life available to people on welfare or unemployment insurance in France or Norway, for example, is much higher than that allowed the subsidized poor in the United States, because France and Norway provide low cost medical care, education and housing in addition to income, while most American states do not. While unemployment due to corporate retrenchment and globalization of trade has occurred in all industrial countries, their effects have been offset, to some degree, by such subsidies. Moreover, the scale and speed of downsizing have been moderated—either because wholesale disposal of surplus employees was discouraged by stigma and shaming (as in Japan), or because union contracts forbid massive layoffs or made them prohibitively expensive (as in Germany, France and Scandinavia) (Abegglen 1975). While few studies have linked social policy directly to crime rates, a recent look at homicide in Norway argues that full employment policies and a relatively egalitarian income distribution can substantially offset the economic and personal strains of unemployment (Stack 1990). (Costs showed up, however, in higher rates of separation and divorce.) The fact that less violent societies have universal health care and parental leaves and more violent ones do not (or, if they do, the programmes are partial and poor), is also worthy of note. Unfortunately, this kind of evidence is suggestive at best. We do not know direction of causality, so we cannot say whether factors such as higher support for the unwaged "cause" lower levels of violence or vice versa. Indeed, we cannot be certain any causal relationship exists—the apparent correlations could be serendipidous. But it does make *a priori* sense to hypothesize that desperate, distraught people are more likely to seek violent solutions to interpersonal problems, for both instrumental and expressive reasons.[22] With collective national or religious identities impaired throughout the west (despite the example of the former Yugoslav states), individual violent acts such as the lone gunman of Dunblane become the primary focus of law enforcement. And there is evidence (Grabosky 1984: 176–8) that violence and punitiveness go up in societies, organizations and families as stress increases. An empirical scale of the "degree of desperation" different societies create, linked to scales of various types of violence, would be a useful measure indeed.

Homogeneity of population is also associated with lower levels of individual and state violence. The people of Japan, Norway and Sweden are similar in religion, ethnicity, heritage and language. Denmark and the Netherlands exhibit more heterogeneity, with visible minorities and ethnic subcultures, yet they remain relatively non-violent societies. In contrast, violent societies such as the United States are extremely heterogeneous (but Canada, the most heterogeneous of all, has homicide rates one quarter those in the United States). Learning to live with difference (in skin colour, sexual orientation, language) without judging it or making it the basis of institutional and cultural ranking systems is clearly difficult for humans (as illustrated by evaluative distinctions made world-wide to differences of gender and age). Levels of population density vary independently, but lower internal levels of mobility are more common in less violent countries. Many people in European societies have roots in their parish, village or county that stretch back many generations. Once again we cannot say that homogeneity and geographic stability automatically produce less violent societies. Indeed, cohesive ethnic, national or religious groups may be more likely to generate *collective* violence against out-groups. But "rootedness" and stability do appear to be associated with lower rates of individual and in-group violence (Christie 1993).[23] The retention of regional identities, the creation of localized cultural or religious bonds that encourage independence from mass culture, and the retention of alternate systems of allegiance alleviate psychic pressures on individuals in times of upheaval. They let some people find sources of meaning and satisfaction even when the forces of global capital (and other natural and unnatural disasters) have taken away economic resources. Alternate identities, then, offer people *psychological* cushions for psychic survival; social safety nets offer them *economic* cushions, both are significant. And both are connected to creating and nourishing less desperate populations.

It is painfully obvious, however, that western societies at present are racing in the opposite direction. Economic "cushions" are under attack and income inequalities are increasing as nation states reduce deficits by eliminating social services, health care, minimum wages, worker protection laws and anything else that adds to the (corporate) cost of production. Removing social safety nets and public services is presented as necessary to allow developed countries (or the national and multinational corporations they shelter) to compete in cut-throat global markets. When capital, investment and jobs can easily be shifted from Birmingham to Bangladesh, they will go wherever the potential for short-term profits is highest, or so we are told. Currency speculators have become key players in this game of capital roulette. George Soros, for example, ex-Hungarian financier, acts as a "global reality cop, pouncing on any government that overvalues or undervalues its currency" (Friedman 1995: A17). To appease investment-bankers and avert potentially disastrous runs on their currency, nation states have systematically begun campaigns to make their citizens less secure and more vulnerable, both psychologically and economically. Developed countries have entered a race to see who can create the most insecure, unhealthy and violence-prone population. The United States is ahead at the moment— but it had a head start, with fewer universal social programmes to dismantle— and Canada, New Zealand and the United Kingdom are catching up fast.

Creating more desperate citizens is not always accomplished without resistance, as the 1995 strike of public sector workers in France and 1996 demonstrations in Germany illustrate. However the removal of public support systems is much farther advanced elsewhere. In Canada, for example, unemployment benefits and federal equalization grants, core programmes to alleviate regional inequality and allow survival outside metropolitan areas, have been dramatically pared. Since jobs are seasonal in much of the country, families would work in tourism or the fishery during the summers, and get by the rest of the year through unemployment insurance, odd jobs, self-sufficiency, lower levels of consumption and family and community networks. In the outports and fishing villages of Newfoundland, for example, the land was exploited for its meagre resources, the sea for the once bountiful cod. Housing costs were low because mortgages were uncommon; people built their own houses.

Interpersonal violence, while not absent, was kept in check by a combination of culture and community traditions (Felt 1987). Thus Newfoundland, always the poorest province in Canada by measures of income, has long had the lowest homicide rates, at 0.69/100,000 in 1994, well below the Canadian average of 2.04, or the 3.08 found in the mobile, heterogeneous and affluent province of British Columbia (Hess 1995: A5). But NAFTA (the North American Trade Agreement) has made government payments to fishers challengeable as unfair trading subsidies. Cutting the deficit to avoid ruinous runs on the Canadian dollar has become the primary way of justifying cuts to federal transfer payments supporting medicare, education, child care and welfare. Public services are costly and inefficient; grants to poor people or provinces erode economic competitiveness and encourage dependence, according to right-wing think-tanks and politicians. But they also allow people to nourish their roots and remain in regions where they have traditions and histories, relatives and support networks. "Subsidies" are important in creating less desperate people.

Psychological "cushions," in the form of identification with values outside mass culture, are also under attack.[24] As many have pointed out, mass culture operates through consumerism, and consumerism works by creating and/or reinforcing personal and social insecurity. People with secure identities, independent of "lifestyle," are harder for advertisers to manipulate, cannot be trusted to buy on cue, may fail to grasp that they are inadequate, inferior and socially irresponsible because they do not own the latest model cars, VCRs and Nikes. Consumerism has to create hierarchies and reinforce individual identities because if I have the fastest car or most fashionable clothes, you obviously do not. This is not a capitalist conspiracy, it is a natural correspondence of interests between privately owned media and capital. Like most ideologies, that of consumerism has a core of truth—many products do save labour, increase comfort levels and make life more pleasant. Add to this the socially created truths of consumerism, that not possessing certain "things" leads other social actors to cast aspersions on your trustworthiness, thrift or credentials as a human being, and you have a very persuasive set of beliefs. But societies made up of people whose identities are solely dependent on purchased commodities are very vulnerable to capital's periodic cycles of contraction and expansion. Combining greater dependence with fewer social and economic supports leads inevitably to greater desperation, and some of this will emerge as increased interpersonal violence.

The content of mass culture is another factor linking desperation to violence. Without exploring the byzantine and endless debates over whether violent videos or television programmes directly incite aggressive acts or produce desensitization, the omnipresence of these messages—the fact that a high percentage of people's leisure time, daily routines and interactions with others revolve around violent events (be they fictional, news events or sports)— indicates that the messages have, at minimum, the power to monopolize human attention. Of course the actual effects of violent media will vary by individual, class, gender, values and role in the community. The food we consume also has different effects depending on body type, mood, age, gender, weight and level of nourishment. But if "you are what you eat," you are even more totally what you direct your attention to, what you think about, and value. And modern cultural diets promote insensitization, the quick 30-minute fix, lists of winners and losers, the unambiguous black and white solution. Compromise means selling out, complexity is denied and violence, when used by "people like us," is a good thing, the only way to surmount omnipresent forces of evil and incompetence.

When all this is added up—polarized politics, an increased focus on individualism at the expense of community, greater heterogeneity, decreased equality and the loss of older identities to mass consumerism—it appears to be a recipe for ever greater violence, deprivation, desperation and pain. It is hard to figure out modes of resistance, let alone transformation. Political parties on the left are demoralized and riven with conflict, some of it between groups that should be allies—unions versus environmentalists, native people against feminists or gays. In the short term, pessimism about the potential of macro-level change in today's nation state or its components is unavoidable. As Glasbeek has characterized the present era: "The employing classes have set out to roll back such gains as the working classes have made" (1995: 128). But none of these developments are new. Individualism, mass culture, consumerism and the decline of collective identities are part of the modernizing forces of industrialism and democracy, producing resistance as well as capitulation, gains as well as defeats. No structure is monolithic or impenetrable—or eternal. Because transformation is a dialectic process occurring from the bottom up as well as the top down,[25] the next section of the paper will look at the potential for change at micro and middle levels.

Building Less Violent Communities and Families

The focus here is on ways of building less violent families. While the difficulty of promoting micro- and middle-level patterns at odds with macro-level forces cannot be underestimated, it is essential to examine the context of subordination and understand the ways in which domination and violence are rooted inside the individual, in the patterns of daily life (Giddens 1981; Smart 1992; Foucault 1982). Thus, even while macro-level institutions are reinforcing one set of social relations, other social relations are undermining class and patriarchy, resisting and refusing hegemonic ways of thinking and acting. Macro-level transformation cannot be effective "if the agents upon whom [transformative politics] depends continue to be governed and defined by the very social contexts they are trying to transform" (Winter 1992: 812). The objective, then, is to examine how practices can be changed to foster subjectivities and identities which reject violent, dominator/dominated roles.

On a purely mechanistic level, attention must be paid to techniques and patterns of socialization. Child-rearing patterns based on rewards or the withdrawal of approval are more effective (that is, long-lasting and efficient) than those based on physical punishment. Practitioners like Spock and Bowlby have demonstrated that guilt- or shame-producing psychological sanctions lead to the development of conscience, while spanking and slapping, which operate primarily through fear of consequences, have erratic effects and sometimes produce retaliatory aggression. Effective socialization produces adults with strong internalized standards of behaviour who refrain from certain acts by "choice," rejecting antisocial behaviours because they feel guilty or evil when they do certain things. Non-violent child-rearing techniques, then, produce better socialized individuals, but less violent people and families will result *only if* violent behaviours are targeted as guilt-producing behaviours, and prohibitions against violence are conveyed to miscreants by role models and significant others—teachers, employers, youth leaders and the like.

However, there is profound cultural resistance to wholesale and unqualified discouragement of individual aggression, particularly in the rearing of sons. Mothers as well as fathers, terrified of boys becoming "wimps," send contradictory messages about the acceptability of bullying and aggression. Only when it becomes extreme, as in the recent murder of a three-year-old child in Britain by two ten-year olds, or when its targets are seen as undeserving, are violent acts unreservedly shamed. To understand why some boys grow up embracing violent acts and identities, others eschew them, and the majority flounder in the middle, one must examine the relationship between micro-level patterns of control and systems of patriarchy. Literature on domestic assault tells us that many of the violent men who have been studied are frustrated individuals who see women as easy, weak and available targets. They are often jealous and insecure, they believe in traditional sex roles and deny, to themselves and others, that their assaults have serious effects on the victimized. Frequently they witnessed or experienced physical or sexual abuse as children. Such men tend to see woman as objects whose duty is to make their men's lives easier, a duty women frequently fail to fulfil being "by nature" unreliable, unfaithful, lazy, etc. Violence for them is instrumental as well as expressive, a method of resolving conflict, establishing dominance, and claiming male entitlement (Tifft and Markham 1991; Dobash and Dobash 1992, 1975; Dekeseredy and Hinch 1991; Ptacek 1988a, b; Stets 1988; Buchwald *et al.* 1993).

However such literatures are often class-biased, and they do not tell us a great deal about pivotal micro-macro links. Works of feminist psychology on the other hand, though typically ignoring structural factors, can be read for insight on the ways that patriarchy becomes embedded in personalities through conscious and unconscious processes of identity formation (Chodorow 1978, 1989). Men construct masculinities in the same way that all identities are built, by choosing among the options they see as available and satisfying for "people like them," people who share their class, race, neighbourhood, family and society as well as gender. In heterogeneous western societies a wide range of masculinities is available, offering much choice—and much confusion. However, the patriarchal man—silent, equipped with the latest $225 Reeboks, emotionally constipated and physically strong—is still the ideal, especially in mass culture. Hegemonic masculinities on this model are heavily promoted in dominant media and sport, and constitute the identities most visible, accessible and appealing, particularly to boys lacking alternative male role models. Peer groups of adolescent males, alienated from mainstream authority, use sport, rap and mass culture extensively to develop ideas of what it means to be a man in this class, race, region, culture and time. Frequently this means borrowing the most violent and misogynous components of mainstream identities on offer. The price of questioning hegemonic masculinities can be high, producing feelings of uncertainty about one's own masculinity, rejection by peers, or even physical attacks. Given dominant value-systems that glorify power as an end in itself, and the undeniable fact that force is useful in getting one's way (for it offers immediate gratification without the need to grovel, negotiate or compromise and, in sexual matters, without vulnerability or risk of rejection), it can be hard for those who buy in to understand why anyone would reject the entitlement offered by hegemonic masculinities. When you can partake of an identity that allows you, by the simple fact of gender, to see yourself as stronger and smarter than half the world, entitled by birthright to deference and power if not wealth, why would you question such beliefs? Dissident males, who by their very existence show that these identities are cultural creations supporting privilege rather than biosocial necessities, threaten the entire structure.

Class and ethnic differences must be figured into this equation because they mediate the appeal of certain masculinities. Poor black or hispanic men in marginalized underclasses, for example, may find identities based on possession of turf or defence of honour appealing, or those that celebrate individualistic and collective force as badges of status, perhaps because a block of contested cityscape, a muscular body and a gun are among the few resources they can claim in such environments (Polk 1994). For men in urban ghettos to claim identities where self-esteem or peer status depends on the successful attainment of professional credentials or higher degrees (as many reformers insist they should) would be psychological and cultural suicide. The economic and educational resources necessary to play this game are simply not available to the vast majority, however intelligent and industrious. The success of the handful who might make it would come at the psycho-social expense of the many who would not.

White working-class American men (and a small percentage of black men) have seen their relatively privileged positions, good wages and strong unions, disappear in recent decades. Some of them have turned to militia-style movements celebrating turf and force (the equivalent of ghetto youth identities but more rural and collective), and/or to nationalistic identities based on citizenship, claiming entitlement as citizens of the richest, best, most powerful nation in the world. Working-class European men, typically less marginalized than urban underclasses in the United States, and better protected from the vagaries of the global marketplace due to the psychological and economic cushions instituted in such states in the post-war period, have often used sport, particularly football (soccer to North Americans), to underpin and reinforce concepts of manhood that contain notions of fair play in addition to celebrating toughness, physicality and the ability to take life's reverses stoically—"like a man" (Williams and Taylor 1994).

For middle-class North American white men, born into settings where masculinities can be centered in occupational success and higher education, dominant masculinities show wide generational splits. Adolescent middle-class masculinity is often premised on physical prowess, strength and sport (all linked to sexual success as a source of status), but with maturity job performance becomes paramount. In the merciless literally accurate language of the metaphor, occupational success "separates the men from the boys." Although phenomena such as the jobless recovery now threaten the economic prospects of the adult middle-class man, mainstream cultural goals of wealth, achievement and success through upward mobility were realistic goals for many decades. There was therefore less need, *as a class,* to cling to older masculinities stressing physical toughness, patriarchal notions based on the power of the male body. Men in this class were not so much learning to labour as learning to rule. This does not mean that middle- or upper-class masculinities reject misogyny or violence on either the personal or professional level (Godenzi 1994); the difference is often one of packaging more than substance. Levi (1994) points out that the City (the financial centre of London) is personalized by corporate executives and traders as a bitch goddess, a fickle female promising much but delivering little. Phrases such as "the City is a place for men, not for boys" (Levi 1994: 241) (and, therefore, not for women at all) suggest a subculture where exchange markets are exclusive boys' clubs, and trading and deals are dominance games, competitions for personal as well as occupational power. The self images of urban currency traders reek of machismo—the cowboy mystique, the swaggering recklessness of the quintessential "25-year olds in red suspenders," the "bad boy" heroes such as Nick Leeson, the 28-year-old bond trader who single-handedly brought down Barings Bank, the power of a George Soros, who "single-handedly broke the British pound" (Friedman 1995: A17). Such warrior power rivals that of earlier male heroes on the battlefields of Waterloo or the Plains of Abraham. Such identities celebrate dominance and patriarchy, but claims are based more on cerebral than physical power. This is hegemonic masculinity globalized.

In modern industrial societies diversity is omnipresent; the identities sketched here are no more than ideal types; the degree to which any particular man buys into them is always partial, fragmented and conditional. Identities and their appeal vary by occupational subculture and change over time. But key common themes can be traced. One is the need to keep certain spheres of thought and action separate and distinct, inviolate, strictly male. Another is the need to dominate one's physical and social environment. Yet another is the celebration of freedom and the related portrayal of women's and family demands—for commitment, labour, permanence—as constraint or fetters that the "real man" must resist and control. A very libertarian rejection of state or female social control pervades western masculinities. Domination by bosses or wives must be resisted, but it is not clear why, to what end, freedom means freedom *from* rather than freedom *to*. Fears of control may also be related to male fears of emasculation which pervade myth, culture and language. However, as discussed earlier, obsessions with criminalization, in the meaning, implications and responses to formal and informal mechanisms of social control, have limited feminist attention to gender differences such as these.

On the level of praxis and policy, any prescription for changing dominant masculinities and identities must be highly speculative: we simply do not understand the roots of these identities, their relation to biology, psychology, the social relations of capitalism or social practice. But the fact that traditional masculine identities are everywhere under attack is a source of hope for those who seek ameliorative social change. It should, it *must* be possible to find ways of being manly that are not misogynous and do not require the repression of every human emotion except anger. It should not be necessary to denigrate male sexuality or insist that it be denied to address misogyny or assault, but it is essential to differentiate the sex drive from the need to dominate. To understand the limits as well as the potential for change it is useful to examine the decline and fall of traditional male spheres of action, male "imperatives" to impregnate, provision and defend females and family groups (Gilmore 1990). These three have been central to male roles, male self-esteem and male identities, historically and cross-culturally, for thousands of years. There is no reason to believe they are epiphenomena, mere social constructions that can be wiped out by laws or political tinkering. Indeed it is more plausible to see the blockage and denial of "maleness" symbolized by the denigration of these roles as fuelling the male rage that animates the late twentieth century. Right-wing, racist, militia-style social movements and the reactionary, punishment-oriented political regimes which are their psychological equivalents (both of which, surveys tell us, are supported by men more than by women), are symptomatic. Male movements such as Promise Keepers and the Million Man March, although different from each other, represent other attempts, by white and black men respectively, to struggle with these issues and reclaim male territory—in this case by redefining the responsibilities, distinctiveness and privileges that defined masculinity in the past.

In less than one generation male prerogatives to impregnate, provide and defend have been radically altered. Take the responsibility to provide for one's family: as we have seen, technologies making many working-class jobs obsolete combined with right-wing policies to accommodate capital's quest for higher profit margins have destroyed union solidarity, wages and benefits, and abolished thousands of jobs. Since few women occupied the well-paid unionized jobs in heavy industry or manufacturing that were the primary targets of this wave of downsizing, working-class men were the main losers. In the 1990s downsizing spread up the class ladder, this time men and women in middle management and public sectors took the hit. The ability to provide for oneself, let alone one's mates and children, was radically altered. Government programmes, the economic cushions, softened the blow to an extent in some European countries, but these are temporary measures at best. To make matters worse, women sometimes found it easier to secure new jobs—they are typically better educated, more willing to accept low wage positions and are sometimes viewed by employers as more reliable and less aggressive (positive traits in the job market of the 1990s for many Mcjobs). In the middle classes, the success of feminism in securing equal opportunity, independence and promotion for women in formerly male domains, while relieving economic stress for men lucky enough to have partners with good jobs, added new stress to the pain of redundance and new fuel to the fires of backlash (Falludi 1991).[26] In North America, women's wages rose relative to men's as various equity programmes made hiring women (and some minorities) beneficial, and their relative scarcity in many traditionally male professions such as science or engineering increased their market value. Thus in the 1990s, just when large numbers of middle-class white men began experiencing intense marginalization for the first time, middle-class women began making real, though often exaggerated, gains.

The imperative to impregnate has become less necessary as well. Advances in technology threaten to make males redundant, with frozen sperm, artificial insemination and test-tube babies replacing humans. Patriarchy's historical monopoly over reproduction and hence over women has been challenged, and contraceptive pills, IUDs and legalized abortion have allowed many women, in the developed world at least, to control when, how and with whom they will reproduce. Backlash and resistance, as in laws requiring the consent of a partner or parent to procure an abortion, or "voluntary chastity" movements, have been largely unsuccessful. The arrival of AIDS has made heterosexual promiscuity, always the prerogative of men more than women, literally life-threatening.

Meanwhile overpopulation has rendered patriarchal structures that value men for the number of (male) offspring they can sire increasingly unfashionable, particularly in first-world countries where each new person consumes 17 times his or her share of the world's resources.

The need to defend oneself or one's mate against natural enemies (fire, flood and wild animals) has largely disappeared as well, particularly in developed and urbanized countries. But the desire for enemies is obvious: invented villains permeate popular culture, and heroes are pressed into service to ward off everything from godless communists, aliens and marauding rapists to killer hurricanes and runaway submarines. Unfortunately fulfilling the male imperative to defend in non-fictive realities runs up against state monopolies over the control of arms and the exercise of interpersonal violence. Thus we see the almost religious significance attached by militia movements to the "right" to bear arms, or the more recent but equally intense reaction to the banning of handguns larger than .22 calibre following the Dunblane massacre in Britain (*Guardian Weekly,* "Guns Go Abroad," 8 December 1996: 24). Public restrictions on private arsenals are essential, but they also benefit women as a group more than men as a group, since women are the more fearful and vulnerable sex. State social control deprives men of the right and obligation to display their (generally) superior physical strength and greater aggressive capacity, and another component of male identity disappears.

So what kind of remedies should progressive movements seek? No one would deny that many of these developments are positive. For people in urban industrialized societies to use violence to settle disputes unleashes cycles of escalating aggression and punishment, as life in many American cities today illustrates, where the wealthy barricade themselves inside armed enclosures and the poor kill each other off in the streets (or die in overheated tenements, too frightened to go outside or even open their windows, as in Chicago's 1995 heat wave). Only arms dealers and politicians who feed off fear benefit from this. And the answer is most certainly *not* to return to a time when female labour was even more underpaid and undervalued than it is now, or to sexual double standards that punished only women.

To my mind the evidence indicates that women, especially feminists, can play only minor roles in struggles to create and define less violent masculinities. The heavy misogyny found in male identity formation is too widespread, culturally and historically, to be wholly accidental. Blatant rejection of femininity and an exaggeration of male-female differences is a primary component of virtually every known male subculture (including those among gay men) (Jefferson 1994). Whether this is biologically or psychologically necessary is not known, nor is it particularly relevant from a utilitarian perspective. What matters is that, to have any appeal to rebellious adolescent males with much clearer ideas of what they reject than what they accept, alternate male identities must be *different* from female identities. It may turn out that the biosocial psychology of male humans, not to mention eons of evolution, make it important for boys to exaggerate gender differences in order to reject the mother-figure and distance themselves from the dependence of childhood. But there is no reason to suppose that the need to create identities that are distinctively different from women's implies a need to hate, devalue or dominate women. The latter are necessary components of patriarchy, not masculinity.

It also seems obvious that boys/men need roles, and therefore institutions and (sub) cultures, that allow them to be aggressive, risk-takers and adventurers (which does not mean that women should be denied such roles). There are few cultural or social spaces in developed societies where boys can be constructively adventurous or aggressive. Fantasy roles abound, from cyber-space to video games, but many of these exploit racism or homophobia rather than satisfying needs. With the disappearance of wild animals, frontiers and unexplored territory, the only adventurous legitimate *jobs* on offer are violent and destructive in nature (such as soldiers, police and/or criminals), or they are restricted to a privileged elite (space explorers today require doctorates in astrophysics). No wonder male police and prison guards cling so desperately to machismo images and subcultures, fighting academic and political directives which would replace warrior roles with service orientations (Heidensohn 1992; Reiner 1992). No wonder, too, that virtually all businesses and political organizations are gendered in ways that relegate women to secondary roles responsible for emotional scutwork, while men claim the adventurous, aggressive roles and the prestige, power and income such roles "deserve" (Hochschild 1983). It is not functionality, capitalism, or the dictates of efficiency that require such subcultures or organizational divisions of labour.

Heterosexual women do have important parts to play in struggles to recast male identities. Too often women as mothers reward violence and toughness in their sons (and weakness in their daughters), or devalue emotionality and vulnerability in men with negative labels. Women as lovers and mates, particularly young women, cannot continue to respond erotically to machismo and reject men exploring alternate masculinities or those who have refused emotional castration. Feminism as a movement is well placed to problematize and consciousness raise around women's roles in reinforcing violent masculinities.

Because knowledge is a form of power, there are important tasks in this struggle for those in the academy as well. New male identities need to be wide-ranging, they will vary with class, ethnicity, orientation, religious identification, occupation and age (to name only a few factors), and they cannot be specified or prescribed in advance. They must be struggled for, forged by trial and error, and based in older masculinities and ways of being. But little is known about the structural and cultural forces forming masculinities and femininities, or about micro-level processes which mediate the process of identity formation among individual men and women (Foucault 1982). Violence has historically been connected with dominance, and both with eroticism, but the roots and consequences of these links are unclear. We know little about the various agendas and interests animating struggles around masculinities today, and we have not adequately explored the social or political consequences of the different visions of male-female natures and relationships now vying for power. Some groups attempting to recast male and female identities, for example, take the partial, political and fragmented bits of biological knowledge we have about sex differences as facts, and argue for conservative policies on this basis (such as forcing women to stay home to bond with infants, or excluding them from higher education in mathematics because of alleged differences in left-right brain functions governing spatial abilities in men and women, for example). Naming the problems, specifying the implications and identifying the interest groups at play is a necessary first step to securing transformative changes and, even more crucial right now, to averting reactionary ones.[27] This is all part of the process of creating alternative models, of envisaging different ways of seeing to counter the dead weight of hegemony, for acceptance of the status quo rests heavily on notions that it constitutes the necessary and inevitable ordering of the world.

Directing greater attention to an "ethics of care" might be a useful component of the process of constructing alternatives (Gilligan 1982; Smart 1989: 72–4; Kellough 1995). Kellough suggests that the intersecting values of capitalism and patriarchy have co-opted, through law, the common human urge to care for others and distorted it into a welfare/dependence frame. Women in particular are forced to choose between independence/autonomy and the obligation to care for others or nurture (Kellough 1995: 382–3). This is a false dichotomy because people must be nurtured (through socialization) in order to become autonomous, so caring and independence are intertwined not juxtaposed. Such a concept is useful insofar as it can be used as a counterbalance to voices advocating penality and revenge, and a challenge to tyrannies of the binary. "Using the need of human beings for the caring attention of others" (Kellough 1994: 383) as a tool to evaluate macro-level processes (laws, structures, policies and institutions) focuses attention on new concepts of human rights, concepts based in collectivist and dualistic rather than individualistic zero-sum terms. We know so little about the activities central to caring, or the institutions and implications of such an orientation, compared to those central to punishing.[28]

An ethics of care also provides entry, on the level of praxis, for an overdue interrogation of the moral basis of capitalism, allowing renewed questioning of the conduct and obligations of capital. A long and difficult struggle a century ago secured minimum levels of health and safety in first-world workplaces and set in place a beneficent cycle redefining the responsibilities of capital to both labour and "society" (Snider 1993: 89–112; Carson 1970, 1980a, b; Paulus 1974). The rise of the global economy has reversed many of these gains. Such downsizing costs millions in direct and indirect costs, through welfare and unemployment benefits, forgone taxes, less productive workforces due to loss of morale, heightened insecurity, and other impacts (Pearce and Snider 1995a, b). It also has significant negative impact, through the removal of economic and psychological cushions on struggles, to create less violent populations. But the right of capital to create disposable people and communities has yet to be seriously scrutinized, much less targeted, by the demoralized political left or progressive social movements.

▥ CONCLUSION

Creating alternative models and shifting attention away from criminal justice "solutions" will not be easy. However, the present era represents a crossroads, a turning point where the potential for ameliorative change increases. It should be clear that criminalization, incarceration and increased punitiveness, while symbolically important, have reinforced right-wing agendas, with little to offer those seeking justice, transformation or remedial action. The failure to theorize social control has allowed a mis-identification of penality and control, and the obsession with punishment has diverted attention from examinations of the causes of violence and from explorations of ways to transcend criminalization to nurture counter-hegemonic change. The paper has explored these issues, asking in a preliminary way how macro-level factors reinforce violence in social orders, and how communities can be restructured and dominant masculinities and identities changed. As always, the bulk of the work remains.

🏛 ENDNOTES

Thanks to Elizabeth Comack, Carole LaPrairie, Gail Kellough and Stan Cohen for comments on earlier drafts, and to John Braithwaite and Peter Grabosky for providing a supportive climate at ANU, where this paper was born.

1   The term "progressive" is inaccurate and pretentious. It seems to imply that only feminists and those on the left care about being humane, while people who identify with other parts of the political spectrum happily go about adding to the sum of human misery. This is obviously not true. However, it is difficult to find any collective term that is more accurate—as postmodernists correctly insist, all generalizing labels are inaccurate. As used in this paper, progressive refers to those people and groups whose work claims to be "critical" (of patriarchy or capital) in theory, and transformative (counter-hegemonic) in praxis.

2   Notable exceptions include the recent works of John Braithwaite and his co-authors (Braithwaite 1989, 1991, 1994, 1995; Braithwaite and Pettit 1990; Braithwaite and Daly 1993); also Brickey and Comack 1987; and the harm-reduction and peace-making schools (Brants and Kok 1986; Dahl 1986; Pepinsky and Quinney 1991).

3   Because it is awkward to put quotation marks around "know" and "knowledge" each time they are used, I have not done so. But they should be assumed, because "knowledge" is never final and it is always fallible, a social construction bound by time and culture. Although this paper is aimed, in part, at constructing arguments that might be "true," the more important goal is to offer alternative conceptions of reality that might be useful, in the struggle to create more humane and egalitarian social orders.

4   Postmodern theories themselves need to be situated to be understood. The insistence that new social movements (nsms) have replaced class-based movements as vehicles of change came out of widespread disenchantment with the left, with the collapse of state socialism and electoral massacres (Hall 1988), and the recognition that global capitalism has robbed nation states of much of their economic and political power. Many on the left welcome the new focus on the politics of identity and on

144

small-scale personal struggles. Foucault's greatest contribution to modern theory was his insight that power is not centred exclusively in the state but dispersed throughout civil society: thus praxis operates through multitudinous theatres of resistance, to constituted authorities of every sort. For him, the key issue is personal identity (Foucault 1982: 211). Similarly, Laclau and Mouffe (1985, 1987), Magnusson (1992) and Offe (1987) celebrate the rejection of state theories, arguing that politics is "inscribed upon the bodies" of human agents, and of the environment they inhabit (Carroll 1992: 16). It is not, in other words "out there." But it is not always clear whether such postmodernists have any vision of building new structures, economies or discourses, or if their only goal is resistance. Resistance to what, for whom, to what end: these are unanswered questions (Wood 1990: 78–9).

5   Many postmodern pieces fail this test. They work well as critiques of dogmatism but fail when they lapse into Dogmatic generalizations such as those condemning all generalizations!

6   As Foucault (1979) and Smart (1989) have pointed out, the disciplines of social science are indeed *disciplines,* and they are central to the promotion of penality. This is particularly true of criminology, which claims to produce useful, scientific laws. Walker (1993) asserts that criminological studies on discretion led to mandatory minimum sentencing and charging policies and to Model Sentencing Codes (thereby increasing sentence length). Similarly, Martinson (1974) receives credit (or blame) for the shift in US prison philosophy from rehabilitation to detention. Such results were neither foreseen, nor necessarily desired by their authors. While empiricist, context-free research often lends itself most easily to such uses, there is no such thing as a study that cannot be used to promote punitive agendas, if only by "proving" it is invalid!

7   Braithwaite's excellent article (1994) on model-mongers provides information on the dynamics of this process. Powerful actors—and countries—are modelled more than less powerful ones; the periphery copies the core. America's dominance allows it to shape everything from fashion trends to scholarship. Intellectuals must publish in American journals and cite American examples. (For non-Americans, being an "internationally recognized scholar" means being recognized in the United States as well as one's own country; Americans are generally spared this cumbersome necessity as recognition in the core alone is sufficient.) Should "good" ideas have the temerity to appear in the periphery, they, and sometimes their originators, are appropriated by power-brokers in the centre, their ideas (inventions, etc.) then become seen as American, and are often reimported by the periphery.

8   Because stranger homicides are less likely to result in arrests than intimate homicides, and because many official studies are based on arrested and/or convicted criminals (it being much harder to gather information on those who have not been apprehended), this increase has often been hidden in official rates. But homicide

clearance rates, a good indicator, have dropped from 91 per cent in 1965 to 60.5 per cent in 1993 and 1994, dipping to 58.3 per cent in cities over one million. The FBI estimates that stranger homicides comprise 53 per cent of all urban homicides in the US (Walinsky 1995: 46), and that "only" 12 per cent of urban homicides take place within the family. Some commentators suggest a feminist conspiracy covers this up because such a statistic downplays domestic assault. It seems unlikely. Women are still more likely to be victimized by men than the reverse. Separated or "unfaithful" women still face much higher risks of being assaulted or killed than unfaithful or separated men (Rodgers 1994; Scull 1983; Wearing 1990; Stubbs and Wallace 1994). And men who kill "in the heat of passion" are still more likely to escape first degree homicide convictions than women who kill to avoid further abuse (Lees 1994). American figures reflect the high rates of homicide outside the family, but low rates *inside* it.

9   The proposal was defeated in Mississippi when the 32-member black caucus, realizing which race was most likely to be whipped and mindful of its historic associations with slavery, took the unusual step of voting against (the legislation as a block.

10   This is all the more ironic when one considers that provincial prisons in Canada are designed for offenders serving sentences under two years. The vicious criminals these crackdowns target, except for a small percentage awaiting trial on more serious offences, are doing time for non-payment of fines, traffic infractions such as driving under the influence (of alcohol) and shoplifting.

11   Mercy is not dead, however. That same day a judge decided it was "too harsh" to fire four Montreal police officers convicted of beating a Haitian taxi driver so severely he never regained consciousness. They were sentenced to 60 or 90-day jail terms, served on weekends, and 180 hours of community service (Picard 1995: A7). Rather than arguing for equity through increased punitiveness, the usual response of progressives, we might instead promote equity by advocating decreased incarceration for the poor and powerless, giving them the same treatment as offenders where mercy is shown to further agendas of hegemonic social control.

12   For example, feminists in Berkeley, California in the late 1960s were so opposed to the punitive arm of the state that the technique they adopted against rapists was to embarrass the offender by visiting his place of residence, en masse, with denunciatory placards (Matthews 1994). An early version of shaming, perhaps.

13   Being rearrested is deemed equivalent to reoffending. Of course it is not, since decisions to call in the authorities and report "offenders" are contingent on social and political factors such as privacy levels afforded by place of residence, alternative resources available to the victim, the parties' past experiences with police, and others. Mandatory arrest policies never deprive police of *all* discretion—the power to respond initially, and to define the occurrence as the type of act covered by mandatory policies remains in their hands.

14   The history of Kingston Penitentiary, Canada's first, established in 1835, is typical. A decade after it opened, the first of a series of Royal Commissions into prison conditions decried the corruption of the warden, the sadistic and excessive use of whipping (the infamous "cat o' nine tails"), the starvation of inmates, physical torture, and corruption of the guards, concluding that inmates were either driven insane or transformed from amateur into skilled criminals (Brown Commission Report 1849, in Cooper 1993: 48). Or consider the Kingston Prison for Women, Canada's only federal penitentiary for women, constructed in 1934 after a hundred years of reports recommending such a prison as a solution to all ills. The first Royal Commission Report to recommend its closure was issued in 1938, a scant four years later (Archambault Commission, in Cooper 1993: 43). And still we do not learn, for as I write plans to replace P4W with five regional facilities (and a healing lodge for Aboriginal women), are underway. The first of these opened three months ago, in Edmonton, Alberta. Meant to be an open facility allowing inmates to learn and grow, it is already under pressure to tighten control because of inmate "escapes."

15   The following definitions are employed in this paper. Violence refers to the infliction of pain, harming others through the use or threat of force. It can be physical or non-physical, and prescribed (legal), for example when police use coercion to subdue suspects, or proscribed (illegal). It can be individual and one-on-one, as in robbery and assault; or collective/corporate, as in manufacturing cars that explode in rear-end collisions or carcinogenic medical implants. Criminal law typically focuses only on the individual, illegal act. Punishment is "the legal process whereby violators of the criminal law are condemned and sanctioned in accordance with specified legal categories and procedures" (Garland 1990: 17). It includes the "linked processes of law-making, conviction, sentencing, and the administration of penalties," the "discursive frameworks of authority and condemnation," and the "rhetoric of symbols," which represent the penal process to its audiences (Garland 1990: 17). Finally social control refers to: "the complex of laws, processes, discourses and institutions involved in criminalizing and sanctioning behaviour" (Garland 1990: 10).

16   The only other success of penality lies in its power to denounce, to convey social disapproval. Criminalization stigmatizes even the most powerful, on the rare occasions it is applied to their misdeeds (Pearce 1989, 1993; Braithwaite 1995). Thus, the evils of hazardous waste or employer negligence are more effectively conveyed through criminal rather than administrative law; the pronouncement of sentence is an august degradation ceremony in and of itself. A strategy of criminalization makes sense if seen as a consciouness-raising device to change public attitudes or highlight the misogyny permeating laws and practices such as the "rule of thumb" on wife beating. However it can be argued that many of the ideological benefits are achieved from the publicity and struggle; it is "success," defined as attaining state monies for criminalization, that is problematic.

17 Penality creates jobs, legitimizes professions, builds major industries. As Christie (1993) shows, the criminal justice system is one of the largest, most prosperous areas of the American economy, one of the few places where jobs can be had, careers built, towns made prosperous, and technological innovations perfected. Penal professionals have their own journals, jargon, conferences and all the detritus of established disciplines. Penal punishment has been refined and rendered scientific, the dispassionate field of experts removed from the emotional excesses of amateurs seeking vengeance and revenge (Garland 1990: 184–5).

18 Arguments on the psychology of offenders are very much in fashion now (Gottfredson and Hirschi 1990). But it should be obvious that many criminal acts—producing, promoting and profiting from selling a drug known to cause cataracts or heart disease, for example, or hiring workers who cannot speak sufficient English to understand the warning labels on the cyanide they are using—require foresight, planning and discipline. Such crimes are more closely related to capitalism and cupidity than to drive fulfilment.

19 I have purposively not defined social control because the definition is part of the problematic. It has been defined so narrowly that it includes only physical coercion, and so broadly every kind of influence, from socialization in family units to brainwashing in total institutions, is covered (Howe 1994: 65–6). Much feminist writing utilizes the broadest definition, implicitly or explicitly, and judges control negatively when exercised over women, positively when exercised by them. It is sometimes suggested that women are imprisoned in familial discourses, for example, because these are shaped by ideals of femininity originating in patriarchy (Howe 1994; Carrington 1990; Benhabib and Cornell 1987). However, if every kind of influence is seen as a patriarchal plot, what, then, is the absence of (social) control? What is the goal of resistance? Is it to create some kind of pre-social, Rousseauian "natural" woman? Feminism needs to sort out which controls must be resisted and which embraced, rather than arguing (apparently) against all the processes of socialization.

20 Conversely it can be argued that men have suffered more than women in the civilizing process described by Elias and Dirkheim since they represent the more aggressive sex. Male definitions of "normal" social control are often used—for example when the level of control applied to girls is described as oversocialization (Hagan 1991). The classic male dream of freedom involves escaping wives and children (deemed responsibilities), pursuing lives where sexual gratification and job-labour are casual, impulsive and commitment-free. Generations of popular culture and literature (male-dominated, aimed particularly at *young* men)—the "Easy Rider," "going down the road" Kerouac-style literatures, the frontier where "a man can be a man"—all celebrate independence from the demands of civilization/ women.

21 Indeed, feminists do well to remember our own culpability—in privileging gender over race, for example, and ignoring the views of many minority women who would see racism as more significant than sexism in their lives (Greer 1994; Matthews 1994; Carby 1982; Williams 1987).

22 They are also more likely to take a job, any job, however menial and poorly paid. This explains, in part, why unemployment rates in the United States have typically been lower than in Europe and Japan, and why employers in general seek to keep support levels as low as possible.

23 This paper looks primarily at reactive, individual violence rather than aggressive collective violence, be it for territory, resources or empire expansion. Both kinds are important in the struggle against violence against women.

24 Earlier collective identities based in craft guilds have largely disappeared. Religion, a primary source of alternative value systems in many parts of the world, has been marginalized in much of Europe and Canada, and "captured" by consumerism and capitalism in the United States (Bibby 1993). There has been talk about the potential of technology (the Net, for example) to recreate community and nourish alternate identities, but since it is still predominantly privileged classes, men, and increasingly commercial interests which are "on line," it is unduly optimistic to see anything "alternative" emerging here.

25 Documentation of the relative futility of starting at the top, in this case with legal reform, is provided by Rosenberg's analysis of judicial activism in the United States (1991). In analyses of school desegregation, abortion, gender discrimination, criminal procedure, reapportionment and environmental protection laws, Rosenberg documents the failure of litigation to achieve substantive results *unless* other factors were present. Incentives for compliance, sanctions for non-compliance, and support from the institutions that would have to implement the reform were necessary prerequisites. In other words, legal victories only change lived realities if the ideological work has already been done, or is well underway.

26 Jobs for married women are not new—all but the most privileged have worked outside the home since the dawn of the Industrial Revolution (except during the most intense periods of child-rearing), but their wages were kept low by a combination of sexism and glass ceilings, and their jobs were more likely to be seen, by women as well as men, as secondary.

27 The struggle for identity, the territory of internal or psychological change, is central to counter-hegemonic and ideological change. And it has not been claimed and politicized to the degree that structure-based change, now the apparently unchallengeable property of those who would make the world safe for profit maximization, has been. It may therefore be fertile soil politically, as well as essential knowledge.

28 Much caring labour, in the private sphere and in mainstream organizations ranging from airlines to government, is done by and expected from women rather than

men (Hochschild 1983). However the consequences and implications this has for social policy, child-rearing, economic reform, and violence are unknown. Do male subcultures and identities lose the potential to express and develop caring identities because of the dominance of women in these spheres? Are women denied the chance to develop more instrumental abilities? With what consequences? The empirical and theoretical territory of caring needs to be explored as carefully as the terrain of penality has been.

⋔ REFERENCES

Abegglen, J. (1975), *Management and Workers: The Japanese Solution*. Tokyo: Sophia University Press.

Adkin, L. (1992), "Counter-Hegemony and Environmental Politics in Canada," in W. Carroll, ed., *Organizing Dissent*, 135–56. Toronto: Garamond.

Adkin, L. and Alpaugh, C. (1988), "Labour, Ecology and the Politics of Convergence," in F. Cunningham, S. Findlay, M. Kadar, A. Lennon and F. Silva, eds., *Social Movements/Social Change*, vol. 4, pp. 48–73. Toronto: Between the Lines and the Society for Socialist Studies.

Alder, C. and Wundersitz, J., eds., (1994), *Family Conferencing and Juvenile Justice*. Canberra: Australian Institute of Criminology.

Allen, J. (1982), "The Invention of the Pathological Family: A Historical Study of Family Violence in New South Wales," in C. O'Donnell and J. Craney, eds., *Family Violence in Australia*, 1–27. Melbourne: Longman Cheshire.

Anderson, K. (1991), *Chain Her By One Foot: The Subjugation of Women in 17th Century New France*. London: Routledge.

Andrews, D., Zinger, I., Hoge, R., Bonta, J., Gendreau, P. and Cullen, F. (1990), "Does Correctional Treatment Work? A Clinically Relevant and Psychologically Informed Mega-Analysis," *Criminology*, 28/3: 369–404.

Appleby, T. (1995), "Crime plummeting across the U.S.," *Globe and Mail*, Toronto, 13 July, A8.

Archer, D. and Gartner, R. (1984), *Violence and Crime in Cross-National Perspective*. New Haven: Yale University Press.

Astor, H., (1994), "Swimming against the Tide: Keeping Violent Men Out of Mediation," in J. Stubbs, ed., *Women, Male Violence and the Law*. Monograph Series 6: 147–73. Sydney: Institute of Criminology.

Australian Bureau Of Statistics (1994), *Crime and Safety in Australia*. Canberra: Supply and Services.

Bagley, K. and Merlo, A. (1995), "Controlling Women's Bodies," in A. Merlo and J. Pollock, eds., *Women, Law, and Social Control*, 135–54. Boston: Allyn and Bacon.

Bartholomew, A. and Hunt, A. (1980), "What's Wrong with Rights," *Journal of Inequality*, 9/1: 1–58.

Benhabib, S. and Cornell, D., eds. (1987), *Feminism as Critique: Essays on the Politics of Gender in Late Capitalist Societies*. Cambridge: Polity Press.

Bibby, R. (1993), *Unknown Gods: The Ongoing Story of Religion in Canada*. Toronto: Stoddart.

Box, S. (1983), *Power, Crime and Mystification*. London: Tavistock Publications.

Boyle, J. (1985), "The Politics of Reason: Critical Legal Theory and Local Social Thought," *University of Pennsylvania Law Review*, 133, April.

Braithwaite, J. (1989), *Crime, Shame and Reintegration*. Melbourne: Cambridge University Press.

Braithwaite, J. (1991), "Inequality and Republican Criminology." Paper presented at Annual Meeting of the American Society of Criminology, San Francisco, November.

Braithwaite, J. (1994), "A Sociology of Modelling and the Politics of Empowerment," *British Journal of Sociology*, 45/3: 445–79.

Braithwaite, J. (1995), "Corporate Crime and Republican Criminological Praxis," in F. Pearce and L. Snider, eds., *Corporate Crime: Contemporary Debates*, 48–71. Toronto: University of Toronto Press.

Braithwaite, J. and Daly, K. (1994), "Masculinities, Violence, and Communitarian Control," in T. Newburn and E. Stanko, eds., *Just Boys Doing Business: Men, Masculinity and Crime*, 189–213. London: Routledge.

Braithwaite, J. and Makkai, T. (1991), "In and Out of the Revolving Door: Making Sense of Regulatory Capture." Unpublished paper. Research School of the Social Sciences, Australia National University, December.

Braithwaite, J. and Mugford, S. (1994), "Conditions of Successful Reintegration Ceremonies," *British Journal of Criminology*, 34/2: 139–71.

Braithwaite, J. and Pettit, P. (1990), *Not Just Deserts: A Republican Theory of Criminal Justice*. Oxford: Oxford University Press.

Brants, D. and Kok, E. (1986), "Penal Sanctions as a Feminist Strategy: A Contradiction in Terms?," *International Journal of Sociology of Law*, 14: 269–86.

Brickley, S. and Comack, E. (1987), "The Role of Law in Social Transformation: Is a Jurisprudence of Insurgency Possible?," *Canadian Journal of Law and Society*, 2: 97–119.

Brodeur, J-P. (1996), "Penal Saturation," in T. O'Reilly-Fleming, *Post-Critical Criminology*, 315–28. Scarborough, Ontario: Prentice Hall.

Brownmiller, S. (1975), *Against Our Will: Men, Women and Rape*. New York: Simon and Schuster.

Buchwald, E., Fletcher, P. and Roth, M., eds. (1993), *Transforming a Rape Culture*. Minneapolis, MN: Milkweed Editions.

Butler, J. (1990), *Gender Trouble*. London: Routledge.

Cain, M. and Harrington, C., eds. (1994), *Lawyers in a Postmodern World*. Milton Keynes, UK: Open University Press.

Calavita, K. (1983), "The Demise of the Occupational Safety and Health Administration: A Case Study in Symbolic Action," *Social Problems,* 30/4: 437–48.

Calavita, K. (1986), "Worker Safety, Law and Social Change: The Italian Case," *Law and Society,* 20/20: 189–229.

Calavita, K. and Pontell, H. (1995), "Saving the Savings and Loans: U.S. Government Response to Financial Crime," in F. Pearce and L. Snider, eds., *Corporate Crime: Contemporary Debates,* 199–214. Toronto: University of Toronto Press.

Canada, Standing Committee on Justice and the Solicitor General (1993), *Crime Prevention in Canada: Toward a National Strategy.* Ottawa: Canada Communication Group, Publishing, Supply and Services.

Canada, Bureau of Competition Policy (1989), *Competition Policy in Canada: The First Hundred Years.* Ottawa: Consumer and Corporate Affairs.

Canada (1988), *General Social Survey.* Ottawa: Statistics Canada.

Carby, H. (1982), "White Woman Listen! Black Feminism and the Boundaries of Sisterhood," *The Empire Strikes Back: Race and Racism in 70s Britain.* London: Hutchinson.

Caringella-MacDonald, S. (1985), "The Comparability in Sexual and Non-sexual Assault Case Treatment: Did Statute Change Meet the Objective?," *Crime and Delinquency,* 31: 206–22.

Caringella-MacDonald, S. (1987), "Marxist and Feminist Interpretations on the Aftermath of Rape Reforms," *Contemporary Crisis,* 12/4.

Caringella-MacDonald, S. (1988), "Parallels and Pitfalls: The Aftermath of Legal Reforms for Sexual Assault, Marital Rape and Domestic Violence Victims," *Journal of Interpersonal Violence,* 3/2: 174–89.

Caringella-MacDonald, S. and Humphries, D. (1991), "Sexual Assault, Women, and the Community: Organizing to Prevent Sexual Violence," in H. Pepinsky and R. Quinney, eds., *Criminology as Peacemaking,* 98–113. Bloomington: Indiana University Press.

Carlen, P. (1991), "Crime, Class, Gender, Race and Racism: Some Reservations about Global and Gender-Centric Theories." Paper presented at International Conference on Feminist Criminology, Mount Gabriel, Quebec, 18–21 July.

Carrington, K. (1990), "Feminist Readings of Female Delinquency," in J. Grbich, ed., *Feminism Law and Society,* 5–31. Bundoora: La Trobe University Press.

Carroll, W. (1992), "Introduction: Social Movements and Counter-Hegemony in a Canadian Context," in W. Carroll, ed., *Organizing Dissent,* 1–19. Toronto: Garamond.

Carson, W. G. (1970), "White Collar Crime and the Enforcement of Factory Legislation," *British Journal of Criminology,* 10: 382–98.

Carson, W. G. (1980a), "The Institutionalization of Ambiguity: Early British Factory Acts," in G. Geis and E. Stotland, eds., *White Collar Theory and Research.* Beverly Hills: Sage.

Carson, W. G. (1980b), "The Other Price of Britain's Oil: Regulating Safety on Offshore Oil Installations in the British Sector of the North Sea," *Contemporary Crises,* 4: 239–66.

Chanteloup, G. (1992), *The Canadian Environmental Protection Act: A Critical Analysis of the Role of Industry in the Legislative Process.* Unpublished MA thesis. Queen's University, Kingston, Ontario, August.

Chodorow, N. (1978), *Reproduction of Mothering: Psychoanalysis and the Sociology of Gender.* Berkeley: University of California Press.

Chodorow, N. (1989), *Feminism and Psychoanalytic Theory.* Cambridge: Polity Press.

Christie, N. (1977), "Conflict as Property," *British Journal of Criminology,* 17/1: 1–14.

Christie, N. (1993), *Crime Control as Industry.* London: Routledge.

Chunn, D. (1992), *From Punishment to Doing Good: Family Courts and Socialized Justice in Ontario 1880–1940.* Toronto: University of Toronto Press.

Clark, I. D. (1989), "Legislative Reform and the Policy Process: The Case of the Competition Act." Address given to the National Conference on Competition Law and Policy in Canada. Toronto: October.

Cohen, S. (1994), "Postscript: If Nothing Works, What Is Our Work?," *Australia and New Zealand Journal of Criminology,* 27/1: 104–7.

Comack, E. (1993), *Feminist Engagement with the Law: The Legal Recognition of the "Battered Woman Syndrome,"* CRIAW Paper No. 31. Ottawa: Canadian Research Institute for the Advancement of Women.

Cooper, S. (1993), "The Evolution of the Federal Women's Prison," in E. Adelberg and C. Currie, eds., *In Conflict with the Law,* 33–49. Vancouver: Press Gang.

Cuff, J. (1995), "TV violence pointless, silly issue," *Globe and Mail,* Thursday, 3 August: C1.

Cullen, F., Link, B. and Polanzi, C. (1982), "The Seriousness of Crime Revisited," *Criminology,* 20/1: 83–102.

Dahl, T. S. (1986), "Taking Women as a Starting Point: Building Women's Law," *International Journal of Sociology of Law,* 14: 239–61.

Dekeseredy, W. and Hinch, R. (1991), *Woman Abuse: Sociological Perspectives.* Toronto: Thompson Educational Publishing.

Dettmer, J. (1995), "Vandals in America could take a caning," *Weekend Australian,* 18–19 March, B1.

Dobash, R. E. and Dobash, R. (1975), *Violence Against Wives: A Case Against the Patriarchy.* New York: Free Press.

Dobash, R. E. and Dobash, R. (1992), *Women, Violence and Social Change.* London: Routledge.

Durkheim, E. (1893), *The Division of Labour in Society.* New York: Free Press (1964).

Durkheim, E. (1990), "Two Laws of Penal Evolution," *University of Cincinnati Law Review,* 38 (1969): 32–60.

Dutton, D. (1984), *The Criminal Justice System's Response to Wife Assault,* Report No. 26. Ottawa: Ministry of the Solicitor-General.

Edgley, C. and Brissett, D. (1990), "Health Nazis and the Cult of the Perfect Body: Some Polemical Observations," *Symbolic Interaction,* 13/2: 257–79.

Edwards, A. (1994), "The Tyranny of the Binary: Social Construction of Gender, Sexuality and Rape in Criminal Trials." Paper presented at Australian Sociological Association Conference, Deakin University, Geelong, Victoria, 7–10 December.

Ekland-Olson, S., Lieb, S. and Zurcher, L. (1984), "The Paradoxical Impact of Criminal Sanctions: Some Microstructural Findings," *Law and Society Review,* 18/2: 159–78.

Ekland-Olson, S., Lieb, S. and Zurcher, L. (1982), *State Formation and Civilization.* London: Oxford University Press.

Elias, N. (1978), *The Civilizing Process.* London: Oxford University Press.

Elias, R. (1989), "Which Victim Movement: The Politics of Victim Policy," in W. Skogan *et al.,* eds., *Victims and Criminal Justice.* Berkeley: Sage.

Ericson, R. and Baranek, P. (1982), *The Ordering of Justice: A Study of Accused Persons as Dependants in the Criminal Justice Process.* Toronto: University of Toronto Press.

Falludi, S. (1991), *Backlash: The Undeclared War Against American Women.* New York: Doubleday.

Feeley, M. (1979), *The Process is the Punishment.* New York: Russell Sage Foundation.

Feeley, M. and Simon, J. (1992), "The New Penology," *Criminology,* 39/4: 449–74.

Feeley, M. and Simon, J. (1994), "The New Penology: Notes on the Emerging Strategy of Corrections and Its Implications," *Criminology,* 30: 449–74.

Felt, L. (1987), "Take the 'Bloods of Bitches' to the Gallows: Cultural and Structural Constraint upon Interpersonal Violence in Rural Newfoundland," *St. John's Institute of Social and Economic Research,* Memorial University of Newfoundland.

Feschuk, S. (1995), "Alberta Jails No Place Like Home," *Globe and Mail,* 15 July, A7.

Foucault, M. (1979), *Discipline and Punish: The Birth of the Prison.* New York: Pantheon.

Foucault, M. (1982), "The Subject and Power," in H. Dreyfus and P. Rabinow, eds., *Michel Foucault: Beyond Structuralism and Hermeneutics,* 194–230. Chicago: University of Chicago Press.

French, M. (1985), *Beyond Power: On Women, Men and Morals.* New York: Summit Books.

Friedman, T. (1995), "Sorry, but this Group of Seven doesn't make the grade." *Globe and Mail,* Tuesday, 30 May, A17 (reprinted from the *New York Times*).

Fudge, J. (1990), "What Do We Mean by Law and Social Transformation?," *Canadian Journal of Law and Society,* 5: 47–69.

Fudge, J. and Glasbeek, H. (1992), "A Politics of Rights: A Politics with Little Class," *Social and Legal Studies,* 1, 45–70. London: Sage.

Galtung, J. (1969), "Violence, Peace and Peace Research," *Journal of Peace Research,* 6: 167–91.

Garland, D. (1985), *Punishment and Welfare: A History of Penal Strategies.* Aldershot, Hants: Gower.

Garland, D. (1990), *Punishment and Modern Society: A Study in Social Theory.* Oxford: Clarendon Press.

Garland, D. (1991), "Punishment and Culture: The Symbolic Dimension of Criminal Justice," *Studies in Law, Politics and Society,* 11: 191–222.

Garland, D. (1995), "Penal Modernism and Postmodernism," in A. Blomberg and S. Cohen, eds., *Punishment and Social Control,* 181–209. New York: Aldine de Gruyter.

Giddens, A. (1981), *The Class Structure of Advanced Societies,* 2nd ed. London: Hutchinson.

Gilligan, C. (1982), *In a Different Voice: Psychological Theory and Women's Development.* Cambridge: Harvard University Press.

Gilligan, C. (1987), "Moral Orientation and Moral Development," in E. Kittray and D. Meyers, eds., *Women and Moral Theory.* New Jersey: Rowan and Littlefield.

Gilmore, T. (1990), *Manhood in the Making.* New Haven: Yale University Press.

Glasbeek, H. (1995), "Preliminary Observations on Strains of, and Strains in Corporate Law Scholarship," in F. Pearce and L. Snider, eds., *Corporate Crime: Contemporary Debates,* 111–31. Toronto: University of Toronto Press.

Godenzi, A. (1994), "What's the Big Deal?," in T. Newburn and E. Stanko, eds., *Just Boys Doing Business?,* 135–52. London: Routledge.

Goff, C. and Mason-Clark, N. (1989), "The Seriousness of Crime in Fredricton, New Brunswick: Perception towards White-Collar Crime," *Canadian Journal of Criminology,* 31: 19–34.

Gottfredson, M. and Hirschi, T. (1990), *A General Theory of Crime.* Stanford: Stanford University Press.

Grabosky, P. (1984), "The Variability of Punishment," in D. Black, ed., *Toward a General Theory of Social Control,* 163–89. New York: Academic Press.

Greer, P. (1994), "Aboriginal Women and Domestic Violence in New South Wales," in J. Stubbs, ed., *Women, Male Violence and the Law,* Monograph Series No. 6: 64–87. Sydney: Institute of Criminology.

Habermas, J. (1968/1971), *Knowledge and Human Interests,* trans. J. Shapiro. Boston: Beacon.

Hagan, J. (1991), "A Power-Control Theory of Gender and Delinquency," in R. Silverman, J. Teevan and V. Sacco, eds., *Crime in Canadian Society,* 4th ed., 130–36. Toronto: Butterworths.

Hall, S. (1988), *The Hard Road to Renewal: Thatcherism and the Crisis of the Left.* London: Verso.

Handler, J. (1992), "Postmodernism, Protests and the New Social Movements," *Law and Society Review,* 26/4: 697–731.

Hanmer, J. and Stanko, E. (1985), "Stripping Away the Rhetoric of Protection: Violence to Women, Law and the State in Britain and USA," *International Journal of Sociology of Law,* 13: 357–74.

Hannah-Moffat, K. (1995), "To Charge or Not to Charge: Front Line Officers' Perceptions of Mandatory Charge Policies," in M. Valverde, L. MacLeod and K. Johnson, eds., *Wife Assault and the Canadian Criminal Justice System.* Toronto: Centre of Criminology: 35–47.

Harper's Magazine (1996), "Does America Still Work? A *Forum* Discussion with R. Blackwell, A. Dunlap, G. Gilder, E. Luttwak, R. Reich and P. Tough," 292/1752: 35–47.

Harris, M. K. (1991), "Moving into a New Millennium: Toward a Feminist Vision of Justice," in H. Pepinsky and R. Quinney, eds., *Criminology as Peacemaking,* 83–97. Bloomington: Indiana University Press.

Heidensohn, F. (1992), *Women in Control.* Oxford: Oxford University Press.

Hess, H. (1995a), "Violent crime rate drops by 3%," *Globe and Mail,* 3 August, A1, and 5.

Hess, H. (1995b), "Babies in first year risk murder most," *Globe and Mail,* 3 August, A5.

Hochschild, A. R. (1983), *The Managed Heart: Commercialization of Human Feeling.* Berkeley: University of California Press.

Howe, A. (1990a), "Sentencing Women to Prison in Victoria: A Research and Political Agenda," in J. Grbich, ed., *Feminism Law and Society,* 32–53. Bundoora, Victoria: LaTrobe University Press.

Howe, A. (1990b), "The Problem of Privatized Injuries: Feminist Strategies for Litigation," in S. Silbey and A. Sarat, eds., *Studies in Law, Politics and Society,* 10: 111–42.

Howe, A. (1994), *Punish and Critique: Towards a Feminist Analysis of Penality.* London: Routledge.

Hurtig, M. (1991), *The Betrayal of Canada.* Toronto: McClelland and Stewart.

Ignatieff, M. (1978), *A Just Measure of Pain: The Penitentiary in the Industrial Revolution.* London: Routledge.

Immarigeon, B. (1991), "Beyond the Fear of Crime," in H. Pepinsky and R. Quinney, eds., *Criminology as Peacemaking,* 69–80. Bloomington: Indiana University Press.

Immarigeon, R. and Chesney-Lind, M. (1992), *Women's Prisons: Overcrowded and Overused.* San Francisco: National Council on Crime and Delinquency.

Jackson, P. (1989), *Minority Group Threat, Crime and Policing: Social Context and Social Control.* New York: Praeger.

Jefferson, T. (1994), "Theorising Masculine Subjectivity," in T. Newburn and E. Stanko, eds., *Just Boys Doing Business?,* 10–32. London: Routledge.

Johnson, H. and Rodgers, K. (1993), "A Statistical Overview of Women and Crime in Canada," in E. Adelberg and C. Currie, eds., *In Conflict with the Law,* 95–116. Vancouver: Press Gang.

Kellough, G. (1992), "Pro-Choice Politics and Postmodernist Theory," in W. Carroll, ed., *Organizing Dissent,* 81–100. Toronto: Garamond Press.

Kellough, G. (1995), *The Abortion Controversy: A Study of Law, Culture and Social Change.* Toronto: University of Toronto Press.

Kesterton, M. (1995), "Income Gaps." *Globe and Mail,* Friday, 27 July, A16.

Kinsey, R., Lea, J. and Young, J. (1986), *Losing the Fight against Crime.* London: Basil Blackwell.

Knopp, F. (1991), "Community Solutions to Sexual Violence," in H. Pepinsky and R. Quinney, eds., *Criminology as Peacemaking,* 181–203. Bloomington: Indiana University Press.

Laclau, E. and Mouffe, C. (1985), *Hegemony and Socialist Strategy: Towards a Radical Democratic Politics.* London: Verso.

Laclau, E. and Mouffe, C. (1987), "Post-Marxism without Apologies," *New Left Review,* 166: 79–106.

LaPrairie, C. (1993), "Aboriginal Women and Crime in Canada: Identifying the Issues," in E. Adelberg and C. Currie, eds., *In Conflict with the Law,* 235–46. Vancouver: Press Gang.

LaPrairie, C. (1995), "Altering Course: New Directions in Criminal Justice. Sentencing Circles and Family Group Conferences," unpublished paper. Ottawa: Department of Justice.

LaRocque, E. (1995), "Violence in the Aboriginal Communities," in M. Valverde, L. MacLeod, K. Johnson, eds., *Wife Assault and the Canadian Criminal Justice System,* 104–124. Toronto: Centre of Criminology.

Lea, J. and Young, J. (1984), *What Is to Be Done about Law and Order?* Harmondsworth, Middlesex: Penguin Books.

Lees, S. (1994), "Lawyers' Work as Constitutive of Gender Relations," in M. Cain and C. Harrington, eds., *Lawyers in a Postmodern World,* 124–54. Milton Keynes, UK: Open University Press.

Levi, M. (1984), "Giving Creditors the Business: The Criminal Law in Inaction," *International Journal of the Sociology of Law,* 12: 321–33.

Levi, M. (1987), " 'Crisis; What Crisis?' Reactions to Commercial Fraud in the United Kingdom," *Contemporary Crises,* 11/3: 207–21.

Levi, M. (1993), *The Investigation, Prosecution, and Trial of Serious Fraud,* Research Study No. 14. London: Royal Commission on Criminal Justice.

MacKinnon, C. (1992), "Pornography, Civil Rights and Speech," in C. Itzin, ed., *Pornography: Women, Violence and Civil Liberties.* Oxford: Oxford University Press.

MacLeod, L. (1995), "Policy Decisions and Prosecutorial Dilemmas: The Unanticipated Consequences of Good Intentions," in M. Valverde, L. MacLeod and K. Johnson, eds., *Wife Assault and the Canadian Criminal Justice System,* 47–62. Toronto: Centre of Criminology.

Magnusson, W. (1992), "Decentring the State, or Looking for Politics," in W. Carroll, ed., *Organizing Dissent: Contemporary Social Movements in Theory and Practice*, 69–80. Toronto: Garamond.

Mandell, M. (1994), *The Charter of Rights and the Legalization of Politics in Canada*. Toronto: Thompson Educational Publishing.

Marsh, J., Geist, A. and Caplan, N. (1982), *Rape and the Limits of Law*. Boston: Auburn House.

Martin, D. and Mosher, J. (1995), "Unkept Promises: Experiences of Immigrant Women with the Neo-Criminology of Wife Abuse," *Canadian Journal of Women and the Law*, 8/1: 3–44.

Martinson, R. (1974), "What Works? Questions and Answers about Prison Reform," *The Public Interest*, 35: 22–54.

Matthews, N. (1994), *Confronting Rape*. London: Routledge.

Mathiesen, T. (1990), *Prison on Trial*. London: Sage.

Maxwell, G. and Morris, A. (1994), "The New Zealand Model of Family Group Conferences," in C. Alder and J. Wundersitz, eds., *Family Conferencing and Juvenile Justice*, 15–43. Canberra: Australian Institute of Criminology.

McBarnet, D. (1981), *Conviction and Law: The State and the Construction of Justice*. London: Macmillan

Melossi, D. (1980), "Strategies of Social Control in Capitalism: A Comment on Recent Work," *Contemporary Crises*, 4: 381–402.

Melossi, D. and Pavarini, M. (1981), *The Prison and the Factory: The Origins of the Penitentiary System*. London: Ink Links.

Messerschmidt, J. (1986), *Capitalism, Patriarchy and Crime: Toward a Socialist-Feminist Criminology*. Tolowa, NJ: Rowan and Littlefield.

Michaud, J. (1992), "The Welfare State and the Problem of Counter-Hegemonic Responses within the Women's Movement," in W. Carroll, ed., *Organizing Dissent*, 200–214. Toronto: Garamond.

Michelman, F. (1979), "Welfare Rights in a Constitutional Democracy," *Washington University Law Quarterly*, 3: 659–93.

Monture-Okanee, P. (1992), "The Violence We Women Do: A First Nations View," in C. Backhouse, ed., *Challenging Times: The Women's Movement in Canada and the United States*. Montreal: McGill-Queen's Press.

Moore, D. and O'Connell, T. (1994), "Family Conferencing in Wagga Wagga: A Communitarian Model of Justice," in C. Alder and J. Wundersitz, *Family Conferencing and Juvenile Justice*, 45–86. Canberra: Australian Institute of Criminology.

Offe, C. (1987), "Challenging the Boundaries of Institutional Politics: Social Movement Since the Sixties," in C. Maier, ed., *Changing Boundaries of the Political: Essays on the Evolving Balance between the State and Society, Public and Private in Europe*. Cambridge: Cambridge University Press.

Ontario Legislative Assembly (1982), *First Report on Family Violence: Wife Battering.* Toronto: Standing Committee on Social Development, September.

Osborne, J. (1984), "Rape Law Reform: The New Cosmetic for Canadian Women," in C. Schweber and C. Feinman, eds., *Criminal Justice Politics and Women: The Aftermath of Legally Mandated Change.* New York: Haworth Press.

Oyserman, D. and Markus, H. (1990), "Possible Selves and Delinquency," *Journal of Personality and Social Psychology,* 59/1: 112–25.

Oyserman, D. and Saltz, E. (1993), "Competence, Delinquency and Attempts to Attain Possible Selves," *Journal of Personality and Social Psychology,* 65/2: 360–74.

Paulus, I. (1974), *The Search for Pure Food: A Sociology of Legislation in Britain.* London: Martin Robertson.

Pearce, F. (1989), *The Radical Durkheim.* London: Unwin Hyman.

Pearce, F. (1993), "Corporate Rationality as Crime," *Studies in Political Economy,* 40: 135–62.

Pearce, F. and Snider, L., eds. (1995a), *Corporate Crime: Contemporary Debates.* Toronto: University of Toronto Press.

Pearce, F. and Snider, L., eds. (1995b), "Regulation Capitalism," in *Corporate Crime: Contemporary Debates,* 19–47. University of Toronto Press.

Pepinsky, H. and Quinney, R., eds. (1991), *Criminology as Peacemaking.* Bloomington: Indiana University Press.

Picard, A. (1995), "Officers shouldn't be fired, union says." *Globe and Mail,* Saturday, 15 July, A7.

Pitch, T. (1995), *Limited Responsibilities: Social Movements and Criminal Justice.* London: Routledge.

Polk, K. (1985a), "Rape Reform and Criminal Justice Processing," *Crime and Delinquency,* 31/2: 191–205.

Polk, K. (1985b), "A Comparative Analysis of Attrition of Rape Cases," *British Journal of Criminology,* 25/3: 280–94.

Polk, K. (1994), "Family Conferencing: Theoretical and Evaluative Concerns," in C. Alder and J. Wundersitz, eds., *Family Conferencing and Juvenile Justice,* 123–40. Canberra: Australian Institute of Criminology.

Pratt, A. (1995), "New Immigrant and Refugee Battered Women: The Intersection of Immigration and Criminal Justice Policy," in M. Valverde, L. MacLeod and K. Johnson, eds., *Wife Assault and the Canadian Criminal Justice System,* 84–104. Toronto: Centre of Criminology.

Ptacek, J. (1988a), "How Men Who Batter Rationalize Their Behaviour," in A. Horton and J. Williamson, eds., *Abuse and Religion.* Lexington, MA: Lexington Books.

Ptacek, J. (1988b), "Why Do Men Batter Their Wives?," in K. Yllö and M. Bograd, eds., *Feminist Perspectives on Wife Abuse.* Newbury Park, CA: Sage.

Rafter, N. (1983), "Chastizing the Unchaste: Social Control Functions of a Women's Reformatory, 1894–1931," in S. Cohen and A. Scull, eds., *Social Control and the State*. Oxford: Martin Robertson.

Rafter, N. (1985), *Partial Justice*. Boston: Northeastern University Press.

Ratner, R. and McMullen, J., eds. (1987), *State Control: Criminal Justice Politics in Canada*. Vancouver: University of British Columbia Press.

Reiner, R. (1992), "Police Research in the UK: A Critical Review," in M. Tonry and N. Morris, eds., *Modern Policing*. Chicago: University of Chicago Press.

Reiner, R. (1994), *Public Knowledge of Crime and Justice: An Inventory of Canadian Findings*. Canada: Department of Justice.

Roberts, J. (1991), *Sexual Assault Legislation in Canada: An Evaluation Report*, vols. 1–9. Canada: Department of Justice, Minister of Supply and Services.

Rodgers, K. (1994), "Wife Assault: The Findings of a National Survey," *Juristat*, 14/9, Canadian Centre for Justice Statistics, March.

Rosenberg, G. (1991), *The Hollow Hope: Can Courts Bring About Social Change?* Chicago: University of Chicago Press.

Rossi, P., Bose, C. and Berk, R. (1974), "The Seriousness of Crimes: Normative Structure and Individual Differences," *American Sociological Review*, 39: 224–37.

Rothman, D. (1971), *The Discovery of the Asylum: Social Order and Disorder in the New Republic*. Boston: Little, Brown.

Rothman, D. (1980), *Conscience and Convenience: The Asylum and Its Alternatives in Progressive America*. Boston: Little Brown.

Sacco, V. and Johnson, H. (1990), "Patterns of Criminal Victimization in Canada," in *General Social Survey Analysis Series*, No. 2. Ottawa: Statistics Canada.

Schrecker, T. (1990), "The Political Enigma of Criminal Justice." Paper presented at 1990 Annual Meeting, Canadian Political Science Association, Victoria, BC, May.

Schrecker, T. (1992), "Facing the Risks of Decline: Can Canada Prosper in the Global Economy?," *Canadian Issues*, 14: 1–29.

Scimecca, J. (1991), "Conflict Resolution and a Critique of Alternative Dispute Resolution," in H. Pepinsky and R. Quinney, eds., *Criminology as Peacemaking*, 263–279. Bloomington: Indiana University Press.

Scutt, J. (1982), "Domestic Violence: The Police Response," in C. O'Donnell and J. Craney, eds., *Family Violence in Australia*, 110–20. Melbourne: Longman Cheshire.

Scutt, J. (1983), *Even in the Best of Homes*. Melbourne: Penguin.

Sherman, L. (1992), *Policing Domestic Violence: Experiments and Dilemmas*. New York: Free Press.

Silberman, C. (1980), *Criminal Violence, Criminal Justice*. New York: Vintage.

Skogan, W. (1990), *Disorder and Decline: Crime and the Spiral of Decay in American Neighbourhoods*. New York: Free Press.

Smart, C. (1989), *Feminism and the Power of Law*. London: Routledge.

Smart, C. (1992), "The Woman of Legal Discourse," *Social and Legal Studies,* 1: 29–44.

Smith, D. E. (1974), "Women's Perspective as a Radical Critique of Sociology," *Sociological Inquiry,* 44/1: 7–13.

Snider, L. (1985), "Legal Reform and Social Control: The Dangers of Abolishing Rape," *International Journal of the Sociology of Law,* 13: 337–56.

Snider, L. (1986), "Legal Reform and the Welfare State," *Crime and Social Justice,* 24: 210–42.

Snider, L. (1990), "The Potential of the Criminal Justice System to Promote Feminist Concerns," *Studies in Law, Politics and Society,* 10: 143–65.

Snider, L. (1993), *Bad Business: Corporate Crime in Canada.* Toronto: Nelson.

Snider, L. (1994a), "Criminalization: Panacea for Men Who Batter but Anathema for Corporate Criminals," in D. Currie and B. Maclean, eds., *Social Inequality, Social Justice,* 101–24. Vancouver: Collective Press.

Snider, L. (1994b), "Feminism, Punishment and the Potential of Empowerment," *Canadian Journal of Sociology of Law,* 9/1: 75–104.

Solomon, S. (1995), *The Confidence Game: How Unelected Central Bankers Are Governing the Changed Global Economy.* New York: Simon and Schuster.

Sorokin, P. (1937), *Socio-Cultural Dynamics.* New York: American Book Company.

Spierenburg, P. (1984), *The Spectacle of Suffering.* Cambridge: Cambridge University Press.

Spitzer, S. (1979), "The Rationalization of Crime Control in Capitalist Society," *Contemporary Crises,* 3/2: 187–206.

Spitzer, S. (1990), "The Seductions of Punishment: Toward a Critical Criminology of Penality." Paper presented to Annual Meetings of American Society of Criminology, Baltimore, November.

Stack, S. (1990), "Homicide in Norway: A Time-Series Analysis." Paper presented at the Annual Meeting of the American Society of Criminology, Baltimore, 7–10 November.

Stanko, E. (1990), *Everyday Violence.* London: Pandora.

Stanko, E. (1994), "Challenging the Problem of Men's Individual Violence," in T. Newburn and E. Stanko, eds., *Just Boys Doing Business?,* 32–45. London: Routledge.

Strauss, M. (1977a), "Societal Morphogenesis and Intrafamily Violence in Cross-cultural Perspective," *Annals of the New York Academy of Sciences,* 285: 717–30.

Strauss, M. (1977b), "A Sociological Perspective on the Prevention and Treatment of Wifebeating," in M. Roy, ed., *Battered Women,* 194–238. New York: Van Nostrand Reinhold.

Strauss, M. and Gelles, R. J. (1990), *Physical Violence in American Families.* New Brunswick, NJ: Transaction Publishers.

Stets, J. E. (1988), *Domestic Violence and Control.* New York: Springer-Verlag.

Stubbs, J. (1995), " 'Communitarian' Conferencing and Violence Against Women: A Cautionary Note," in M. Valverde, L. MacLeod, K. Johnson, eds., *Wife Assault and the Canadian Criminal Justice System*, 260–92. Toronto: Centre of Criminology.

Stubbs, J. and Wallace, D. (1994), "Domestic Violence: Impact of Legal Reform in New South Wales," in J. Stubbs, ed., *Women, Male Violence and the Law*, Monograph Series No. 6. Sydney: Institute of Criminology.

Thomas, P. (1994), "U.S. Prison Population, Continuing Rapid Growth Since '80s, Surpasses 1 Million," *Washington Post*, 28 October, A3.

Thompson, E. P. (1963), *The Making of the English Working Class*. London: Gollancz.

Thompson, E. P. (1975), *Whigs and Hunters: The Origin of the Black Act*. New York: Pantheon.

Tifft, L. and Markham, L. (1991), "Battering Women and Battering Central Americans," in H. Pepinsky and R. Quinney, eds., *Criminology as Peacemaking*, 114–53. Bloomington: Indiana University Press.

Tombs, S. (1990), "Industrial Injuries in the British Manufacturing Industry," *Sociological Review*, 38/2: 324–43.

Tombs, S. (1995), "Corporate Crime and New Organizational Forms," in F. Pearce and L. Snider, eds., *Corporate Crime: Contemporary Debates*, 132–46. Toronto: University of Toronto Press.

Tripp, R. (1996), "Dollars and Pain; The Economics of the Justice System," *Kingston Whig-Standard*, Monday, 25 November, A1.

Ursel, J. (1986), "The State and the Maintenance of Patriarchy: A Case Study of Family, Labour and Welfare Legislation in Canada," in J. Dickinson and B. Russell, eds., *Family, Economy and State*, 150–91. Toronto: Garamond.

Ursel, J. (1992), *Private Lives, Public Policy: 100 Years of State Intervention in the Family*. Toronto: Women's Press.

Walinsky, A. (1995), "The Crisis of Public Order," *Atlantic Monthly*, July: 39–54.

Walker, S. (1993), *Taming the System. The Control of Discretion in Criminal Justice, 1950–1990*. Oxford: Oxford University Press.

Wearing, R. (1990), "A Longitudinal Analysis of the 1987 Crimes (Family Violence) Act in Victoria." Unpublished Report, Criminology Research Council, Canberra.

Whynhausen, E. (1995), "Fuelling a Fear of Crime," *The Weekend Australian*, 18–19 March, 25.

Williams, J. and Taylor, R. (1994), "Boys Keep Swinging: Masculinity and Football Culture in England," in T. Newburn and E. Stanko, eds., *Just Boys Doing Business?* 214–34. London: Routledge.

Williams, P. (1987), "Alchemical Notes: Reconstructing Ideals from Deconstructed Rights," *Harvard Civil Rights: Civil Liberties Law Review*, 22: 401–27.

Wilson, J. Q. and Kelling, G. (1982), "Broken Windows," *Atlantic Monthly*, March, 29–38.

Winter, S. (1992), "Don't Trust Anyone Not Over the Sixties," *Law and Society Review,* 26/4: 789–818.

Wood, E. (1990), "The Uses and Abuses of 'Civil Society,' " *Socialist Register,* 62–81.

Yeager, P. (1991), *The Limits of Law: The Public Regulation of Private Pollution.* Cambridge, MA: Cambridge University Press.

Zipper, J. and Sevenhuijsen, S. (1987), "Surrogacy: Feminist Notion of Motherhood Reconsidered," in M. Stanworth, ed., *Reproductive Technologies.* Cambridge: Polity Press.

PART 3

NEW ISSUES:
HOW COULD PENALIZATION
OF "SUITE CRIMINALITY"
BE ABOLISHED?

9

Caging the Poor:
The Case Against the Prison System

John McMurtry

🏛 INTRODUCTION

We need to understand from the outset that prisons are not there for the reasons they are usually said to be there. In truth, they do not morally reform lawbreakers. They do not protect society from violent criminals. They are not retributive institutions. All of these rationalizations of the prison system are myths. This paper will refute each in turn, and then explain the underlying function of the prison system, which has not yet been recognised.

For over two centuries, theoretical justifications of prisons have expended their time in arguing *which* of these competing myths is valid. They have not considered that none of them are valid. Scientific criminology studies have assumed the prison institution as a given, and then attended to the institutional details of the various steps and types of its incarceration regime.[1]

We have seen the same structure of narrow thought in oppressor institutions for an epoch—in the enslavement of foreign peoples as "civilization," in public executions of the unemployed as "the law of the realm," and in the savage beating of children as "parental correction." We see now the same conventionalised cruelty in caging people to "make them more fit for society."

🏛 PRISONS AS A "CORRECTIVE" SYSTEM

Let us consider first of all the claims that prisons are *corrective* of behaviour that is harmful to others. Although this ideal is the official category of description for the prison system—"the corrections system," "reformatories," "correctional facility," "penitentiary," and so on—the moral reform function, which is affirmed of the prison system, does not stand up to elementary scrutiny, as either an organisational goal or, as a plausible pattern of outcomes. This is not surprising. The Tower of London was not intended to rehabilitate, nor was the Bastille of France, nor are the mushrooming prisons of North America today. There is no body of evidence ever compiled that shows any lock-up prison system to be rehabilitative in its regulating aim, or effective result. All the evidence we have suggests the opposite. Prisons dehumanise. Lawbreaking behaviours persist after imprisonment, intensify and spread as an effect of the pathology of the prison's totalitarian regime.

This outcome is perhaps predictable. Depriving individuals of all responsibility does not and cannot teach individual responsibility. Caging persons while intermittently threatening them with further violence and deprivation cannot teach them respect for others' rights. Yet the prison regime abolishes self-directed action as well as respect for other humans. To imagine that such a system can evolve responsibility or civility is obviously delusional.

From the standpoint of scientific reason, what more efficient method could there be for constructing a sociopathic character? From the standpoint of normative structure, how can the removal of all civil rights and responsibilities with force and contempt as the ruling currency of interaction ever develop anything but a similar culture in those regulated in this manner? Such a system is bound to create monsters or human wrecks, and it does.

What, we might ask, would we think of a criminal gang who abducted, caged and terrorised people for years because they broke a gang rule, and then declared to us that this was all for the victims' "own good." We would think they were criminally insane. Yet is what the prison system does to mostly non-violent offenders so different? What, we must eventually come to ask, most needs reform—prison populations, or the prison system itself?

🏛 PRISONS AS "PROTECTION" FOR SOCIETY

The dominant justification of prisons today, as we know, is no longer rehabilitation of the prisoner. The dominant rationale is that putting criminal offenders into prison "*protects society by putting them behind bars.*" Given the pattern of corporate media presentation of underclass convicted offenders as violent madmen, and the systematic defunding of life-serving social programs, we might decode the new prevalence of this rationalization as an expression of *a deeper-lying pattern to replace the welfare state with more police and prisons.* To confirm this pattern, just track where more and more public revenues are going—to police and prisons, even while violent crime falls; then track where much greater public revenues are being taken—from social programs serving the needs of the less privileged.

The *claim* that prisons protect society is really a cover story for a deeper design. The state is being restructured from its progressive post-war function of serving the disadvantaged with life-enabling benefits at a cost of higher corporate taxes to locking the offensive poor in prison in ever greater numbers for corporate profit.[2]

Thus, the "prisons are to protect society" justification is what we might expect from corporate-funded politicians and mass media vehicles in a time when less and less social connection remains between the increasing underclass with less money than they need, and the simultaneously increasing financial and business class who have ever more money than they need. This is *the ultimate dividing line between those who end up inside prison and those who almost certainly never will,* and its increasing obviousness requires a marketable justification to sustain it.

If increasing profits can be made from a privatised prison industry, *and* media violence entertainments in which the targets and victims of the exponentially expanding prison system can be demonized and blamed at the same time—that is what might be called a "perfect market." Its implementation will keep "growing business" the more the poor are impoverished and perceived as threatening. This is not to mention the simultaneously increasing domestic and foreign markets for armed forces, private weapons and security commodities. That is where we are today.

We must bear in mind that the underlying function of prison systems since their inception *has been a way of walling off the rebellious poor as a nuisance to those with property.* Prisons remain in general what they always have been—a legal licensing of abduction and institutionalised caging of those perceived by the privileged classes to be a threat to the invulnerability of their social privileges. The "keep them behind bars" slogan marketed to unthinking members of the working and lower middle classes is a manifest expression of the latent function of keeping the insurgent poor in their place.

If one doubts this deep-structural function, try to find a legal jurisdiction anywhere in the Americas in which ninety percent or more of all prison inmates do *not* come from the poorer and more deprived groups and families. The figures for the prior income level of those found guilty of crimes, are not officially available. One can conjecture that this is because transparent public records of the consistently low and insecure income of those who are imprisoned would expose the nature of the prison system: that the blind scales of justice which put them are, in fact, weighted so as to select the poor. The parallel court, prison and criminology systems are, *specifically structured not to see that the basic determinant of imprisonment is the poverty of those imprisoned.* And so figures are even now not officially kept which lay bare this deep-structural general fact. Yet other figures do allow us to infer its underlying pattern. Thirty-six percent of those caged in Canada, for example, have less than a grade nine education. At the same time fifty-two percent of all prisoners in Canada had no job prior to the offence for which they were imprisoned.[3]

On the other hand, try to find anywhere where *the privileged and rich of society*— those with at least two times the national average of income—have *any* members in that society's prisons. We need to keep in mind here that those who do the most premeditated grievous harm to society are almost always from this group, and are almost never imprisoned for their actions which are primarily responsible for systematic and extreme violence to persons and environments. This freedom from prison remains even if these richer offenders are convicted despoilers of entire ecological systems or the killers of thousands of innocents by illegal working conditions and criminal wars.[4] If prisons were really there to prevent violent criminals from continuing their violence against innocent persons, then this class of persons who are the most dangerous to society and who are uniquely sensitive to this penalty as a deterrent, would be in prison, but they are not. So the protect-society rationalisation of the prison system fails most of all in the cases where it could be most plausibly defended.

The hard fact is that prison is *not* the place where the most premeditatedly vicious are "kept behind bars," nor is it remotely designed to serve this claimed function. Nor is "society protected" by those who *are* identified as criminals and thrown into prison. The myth that it is the most violent criminals who are behind bars rivals the claim centuries ago that it was those who Satan most possessed who were burnt at the stake.[5] The great murderers and robbers are almost always found at the top of the system that imprisons the most people—as the last 50 years of Nazi, Stalinist and neo-colonialist rule have shown us more clearly than at any time in history. If the enormity of this general pattern is not registered, society will continue to develop an ever more effectively enslaved population, in fact, quadrupling prison populations over the last 20 years in the U.S., for example, while simultaneously terrorising ever more of the unimprisoned young, poor and non-white members of society.[6]

At the bottom of the prison institution's monstrous construction are two complementary facts refuting its primary justification:

> *Jails and prisons: (1)* do not confine those who most threaten society with violent and life-destructive crimes;[7] *and*
> *(2)* the majority of those they do confine are neither violent nor life destructive.[8]

The worst crime of all according to law and custom is *murder*, and it becomes worse in proportion to the murders. But no war crime or crime against humanity, the ultimate crime of violence, has—outside African Hutus and former Yugoslavians—yet been subject to application of law and imprisonment to those planning and commissioning the crimes since the internationally binding terms of the Nuremberg Charter and Tribunal over 50 years ago.[9] Reflect on that fact, then add to it the immediate and locally present mass and serial killings caused by identifiable wealthy corporations in the US and elsewhere by deadly labour conditions in violation of law and established norm, lethal products scientifically known to poison and kill their users, and calculated actions that deprive people of their livelihoods and security so as to cause disease and death in predictable numbers. None of the continuing perpetrators of these murderous crimes normally goes to prison to protect society. Yet they tend to be at the forefront of barking for stricter punishment by imprisonment for others who are not nearly so dangerous to innocent others, but are poor, younger and of colour.[10]

Now consider the most compelling, and appalling, refutation of the "protect society justification" for putting people into prison. The imprisoned are not just the less moneyed and less dangerous to others. They are dominantly *the criminally harmless*. According to the most recent F.B.I. statistics in the U.S., 88 percent of the 680,000 people arrested for criminal offences in 1999 were charged with possession of marijuana.[11] Here we see the clearest expression of the underlying logic of the *criminal-charge system* selecting for people to put into jails and prisons. This system is not structured to protect people from violent offenders at all. For marijuana possession is a *victimless offence*. There is also little or no scientifically sound evidence that it is harmful even to its users.[12] But what is very clear is that it is the *categorisation of an offence as criminal* that drives public acceptance of the prison system. For it spreads stigma over all offenders, permitting almost any offender to be caged by the discretion of the sentencing system. This system, incredibly, *does not require violence to persons as a qualifying condition for being locked up*. This is perhaps the most alarming irrationality and absolutism of the entire regime. It not only contradicts the public presumption that it is the dangerous and violent who are imprisoned, but it opens the gates to the discretionary power of those in police uniforms and judges' robes who can as they choose put others in cages and destroy their lives *although they have committed no crime against the person or even raised a complaint of harm*. Almost anyone without the income resources to defend him or herself is, thus, made vulnerable to forcible seizure, imprisonment and permanent social stigma for a purely self-regarding choice or an other-harmless transgression (e.g., a private act of consumption or exchange, or a petty infringement of public property). When this brutally indiscriminant system of institutional cruelty has been left behind, can there be any doubt that this arbitrary power to arrest and cage persons by the millions for non-injurious acts will be regarded as a cultural barbarism?

How could such a structure of affairs be accepted in an age which, at the same time, is distinguished by its repudiation of practices of arbitrary cruelty as uncivilised? The reason is that not only is this nature of the prison regime unrecognised, but it invisibly serves the private sectarian powers of ascendant groups and their followers to oppress different and weaker out-group members of society. That is its unseen and regulating function, a caste function if you will against the designated "untouchables" of our era, the poor and the marginalized. Categorisation of a non-conventional behaviour as a criminal offence, that is, *achieves an omnibus function of wide-cast vulnerability, accusation, charge, stigmatisation, unaffordable costs and threat of imprisonment for any transgressor of ruling norms: but essentially the legal destruction of almost any person who is poorer than the most privileged* (i.e., those without a private home or secure employment). The great majority of young poor people between 15 and 30 with even marginally rebellious tendencies are thus made vulnerable to criminal charge and prosecution *although they harm no one*. The crime-and-imprisonment regime becomes in this way the modern counterpart of the *lettre de cachet* of the *ancien regime* of France. The jail or imprisonment to which a criminal charge may lead is a veiled threat of terror for anyone—in particular poor youths—who might get out of line.

The deeper substructure function of the prison system to keep the poor and the marginalized in their place here emerges into light. The terror of being caged and brutalised applies to all who are *not* in prison as an ever present shadow of what can happen to anyone without a lot of money/demand who transgresses the system and, in particular, who might offend or cross police or juridical figures who are permissively armed with great latitudes of discretionary power to lord over, violate and subjugate them, and perhaps destroy their lives. The young without private homes of their own are the most vulnerable target group. From pre-Revolutionary France to the late-capitalist order, the prison system is in its most general function terrorism, selecting most of all from those whose sin is to be poor. But now as then, even the privileged can be put behind the bars of the prison cage if they publicly defy the ruling system *on behalf of* the dispossessed—as demonstrators against state policies to dispossess the poor of their jobs, traditional rights, social benefits or public space learn across the world every day in the "new world order."[13]

What normally *legitimates* the inhuman act of putting people into cages is that a criminal charge has been judicially proven against the victims. Since the word "criminal" connotes a dangerous offender, this legitimation translates into the now dominant *justification* of prisons as "putting proven criminals behind bars where they belong." This rationale becomes credible for an unexamined reason. People unthinkingly *assume* a non sequitur as a self-evident truth. The reasoning is this: If a criminal charge has been laid against a person, and that criminal charge has been upheld by a court of law, the offender *must therefore be a threat to others*.

That is the great and hidden *mind-slippage*, which single-handedly sustains the prison system as justifiable in the group mind.

The assumption represses basic inferences that do not begin to follow. If, for example, a young person without financial resources is charged with possession of a forbidden substance or with trespass to defend environmental or human life, the danger to others of this act is *not even alleged by the charge*. Yet 88 percent of all criminal charges in the U.S. now are, as we have seen, for the private possession of marijuana alone. This is the most overwhelming refutation of the "protect society" justification of prisons one could imagine. *For it is refuted by the nature of the criminal charge itself which does not anywhere allege, imply or require to prove any damage of any kind whatever to anyone.*

This undermining of the integrity of the criminal law is itself an immeasurably harmful practice of violence against the person. It could be corrected easily by withdrawal of the barbaric right to sentence to jail or prison anyone who has done no harm to anyone. Yet the use and threat of jail or prison for those who have not harmed anyone is not the exception in our contemporary criminal justice systems. It is *the general rule.* And this general rule fills jails and prisons everywhere with poorer people who are not dangerous to any citizen or other's wellbeing. *Ninety-seven percent of police-reported U.S. crimes involve no injuries at all to victims, and in 86 percent no violence whatever to another person is involved.*[14]

🏛 PRISONS FOR VIOLENT OFFENDERS

Those who are seriously violent to others, especially to unprivileged others who pose no threat to them, are not defended by this argument. From one standpoint, they deserve the worst from society in proportion to the damage they do to innocent and helpless others. But a broader view would question the social order that produced such vicious behaviour, and then seek to ensure that conditions did not arise which produced such crimes. A *responsible society*, that is, would not identify only one condition of a crime as the sole condition that produced it.[15] It would be more impartial, and not seek only to attack what may only be the individual symptom of an underlying social disorder. For there can be little doubt that behind most heinous crimes of individuals in a society lurk accepted social conditions by which it was caused to grow—for example, permitted parental violence against children which is almost invariably the causal background of violent criminal offenders.

But, in fact, only a few percent of prison inmates are there for violent crimes. According to Goldberg and Evans, only a very few are in prison in the current U.S., which has "the highest per capita incarceration rate in the history of the world," for their violence against innocent and helpless others, and almost 90 percent of the remainder are in prison for no violence to the person at all.[16] Prisons, it seems, are not truly directed against violence, but are *themselves the primary producer of systematic violence against persons.*

There are vicious killers, rapists and extortionists who do belong behind locked doors—not only to protect society, but also to learn what has gone wrong in the social background and mind-set that produced their pathological behaviours. But such exceptions cannot justify the caging and torment of the majority who are not violent offenders. Again we see behind the most compelling justification of prisons and jails the very reverse of the justification. As with slavery, which imprisonment reproduces in contemporary form, a presupposed social program still confines the group-mind within blind reflexes of reaction.[17]

ᾓ PRISONS AS "RETRIBUTION"

What is the way out of a cultural insanity? The prison institution survives only because it is still socially acceptable. It is socially acceptable, in turn, for only one reason. Citizen bodies have, as a whole, not yet consciously recognised its underlying terrorist function selecting against the non-violent poor.

Yet there remains the most venerable justification for imprisoning people of all—that the terror of imprisonment is a *just retribution for their crime*. "An eye for an eye, a tooth for a tooth," in the words of this justification's most ancient formula. People who see through other excuses for putting people in cages are apt to retreat to the retribution justification as a final refuge of mental comfort in the face of a socially accepted institution of cruelty to the weak. This is a brutish inheritance. Torture of children, the burnings of witches, and the right to kill inferiors have all been justified as right and good by intelligent people, and prisons are no exception to this pathology of instituted structures of terror and violence against underclasses.

Retributivists, however, never mention that only the poor are likely to be imprisoned—even if all of the prison population comes from the bottom economic classes. The facts are obscured in striking back at those whose life condition is a remonstration to the more privileged. For the facts *cannot* be seen if the retribution justification is to make any sense. The rich offender deserves under any coherent retributivist argument far more punishment than the poor offender does because his criminal intention is formed with lawful options amply available. But that does not awaken the retributivist from the comforts of punitive dogma. The retribution argument is especially popular among philosophers and theorists who exclude social circumstances as a method.[18]

Yet even the fact-blind retributivist cannot ignore the *internal* incoherence of the retributivist argument. For to *re-tribute* is to *pay back*, and there is no pay-*back* in caging and ritually bullying someone for years in return for their petty theft or possession of a prohibited plant substance. In fact, one can go through almost the entire roster of imprisonable offences and not see a single imprisonment that is deserved as *re-tribution*. The "debt owed to society" and "paid" by "time in prison" is, in fact, not like a debt or payment at all. For the payment of one's life being caged is absolutely incommensurable with any offence it is imposed for. The loss of the mind in such a metaphor of exchange that makes no sense whatever, but is conditioned into social consciousness as self-evident axiom, should jolt us into recognition of the madness at work here. But it is not yet seen in the field of daily affirmation of the prison system in every newspaper and police television show. When one examines its *moral exchange*, however, the retribution argument is seen for what it is. It is insanely unbalanced—assuming as certainly right a wild disproportion between a person's probably non-violent transgression of a law and being caged in return. There is no intelligible similarity or proportion here between offence and the re-*talis* for it. It is not an eye for an eye, but the loss of all rights of personhood for what is in most instances a violent offence against no person. It is not a holding another responsible for their offence by punishment. It is an abolition of their conditions of responsibility.

The retributivist justification of prisons is not only unbalanced. It is also vicious and violent in its own right. It demands as "just" the seizure, torment and forcible imprisonment of millions of people in exchange for nothing remotely similar in violence from them, and in the majority of cases, no violence at all. As with past monstrous systems of cruel and systematic oppression, we see how morally blind the conventionalised mind-set can become.

⛫ PRISONS' FUNCTION IN THE "ANNIHILATION OF HUMANITY"

At the bottom of the mental impasse is a missing link. The primeval function of prisons from their inception has never been recognised. It is the brute right of established ascendant force *to publicly defeat any perceived adversary by a victory of force so total that not a single accessible dimension of autonomous human being remains.*

The hidden ruling principle of the prison regime is not to punish, to discipline into order, to pay back, or to protect society—the competing rationalisations that have distracted critical analysis from Locke to Foucault.[19]

All are false to the actually ruling goal. It is *to break human beings into subjugated animals.*

Every moment of the imprisonment ritual and ceremony, every overt and covert operation of the prison process afterwards, every commanded surrender of prisoner movement and position by the guards serves and is exactly regulated by this overriding but never stated purpose: the *total defeat of the human status of the prisoner.* One cannot begin to make sense of the panoply of oppressions at work in every moment of the subterraneanly evolved prison subjection until one recognises this underlying principle by which all are unified as a single unstated *program*—the breaking of all connections and rights whatever to human being, the reduction of an individual person to an inhuman body.[20]

Consider the exactly ritualised procedures that deconstruct the prisoner. The inner logic of every step is to relate to *every distinct capability of being human so as to annihilate it*—to manacle the human hands and its opposable thumbs, to reduce the upright carriage to animal postures at command, to control the wide-spectrum eyes and the bipedal walk within mechanical ranges, to forcibly disconnect the prisoner from family, friends and every human relationship developed over a lifetime, to prohibit all privacy from being watched, to abolish the right to human voice and language by enforced silence and obedient sounds, to remove all the clothes and signs of individual and juridical identity, to liquidate all free access to humanity's civilised tools of reading, writing and creative inscription, and above all to deprive the huge 150,000,000,000-neuron brain of the evolved human of its every normal stimulus, space, time and medium to connect, to self-direct, and to create.

It is the human's unique powers of thought and sensibility that the prison-cage is most of all structured to put on the rack of continuously shackled time and break. Its presupposed regime is to lay waste human identity itself. For it is only in terms of this covertly regulating principle that the jail and prison regimes can be understood, that all their constitutive steps cohere. Their spaces and order systematically and pervasively deprive the individual of every outlet, choice or relationship by which to live and think *as* human, and their enforced routines close down every aspect and step of free will around the clock and into every region of life. The confinement to the "hole" for any assertion of human resistance to the program, the living amidst one's body waste as an animal, the ever-present terror of attack or animal rape from the jungle all around—all of these are signs pointing to the underlying master program. From start to finish, the regulating design that operates beneath speech or written code is to strip the prisoner of human status. *To crush it* absolutely. The prison system is the reduction of the person to an animal's body at the feet of the omnipresent sovereign.

ɱ PRISONS FROM "HOLDING PLACES OF THE CONDEMNED" TO "CAGES FOR THE POOR"

The prison system thus remains in a way the judicial murder it began as a first step of—the holding place for the condemned before execution. The former ritual of the sovereign's vanquished adversary—to be publicly mutilated, hanged, beheaded, drawn and quartered—is here drawn out as a set time of *the living death of human being.* The reforms of this mad triumphalism of absolute power have been significant over the last 300 years. The hideously sadistic violence as show of majesty has been discontinued because of rising human repulsion. Public executions have been abolished altogether, or reduced to the crime of murder, and taken behind closed doors for ritualised enactment still reeking of the medieval past. But the propertiless poor are more and more mass imprisoned instead. Their bodies are made first inhuman, and then chained and guarded functions to labour as beasts.

We still face the deep obscenity of the privileged savagely avenging themselves on the poor to show their superiority, with the dehumanization of them by cages instead of scaffolds as the means of reduction. The prison thus remains in principle what it started as—the impress of absolute power on the subjugated to dispose of at will as bodies.

The recent movement beneath public debate to private-profit prisons should be seen in the light of the prison's history. Like the rest of the life-blind corporate agenda of which it is part, it is an atavistic throwback to the rule of sadistic absolutism in which the first prisons incubated. It is a turning of the clock back to convict galleys and workhouses for the poor, and the use of their living bodies for slave-labour inputs instead of scaffold detritus, a regression back to the methods of vampire capital centuries ago.

A revealing marker of this New Dark Age is that the emerging corporate workhouses multiply their caged inmates—by three to four times in the U.S. since 1980—even while violent crime rates unprecedentedly drop in an aging population. From a rational point of view, this contradiction between ever more prisons for a decreasingly violent population demography is sheer insanity.

But from the point of view of transnational corporate stockholders, who are beneficiaries of costless slave labour and rising public monies to house it, it is a bull market.

Let us then consider the bigger picture within which the corporate prison is an incubus. *The public purse was in 1980 the biggest unopened revenue source and market since the age of overseas colonies began in the sixteenth century.* Better still, far more than the money-demand equivalent of past Americas gold was in the U.S. orbit of industrialised countries themselves—lying piled high and apparently forever in the limitlessly rich public coffers of governments spending on social services, with the majority world following suit. Next to the inexhaustible supply of wealth here, gold in the Americas was hinterland fortune. The military took most of it in the U.S., and then tripled the amount after the Reagan administration began the counter-revolution in 1980. Bondholders received 25 percent-plus compound interest accumulating on a trebling debt at the same time. Stockholders of the 1990s hollowed the rest out as beneficiaries of world-wide "structural readjustments," which massively privatised public services, slashed reduced taxes for the corporations and the rich, and opened up trillions of dollars of public revenues for education, health, diplomatic, transportation, resource, pension and other public budgets to corporate control and appropriation. All of this was permitted, and then enforced by, trade-and-investment deregulation across the world.[21]

The gargantuan and insatiable feeding frenzy by rootless financial and business classes on the world's public sectors for the last twenty years knows no remote parallel in modern history, and perhaps all of history. From this condition, the tumorous growth of corporate prisons is more or less to be expected. The fact that there is a $50-100,000 public payout for every *individual* in prison is not a fact that could escape any corporation geared to bid on escalating public revenues for "getting tough on crime." Underclass prisoners, worthless in the market with little or no money demand, now multiply their worth by what can be charged to the public purse to lock them in prisons. Corporate media and law-and-order politicians accordingly demand and get "tougher penalties for criminals"—changes in the laws, longer terms, three-strikes legislation, target programs, bigger budgets for non-pharmaceutical drugs, larger multilevel super prisons, more military ordinance—all of which translates into ever more public monies spent on the prison system, and correspondingly more police to catch and put people into them. The military-industrial complex long secured endless demand for expensive weapons by talking up the dangers of "communism" and, now, "rogue states." The prison industrial complex can deploy the same tried-and-true formula of bleeding the public purse and victimising the poor by selling the same line about "criminals."

There is no internal limit to this game. You can put every second poor person into prison for whom there is no job—and you get an ever wider-mouth siphon into present and future public revenues, plus a multiplying army of slave labour. It is the ideal circuit for what I have elsewhere analysed as "the cancer stage of capitalism," feeding on the social body the more its invasions deprive formerly contributing functions of their means of life. The lock-in of this circuit occurs when the game is then sold to the insecure and angry as "getting tough on crime." The success of this story, in turn, opens up more markets for violence entertainment on hunting down and hog-tying the poor who step out of line, and for selling private weapons and security devices to protect against them when they get out from behind bars. The death-spiral of the system deepens as oppression itself becomes more and more a growth industry.

When the prisoner has risen above the worst that others can do to him by an integrity of being that cannot be shaken, the system begins to collapse from within. In the twentieth century, Antonio Gramsci, Dietrich Bonhoeffer, Mahatma Gandhi, Nelson Mandela, George Jackson, Aung San Suu Kyi and Ken Saro-Wiwa are famous prisoners who would and could not be broken because they were fighting a war for freedom from the larger social prison around them. Few of these social prisons stand for long once such stand-ups begin within the inner sanctums of their oppression.

Today the social prison is held in place by the manacles of the mind. They keep the public captured within a program of conditioned appetite and obedience, in "freedom" outside of the dread place where offenders against the system go. But as these manacles of the mind are recognised for what they are, and confinement within the mental prison awakes to the primeval brutality of the iron prison behind it, the connection across walls opens up a common human cause. As the Bastille of two centuries ago, the prison system we know today is the nadir of a larger oppressor structure that has delinked from shared responsibility for the world of life. Sustaining its regime of cruel indifference and life-blindness are history's deepest and most incorrigible criminals—those who seek in no way to serve the better life of all, but only to deprive the most deprived more for their private gain. Only they can be justly imprisoned, but even they are unlikely to benefit from it. The prison is an historical anachronism of the absolutism of power, and must be abolished—step by step.

Abolition will begin with the principle of imprisoning only those who are deliberately and physically injurious to others—the bestial people of all classes who are still with us. This civilizing of a barbaric institution of the past can be achieved in a single stroke by exact judicial and sentencing standard.

Abolition will continue by a mounting social intolerance of the role models and conditions of mindless cruelty and deprivation out of which violent criminals of all kinds develop on both sides of the prison's walls.

🏛 ENDNOTES

1   In general, we can discern in criminology the *structure of not seeing* by which all oppressor institutions are sustained. The statistics and studies of prison systems are regulated by the presupposition of the prison system as a set of scientific facts. Then analytic attention is preoccupied by "security" procedures, classifications, populations and results, while the dominant pattern of millions of persons being caged for no violent offence never arises as an issue.

2   Telling indicators of this pattern are that black women are the fastest growing prison population in the U.S. in a two-million prison population that is 70 percent non-white, and that prisoners have multiplied by eight times since the height of the "war on poverty" began to wind down in 1970. Under the 1995 U.S. Welfare Bill, 11 million poor American families lost income, 2.6 million people and 1.1 million children dropped below the absolute poverty line, and 8 million families lost an average of $1300 (U.S.) each in food stamps. (These figures are drawn from Avery Gordon, "Globalisation and the Prison-Industrial Complex: An Interview with Angela Davis," *Race and Class*, 2/3 (1998-99), 145-46 and "Do-Gooders Rally To Plight Of The Poor," *Washington Post*, May 4, 1997). The *general hypothesis* suggests itself here that there is a direct, inverse correlation between increase of public funds spent on police and prisons and decrease of public funds spent on social programs directed at the poor. See my *The Cancer Stage of Capitalism* (London: Pluto Press, 1999) for the inner logic of the systemic societal pathology of which this pattern is an expression.

3   Figures are drawn from Canadian Centre for Justice Statistics, *The Jurisdat Reader: A Statistical Overview of the Canadian Justice System*. Toronto: Thompson Publishing, 1998. See also Jeffery H. Reiman, *The Rich Get Richer and the Poor Get Prison*. Boston: Prentice-Hall, 1998.

4   An estimated 500,000 deaths a year in the U.S., prior to the full effects of deregulation by the Reagan regime, were "attributed to occupationally related diseases, the majority of which are caused by knowing and wilful violation of

health and occupational safety laws by corporations." (R. Kramer, "Corporate Criminality" in E. Hochstedler (ed.), *Corporations As Criminals* (Beverley Hills: Sage Publications, 1984, p. 19). Fifty-six thousand U.S. citizens die annually from such diseases while on the job ("10 Worst Corporations of 1996," *Multinational Monitor*, Dec. 23, 1996). As for war crimes and crimes against humanity by U.S. and/or allied forces in the third world since 1945, there were millions of such deaths commissioned in Indonesia, Vietnam and Cambodia alone between 1965 and 1973, while war crimes or crimes against humanity in Chile, Guatemala and Iraq (the list is long), run in the hundreds of thousands. With a very few exceptions, there has been no imprisonment of those legally responsible for these crimes of murder and extermination.

5   The most vicious human cages today are short-term jails within which three to seven million people a year are confined every year in the U.S. (in addition to those already in federal and state prisons). Although "the cruellest form of imprisonment," sociologist John Irwin tells us, "jails operate as "catchall asylums for poor people." "With few exceptions, the prisoners are poor, undereducated, unemployed, and belong to minority groups." They are more subject to "discretionary abuse and intentional meanness," have "less space and fewer resources and amenities," and are "sought out" by the police who "never patrol used car lots—and never raid corporate board rooms" but who "are always on the lookout" for the poor committing petty offences (John Irwin, "The Jail," in T.J. Flanagan, J.W. Maruart, K.G. Adams (ed.), *Incarcerating Criminals: Prisons and Jails in Social and Organizational Context*. New York: Oxford University Press, 1998, pp. 227-35).

6   Angela Davis points out that, "More than 70 percent of the imprisoned population [in the U.S.] are people of colour," and argues (my emphasis) that *"an explicit linkage between slavery and punishment was written into the U.S. constitution precisely at the moment of the abolition of slavery*. In fact, there was no reference to imprisonment in the constitution until the passage of the Thirteenth Amendment declared chattel slavery unconstitutional. The Thirteenth Amendment read: 'Neither slavery nor involuntary servitude, except as a punishment for crime—shall exist within the United States or any place subject to their jurisdiction" ("Globalism and the Prison Industrial Complex," *Ibid*, pp. 146-151).

7   As Chair of Jurists of the Crimes Against Humanity and War Crimes Tribunal at the 1989 Toronto World Summit of international heads of state, I heard days of testimony by eyewitnesses of crimes against humanity in which these heads of state were indicted by extensive documented evidence of (I quote from "international law recognised by the community of nations") "murder, extermination, enslavement, deportation, persecution or other inhumane act or omission that is committed by against any civilian population or any identifiable group of persons" (*Canadian Criminal Code*, Chapter 37.1.96) as well as or including (I quote from the Nuremberg

Charter and Geneva Convention derived articles, now enforceable under Article 2 and 3 of the International Criminal Tribunal For The Former Yugoslavia at the Hague) "the wilful killing of civilians and the wilful infliction of great suffering and serious injury, wanton destruction of civilian property not justified by military necessity," "the wanton destruction of cities, towns and villages and devastation not justified by military necessity," and "the employment of poisonous weapons and weapons calculated to cause unnecessary suffering." The evidence of these very grave and systematic crimes of violence against the person on a serial and mass basis was then and since well documented, but is almost nowhere reported in any mass media, including those who provide readers with a daily diet of crime and violence altogether trivial in comparison. Such is the pattern of selection of dominant opinion that expresses its concern to "protect society against violent criminals."

8   Most people who are imprisoned are not only jailed for victimless or non-violent offences (i.e., for personal possession of banned substances or for petty property offences), but are besides selected for imprisonment because they are non-white and/or younger than average. Canadian statistics show that only 29 percent of "high risk" offenders are incarcerated for "a crime against the person," while for 51 percent of all prisoners there is no conviction for such violence (*Jurisdat*, pp. 59-60). (Note here that prisoners whom the system deems "*high risk*" and, thus, to which it assigns *more stringent "security" measures*, are far *less likely to be convicted for "violence against the person*.") As for the less powerful groups whose members are more likely to be in prison, Canadian prisons as a whole house more than eight times as many indigenous persons as non-indigenous persons, and select for those aged 20-24 (almost a quarter of all prisoners: *Jurisdat*, p. 57). Seventy percent of Saskatchewan's prison population are First Nations' people, while Canada's Young Offenders' Act—continuously charged with being "too soft on crime" although Canada's violent crime is one-quarter of the U.S.'s—allows criminal charges for such offences as eating crab-apples off a tree (Felicia Daunt, "At War With Our Kids," *Briarpatch*, November 1998, pp. 3-4).

9   The binding nature of this criminal law is often overlooked. But see the terms of Chapter 37.1.96 of the *Canadian Criminal Code*, for example, cited in Note 7.

10   See Note 4.

11   C.N.N. News, October 11, 1999. The 88 percent figure of total arrests reported by C.N.N. is not, as it may seem, inconsistent with the much lower percentage of marijuana offenders in prison. Although U.S. drug arrests have stunningly multiplied by more than nine-fold since 1968 (from 162,000 to 1,476,100 by 1995: Jeffrey H. Reiman, *The Rich Get Richer And The Poor Get Prison: Ideology, Class and Criminal Justice*. Boston: Allyn and Bacon, 1998, p. 37), by no means all arrests on marijuana charges end with the arrested person in a federal or state prison. This is a crucial point to bear in mind in understanding that prison is only the end-point of an

escalating system of terror in which abduction and temporary imprisonment by arrest has many points between it and the full caging of the convicted person. The arrest for the alleged offence must extend into formal charge. The formal charge must continue to be pressed past possible ties with people in the system, legal representation or other successful external assistance. There must then be movement to legal trial on the charge without other disposition of the case in the interim, trial without plea-bargain release, finding of guilt rather than innocence on the charge, and, finally, imprisonment rather than conditional discharge, probation or other penalty in place of full caging. Each of these steps of the caging system selects for the young and poor, and is open to discretion of officers in charge at various levels—a point that is not lost on either side in the long and harrowing process of stigmatisation and subjugation from initial arrest to conviction behind bars. It is this larger system of social terror, which can target a large part of the population at any time, which needs to be recognised in the full extent of its oppression, although prison proper be only the final, total subjugation for those arrested on "a marijuana offence."

12   The justification for claiming harm in these cases is examined in John McMurtry, "The Ethics of Compulsory Drug Testing," *Westminster Review* 1:1 (1987), 3-4. While the mainly poor are being imprisoned for drug possession—400,000 in U.S. prisons in 1999—the pharmaceutical corporations quadrupled their inflation-adjusted revenues between 1970 and 1998, "24 percent of these affecting the central nervous system." "The drug wars and the drug boom are interrelated," contends *Harper's* Joshua Wolfe Shenk. Leading "the drug-free America" crusade are "the former C.E.O. of Johnson and Johnson [and]—the philanthropic arms of Merck, Bristol-Myers Squibb and Hoffman La Roche." Yet "legal medications are the principal cause of between 45,000 and 200,000 American deaths each year—[and] no federal agency collects information on deaths related to illegal drugs" (*Harper's Magazine*, May 1999, pp. 38-50).

13   An unpublicized feature of demonstrations of this sort which I have observed over 30 years of eyewitness and on-site camera footage is the structuring of police systems *to* terrorise lawful participants in assembly against long documented, institutionalised oppressions—by massive display of weapons of violence, masked black-uniformed squads, lines of armoured vehicles and prison vans, senseless discharges of toxic sprays and club-swingings against non-violent citizens, and maximally painful, limb-torquing manacling of passive resisters before caging. Here the terrorist function of the imprisonment system is clear independent of any dangerous behaviour by its victims. Its most recent publicly observable display, but not observed by media commentators, was in Seattle, December 1-2, at the World Trade Organisation meetings where over 700 persons were arrested and imprisoned.

14 These figures are taken from the superb documentation of Eve Goldberg and Linda
    Evans of the Prison Activist Resource Center, Berkeley California, "The Prison
    Industrial Complex and the Global Economy," *Nexus* (June-July) 1999, 17.

15 When I wrote my M.A. thesis in philosophy on the concept of causation many
    years ago, I learned a remarkable conceptual fact. Our notion of "cause" derives
    from the etymological root of "accusare," and what is accused, the cause, is
    determined by the principle of *what deviates from the norm*. See, for example, Hart
    and Honore's classic study, *The Concept of Causation* (Oxford: Clarendon Press,
    1957).

16 "The Prison Industrial Complex," p. 17.

17 The key to understanding the prisoner-state relationship is that the prisoner is the
    property of the state (or its delegated stand-in as with new corporate prisons).
    Property means the right to exclude all others from the object of property, including
    the prisoner. There seems to be a deep structure of consciousness in which thus
    "owned," anything can be done to the object owned, even humans, who have as
    property no civil or human rights as persons. This is the legal moment of the
    reduction of the prisoner to non-human, which is analysed ahead. It is also the lock
    on the unthinking mind which cannot get beyond the regulating mind-sequence
    of criminal = violent = rightfully owned body of the state = no treatment of this
    object can be wrong.

18 It is interesting to note in this connection that not only judges, but the law itself is
    structured to select poor people for prison by, for example, requiring *one one-
    hundredth* as much cocaine possessed by crack possessors to receive a mandatory
    prison sentence as for pure cocaine powder, the choice of the rich (cited in Goldberg
    and Evans, p. 19). Jeffrey H. Reiman provides ample documentation of the wildly
    discriminatory treatment between white-collar criminals and the poor in their
    judicial sentences (*The Rich Get Richer And The Poor Get Prison, passim*).

19 Foucault writes in a summation of his *Discipline and Punish: The Birth of the Prison*:
    "The perpetual penalty that traverses all points and supervises every instant in the
    disciplinary institutions compares, differentiates, hierarchizes, homogenizes,
    excludes. In short, it *normalizes*" (Foucault's emphasis, Paul Rabinow (ed.), *The
    Foucault Reader*. New York: Pantheon Books, 1984, p. 195). Foucault does not
    penetrate the prison institution deeply enough. Its regime precisely does *not*
    normalise. It *de*normalises at the profoundest level possible, reducing the human
    person to the *non*-human. In his post-modern impulsion to attribute all brutality
    to the ordering forces of totalizing scientific modernity, Foucault misses the primeval
    and subterranean nature of the prison system.

20 Angela Davis comes closest to penetrating this inner logic of the prison cage by
    aligning imprisonment to slavery. But the key difference is that no slave was kept
    who was not an *instrument* of the private owner's will, normally for a productive

purpose. Prison reduces to animal status prior to and independent of the prisoner serving any *productively instrumental* function to the prison's masters. Indeed, prison typically *prevents* productive function *and* vastly increases input costs by its regime of absolute repression of human properties. The corporate prison seeks to extract productive labour and money profits, but its greatest cost is in the reduction of prisoners to animal status, a cost far beyond productive enslavement that even corporate cost-cutters do not question.

21   The historical trends here within which the corporate prison has incubated are explained in detail in my *Unequal Freedoms: The Global Market as an Ethical System* (Toronto and Westport Ct.: Garamond and Kumarian Press, 1998, pp. 215-97). The economic paradigm shift within which these trends unfolded is explained in *The Cancer Stage of Capitalism*, Ibid, pp. 132-190.

10

Regulating
Toxic Capitalism

Frank Pearce and Steve Tombs

�🏛 INTRODUCTION

This paper addresses the nature and possibilities of regulating "toxic capitalism," by which we mean the various aspects of threats to human and environmental well-being, and particularly to occupational health and safety, posed by industries (Pearce and Tombs, 1998). We note a number of trends towards the criminalization of safety crimes in both the UK and the US, and document the crucial role in these and other trends played by a range of popular pro-regulatory forces engaged in activities of resistance, which take law as one, but not their only focus. We argue further that a more punitive regulatory approach must be combined with other regulatory techniques, many of which are currently in existence in various nation-states and regions, and a changed prosecutorial policy. In particular, we argue for an overall regulatory strategy which is based upon the principles of deterrence and rehabilitation, developing an understanding of regulation that is both facilitative and positive rather than merely limiting and negative, as it has historically been viewed.

ᠬ REGULATING CAPITAL

In this section, we discuss the regulation of crimes against human and environmental health and safety; some of the arguments proposed here are of more general relevance for the effective regulation and sanctioning of corporate crimes in general. However, to emphasise a point we suggest throughout: while it makes sense to delineate a form of illegality which we have referred to as corporate crime, such crime cannot always be treated usefully as if it were homogeneous in its nature and effects. This is certainly the case when considering forms of regulation (Snider, 1991). Thus, some varieties of corporate crime have undoubtedly been hoisted onto social, political and legal agendas, notably "economic" crimes such as "insider trading" or pensions fraud. We should not be surprised that it is these kinds of corporate illegalities that have been subject to criminalization.

Economic illegalities, certainly those within and between corporations, may be inimical to the "effective" functioning of, and also maintenance of legitimacy for, contemporary capitalism (Pearce, 1976). It is hardly a coincidence that the past decade has seen a mushrooming of both academic and governmental concern with "economic" crimes in North America and Western Europe, in particular the UK. While these responses have been represented as being designed to protect the investments of *all* sections of the population—such as house or share owners, pension or insurance contributors—there is no doubt that they also helped to provide a more "predictable and controlled business environment" for financial corporations (Szasz, 1984: 114). Of further interest for us, however, is that although none of these reforms have been unequivocally successful (and some are too recent to allow us to make a judgement) the fact that they have had some impact does support the argument that more effective regulation of corporate activity, and the prevention, detection and sanctioning of corporate crime is feasible. It is no surprise that research from North America should claim that the regulation of economic crimes is likely to be more successful than the enforcement of so-called "social" regulation (Snider, 1991).

Indeed, the very distinction between economic and social regulation is an interesting ideological mechanism whereby certain forms of regulation are accorded greater legitimacy than others. Moreover, it is of course the case that even within social regulation, there are differences between the nature and efficacy of regulatory strategies. As we have noted (Pearce and Tombs, 1998: chapter 5), environmental degradation and environmental crimes have received far greater priority in both North America and the UK in the past decade or so, although the record of regulatory enforcement hardly points towards any unequivocally positive judgement (Barnett, 1995; Edwards et al. 1996; National Institute of Justice, 1993). The record of protecting workers' health and safety is an even poorer one (Noble, 1995; Pearce, 1995; Tombs, 1995a, 1995b; Tucker, 1995). Despite some real improvements, not least those reforms aimed at more effective regulation of chemicals industries. However, what is frequently referred to as social regulation—such as the regulation of occupational safety and environmental protection—is likely to be *relatively* ineffective since it may impinge upon "the most minute details of production," rendering such regulation fundamentally "antagonistic to the logic of firms within a capitalist economy" (Szasz, 1984: 114; and see Snider, 1991). Nevertheless, it is also undoubtedly the case that effective safety regulation *can* be functional for capital, albeit under certain conditions, for certain companies, over limited periods of time (Tombs, 1989). This latter point can be illustrated through reference to the complexities of regulating occupational safety.

This is one reason why environmental and safety crimes or accidents can be understood simply in terms of a safety-profits dichotomy. Four points are worth making explicit here, since these bear upon these complex relationships. *First*, if more effective regulation of occupational safety is in the interests of some corporations, it remains the case many companies either fail to understand the costs of accidents, or do not act upon such understandings (HSE, 1993). *Second*, and relatedly, the benefits of more effective safety regulation may not be recognised by many corporations precisely because of their inability to see safety as anything other than an avoidable cost (such short-termism being particularly characteristic of British companies). *Third*, and as documented by Marx in Volume I of Capital, individual employers are likely to resist the development of safety regulation on the grounds that it creates unequal conditions of competition; and it is still claimed by many larger, more visible corporations that while they are likely to have to meet such regulations, other, often smaller enterprises, are less likely to comply given their relative invisibility to regulators (National Institute of Justice 1993: 7-10). *Fourth*, both for individual corporations as well as for capital as a whole, more effective forms of "social" regulation raise a real contradiction between the twin exigencies of capitalist production, namely, the need to accumulate capital and the need to manage (and thereby maintain control over) labour processes.

Such complexities of safety regulation for management, and for capital in general, indicate the need to avoid any naive functionalism, and to recognise the potential significance of gains that workers and their allies might win on the basis of "agency, struggle and resistance" (Snider, 1991). There are clearly objective and subjective differences in "interests" between corporations of different sizes, operating in different countries or markets, in different sectors, and so on. That is, we cannot consider capital or the corporate sector as simply homogeneous; the state and regulatory agencies often act as hegemonic apparatuses (Pearce and Tombs, 1998). Finally, they sensitise us to the need to view the state's actions or inactions in this sphere in a way that transcends a narrow instrumentalism. That is, all things being equal—and as the above points indicate, all things are often not equal—the preference of capital is for less rather than more regulation.

𝕞 REGULATING CAPITAL: THE POLITICS OF CRIMINALISATION CAPITAL/ THE POLITICS OF CRIMINALISATION

Recent experience in the UK lends weight to Snider's claims, while her own analysis is developed on the basis of recent trends in the US and Canada. Since Snider has provided an excellent analysis of these trends in the context of North America, (and since we have treated these elsewhere: Pearce and Tombs, 1998: chapter 8), we shall confine ourselves here largely to a consideration of such trends within the UK.

The UK has witnessed a series of regressive measures in relation to occupational safety regulation, yet certain factors allow some optimism. Because of "public crises" and "union agitation," there exist opportunities for securing improved protection from harmful corporate activities. This section examines recent and continuing developments in the regulation of occupational safety in the UK, and argues that law is an important site of struggle for safer workplaces.

In the UK, for example, we have noted how the late 1980s' arguments for the prosecution of "corporate manslaughter" began to be strongly articulated in the UK. Probably more important as a catalyst here than a half decade of rising injury rates were a series of highly publicised disasters and subsequent inquiries and reports that occurred so frequently in UK in the latter half of the 1980s (see

190

Harrison, 1992; Slapper, 1993; Wells, 1993). Slapper has recently provided a useful catalogue of these:

> *Zeebrugge, where 193 died in March 1987: the Kings Cross fire, 31 deaths in November 1987; the Piper Alpha oil rig fire, 167 deaths in July 1988; the Clapham train crash, 35 deaths in December 1988; the Purley train crash, 5 deaths in March 1989; and the sinking of the Marchioness, 51 deaths in August 1989. (Slapper, 1993: 424; see also Harrison, 1992; Wells, 1993)*

In each case, evidence and official enquiries inculpated the relevant companies as significant contributors to the cause of death (Slapper, 1993: 424). Importantly, most of the above events led to the loss of lives of those other than workers. They helped to "impress" upon the public consciousness that occupational accidents did not have their effects confined within "the factory fence"; public and worker safety became linked, and were politicised. Their cumulative effect was to raise the profile of the *public* harm that economic activities caused, often seemingly needlessly, demonstrating that corporations act irresponsibly, sometimes illegally; this at a time when environmental issues also had their highest political profile in the UK (McGrew, 1993). Moreover, Conservative governments were implicated in many of the above disasters—whether generally, through attacks upon the consequences of their promotion of the enterprise culture, or specifically because some occurred in sectors which they were responsible for funding—notably public transport—or in which their interests were manifestly imbricated—for example, the extraction of North Sea oil.

It was in this context, most notably around the Zeebrugge disaster, that the charge of corporate manslaughter received its most public airing. Some of the legal complexities in pursuing the charge of corporate manslaughter have been discussed elsewhere (Pearce and Tombs, 1998, Bergman, 1991; Moran, 1992; Pearce, 1993; Slapper, 1993; Wells, 1993). That this charge has now been successfully pursued (see below), must be seen as a result of struggle, rather than any simple, teleological unfolding of progressive opportunity that remained implicit within law (see Tombs, 1995b).

Thus at the end of 1994 there occurred a possible landmark event, the first ever successful conviction for corporate manslaughter in English legal history, against OLL Ltd. The managing director of an activity centre was given a custodial sentence following the death of four teenagers in a canoeing accident. Certainly, the case was emotive as it involved young people away from their homes, seeking to "have fun" in the "charge" of others; crucially, it also involved a small company, where the identification of an individual controlling the corporation is relatively easy; and there was also extremely clear evidence that the managing director had knowledge of the risks that led to the deaths (Slapper, 1994). This combination of factors makes the case slightly unusual; it certainly has symbolic significance, though its effect upon the number of future prosecutions for corporate manslaughter "can only be properly judged in time" (ibid.: 1735). One further successful prosecution of corporate manslaughter has followed the OLL judgement. This latter case, against Jackson Transport (Ossett) Ltd., was perhaps significant in that it followed the death of a *worker*, and centred around failings in supervision, training and protective equipment. On the other hand, it again involved a small company; Jackson Transport employs just 40 people (*The Safety and Health Practitioner*, December, 1996: 3).

It is important to recognise that the revival of the issue of corporate manslaughter in the UK in recent years is largely a consequence of political action by a range of groups including trades unions, "Hazards" groups, and victims groups (such as the Herald Families Association and Disaster Action). The disasters acted as a catalyst for new groupings and new demands, and provided a larger and perhaps more receptive political audience for more longstanding activists and activities. Many of those involved in struggles following these disasters were already active in relation to occupational safety, organising around other "mundane" sites of employee death and injury, perhaps most notably in the construction industry. The construction industry is significant, for while organised labour has historically been in the forefront of struggles around occupational safety in the UK, this industry is one in which rates of unionisation are low, and employment is fragmented and fragile. The fact that pressure has been applied upon employers here attests to the potential efficacy of resistance by social groupings beyond, but including, trades unions (here, mobilised through the Construction Safety Campaign). Thus, disasters need to be used as opportunities to organise around "*resonances already present in social discourse*" (Hadden, 1994: 108; see also Sarangi, 1996: 106-7).

The substantive outcomes of these struggles are of course important in their own right. But more generally, they also indicate that while predominant ideological representations of what constitutes" "real" crime are powerful, they can be challenged and changed (Pearce and Tombs, 1990, 1991). Indeed, even the emerging use of terms such as "safety crimes" and "corporate manslaughter" is significant, given the social power of language (Wells, 1993).

In conjunction with the above developments, there has also emerged the language of criminalisation in relation to the most common sanction currently employed following prosecution of safety offences, namely, monetary fines. Now, there is no doubt that fines in both the UK and the US remain pathetically small. Even some unprecedentedly large fines remain completely unexceptional taken in the context of the annual turnover and profits of the companies involved (Bergman, 1994: 96; Slapper, 1993: 430).

Other points emerged from these signs of criminalisation for corporate offenders which are of particular interest. First, given the reluctance to link fines to "ability to pay" (in terms of corporate assets, sales, turnover, or some measure of profitability). Increased levels of fines may, as in the development of charges of manslaughter in the UK, noted above, work to the relative interests of larger corporations as opposed to smaller firms. Second, exceptional fines against a few individual employers constitutes no challenge to capital as a class, and again may actually strengthen its legitimacy through the symbolic effects of apparently class-neutral law and its enforcement. At the same time, however, some of these legal developments may pose a threat to capital should they become generalised or widespread. The prosecutions of OLL Ltd. and Jackson Transport in the UK, for example, may prove significant as legal precedents if they signal a new, generalised vulnerability of corporate entities to successful prosecution for manslaughter. Third, the pronouncements of senior regulators which accompanied these changes constitute interesting endorsements of deterrence theory, which clearly links individual offenders with a potentially offending group or class of offenders.

There have been perhaps more significant shifts towards criminalisation in the US. For example, prosecutions of Ford Motor Company and Film Recovery Systems. The most important developments, however, have occurred at local levels. For example, while Federal OSHA recommended just nineteen cases for prosecution between 1981-1988, CAL/OSHA recommended 292 during this same period, almost 40 per cent proving successful (Brill, 1992: 67); moreover, these cases have involved large as well as small companies (Reiner and Chatten-Brown ,1989).

Some analogous developments can be found with respect to environmental regulation in the US. It is at local levels that attempts to more effectively criminalise and prosecute environmental offenders are developing, notwithstanding considerable obstacles (National Institute of Justice, 1993).

Some "caveats" should be entered. For example, none of the above points imply an evolution towards the criminalisation and more effective and punitive prosecution of safety violations. It remains important not to underestimate the individualistic nature of bourgeois law which makes it difficult to establish legal liability or responsibility of corporations (Sargent, 1990), especially those which are large and complex. Thus, for example, the shift from the prosecution of OLL Ltd for corporate manslaughter to the successful prosecution of a large multinational would be a qualitative rather than simply a quantitative one. However, lest we prove complacent concerning some ineluctable trend towards more effective legal treatment of safety crimes, we should be aware that legal developments that appear progressive can be reversed (see Harrison, 1992; James, 1993). However, to recognise that legal reforms which apparently constrain capital can be turned against labour should not be taken as an argument for refraining from struggles for such reforms. This recognition is, however, a reminder, if it is needed, that legal reform is not an end in itself; that our contemporary legal systems are not of (class-) neutral institutions; that it is vital not to underestimate the versatility of capital and its allies, not least those in the legal profession (Mann, 1985), and that gains won within capitalist structures have contingent conditions of existence. It is also important not to underestimate the extent and power of more general obstacles that such attempts at criminalisation still face (see Bergman, 1991, 1994). Nevertheless, the preceding observations do emphasise that relationships between criminalisation, the criminal law, and health and safety offences are far from static or immutable: while predominant ideological representations of what constitutes real crime are powerful, they can be challenged and changed (Pearce and Tombs, 1990, 1991). Moreover, that these changes have occurred in highly unfavourable economic and political contexts indicates that hegemony is never secure. Thus while economic and political factors constrain, they do not determine the nature and extent of agency, struggle, and resistance (Snider, 1991). If the law is an object of such struggle, it may also serve as a element within it.

ꟿ REGULATING CAPITAL: THE POLITICS OF DETERRENCE AND REHABILITION

There are, then, in both the UK and the US some nascent signs of the criminalisation of safety offences. Criminalisation reflects, for us, one of three key principles upon which more effective regulation must be organised. Criminalisation represents punitiveness. It is significant in its own right, since a more punitive approach to corporate crime, inegalitarian in its effects, represents a shift towards greater social justice. Yet it is also significant in a slightly different sense. A punitive response to corporate crime helps to break down the ideological distinction between "real" and "regulatory" crime (a distinction upon which so much rests, as we have argued throughout). In particular, it breaks into the (powerful) tautology that real crimes are those for which there is a punitive response, so that regulatory crime is not real crime since it does not provoke a punitive response.

However, criminalisation is not an end in itself and needs to be related to two further principles underlying a more effective regulatory strategy, namely, deterrence and rehabilitation. We shall approach these issues by asking how criminalisation might play a role in making workplaces and local communities safer in particular, and preventing corporate crime in general.

Let us clarify further what we mean by the term "criminalisation" here. For us, this refers to three, intimately related, but not synonymous, phenomena: (1) the adoption by regulatory agencies of a more punitive-oriented approach to enforcement, so that regulators act more like some form of "police force" for industry (a regulatory approach discussed at length in Pearce and Tombs, 1998: chapter 7); (2) the term criminalisation here implies that sanctions, where these are invoked, involve a deterrent element; (3) that criminal prosecution must be included in the range of sanctions.

Let us examine the second issue first. It has long been accepted by most criminologists that deterrence fails when aimed at individual "street" offenders. However, some have argued that corporate illegality offers a sphere in which deterrence is much more likely to be effective. This is clearly the implication of Sutherland's characterisation of the corporation as coming "closer to economic man and to pure reason than any person or any other organisation" (Sutherland, 1983: 236-8), a view of the corporation which, as we have argued, we find persuasive in as much as it represents that which corporations are capable of, and strive towards, even if they do not always achieve this level of rationality and calculability. It is these very features of the corporation which render it potentially liable to deterrence-based sanctions (Croall, 1992: 147).

However, the applicability of deterrence theory in the context of corporate crime has been contested by others, certainly by those who do not cast the corporation as a rational, calculating entity. For example, some have argued that deterrence and more punitive modes of enforcement are neither desirable nor feasible. Yet on this specific point of deterrence, even within such work there are recognitions both that most firms try to avoid prosecution of violations of safety law (Hawkins, 1990: 450), and that the vast majority of firms comply with regulations only if they believe that those transgressions will be detected and sanctioned (Bardach and Kagan, 1982: 65-6). A number of significant points can be made regarding latter, much more significant concerns, vis-à-vis deterrent sanctions. Braithwaite et al. have argued that at least for certain kinds of economic actors, the use of deterrence is an effective means of achieving compliance (Braithwaite et al., 1993; Braithwaite and Makkai, 1994). Indeed, Braithwaite and Geis have argued that "the discredited doctrines of crime control by public disgrace, deterrence, incapacitation, and rehabilitation can be successfully applied to corporations" (Braithwaite and Geis, 1982: 293). This general proposition is itself based upon the arguments that "corporate crime is a conceptually different phenomenon from traditional crime" (Braithwaite and Geis, 1982: 294). Thus corporate criminals may be "among the most deterrable types of offenders ; they do not have a commitment to crime as a way of life, and their offences are instrumental rather than expressive" (ibid.: 302-3). Indeed, in relative terms they "usually have a good deal more than their fair share of the world's goodies, and they will be reluctant to risk losing what they have" (Geis, 1996: 258).

We agree that deterrence is fundamentally flawed both as a practical strategy, and indeed at a conceptual level, when directed at "street" or "traditional" crime, a view commonly expressed within criminology, and which finds its most thorough and eloquent expression in the work of Mathiesen (1990). However, deterrence has a rather different potential with respect to corporate crime. There are four aspects to this rather different potential, which we present in relation to Mathiesen's cogent rejection of the principle and practice of deterrence.

First, occupational or environmental safety crimes tend not to be single acts of commission, but are actually ongoing states or conditions—for example, chronic exposures because of a faulty plant, an absence of legally required guards or other forms of protective hardware, a failure to provide information or training, unsafe systems of work, and so on. What Mathiesen (1990: 54-7) refers to as the *"low detection risk"* of crime (and see also the claim made by Braithwaite and Geis, 1982: 294-6)—one of the factors which in his analysis renders general prevention (deterrence) unworkable—does not usually apply in this context. Thus it is important to note that we are arguing here about safety and environmental crimes, although we should also note that not all these are readily detected.

Mathiesen refers to "modern economic crime" (1990: 68, 71-2) as being difficult to detect and deter.

Second, the requirement for a proactive inspectorial and regulatory strategy raises the issue of enforcement resources. Certainly, as in all social activities, there is a minimal level of resource required to make regulation effective, as opposed to merely gestural or symbolic (Pearce, 1996). More specifically, adequate resources are required to maintain routine, or preventive, visits, and to prepare prosecutions.[1] We are thus led to a (familiar) demand for greater (here, regulatory) resources in the name of crime control. Again, however, it is worth distinguishing the contexts of corporate and street crimes. Since many corporate crimes do not pose the same problems of detection as street crimes, then greater regulatory resources *would* increase detection (Levi 1987: 281-4; Croall 1992: 154-6); this is quite distinct from the relatively marginal effect of increased resources for policing on levels of many kinds of traditional crime.

Third, a further objection raised by Mathiesen to the principle of general deterrence—namely that the "message" of deterrence is not communicated to those who need to receive it (Mathiesen, 1990: 58-69)—is also largely inapplicable in the context of safety, health and environmental crimes. Certainly, the symbolic effects of punitive sanctions against highly visible corporate offenders is one that should not be too easily dismissed.

Fourth, in the context of corporate crime, deterrent forms of sentencing should not serve to exacerbate social inequality, as seems to be the case for traditional crimes (Mathiesen, 1990: 72, 97, and passim).

Taken in combination, the above points indicate that deterrence as a principle informing enforcement activity and the sanctioning of corporate crime has considerable potential. Yet in contrast with the treatment of traditional crime, deterrence has rarely been used, nor its effects studied, in the context of regulating corporate crime. Notwithstanding this fact, there is evidence of its practical efficacy, not least in the context of health and safety regulation (Morgan, 1983; Health and Safety Executive, 1985; Pearce and Tombs, 1990, 1997; Tombs, 1995b).

What we are proposing, then, is not simply that deterrent sanctions represent a rational, just and effective response to corporate crime; but that effective forms of deterrence constitute a condition of existence for law-abiding behaviour on the part of organisations or corporations: that is, the existence of a likelihood of detection and credible sanctions following successful prosecution makes it possible for corporations to obey the law. This is consistent with our conceptualisation of corporations as amoral calculators. It is also consistent with the empirical evidence of the concerns of corporate capital over competitive advantage. Further, it is consistent with empirical work on the internal dynamics of corporate crime, which almost always identifies the existence of socially responsible individuals or groups within and around corporations, typically drawn from compliance or safety officers, engineers, middle or lower-level managers, workers, or local publics.[2] Deterrence can help to empower such individuals and groups, through creating conditions where their voices receive a hearing in the interests of the corporation as a whole. In a sense, then, deterrent law has the same characteristics that we would ascribe to law in general, namely, that it is facilitative and productive as well as being constraining and negative.

Notwithstanding these previous points, it is clear in any case that it would neither be feasible nor desirable to rely *solely* on the principle of deterrence as the basis of any sanctioning strategy. Two points seem clear. First, that any effective regulatory strategy must include a range of regulatory tools and techniques—and there are many examples of effective regulatory mechanisms. Second, that some principle of deterrence should form part of any regulatory strategy, even if this principle is not inherent in each particular mechanism of which that strategy is comprised.

Now, it is not an aim of this paper to consider in detail regulatory techniques *per se* (but see Pearce, 1990; Pearce and Tombs, 1994). Rather, we seek here to set out the principles upon which a regulatory strategy should be based. Crucial here is that once existing constraints on forms of regulation are recognised not as necessary but as related to contingent, though obdurate, material and ideological factors, then the appropriateness of a range of regulatory techniques can then be given serious consideration.

John Braithwaite, working with various colleagues, has been particularly active in considering the range of regulatory forms, both in isolation, and as part of an overall regulatory strategy (see, particularly, Ayres and Braithwaite, 1992; Fisse and Braithwaite, 1993). Arguing that deterrence is not effective in all contexts, Braithwaite and colleagues have urged the use of a "pyramid" of enforcement action and sanctions, where non-compliance results in regulators progressively shifting from one level of sanction up to a more punitive level (Ayres and Braithwaite, 1992). Essentially, Braithwaite has argued that compliance is more likely where regulators have at their disposal a range of credible enforcement techniques which allow an escalation in severity of sanctions in response to uncooperativeness on the part of the regulated. There is much within Braithwaite's arguments for an enforcement pyramid with which we are in agreement. Certainly it is crucial that any sanctions that are formally at the disposal of regulators be credible ones—that is, that it should be accepted that such sanctions may be, and are, used in the face of non-compliance. Secondly, and (from the point of view of general deterrence) crucially, we concur with Braithwaite's exigence that it is important "to transcend models of regulation as games played with single firms" (Ayres and Braithwaite, 1992: 39). Third, we also find that many corporations do make *explicit* calculations regarding the costs and benefits of compliance/non-compliance. Thus, while regulators are dealing with rational, calculating corporations, then

> *the greater the heights of punitiveness to which an agency can escalate, the greater its capacity to push regulation down to the cooperative base of the pyramid. (ibid.: 40)*

Thus for these authors, and for ourselves, a deterrent, potentially punitive regulatory strategy can be cost-effective in that "the bigger the sticks, the less they [the regulators] have to use them" (ibid: 40-41). Thus there are some complementarities between our general argument, and Braithwaite's claims for the efficacy of what he terms a pyramid of regulatory enforcement. However, we depart from his analysis in several respects. One issue relates to the speed with which such escalation will or should occur. This is not a minor point, since without a commitment to a real, and rapid, escalation of enforcement tactics as part of an overall strategy, then there is a real likelihood that the regulatory pyramid will start to resemble the most lax form of compliance strategy. Second, we depart significantly from Braithwaite and his colleagues in their argument that the first stage within their regulatory pyramid should be to allow corporations to self-regulate, and that only upon failing in this will escalation within the pyramid be triggered. *There is simply no evidence to support claims to the abilities or willingness of corporations to self-regulate.*

Finally, then, we believe that arguments for self-regulation in a hostile economic and political climate are likely to be expropriated, by dominant economic and political forces, and used in ways that differ markedly from the intentions of those who had originally espoused them.

We have already accepted, however, that deterrence will not be effective in all instances. Yet even in its inefficacy in achieving its explicit goal, it still provides a challenge for corporations; it calls the corporate bluff (Pearce, 1995).

And to challenge or to expose corporate rhetoric in this way is a key element of hegemonic struggle, exposing contradiction within dominant representations of how corporations operate and what they are. Interventionist strategies represent, in essence, attempts to operationalise the principle of rehabilitation. That is, they are attempts to reorder, reconstruct or reconfigure a corporation's structure, functions, activities; in this respect, corporations are much more prone to rehabilitation than are individual offenders. Although the means towards, and the potential efficacy of, rehabilitation is often subject to question in the case of individual human beings, rehabilitating the corporation itself is a different matter (Braithwaite and Geis, 1982: 309). Lofquist (1993) has recently considered the innovatory potential of corporate probation, precisely as a form of "rehabilitative and interventionist sanction" (Lofquist, 1993: 161-3).

Now, if we turn to the UK, it is undoubtedly the case that the EU has become highly significant as a source of potentially progressive and protective safety, health and environmental legislation in the UK in recent years (HSC, 1991: 19; McEldowney and McEldowney, 1996), and that this is more interventionist and prescriptive than the legislation that has typically emerged in the UK, the latter typically being overly flexible and reflecting a more laissez-faire approach to the regulation of hazards.

This opposition emerged despite the fact that any potential efficacy of such regulation in the UK remain limited by the lack of any specific right-to-know (RTK) legislation, or any general Freedom of Information legislation. By contrast, the latter has long existed in the US, while the former, namely RTK legislation, has mushroomed following Bhopal, then Institute in the US (Lewis and Henkels, 1996; Foveux, 1986; McCurdy, 1986). Capitalist corporations function on the basis of the disempowerment of the views of a range of stakeholders (Pearce and Tombs, 1998). And we have also argued that this disempowerment is a condition of their existence rather than an epiphenomenon. Thus any generalised attack upon the hierarchical and exclusive nature of corporate organisation and control is an attack upon the capitalist corporate form itself.

It is also possible to see this form of activity, to the extent that it occurs on a generalised scale, as one element towards what Adaman and Devine have called "participatory planning." Production organised according to this principle would enable "tacit knowledge to be articulated and economic life to be consciously controlled and coordinated in a context that dispenses with coercion, whether by state or market forces" (Adaman and Devine, 1997: 75).

This integral role for people in general might also be developed in the context of licensing systems, a further current form of regulation which has an interventionist element and potential. There is no doubt that at present these are often used formalistically, but this need not always be the case, and in potentially opening up the minutiae of compliance and more general hazard and risk management to external bodies, they are of enormous potential significance. Thus thoroughgoing forms of intervention have been introduced in some US states, in the form of licensing arrangements for hazardous facilities (Deieso et al., 1988: 444). Moreover, the use of licensing also greatly augments the power of formal regulatory bodies, and thus represents a regulatory tool of more general significance.

Finally, in terms of developments which might legitimate interventionist strategies, it is worth noting the emergence in both the US and the UK of debates around corporate governance. At one extreme is a series of attempts to urge corporations to act more ethically, more responsibly, as a more effective citizen, etc. In short, they reflect many of the claims that capitalist corporations can and will simply decide to moderate their profit-seeking tendencies. They are based upon contradiction, and are doomed to failure. At the opposite extreme are arguments for capitalist corporations to function as (neoliberal) capitalist rhetoric claims—at the behest of the wishes of shareholders. But these debates express the concern that shareholder wishes should somehow be met, and these should not be confined to those of the dominant, most powerful institutional investors.

These latter demands are typically resisted most keenly by corporate representatives. Yet such reforms are now on corporate and political agendas. Of course, any reforms won through such initiatives are strictly capitalistic, are certainly precarious, and cannot be ends in themselves. Given the inherently destructive features of capitalist markets, and of the social divisions of labour upon which capitalist markets are constructed, then even radical demands around corporate governance are likely to be highly reformist. This criticism extends even to the most progressive of these arguments which advocate extensive employee share ownership, subsidised by the state, thereby extending rights of "control" to large groups of employees (Gamble and Kelly, 1996). Nevertheless, at least such arguments raise the issue of ownership together with that of control—and it is clear that without an attack on private ownership, gains made on the issue of control remain vulnerable to reversal (this was, of course, illustrated in the failures of Swedish social democracy; see Pearce and Tombs,

1998: chapter 2). Yet even arguments about control, framed around corporate governance, have potentially important effects. They do raise important tensions which corporate capitalism cannot resolve, so that such forms of corporate governance offer two possibly complementary possibilities. First, they expose contradictions within neoliberal rhetoric that capitalist firms can operate in the interests of the majority of shareholders. Second, they raise the issue of corporate accountability and democracy—and these are issues which cannot be resolved within capitalist forms of the corporation.

Certainly, interventionist forms of regulation have the general potential to force companies to adopt different business strategies, and the particular possibility of forcing them to internalise legitimate costs of production. In this latter respect, if this internalisation of costs is pursued, this will help to alter popular understandings of the successes of capitalism (such as those referred to in Pearce and Tombs, 1998: chapter 1), by contrast raising to greater prominence the costs of such "successes" (see Pearce and Tombs, 1998: chapter 2). That is, effective forms of regulation expose some of the present contradictions within a system of production that allows enormously rich private actors to generate benefits while socialising much of the costs of their activity. To the extent that regulation forces the costs of production back onto corporations, then it exposes how unsustainable present modes of economic organisation are; thus, effective regulation may be prefigurative. This is clearly the case even if some aspects of the regulatory strategy as we have indicated, rely on private or market-based approaches. Both developments within tort law and the activity of some insurers have forced more progressive forms of regulation of chemicals companies (Pearce and Tombs, 1998: chapter 8). This is not to argue that tort and private insurance are unequivocally progressive; but we also need to recognise that the potential in such developments is not exhausted by their design.

ᛗ REGULATION, DEMOCRATISATION AND SOCIALISATION

These considerations on the regulatory principles of punitiveness, deterrence and rehabilitation lead us to a general, and crucial point. Effective regulation is never a question of punitive versus compliance-oriented regulatory approaches, nor based upon deterrence in any simplistic fashion, nor one which relies solely and simply on rehabilitation. Moreover, we would argue that effective regulation does not require us to think in terms of a strict dichotomy between state or market mechanisms. Thus the present conjuncture requires more effective regulatory strategies which combine state (national and local) regulatory techniques with private, or market-based, approaches (Paehlke, 1995).

If more progressive regulatory reform is feasible, as we have indicated here, and argued in detail elsewhere (Pearce and Tombs, 1990, 1991), it must also be clear that legal regulation can only be a means rather than an end. Yet even where regulators fail adequately to enforce, the very existence of such law can be utilised in both a material and ideological fashion since it provides both "leverage" and a "moral legitimacy" for pro-regulatory forces (Snider, 1991: 221).

This is a specific instance of the potency of the discourse of collective rights, which should not be underestimated (Woodiwiss, 1990); it is quite possible to seek reforms without descending into reformism (Gorz, 1980). On the other hand, it is important to guard against mere reformism. Rights politics— the right to a safe and healthy working environment, to clean air, water, land— can not be an end in itself, since to seek such rights as ends is to leave them always precarious.

However, effective prevention and sanctioning of corporate crime, whether safety crimes or other forms of such crimes, means that we must move beyond criminology and considerations of crime and the criminal justice system. We need to consider a more general political economy of regulation.

As we have indicated here, both Snider and Mahon have highlighted the need to examine regulation, and regulatory reform, in terms of struggle, and, in particular, struggle in which a (albeit more or less) precarious hegemony is at stake. To this end, as Snider sets out, considerations of regulatory reform need to address sets of actors in at least three locations—within *states* (be these international, national or local), *corporations* (where there are clearly fissures and contradictory sets of interests), and *pro-regulatory forces*. Snider also argues that the most effective of the latter outside the corporate sector have been organised labour or trades unions—that is, despite their vulnerability to the charge of sectionalism, trades unions remain the key vehicle of collective resistance, with historically developed, and institutional, power bases. This is not to argue, of course, that struggles will be confined to struggles of labour; but it is to argue that class politics remains essential, and that in its absence, forms of resistance expressed through individualism, fragmentation, new social movements, identity politics, and so on, amount to little more than a "pluralist struggle for democracy"

(Fudge and Glasbeek, 1992: 62). And such a form of politics, whereby a pluralist democracy—however radical—is an end rather than a means, represents no fundamental challenge to a capitalist economic and social order.

Interestingly in this context, trends towards the internationalisation of capitalist economic and political institutions contain fundamental contradictions which are liable to exploitation by pro-regulatory forces in general, and organised labour in particular. There are at least three inextricably linked types of internationalising trends which create both opportunities and challenges for pro-regulatory forces. And even a cursory indication of these highlights a (perhaps increasingly) complex, and contradictory, set of relationships between pro-regulatory forces, national state bodies and those institutions and practices which we might refer to as the "international state" (Picciotto, 1991).

First, we have argued that the international economy is less adequately understood in terms of a "global economy," more accurately represented in terms of three increasingly dominant trading blocs, namely, the Americas (within which the US remains hegemonic), Western Europe (within which the Franco-German axis is crucial) and the Pacific Rim (dominated by Japan) (see Pearce and Tombs, 1998: chapter 2, and Hirst and Thompson 1996: 199 and passim). If this representation of the international economy is accepted, it is likely that there will also develop bodies of law which operate on a transnational basis within each of these three trading blocs. Initially, these facilitate the very structures within which nation-states have imbricated themselves—this was the origin of the EU, of course, and we can see NAFTA as a regulatory framework for trade in the Americas. But this then creates at least two interesting and complementary possibilities. First, that the development of so-called social regulation will follow economic regulation in such blocs, signs of which are clear in the context of both the EU and NAFTA, albeit to differing extents. Second, that there may develop the coordination of actions by organised labour and allies within various social movements across nation-state boundaries. Here, the internationalisation of economic and political structures creates new objects of struggle and gives impetus to the development of forces in that struggle.[3]

Second, the emergence of more truly transnational corporations has been accompanied by a proliferation of what Picciotto (1991) has termed international economic soft law. Picciotto makes a series of important points on the emergence and nature of such law. First, he relates its emergence to the technical inefficiency—and subsequent legitimation problems—which were apparent in attempts of national state bodies to develop an international regulatory framework for international capital. Second, he notes that much of this emergent "oft law"—certainly the Codes of Conduct for transnational corporations— was itself sponsored by international business concerns in the face of such challenges to legitimacy. Third, that even in the ineffectiveness of this latter body of "regulation," even if it were to be dismissed as purely symbolic, there has been provided a focus of political action for "pressure groups, trades unions and other bodies" (Picciotto, 1991: 58; Sklair, 1995). This political action represents a critical response to a range of issues related to the social impacts of transnational corporations, and has been:

> *based on notions of popular power, aiming to democratise both the political structures of the state and the international system, as well as the production dominated by the TNCs (Picciotto, 1991: 58).*

Moreover, such political action will exploit a key contradiction at the heart of corporate capitalism, even in its international forms—namely, that however "global" capitalism becomes, it can only globalise, and maintain global activities, on the basis of regulation. The development of international regulation— whether sponsored by national state actors or new forms of international institutions—simultaneously creates new sites of potential resistance.

Third, internationally-based resistance shifts the balance of power away from particular national state bodies and "domestic" capital. The former is much trumpeted in the more exaggerated claims of globalisation (Horsman and Marshall, 1994), yet it is interesting that such arguments rarely examine the effects of any global, or even internationalising, economic order upon nationally-tied capital. Yet it is surely the case that resistance which is organised beyond the level of any one nation-state, and operates outside the structures of international or national regulation or international "soft law," may compromise or undermine the ability of particular states or *particular nationally-based corporations* to pursue autonomous agendas.

While these trends and factors can only be indicated here, they highlight both that pro-regulatory activity *needs* to be internationalised, and that there are forces that are furthering this internationalisation. Thus Elling has observed that the internationalisation of "the capitalist political—economic world system" may carry with it "much of the counter culture of resistance forces from one core country to another as well as to semi-peripheral and peripheral countries" (Elling, 1986, cited in Carson and Henenberg, 1989: 130).

To emphasise. Such international forms of resistance exist, even if labour has traditionally organised less effectively than capital at such a level. There is some evidence that trades unions have begun to systematise forms of international coordination around health and safety issues, through initiatives such as the European Work Hazards Network, an ICFTU coordinated information exchange between International Trade Secretariats, and international campaigns on specific issues (for example, the hazards of Free Trade Zones). We do not share the view that labour has, either inevitably or necessarily, "failed" in its opposition to global capitalism (Sklair, 1995).

Thus, as Fudge and Glasbeek have argued, people will, indeed must, "fight their oppressions as they experience them" (Fudge and Glasbeek, 1992: 66). But this does not remove wider connections between such oppressions; it indicates the significance of the exigence to "think globally, act locally." Moreover, to the extent that such resistance to oppressions focuses upon capital, in national and international manifestations, then this resistance immediately takes on class dimensions. Given that it is workers and the poorest sections of any society who are likely to be those who must endure dangerous working conditions, live in close vicinity to hazardous production plants and sites of waste disposal, be denied access to clean air, water and land, then such resistance again has a class dimension, and is likely to emerge with a class-basis. The resistance of corporate capital to control of its activities in these kinds of areas is likely to be particularly trenchant. This might be contrasted, as we have noted above, to state and subsequent corporate responses where small-scale capital is involved— where the homes, pensions, and shares of the middle classes who see themselves with some financial investment in capitalism have been placed at stake, then regulation has been more likely to ensue.

Relatedly, thinking globally/acting locally requires that those who push for improved corporate performance in respect of hazardous and criminal activities must recognise that a consequence of "successful" pressure may be displacement of such activities from one location to another; thus the prevention of the export of hazard, either intra- or inter-nationally, must be a key element of the discourses of resistance.

Further, activities of resistance must continue to focus upon (but not be restricted to) formal political groupings, namely parties, and this focus needs to be maintained at local, regional, national and international levels. Moreover, given the existence, but often marginalisation, of more socially responsible individuals and groups within corporations, pro-regulatory forces need to seek to develop alliances *within* corporations.

Real, long-term improvements in conditions for working men and women have not emerged via any evolutionary processes, nor via enlightened or socially responsible capitalism. Capitalist corporations are essentially amoral, calculating entities; they will only act "responsibly" or in an enlightened fashion when the costs of, and opportunities for, doing otherwise are raised. Thus, in an assessment of the dynamics of regulatory effectiveness in general, and the prospects for improved levels of corporate performance with respect to social regulation in particular, Snider has pointed to the significance of pro-regulatory pressures on both corporations and the state. Such pressures emanate particularly from employees and their representatives, from local communities, from various interest/pressure groups, from some formal political representatives, and even from some academics.

Such struggles are not simply confined to the legal sphere. Without returning to past debates, it is only by recognising that law is not *simply* a bourgeois tool, is not *simply* a reflection of economic relations, that its potential as an element of working class struggle vis-à-vis capital can be appreciated. Law can of course constrain, but it also creates possibilities, through creating unstable and contested spaces (Moran, 1992; Pearce, 1989; Woodiwiss, 1990).

Clearly there are specific legal measures which would further these processes. Some are already in place in some states, but barely used, others would require reform of existing law. For example, we would advocate the development of charges of corporate manslaughter and reckless employing; disqualification of named employers and/or directors of successfully prosecuted companies; and the development, or external imposition if necessary, of clear lines of accountability and responsibility in corporations. Further, there is a need for greater experimentation with licensing systems and other forms of interventionist regulation, accepting that the principles of public participation, access to information, and social dialogue are crucial to such forms.

CONCLUSION

Central to our argument here is the need to reassess what we understand by the term "regulation." Historically this has referred to aspects of administrative, civil and criminal law and their enforcement. However, as the preceding demonstrates, regulation can only be understood as a process that involves the widest possible range of social actors and social relations. At present, corporations and their representatives themselves play dominant, often covert, roles in the development of regulations to which they are then subjected; they then play key roles in negotiating the ways in which, and the extent to which, such regulations are actually enforced. We have argued that both in the development and enforcement of regulation, there are crucial roles to be played by workers, local communities, and various activist groups. Effective regulation of criminal corporate activity, one aspect of which must be control of hazards associated with production, requires corporate and social democratisation. This is also a matter of social justice

Neither the unequal distribution of the effects of hazardous production in particular, nor the control of corporate crime in general, will be genuinely achieved without controlling corporations. And control of the corporation requires new forms of ownership, forms of ownership which must, in effect, dissolve the corporate form. This is, to say the least, a long-term project, and, as we speak, one to be conducted in a highly unfavourable economic-political conjuncture. Yet there are signs of a general popular intolerance with the criminal activities of corporations. It is clear that neoliberalism remains insecure, and that contradictions between its rhetoric and the actual practices of corporations will perhaps be exacerbated. It is clear that the science-technology paradigm is increasingly questioned. And it is clear that in internationalising economic activity, corporations also create the conditions whereby international forms of resistance are at least more likely. None of these trends are simple, and they are certainly not unilinear. But they are real, and they offer hope.

ṁ ENDNOTES

1   The extent, and effect, of the inadequacy of resources is sometimes graphically illustrated. For example, the Offshore Safety Division of the UK's Health and Safety Executive, established by the Offshore Safety Act following the Piper Alpha disaster in which 167 lives were lost, is unable to visit offshore installations without giving prior notice to employers. This is due simply to the fact that the OSD does not have the resources to own a helicopter, thus requiring its inspectors to arrange to fly on helicopters owned by oil companies, thereby granting advance notice of any "proactive" inspection.

2   The potential significance of dissension amongst such groups within and around corporations involved in criminal activity is clearly illustrated in many of the "classic" studies of corporate crime. On the warnings and dissension of compliance or safety officers, see Braithwaite's study of corporate crime in the pharmaceutical industry (Braithwaite, 1984), or the documented histories of the design and production of the Ford Pinto (Cullen et al., 1987); the dissenting voices of groups of engineers is documented by Vaughan in the case of the Challenger launch decision (Vaughan, 1996); on middle and lower-level managers, see Wells's (1993) discussion of the sinking of the *Herald of Free Enterprise*, or Vandivier's (1982) account of the Goodrich Brake Scandal; as we have noted in this text, workers and local publics had consistently raised concerns about the operation of Union Carbide's Bhopal plant (see Pearce and Tombs, 1998: chapter 6; also, Chouhan, 1994; and Jones, 1988).

3   This argument is hardly a new one, of course, having been developed in outline by Marx ([1872] 1971).

⋔ BIBLIOGRAPHY

Adaman, F. and Devine, P. (1997) "On the Economic Theory of Socialism," *New Left Review*, 221, January/February.

Ayres, I. and Braithwaite, J. (1992) *Responsive Regulation: Transcending the Deregulation Debate*, Oxford: Oxford University Press.

Bardach, E. and Kagan, R. (1982) *Going by the Book: The problem of Regulatory Unreasonableness*, Philadelphia: Temple University Press.

Barnett, H. (1995) "Can Confrontation, Negotiation, or Socialisation Solve the Superfund Enforcement Dilemma?", in Pearce, F. and Snider, L., eds., *Corporate Crime: Contemporary Debates,* Toronto: University of Toronto Press.

Bergman, D. (1991) *Deaths at Work: Accidents or Corporate Crime?* London: The London Hazards Centre / Workers' Educational Association.

Bergman, D. (1994) *The Perfect Crime? How Companies Can Get Away with Manslaughter in the Workplace*, Birmingham: West Midlands HASAC.

Braithwaite, J. (1984) *Corporate Crime in the Pharmaceutical Industry*, London: Routledge and Kegan Paul.

Braithwaite, J. and Geis, G. (1982) "On Theory and Action for Corporate Crime Control," *Crime and Delinquency*, 28.

Braithwaite, J. and Makkai, T. (1994) "The Dialectics of Corporate Deterrence," paper presented at the Annual Meeting of the Academy of Criminal Justice Sciences, Chicago, 8-12 March.

Braithwaite, J., Makkai, T., Braithwaite, V. and Gibson, D. (1993) *Raising the Standard: Resident-Centred Nursing Home Regulation in Australia*, Canberra: Australian Government Publishing Service.

Brill, H. (1992) "Government Breaks the Law: The Sabotaging of the Occupational Safety and Health Act," *Social Justice*, Vol. 19, No. 3.

Carson, W.G. and Henenberg, C. (1989) "Social Justice at the Workplace: The Political Economy of Health and Safety Laws," *Social Justice*, 16, 3.

Croall, H. (1992) *White Collar Crime*, Buckingham: Open University Press.

Deieso, D.A., Mulvey, N.P. and Kelly, J. (1988) "Accidental Release Prevention: a Regulator's Perspective," in *Preventing Major Chemical and Related Process Accidents. IChemE Symposium Series No. 110*, Rugby: IChemE.

Edwards, S.M., Edwards, T.D. and Fields, C.B. (1996) *Environmental Crime and Criminality: Theoretical and Practical Issues*, New York: Garland.

Elling, R. (1986) *The Struggle for Workers' Health*, New York: Baywood Publishing.

Fisse, B. and Braithwaite, J. (1993) *Corporations, Crime and Accountability*, Cambridge: Cambridge University Press.

Foveaux, M. (1986) "A Field Day for Legislators: Bhopal and its Effect on the Enactment of New Laws in the United States," in Smith, M.A., ed., *The Chemical Industry After Bhopal*, London: IBC Technical Services Ltd.

Fudge, J. and Glasbeek, H. (1992) "The Politics of Rights: a politics with little class," *Social & Legal Studies*, 1, (1), March.

Gamble, A. and Kelly, G. (1996) "The New Politics of Ownership," *New Left Review*, 220, November/December.

Geis, G. (1996) "A Base on Balls for White-Collar Criminals," in Shichor, D. and Sechrest, D.K., eds., *Three Strikes and You're Out: Vengeance as Public Policy*, Thousand Oaks, CA: Sage.

Gorz, A. (1980) *Ecology as Politics*, London: Pluto.

Harrison, K. (1992) "Manslaughter by Breach of Employment Contract," *Industrial Law Journal*, 21, 1.

Hawkins, K. (1990) "Compliance Strategy, Prosecution Policy and Aunt Sally: A comment on Pearce and Tombs," *British Journal of Criminology*, 30, (4), Autumn.

Hirst, P.Q. and Thompson, G. (1996) *Globalisation in Question*, Cambridge: Polity.

Horsman, M. and Marshall, A. (1994) *After The Nation-State: Citizens, Tribalism and the New World Order*, London: Harper Collins.

HSC (1991) *Plan of Work 1991/92 and Beyond*, London: HMSO.

HSE (1985) *Measuring the Effectiveness of HSE Field Activities. HSE Occasional Paper 11*, London: HMSO.

HSE (1993) *The Costs of Accidents at Work*, London: HMSO.

James, P. (1993) *The European Community. A Positive Force for UK Health and Safety Law?*, Institute of Employment Rights: London.

Levi, M. (1987) *Regulating Fraud*, London: Tavistock.

Lewis, S. and Henkels, D. (1996) "Good Neighbour Agreements: A Tool for Environmental Social Justice," *Social Justice*, 23, (4).

Lofquist, W.S. (1993) "Organisational Probation and the US Sentencing Commission," in Geis, G. and Jesilow, P., eds., *White Collar Crime,* Newbury Park, CA: Sage.

Mann, K. (1985) *Defending White-Collar Crime,* New Haven: Yale University Press.

Marchington, M. and Parker, P. (1990) *Changing Patterns of Employee Relations,* Hemel Hempstead: Harvester Wheatsheaf.

Marginson, P. (1994) "Multinational Britain: Employment and Work in an Internationalised Economy," *Human Resource Management Journal,* 4, (4).

Marx, K. (1867/1976) *Capita, Volume 1,* Harmandsworth: Penguin.

Marx, K. and Engels, F. (1872/1971) *Manifesto of the Communist Party,* Moscow: Progress.

Mathiesen, T. (1990) *Prison On Trial,* London: Sage.

McCurdy, P. (1986) "The Challenge to Communications: Communications in a Right-to-Know Era," in Smith, M.A., ed., *The Chemical Industry After Bhopal,* London: IBC Technical Services Ltd.

McEldowney, J.F. and McEldowney, S. (1996) *Environment and the Law,* Harlow: Addison Wesley Longman.

McGrew, A. (1993) "The Political Dynamics of the 'New' Environmentalism," in Smith, D., ed., *Business and the Environment: Implications of the New Environmentalism,* London: Paul Chapman.

Moran, L.J. (1992) "Corporate Criminal Capacity: Nostalgia for Representation," *Social & Legal Studies,* 1, (3).

Morgan, P. (1983) "The Costs and Benefits of the Power Presses Regulations," *British Journal of Industrial Relations,* (2).

National Institute of Justice (1993) *Local Prosecution of Environmental Crime,* Washington, DC: US Department of Justice.

Noble, C. (1995) "Beyond OSHA: Regulatory Strategy and Institutional Structure in the Work Environment," in Pearce, F. and Snider, L., eds., *Corporate Crime: Contemporary Debates,* Toronto: University of Toronto Press.

Paehlke, R. (1995) "Environmental Harm and Corporate Crime," in Pearce, F. and Snider, L., eds., *Corporate Crime: Contemporary Debates,* Toronto: University of Toronto Press.

Pearce, F. (1976) *Crimes of the Powerful,* London: Pluto.

Pearce, F. (1989a) *The Radical Durkheim,* London: Unwin-Hyman.

Pearce, F. (1989b) "Socially Responsible Corporations Need Strong and Independent Regulatory Agencies," paper presented at a symposium on The Management of Safety, Society of the Chemical Industry, London, April 25.

Pearce, F. (1990) "Responsible Corporations and Regulatory Agencies," *The Political Quarterly,* 61, (4).

Pearce, F. (1993) "Corporate Rationality as Corporate Crime," *Studies in Political Economy,* 49, Spring.

Pearce, F. (1995) "Accountability for Corporate Crime," in Stenning, P., ed., *Accountability for Criminal Justice,* Toronto, University of Toronto Press.

Pearce, F. and Tombs, S. (1990) "Ideology, Hegemony and Empiricism: Compliance Theories of Regulation," *British Journal of Criminology*, 30, 4.

Pearce, F. and Tombs, S. (1993) "US Capital versus the Third World: Union Carbide and Bhopal," in Pearce, F. and Woodiwiss, M., eds., *Global Crime Connections*, London: Macmillan.

Pearce, F. and Tombs, S. (1994) "Class, Law and Hazards," a Submission to the Permanent Peoples' Tribunal, Industrial Hazards and Human Rights, 28th November-2nd December, London.

Pearce, F. and Tombs, S. (1997) "Hazards, Law and Class: Contextualising the Regulation of Corporate Crime," *Social & Legal Studies*, 6, (1).

Pearce, F. and Tombs, S. (1998) *Toxic Capitalism*, Aldershot: Dartmouth.

Picciotto, S. (1991) "The Internationalisation of the State," *Capital & Class*, 43, Spring.

Reiner, I. and Chatten-Brown, J. (1989) "When it is Not an Accident but a Crime: Prosecutors Get Tough with OSHA Violations," *Northern Kentucky Law Review*, 17.

Sarangi, S. (1996) "The Movement in Bhopal and its Lessons,"*Social Justice*, 23, (4).

Sargent, N. (1990) "Law, Ideology and Social Change: An Analysis of the Role of Law in the Construction of Corporate Crime," *The Journal of Human Justice*, 1, 2.

Sklair, L. (1995) "Social Movements and Global Capitalism," *Sociology*, 29, (3).

Slapper, G. (1993) "Corporate Manslaughter: An Examination of the Determinants of Prosecutorial Policy," *Social & Legal Studies*, 2.

Slapper, G. (1994) "A Corporate Killing," *New Law Journal*, December 16.

Snider, L. (1987) "Towards a Political Economy of Reform, Regulation and Corporate Crime," *Law & Policy*, 9, (1).

Snider, L. (1991) "The Regulatory Dance: Understanding Reform Processes in Corporate Crime," *International Journal of the Sociology of Law*, 19.

Sutherland, E.H. (1983) *White Collar Crime: The Uncut Version*, New Haven: Yale University Press.

Szasz, A. (1984) "Industrial Resistance to Occupational Safety and Health Legislation 1971-1981," *Social Problems*, 32, (2).

Tombs, S. (1989) "Deviant Workplaces and Dumb Managements? Understanding and Preventing Accidents in the Chemical Industry," *Industrial Crisis Quarterly*, 3, Autumn.

Tombs, S. (1990a) "A Case Study in Distorted Communication," in *Piper Alpha - Lessons for Life-Cycle Safety Management, Institution of Chemical Engineers Symposium Series No. 122*, Rugby: IChemE.

Tombs, S. (1990b) "Industrial Injuries in British Manufacturing Industry," *Sociological Review*, 38, (2).

Tombs, S. (1994) "Strategic Failures? Managing Environmental Protection, Managing Safety," *Industrial & Environmental Crisis Quarterly*, 8, (3).

Tombs, S. (1995a) "New Organisational Forms and the Further Production of Corporate Crime," in Pearce, F. and Snider, L., eds., *Corporate Crime: Contemporary Debates*, Toronto: University of Toronto Press.

Tombs, S. (1995b) "Law, Resistance and Reform: 'Regulating' Safety Crimes in the UK," *Social & Legal Studies*, 4 (3).

Tucker, E. (1995) "And Defeat Goes On: An Assessment of 'Third-Wave' Health and Safety Regulation," in Pearce, F. and Snider, L., eds., *Corporate Crime: Contemporary Debates*, Toronto: University of Toronto Press.

Wells, C. (1993) *Corporations and Criminal Responsibility*, Oxford: Clarendon Press.

Woodiwiss, A. (1990) *Rights v. Conspiracy: A Sociological Essay on the History of Labour Law in the United States*, New York: Berg.

11

Reconciled with Whom?
Wrong Criminals, Wrong Goal

Ruth Morris

🏛 PROPHETIC VOICES, EMPEROR'S NEW CLOTHES

Most people know the story of the Emperor's new clothes. The Emperor in this fable was conned by a tailor who claimed to be making clothes visible only to those with special vision. Courtiers were afraid to say they saw a naked emperor, and it took a little child to say, "But the Emperor has no clothes!" Today we live in a world order that is naked, with a justice system that is naked of justice and compassion. For years I have compared my role to that of the little child, saying to the justice system, "But the Emperor has no clothes!" Today however, after several years of reading and praying about the world economic crisis, I find myself in the unenviable position of declaring, "The whole court is stark, staring naked!"

When I read the Bible, I am struck by how unanimously the prophets God called didn't want the job. They weren't stupid. They knew being a prophet put you on a collision course with the worldly powers of the day. But even more, none of them felt worthy enough, eloquent enough, strong enough to be the ones God calls to preach truth to a world living in the shadow of untruth, oppression, and idolatry. And today, all of us continue to say, "Not me, God. Find someone more qualified."

We Quakers believe we are *all* called to listen to the voice of God in us. I have come to believe that God calls every one of us to prophetic words and roles and utterances at times, but some of us are more expert at turning a deaf ear to God than were the Old Testament prophets. I have a feeling that if Jesus were to walk among us today and call us personally to be one of his chosen disciples, we would find good reasons to excuse ourselves.

So today, I wish I could stand up here and give you a nice, heart-warming talk about how you can be a little kinder, more patient, and more successful in reaching out to the fallen in prisons who are ready for the gospel message. It is a good thing to minister to the lost souls in prison, who yearn to be a part of both God's kingdom, and also part of our much more rejecting society. That ministry has been an important part of my journey forward. But today, I see a much larger challenge for all of us: to free ourselves from the prison we are building in the world, a prison of ungodly greed, from which the prisons in which we work emanate.

My talk will challenge you to open those larger prison doors that are entombing us all, and I am afraid. I am afraid I will offend some of you, and that some of you will be disappointed that I didn't talk enough about the work you and I do in prisons directly. I'm sorry about that, but I have to answer the call I get from that Inner Voice that I believe is God calling. We Quakers say, "The water tastes of the pipes." My message of God's call will have a Ruth Morris flavour. Your listening will also be affected by who you are, which enables you to hear some ideas more than others. But I'll keep the pipes as clear as I am able, and I'm asking you to keep your listening pipes as open as you can. Please ignore the flavour of me, and listen for the savour of God's truth. We are all thirsty for Christ's water of life, which is here for each of us today.

𝍇 WHAT'S WRONG WITH OUR SYSTEM?

A Costly, Unjust, Immoral Failure

For many years, I used to give talks in which I said, "There is nothing at all wrong with our justice system, except that it is an expensive, unjust, immoral failure." Then I devoted the rest of the talk to expanding on those four key words:

Expensive

Prisons in Canada cost $70 to $200 per day for each soul we incarcerate there, not because they are full of luxuries, but because it costs a lot to pay for guards to keep a human being in a cage. Strangely enough, people don't like being caged, so it takes a lot of "security" to keep them in one. Although the cost varies around the world depending on the local wage and building costs, always and everywhere prisons are far more costly than community alternatives. A pre-trial Bail Program I headed cost three dollars a day, one twentieth as much as incarceration did! For that tiny amount, we were able to provide support in housing, finding treatment, new educational plans, addiction advice, and general supervision. One of the ironies of the world is that poorer countries often do better in our field than wealthier countries, because poorer governments can't afford as much of the colossal waste that prisons are, so they look more seriously at community options. We could save huge amounts of government budgets if we just used existing community alternatives more effectively for the many prisoners who, by any reasonable standard, would be far better off in the community.

Unjust

Around the world, prisons are full of the poor and of racial minorities: indigenous people and people of dark skin. This is not because these groups are more criminal, but because they are more marginalized. incarceration rates don't correlate with crime rates. Instead, consistently, they relate to two population variables:

- Unemployment rates
- Proportion of people of minority race in the population

Prisons are where we store our surplus unemployed racial minority poor. Studies of drug use in the USA consistently show that illegal drug use is approximately equal between blacks and whites. But because police do sweeps in black neighbourhoods, because courts prosecute blacks more consistently and vigorously, because judges sentence them longer, the prisons have ten times the rate of black people for drug crimes as white. A similar picture exists in other countries. I won't even delve into the big issue of wrongful convictions, but the most conservative estimates are that three to five percent of the prison population is wrongfully convicted by any standard. Students of the subject put the figure much higher. What is more, the more serious the offence, the greater the probability of a wrongful conviction, because the police and courts want to prove to the public they can solve this crime, and getting anyone inside eases public fear. Above all, the poor are sifted in and the rich are sifted out. The book title *The Rich Get Richer and The Poor Get Prison* sums it up precisely.

Immoral

You may think immoral is the same as unjust, but it isn't. Even if justice were meted out in exactly equal measure to rich and poor, blacks, native people and whites, and all accused persons had equal representation, and no wrongful convictions occurred, the system would be immoral because it is based on revenge. God said it loud and clear, "'vengeance is mine!' saith the Lord God." Whenever we dabble in revenge, it is like the Hebrews touching the sacred Ark of the Covenant—we are jolted back by a powerful voltage, because we are not meant to handle that. Which of us is without sin, that we can mete out punishment to our fellows? Restrain wrong behaviour, yes. Revenge, no.

A related issue is deterrence. It is immoral for me to hurt John in order to deter Mary from offending, because that is using John—a sacred human being—as a means to an end. Hitler did it lots: he would execute a hundred innocent people to deter a village from sabotage. In the justice system, the whole theory of deterrence is a milder form of Hitler's approach. Revenge satisfies the core needs of neither victims, nor offenders, nor society. Moreover, the great majority of those charged as offenders are young people whom society has failed to protect from abusive homes, bad foster homes, or sterile institutions. Our failure to provide them with UN minimum standards for the rights of a child does not entitle them to engage in crime. But it doesn't put us in a morally defensible position to wreak lifelong revenge on them through the tragic police-court-prison vicious circle.

Failure

Prison claims to do four things: deter others, protect the public, rehabilitate offenders, and punish people. It achieves only the last. Its failure as a deterrent and its failure to protect the public are well documented. You cannot put a person into a violent, destructive, humiliating, isolating environment and expect them to be improved. Recidivism rates vary from 40-85 percent in most prisons. One educator commented that we should study prisons because if we could get return rates like they do we would have achieved something!

Those four points used to be the main part of my talk. Most of you are familiar with them. But today I sum up what's wrong with the justice system with two big ones:

- Wrong Goal: Revenge
- Wrong People in the Dock: The Marginalized

It is hard to get across both those profound points in the same talk, because both of them challenge fundamental errors of our culture. We think, self-righteously, that it is our job to play God and do the punishing in this world. And we fall into the trap of persecuting the marginalized instead of stopping the powerful whose wrongdoings eclipse those of all the prisoners in the world. Let's look for a few moments at corporate crime.

🏛 STORIES OF CORPORATE CRIME

And now, a few stories of corporate crime; stories that make my blood run cold, except when it is boiling with rage. For we are surely entitled to be angry when those who are already wealthy choose to add to their wealth by attacks on innocent consumers, employees, and bystanders.

- Dow Chemical always maintained dioxin was harmless, except for "a possible skin disease." By the late 1970s, Vietnam veterans reported soft-tissue cancers, birth defects, and shorter life spans. Twenty thousand veterans launched a class action suit showing that chemical firms knew of these dangers in the 1930s and the US army knew of them by 1959. Despite some damages won by the veterans, Dow persuaded the Reagan government not to ban dioxin and inspectors testified they were ordered to change reports to comply with Dow's wishes.
- Each year in the world, 375,000 people are poisoned, 10,000 of them fatally, by exportation of hazardous and lethal chemicals. According to the World Health Organization, pesticides kill 20,000 people per year in the third world, and cause illness to several hundred thousand. American firms continue to export banned DDT to the third world.

- Much more is lost in money and health through pollution, than crimes of street violence, yet only the latter is defined officially as violence… Why is it a crime for an individual to relieve himself in Puget Sound, when a corporation can do it 24 hours a day? Can you imagine the poor polluting the streams of the rich, and instead of getting charged for it, being paid by the rich through the government for cleaning up their own pollution? That's what corporations do all the time!
- Between 1960 and 1972 Reed Paper Company released 900 kilograms of mercury into river and lake systems of Canada, polluting them to double safe levels. Some fish had sixteen times the safe level. Despite a 1970 government ban, Reed continued to discharge mercury, destroying the native fishing economy, and causing deafness, muteness, blindness, and destruction of brain tissue.
- One text on corporate crime lists over 50 major corporations that have admitted making illegal bribes. Most of them listed the bribes as business expenses, and got a tax deduction for them!
- Clinard and Yeager studied seventeen pharmaceutical companies, and found in two years *every* company violated the law at least once, and two had over twenty violations. Lilly's Oraflex killed 49 in the USA, several hundred worldwide, and caused thousands of nonfatal liver and kidney failures. They were fined $25,000, and made a $3.1 billion profit.
- US Congressional studies in the 1980s put the costs of corporate crime between $174 billion and $200 billion per annum—far more than all other crime and the cost of running the criminal justice system, combined.
- Firestone was aware of extensive failure problems with its 500 belted tires, by 1975, but continued to sell millions. They refused a government request to recall the defective tires, defended their right to keep very critical customer surveys secret, and when the facts leaked out, they dumped the tires on the market at clearance prices! A House of Representatives Committee said the tires had caused "34 known deaths and thousands of accidents."
- Winstrol, found to stunt growth in American children, is sold in Brazil as an appetite stimulant for children. Other products known to cause death in North America and then exported to the third

world include chemical pesticides, birth control devices, baby pacifiers, and a wide variety of legal drugs.
- Nestlé, the biggest criminal of them all, has over the past twenty years killed two to three times as many people as perished in the Holocaust of Hitler. They have done all this knowing that their policy of promoting formula to third-world mothers who cannot afford to buy enough to nourish the babies is starving to death a million babies a year. Nestlé puts all the serial killers in the world's prisons in the shade.

I could go on for a long time with these and other sickening stories. But you may be asking, "What is the point of all this? What does it have to do with our work or with 'Reconciling and Restoring Relationships?' Each of you will have to answer those questions for yourselves, but for me, these stories raise the question of *who* are the most serious criminals in our society, *why* our prisons are full of offenders who could not equal any of these killers, and *how* we can be reconciled to corporations that show no remorse at their continual taking of human life for the sake of maximizing profits.

🏛 QUOTES ON CORPORATE RULE

For we live in an age of corporate rule, and the sooner we face that fact the sooner we can begin to challenge the major obstacles to peace and reconciliation in this world. We are meeting in Mexico, the first country in the world to be forced to its knees and driven into desperate hunger and poverty by the International Monetary Fund's "structural adjustment formula." Structural adjustment guaranteed that investors like me get paid handsome profits, while more and more of the children of Mexico go hungry. Let's contrast the advice of Jesus with the realities of corporate rule today.

Jesus said, "Oh Jerusalem, Jerusalem, how often would I have gathered ye to me, but ye would not"—but corporate rule promotes idolatry of the false gods: money and market

Unlike the New Testament God, the market God is jealous and unforgiving. The penalties are strict: poverty, malnutrition, starvation, death, or as the current lexicon of terrors warns us collectively "Social shock treatments—slashings, axings." The more that sacrifices are demanded, the more humanity is subjugated to the demands of the market, the more terrorist the prescriptions seem to become. In the 1990s, the starvation conditions of a quarter of the world's population and the unemployment of a third, became a daily warning to all that they could be next… "The World Bank referred to the sudden fall into unemployment of 15 percent of Mexico's population, and the fall of real wages by 30 percent, a harsh punishment imposed on workers for the sudden departure of transnational mobile capital from the country. The global market order is not sparing in its punishments. Most people in the world seem to have been disobedient, according to its judgements, because most people are suffering cutbacks to their life incomes and entitlements" (McMurtry, 69).

Jesus said, "Comfort ye my people"—but corporate rule promotes oppression of the poor.

The focus has been on the propertyless—students, the disemployed, and the old—to "be responsible for their burdens on society" and "learn to pay their own way." A society's environmental resources may be polluted, degraded, and exhausted by private corporate exploitation, with no requirement to pay damages or to ensure the prevention of these problems. Those who seek to stop environmental degradation are themselves prosecuted by the state. Rootless corporations may deprive whole communities of their livelihoods and security… This destructive process is neither recognized nor deterred by current law or regulation…

"The world's multiplying Free Trade Zones, particularly the Maquiladora zones on the border of Mexico and the USA, make explicit this absolute refusal of responsibility. These zones grant private foreign corporations the freedom not to pay taxes, not to reinvest capital, not to allow labour unions, not to be subject to national pollution laws, not to pay minimum wages, not to have maximum work days or weeks, not to be bound by any rule to pay for what they receive…" (McMurtry, 116).

"Progress in social responsibility… has been imposed on the market only in the face of fierce resistance from profit-seeking investors… Conventional market doctrine does not in principle rule out any form of free-market profit. It is perfectly consistent with this doctrine that humans are sold as slaves, lethal narcotics and toxins are sold for mass consumption, and lethal weapons are marketed across the world. Slavery was defended for centuries as the very core of private property and right… Unconditional greed is thereby justified as the providential working of the invisible hand" (McMurtry, 117).

"If in the past, it was, 'We must burn your body, but it is for the salvation of your immortal soul,' today it is, 'We must axe your supports of life, but it is for the good of making the economy competitive'" (McMurtry, 22).

Worthlessness of the poor and their sins in market idolatry vs. Jesus' love for the widow, the fallen: "Consider the lilies of the field, they toil not neither do they spin, yet I tell you that Solomon in all his glory was not arrayed as one of these." Contrast this: "A gold-plated toilet in a private jet is worth a thousand times a village well in a poor village in India, because only demand counts, not need. If one does not have money, one has no value, only "dependent want" the opposite of "effective demand." There is nothing to be gained from such beings in the market, only trouble from their attempts to go on living in some other way—by demands for welfare, "scrounging in garbage, panhandling, or other impecunious efforts to survive. Therefore, the poor are pronounced bad. Poverty is the one sin that market theory cannot forgive... This is a principle of badness that admits of degrees. As the world turns, ever more people have less money, even in the world's richest market, where the bottom 40 percent of workers have seen their real wages fall by more than 20 percent in the last two decades. People learn in such a value system to be ashamed of not having enough, or even as much, money as others. They show it on their faces, and in their body movements, and they are gnawed by it within. The less money one has, the less worthy... one is. That is why people are terrified of losing their source of income, and that is why they count money loss as always bad and money gain as always good..." (McMurtry, 161).

⋔ THE WORLD'S PRISONS

This brings us back to where you and I work: the world's prisons. "But another wrong is still greater than having no money, and that is to take money from those who have it. The global market's prisons bulge with the perpetrators of this double, unforgivable sin. White-collar criminals are not such a problem... They still fit into the market ethic as people *with* money, wanting *more* money.... But those who have no money and take it from others who have it, have no redeeming trait in the market morality. Such miscreants are duly incarcerated, and if need be, killed" (McMurtry, 161-162).

Remedy Of Penal Retribution

"Common sense recognizes that there are life needs a society's economy should be geared to meet—for example, the needs of its children and next generations to reproduce in a healthy state. The global market has no measure for these needs. From its value system, staggering growths of child poverty, while profits and stock-market values skyrocket, pose no problem. They only pose a problem... to the extent that more and more children without the means to live may cause "instability for investors." For this, there is the remedy of "getting tough on juvenile crime."

RELEVANCE TO CRIMINAL JUSTICE

Let me try again to explain how all this relates to the Christian responsibility to reconcile and restore relationships, and our work with the penal system. Jesus was a victim of retributive justice, and of self-righteous officials who punished dissidence, just as people who defend the rights of the homeless are attacked today by our justice systems. Recently 200 peaceful protestors camping with our homeless in a "safe park" were arrested and charged by police in Toronto. It's the same story around the world. Jesus was a problem to authorities because he did not reinforce the structural barriers so essential to those deluded by the corruption of power. Those who follow Jesus far enough today always run into the same difficulty, and many of them will be found in our prisons, around the world.

Am I suggesting that the petty thieves in our prisons are there because of some lofty moral principles? No, what they did was wrong, too. But in unravelling the fabric of social injustice in our world, their part is small, compared to the unchallenged continuing crimes of the powerful. So to be reconciled, we have to be truthful, and we have to acknowledge that the vast chasms between rich and poor, the promotion of greed, the worship of money and the market, are the great barriers that stand between us and Christian reconciliation.

We have to reclaim honesty in language: Welfare "reforms," that make Christ's beloved poor more hungry and more homeless are a *de*formation of Christian mercy and justice. "Tenant protection acts" that eject many tenants into the streets are tenant *re*jection acts. "Justice systems" that systematically penalize the poor and racial minorities, to protect wealth and greed, are *in*justice systems.

An indigenous friend of mine says, "Stop calling our systems alternative. We were there before you. Ours is the way of community, yours is the failed alternative."

WRONG GOAL: RETRIBUTION VS. FORGIVENESS

But despite the horrors of the crimes of the powerful, we must not seek revenge toward them either. Control, yes, and new systems that reject greed and embrace compassion. But if we seek revenge toward the powerful who are laying waste this planet and its people, we reduce ourselves to their level. Reconciliation is about ending wrong behaviour, while acting in compassion toward the wrongdoer.

When I first began to study the literature on victim needs, I was surprised to find revenge was not listed as a primary need. From the various studies, I found five core needs of victims. Every one of us experiences traumas, and every trauma makes us feel victims:

- Answers
- Recognition Of Wrong
- Safety
- Restitution
- Meaning Or Significance

When these five needs are met promptly, respectfully, and fully, victims are freed up to walk more easily the wonderful path of forgiveness. When they are not, we make it harder for victims to move forward on that path. So whether we are talking about the typical small criminal you meet in prison, or the big corporate criminals I look at, revenge cannot be the name of the game. As Howard Zehr has said so eloquently, "Instead of asking 'Who done it, and how can we hammer them?' we should be asking, 'Who has been hurt, and how can we heal them?'"

For many years I have been fascinated by forgiveness. I believe it is one of the most fundamental lessons God put us in this world to learn, and it has so many nuances, colours, challenges, sorrows and beauties, it is like a mosaic of all of life. One day I realized something about the word: *fore*-giveness means *giving before* you receive. We are so ready to say, "When the other party comes to me and apologizes, then I will forgive." But most of the forgiving I've had to do is the hard kind: unilateral work, with the other party taking little or no responsibility, and not helping me forward. It's tougher, but it's still very liberating, and every step we take along that road is a step in the Kingdom of God.

⛪ CONCLUSION

I began by saying I was afraid I would offend some of you with this talk. I am also afraid I have not been clear enough about why I had to challenge the sins of corporate rule, in speaking about reconciliation and restoring relationships. There is a frequent chant in demonstrations I have walked in: NO JUSTICE! NO PEACE! NO JUSTICE! NO PEACE!

The prisons in which you and I work are cesspools of injustice. The people who fill them must take responsibility for their sins, but so must we all. Until our criminal justice systems have more to do with Christ's compassionate call to justice and relief to the oppressed, and less to do with maintaining the barriers of racism and classism in our world today, we are not on the path of reconciliation.

If some of us are glutting ourselves with private swimming pools, fancy jets, and costly clothes while the children of others are hungry, we cannot be reconciled. Let us take a step on the road to reconciliation by honestly confronting the injustice and inequality in our world, and daring to challenge it. The Bible enjoins us, "If thine enemy hungers, feed him." But we countenance an economic system where we don't even feed millions of children of our friends!

Beginning with honesty, enriched by compassion and humility, every one of us can be builders of Christ's Kingdom on earth. For we are all, rich and poor, judge and prisoner, priest and follower, children of one loving Father.

> We are one in the spirit, we are one in the Lord,
> We are one in the spirit, we are one in the Lord,
> And we pray that our unity may one day be restored,
> And they'll know we are Christians by our love, by our love,
> Yes they'll know we are Christians by our love.

𝍔 ENDNOTES

This paper was first given in September 1999 in Mexico City at the World Conference of Catholic Prison Chaplains.

𝍔 BIBLIOGRAPHY

John McMurtry, *Unequal Freedoms, The Global Market as an Ethical System*, Toronto: Garamond, 1998.

David C. Korten, *When Corporations Rule the World*, West Hartford, CT: Kumarian Press, 1995.

12

Relocating Law: Making Corporate Crime Disappear

Laureen Snider

The study of corporate crime provides a dramatic illustration of the influence hegemonic class interests exert over law. Many of the essays in this book show how difficult it is to apply the promises of Western legal systems embodied in what is called "the Official Version of Law"—its claims of universalism and equality, the notion that justice is "blind" to class, race and gender; in other words, to workers, people of colour and women, groups with little ideological and/or economic power. But the most cursory attempt to use the Official Version of Law to explain the passage or enforcement of laws governing the antisocial, acquisitive acts of business quickly illustrates the overwhelming, and overt, failure of law to impose meaningful limits on the offences of corporations. State law has consistently, though not exclusively or simplistically, accommodated the interests of Canada's economic elites, particularly where they spoke with unanimity on issues they saw as important. In the last two decades, this has meant that the few laws and weak enforcement mechanisms which were enacted to control corporate crime—themselves the product of a century of struggle by employees, consumers, feminists, environmentalists and others—have been systematically repealed and dismantled.

From Elizabeth Comack, ed., *Locating Law: Race, Class and Gender Connections*, Fernwood Publishing, 1999. Reprinted by permission.

In direct contrast to state law in every other jurisdiction, which has become ever more intrusive and increasingly punitive (with rates of incarceration spiralling for all traditional offences despite falling crime rates (Rothman 1995; Snider 1998)), laws governing corporate crime have become more lax and lenient, and many types of corporate crime have entirely disappeared from the law books.

This disappearance has not happened because corporate crime—defined as "white-collar crimes of omission or commission by an individual or group of individuals in a legitimate formal organization—which have a serious physical or economic impact on employees, consumers or the general public" (Box, 1983: 20)—has ceased to be a problem. The toll of lives lost, injuries sustained, species obliterated, watercourses decimated, savings and pensions destroyed and life chances ruined by the various types of corporate crimes has dramatically increased with the advent of the global marketplace, the spread of capitalist workplaces and production to Third World countries, the new-found dominance of finance capital, and the decline in the power of the nation-state. It has happened, rather, because a successful corporate *counter-revolution* has succeeded in reversing progress towards a more egalitarian society, by taking back "such gains as the working classes have made" (Glasbeek, 1995: 112). In the latter half of the 1970s, the margin of profitability—that is, the surplus value accruing to capital determined by the difference between the all-in costs of production and the all-in profits of production (per unit)—began to decline. From roughly 1980 on, signalled by the election of right-wing governments under Ronald Reagan in the United States and Margaret Thatcher in the United Kingdom, the owners and controllers of capital and their allies in political, media and knowledge elites have waged a highly successful campaign to increase the margin of exploitation, the absolute and relative profitability of capitalist enterprises. This has meant decreasing the incomes and life chances of the bottom 75 to 80 percent of the population to benefit the top one to two percent.

Thus we have observed that, over the last twenty years, rates of inequality have dramatically increased. In the bellweather United States from 1977-89, the top one percent of American families received 60 percent of after-tax income gains while the incomes of the bottom 40 percent went down, in real (absolute) as well as relative dollars (Miyoshi, 1993: 738). In Washington, D.C., for example, the top 20 percent of families today have incomes 28 times larger than the poorest 20 percent. The bottom quintile take home an average of $5290 per year, nearly $2000 less than they received 20 years ago (*Globe and Mail,* December 23, 1997, A13). In Canada, between 1977 and 1991, the average total family income for the bottom fifth of families stood at $17,334 in 1996, a 6.1 percent share of the national income, the lowest in two decades, while the average income of the top fifth rose to $114,874, a 40.6 percent share, the highest in two decades (Statistics Canada, 1997). Meanwhile the size, power and profitability of corporations has dramatically increased—the total wealth of the world's 385 billionaires equals the combined incomes of 45 percent of the world's population or 2.3 billion people (United Nations, 1996). Corporate salaries, perks and bonuses totalling $3 million a year for Chief Executive Officers are not uncommon in Canada; in the United States CEOs routinely get double and triple this (*Globe and Mail*, May 5, 1998: B16; June 22, 1998: A1). World-wide, the top 20 percent of the world's population increased their share of total global wealth from 70 percent in 1960 to 85 percent in 1991, and the share "enjoyed" by the poorest 20 percent actually *declined* from 1960 to 1991, falling from 2.3 percent to 1.4 percent (United Nations 1996). "The richest 200 largest corporations [now] have more economic clout than the poorest four-fifths of humanity" (Dobbin, 1998: 74-5).

Getting rid of laws to control the acquisitive and antisocial acts of business, in general, and corporations, in particular, has been an essential component of this counter-revolutionary reversal. Historically, one of the main tasks of the nation-state has been protecting citizens from the harm caused by corporations. This was, however, a duty that capitalist states undertook with the utmost reluctance. Typically such laws were passed only after major environmental or industrial disasters made some sort of state response imperative (Snider, 1991 and 1993). Thus, it is not surprising that national governments in the 1980s and 90s, facing deficits and declining revenues (caused, in large part, by another successful corporate initiative, this one reducing the tax rates of corporations and the rich), have been quick to repeal laws which restrict and criminalize potentially profitable acts and thereby annoy the corporate sector. For corporate crimes—ignoring costly regulations on mine safety, not paying overtime wages, marketing drugs with harmful side-effects, conspiring to increase the price of necessary goods—are always committed in order to increase profits or prevent losses (and they usually do). By abandoning efforts to prevent, monitor or sanction such acts, the nation-state signals its acquiescence to corporate (and corporatist) agendas and acknowledges its inability (or disinclination) to protect its own citizens from the predations of the global marketplace. In the race to achieve maximal profitability, destroying profit threatening measures such as environmental restrictions and the minimum wage shows that a country is, in the immortal words of former Prime Minister Brian Mulroney, "open for business." It signals that a century of struggle to use the laws of the nation-state to force capital to meet certain standards of behaviour and impose limits on the exploitation of human and natural resources has been abandoned.

This essay has two objectives: first, to document the disappearance of state law over corporate crime; and, second, to examine its significance. What are the implications for those who seek to force Western legal systems to live up to their promises of universalism and equality, their obligation to protect citizens from the harmful antisocial acts of senior executives in transnational corporations as well as biker gangs? And what does this disappearance say about the relations between state law and capital, or about the potential of law to challenge the corporate counter-revolution and promote a more equitable distribution of the spoils of capitalism in the developed world?[1]

ᨎ THE DISAPPEARANCE OF CORPORATE CRIME

Item:

Bolar Pharmaceutical Company admitted to selling adulterated and mislabelled drugs, and lying to investigators from the federal (U.S.) Food and Drug Administration about the quality and origin of the medicines (*New York Times*, March 24, 1991: 26; *Orlando Sentinel*, February 28: A17).

Mer/29 (triparanol), a drug developed by Richardson Merrell to reduce cholesterol levels, went on sale in United States in 1960. When skin damage, cataracts and changes in reproductive organs were reported in patients, investigation revealed that Richardson Merrell knew about these side effects (through animal tests done in its own labs) but suppressed the damaging evidence (Clarke, 1990: 205).

Every year thousands of Canadians suffer adverse drug reactions; ineffective, impure and unsafe drugs cause much human anguish and cost millions of dollars. From the Dalkon Shield (an intrauterine device that caused miscarriages, sterility, pelvic infection and several deaths) to the Meme breast implant (a silicon gel coated with polyurethane foam that decomposed under certain conditions to produce a dangerous chemical, finally banned by Health and Welfare Canada in 1992), to defective heart valves and surgical gloves (more than half of the latex medical and surgical gloves failed quality tests), unmonitored, unassessed medical devices have "killed, mutilated, electrocuted, blinded, burned and injured hundreds, if not thousands, of Canadians (Regush, 1991: 9). Every year hundreds of new medical devices, products ranging from heart valves to incubators, are brought into Canada, a business worth more than $2 billion with 300,000 medical devices produced by some 6595 manufacturing companies, the vast majority in Third World countries (Regush, 1991: 16).

However, in the summer of 1997 Health and Welfare Canada closed down its research laboratories, known as the Bureau of Drug Research, eliminating 68 jobs and saving the federal government $2 million (*Globe and Mail,* July 11, 1997: A1). Laboratories and programs in the food directorate, which sets standards for acceptable levels of chemical residues or growth hormones in food, have also been cut. The Bureau of Drug Research had been the agency responsible for investigating the safety and effectiveness of drugs sold in Canada, and for monitoring problems after medications were approved. Drug safety will henceforth depend on the validity of research conducted by pharmaceutical companies, and their truthfulness in reporting adverse findings and risks. This research is either conducted by scientists employed by these companies, or on contract to them.

Item:

Taking Stock, a report released by the NAFTA Commission for Environmental Cooperation, identified seven Canadian facilities in the top 50 polluters in North America. A recent study of Environment Canada's Environmental Assessment process called it "a disaster." Standards and penalties are absent, and companies seeking Cabinet approval for proposed developments (such as mining the Bedford Sea or logging old growth forests) are free to shop for whatever industry-friendly scientists are available. The lack of standards allows scientists to "sell out to the highest bidder" (Nikiforuk, 1997: 17).

Canada has admitted its failure to meet the international obligations it agreed to at the Earth Summit in Brazil in 1992. Canada's output of greenhouse gases will *increase* by ten percent from 1990-2000. Already it appears that commitments to environmental protection made at Kyoto in

December 1997 will not honoured (*Globe and Mail,* August 15, 1997: A-14; *Globe and Mail*, October 4: D1; *Toronto Star*, April 11, 1998: E-5; Gallon 1996).

Less than nine percent of Alberta's boreal forest remains; it is disappearing as fast as the Amazon rain forest (*Globe and Mail*, June 22, 1998: A1).

However, in 1993-94 Environment Canada lost 30 percent of its budget under the *Regulatory Efficiency Act* passed by the federal Liberal government. In 1995-96 the budget was chopped from $705 million to $507 million. Staff was slashed from 10,000 to under 4000 people, and in 1997 Environment was demoted, from a senior to junior ministry (a loss of prestige and clout, plus staff and budget). In the seven year period from 1988-95 the Department launched a total of 63 prosecutions for environmental offences for the whole of Canada, an average of 7.2 per year.

Item:

Owners and operators of nearly half of all underground coal mines in the United States have systematically tampered with coal dust samples sent to federal safety inspectors and monitored to control black lung disease. More than 5000 incidents of sampling fraud have been discovered thus far (*Washington Post*, April 4, 1991: 1).

Approximately 4000 coal miners die every year from black lung disease, 4.5 percent of the workforce have contracted it (Cullen et al, 1987: 69).

In 1992, the Westray Mine in Pictou County, Nova Scotia exploded, killing 26 miners. Subsequent investigations showed that the owners of Westray routinely violated safety laws and failed to make essential repairs. Inspectors for the province of Nova Scotia provided advance notice of impending visits, routinely overlooked minor and major law-breaking, and generally adopting the perspective of management, whose goal was to minimize the costs of production. Workers who reported unsafe conditions were seen, by both government and industry (and sometimes by their peers as well) as malcontents and rabble-rousers (Richard, 1997; Comish, 1993). By July of 1998, all of the 52 non-criminal and three remaining criminal charges laid against the owners and managers of the mine and the government inspectors had been dropped (*Globe and Mail*, July 1, 1998: A1; Jobb 1998).

Nova Scotia, and virtually every other province, has consistently cut the budgets and workforce of regulatory agencies charged with protecting the health and safety of employees. Self-regulation, a system which asks workers and managers to regulate themselves, with minimal government oversight, has become the norm in virtually every industry (Tucker, 1995; Walters et al., 1995; Noble, 1995). Between 1976 and 1993, almost 16,700 people died from work-related causes, an average of more than two deaths per day. The average annual rate of seven per 100,000 (1988-93 data, all industries) is four times greater than the average homicide rate (which hovers around 2.2 per 100,000). Two-hundred and eighty-one of every 100,000 miners died as a result of their work in the 1988-93 period (Statistics Canada, 1996; *Globe and Mail*, August 10, 1996: A6).

Item:

British Columbia has the highest fatality rates in Canada for on-the-job deaths in construction, forestry, and transportation, with deaths per 100,000 double and triple those of other provinces (Statistics Canada, 1996*)*.

On July 17, 1997 British Columbia bowed to heavy, unrelenting business pressure and withdrew Bill 44, a law that would have increased the power of workers to refuse to work in unsafe conditions. The Bill aimed at improving workplace safety by creating new rights for workers in service industries and strengthening laws in other areas. However, campaigns orchestrated by the Coalition of BC Business charged that the proposed law would scare off investment and increase (their) costs. The NDP government was vilified in the business press as a "crank government" conspiring with "Big Labour" to destroy small business and "enslave the private sector" (*Globe and Mail,* July 17, 1997: B2).

Item:

Taking Stock, a report released by the NAFTA Commission for Environmental Cooperation, identifies Ontario as the third-biggest polluting jurisdiction in North America, behind only Tennessee and Texas in contributing to air, water and land pollution. Ontario Hydro dumped at least 1800 tonnes of heavy metals into Lake Ontario in the last 25 years. Smog alone kills 1800 people per year in Ontario (*Globe and Mail*, July 30, 1997; also January 13, 1997: A15; July 30, 1997: A3; August 19, 1997: A1; June 22, 1998: A1).

However, fines against polluters in Ontario declined to $955,000 in 1997, the lowest in more than a decade, less than one third of the 1995 amount. Since 1995 the province's Environment Ministry has lost 45 percent of its budget and 32 percent of its staff; the allied department of Natural Resources has dropped 19 and 30 percent respectively (*Globe and Mail*, June 22, 1998: A1). The number of charges laid against polluters has been cut in half since the Progressive Conservatives took office in Ontario, dropping from 1640 in 1994 to 724 in 1996. The average fines on polluting companies dropped from a high of $3,633,095 in 1992 to $1,204,034 in 1997. According to Premier Mike Harris, many of Ontario's rules frighten away investment because they are "extreme" (*Globe and Mail*, November 14, 1996).

Item:

Two hundred people died when the appropriately named "*Herald of Free Enterprise*," owned and operated by Townsend Car Ferries Ltd., went down in the English Channel in 1987. The accident occurred when the ferry left the dock before the bow doors were properly secured. Subsequent investigation showed that there was no means by which those who piloted the ship, on the bridge, could communicate with those responsible for closing the doors in the bow. Requests from employees for a system of signal lights to remedy this dangerous situation were rejected by the company in "authoritarian and contemptuous terms" (Clarke, 1990: 203-4). Such a system would reduce profits and increase costs. Investigations showed that the system would have added less than 1 percent to the price of a ticket.

The subsequent legal report concluded that "a company could not in law be indicted for manslaughter" (Queen's Bench Divisional Court, October 6, 1987). In 1990, the British government awarded a peerage to the Chairman of the company that owned the "*Herald of Free Enterprise*," elevating him from Sir to Lord (Pearce 1993).

Item:

On Sunday December 2, 1984, a choking cloud of toxic fumes from the Union Carbide pesticides plant leaked through Bhopal, India. Methyl isocyanate and hydrogen cyanide gases burned the lungs of all who breathed it. By Monday morning more than 2000 people were dead. In addition, tens of thousands were left with wrecked lungs and impaired vision, and subsequently developed cataracts, tuberculosis, breathlessness and reproductive disorders. More than 5000 have died in the intervening years (*Guardian Weekly*, August 30, 1998: 24).

Subsequent investigation found that Union Carbide, with declining markets for carbamate pesticides, cut costs by employing fewer staff, reducing the training time offered new employees and cutting back on plant maintenance. Plant instrumentation and back-up systems were inadequate, workers were not properly trained or monitored, and the refrigeration plant was not powerful enough to cool the gases stored there.

The company attributed the accident to incompetent employees and accused the Indian government of negligence (for failing to enforce its own regulations—which Union Carbide strove mightily to avoid!). On February 14, 1989, a deal was negotiated with the government of India (not with the victims) to pay $470 million in damages. India accepted the settlement even though it had originally requested the "anything but excessive" sum of $3.3 billion, roughly comparable to the $2.9 billion received by some 195,000 victims of A.H. Robbins' Dalkon Shield (an intrauterine device deemed responsible for "only" seventeen deaths (Pearce and Tombs, 1998: 211). However, the Dalkon Shield case was heard in American courts, known for more generous settlements, and the victims were primarily First World, white women. Union Carbide fought hard (and successfully) to keep the Bhopal case out of North American or European courts. A deal was ultimately negotiated with the Indian government, it gave Union Carbide immunity from all future claims. In addition, the corporation received a guarantee that no criminal charges would (ever) be laid against it.

It is no secret that corporations set up plants in the Third World to get away from regulation, because obeying regulatory laws adds to the cost of production. The chemical industry spends less than half as much on pollution and safety control in its overseas operations as it does in the United States (Pearce and Tombs, 1998).

Corporate crime, then, causes injury and death. It is also incredibly costly, defrauding hundreds of thousands of people of millions of dollars. The average amount stolen annually by bank robbers makes up well under five percent of the totals stolen by white-collar and corporate criminals (Snider, 1993: 4-5; Reiman, 1994). Some recent examples of the harm done and losses incurred in financial corporate crimes are outlined below.

Item:

With the advent of global capitalism and the new-found dominance of financial capital, trillions of dollars circulate daily throughout the stock exchanges and currency markets of the world. Individual traders in these markets buy and sell thousands of shares each day, seeking to maximize their own profits and increase their personal fortunes. Traders, essentially unregulated actors, have the power to bankrupt individuals, companies and countries—and have done so, most recently by driving the value of the Russian ruble down 90 percent in less than a week. In the last five years, Indonesia, Japan and many Asian countries, and Mexico have suffered similar fates. The decision to "set capital free" and facilitate millions of untaxed, unregulated trades has destroyed the standard of living of hundreds of thousands of people in many parts of the world, producing starvation and revolution in some countries, the destruction of personal savings, destitution and penury in others.

Much of the harm done by such actors is not defined as criminal. However, scams such as insider trading, falsifying records, failure to disclose and outright fraud (as in the alleged "salting" of gold samples taken from the Busang site at Bre-X, inflating the value of Bre-X stock by millions of dollars and fleecing countless of innocent investors) have been criminalized in many countries. While most stock market traders are closely allied with multinational capital, "rogue traders" have the power to destroy centuries-old institutions, as Nick Leeson did at Barings Bank in the United Kingdom or Yasuo Hamanaka at Sumitomo Incorporated in Japan. Financial corporate crime has gone global: the BCCI bank, which imploded causing an estimated $15 billion in losses, was organised to be off-shore everywhere. Corporations have always attempted to incorporate in jurisdictions with the lowest taxes and the fewest regulations, but the BCCI shows that it is possible to avoid all nation-state restrictions.

The systematic removal of regulatory controls over financial institutions and stock exchanges has been a cherished component of those leading the corporate counter-revolution. Thus, when the Reagan government took office in the United States in 1980, it repealed regulations and fired regulators responsible for overseeing stock exchanges, such as the federal Security and Exchange Commission (SEC). Staff at the SEC fell by 300, while the number of securities requiring monitoring doubled from 1981-86. In the financial arena, a series of restrictions on institutions known as Savings and Loans companies were removed, leading to the most costly series of corporate crimes ever, with estimated losses topping $500 billion (see below). This caused some momentary re-regulation; however in 1994 the U.S. House of Representatives again loosened controls on banks, and in 1995 it tabled legislation to gut the SEC once again (Calavita et al., 1997).

Item:

The S & L Fraud, the collapse of the Savings and Loans companies in the United States, occurred when laws limiting the kinds of investments these companies could make, and laws setting out minimum capital requirements to be maintained, were repealed in the counter-revolutionary de-regulatory drive of the 1980s. The problem was compounded when federal insurance on losses was retained while federal regulators were removed.

The most common frauds were of three types: *Hot Deals*: The owners of Savings and Loans institutions engaged in land flips, nominee loans and reciprocal lending (huge sums were "lent" in return for deposits). *Looting*: Owners siphoned off funds, paid themselves huge salaries, took expensive holidays or bought yachts, women, [2] limousines and other "luxury" goods from company money. *FalsifyingRecords*: False audits created the appearance that the companies were well managed and fiscally sound. The notion that such behaviour is rare in business is put to the test by the fact that every major accounting firm in the United States but one was implicated in the production of false, dishonest, misleading accounts.

Although estimated losses exceed $500 billion, the mean loss per institution was put at $12,420,065; the estimated cost to each American household at $5000. Two-hundred and eighty-four Savings and Loans institutions went bankrupt, the bulk of them in Texas and California. Thousands of individuals lost their life savings, with most of the "little guys" recovering only a fraction of their money back—the bulk of the federal insurance went to compensate "secured" creditors, typically large (corporate) institutions (Calavita et al., 1997; Zey 1993; *New York Times,* June 10, 1990; *Observer*, April 8, 1990).

Item:

Competition/Combines Offences are anti-competitive practices designed to inflate profits through such deceptive practices as conspiracy to restrict trade, mergers and monopolies, predatory pricing, price discrimination, resale price maintenance and refusal to supply. False Advertising, an allied offence, refers to deceptive trade practices such as inflated claims about a product's effectiveness, or misleading consumers by misrepresenting a product's regular price as a sales price.

Combines, mergers and monopolies were outlawed in Canada's first piece of corporate crime legislation, the Combines Investigation Act, passed in 1889. It was regularly amended and enlarged (though never effectively enforced) from that time until 1976.

Shortly after its election in 1968, the Liberal government under Pierre Trudeau decided to strengthen the legislation and commissioned a white paper, the *Interim Report on Competition Policy.* The paper caused "all hell to break loose" (according to Ian Clark, the Deputy Minister of the Department responsible at the time), as business and its spokespeople lined up to condemn the government's "radical" proposals for reform (which were really very modest). Three Ministers of Consumer and Corporate Affairs were appointed and deposed in short order, several versions of a bill, each weaker than the last, were put forth but none passed.

In January of 1976, the legislation was split in two, all efforts to reform laws on restraint of trade were dropped. An amended act was finally passed which called for increasing maximum fines for False Advertising, extended Price-Fixing regulations to cover services (such as real estate or lawyers) as well as products, and prohibited sales practices such as Bait and Switch, Bid-Rigging and Pyramid Selling.

In 1984, the new Conservative government under Brian Mulroney officially declared Canada "open for business," and a "blue ribbon" committee was appointed to recommend revisions in legislation on mergers and monopolies.

The Committee consisted entirely of representatives of (big) business, from the Canadian Manufacturers Association, the Canadian Chamber of Commerce, the Business Council on National Issues and, added later, the Grocery Products Manufacturers of Canada and the Canadian Bar Association. No labour or consumer groups were represented on the Committee (but the Deputy Minister swore that the Consumers Association of Canada and "interested academics" were "also consulted").

In 1986, new legislation was passed in the House of Commons, abolishing the Combines Investigation Act. Its replacement, the Competition Act, had a very different mission: "to improve and facilitate corporate operations" *not* to control or sanction conspiracies to restrict trade, drive up prices or engage in monopolistic, predatory practices. To this end:
- Criminal sanctions were *removed* from merger/monopoly sections.
- "The Public Interest" was *removed* as a criterion or directive to be used in evaluating a proposed merger.
- A "compliance-centred" approach was adopted to deal with "clients" (who were no longer "offenders" suspected of "crimes").[3] The new goal of law was to provide a stable and predictable climate for business, with the promotion of business prosperity made key.
- Prosecutions for conspiracy, discriminatory and predatory pricing, misleading or deceptive practices and price maintenance dropped from 37 in 1982-84 and 36 in 1984-86 to 23 in 1986-88. By 1995-96, all regional offices of the Competition Bureau were terminated; the number of inquiries commenced dropped from 82 to eight in the

four year period from 1991-92 to 1995-96, the number of cases referred for prosecution dropped from 55 to seven, prosecutions declined from 44 to seven, and convictions dropped from 43 to fourteen (Canada 1997: 36). In the spring of 1998, a bill was introduced to further decriminalize misleading advertising and deceptive marketing practices (*Globe and Mail,* May 5, 1998: B3; Canada 1998: 3).

- From 1986-89, 402 merger files were opened, 26 "monitored," seven abandoned, nine mergers were restructured, five went to Competition Tribunal and two were under appeal. By 1996-97, the Competition Bureau reviewed a total of 319 mergers, but only 23 were deemed problematic enough to require follow-up. There are 369 slated for review in 1997-98 (*Globe and Mail*, March 30, 1998: B4), a record the aforementioned *Globe* decries as "Cracking Down" by "Competition Cops" (Milner, 1998) (*Sources*: Snider, 1993 and 1978; Stanbury, 1977, 1986-7 and 1988; Canada, 1989; Varrette, 1985; Goldman, 1989).

Monopolistic markets have become a fixture of the developed world. They mean that the power of capital is increasingly concentrated in the hands of a small number of transnational corporations with monopolistic control over the life-style and life-chances of most of the world's citizens. No representative citizenry elect the owner-controllers and, increasingly, no public body regulates their actions or behaviour. Fifty-one of the largest economies in today's world are not countries but corporations (Dobbin, 1998; McQuaig, 1997). In Canada in 1991, a mere ten corporations (excluding banks) made up more than one-fifth of the Gross National Product. (Many are transnationals such as General Motors of Canada, Chrysler, Ford and Imperial Oil; others such as Bell Canada, Noranda, George Weston and Thomson are nominally controlled in Canada.) Monopolistic, mammoth companies do not provide a commensurate number of jobs—the top 200 transnational corporations, with sales accounting for 28.3 percent of the world's GDP, employ less than one percent of its workforce (Dobbin, 1998: 76). Nor do they pay a commensurate share of taxe—Nortel, for example, received "at least" $880 million in federal research and development tax credits, but paid a mere 0.4 percent of its total revenue back in income tax; as of 1996 it owed $213 million in deferred taxes (Dobbin, 1998: 78).

WHY DOES IT MATTER?

Thus far, this essay has documented the harm caused by corporate crime and the virtual abandonment of attempts to proscribe or sanction it. The nation-state has, in effect, given up the struggle to control corporate criminals through law. The disappearance of corporate crime matters—but not because state law was ever particularly successful in punishing it. Because of the power of the perpetrators and the collective weakness of the victims, laws governing corporate crime have always been full of loopholes, regulating authorities starved for funds, convictions few and far between, and sanctions totally incommensurate with the damage inflicted.[4] It matters because this retreat is part of an ideological retrenchment whereby the ability to censure, monitor or signal disapproval of the antisocial acts of capital is being lost. So is legal recognition of the fact that corporate acts cause harm. It matters because "the growing incapacity of sovereign states to control the behaviour of corporations" (Reiss, 1993: 190) is a created event, not an inevitable, unalterable fact (McQuaig, 1997).

And it matters because the data to counter heavily promoted business claims that corporate crimes are no more than one-time accidents, committed by "good citizens" rather than "criminals," disappear. This argument is both beside the point and incorrect. Beside the point because many traditional offences are equally unintentional, but intention is no defence *except* where the crimes of corporations are at issue. Drunk drivers who "didn't mean to hurt anyone" face charges of criminal negligence and long prison terms if convicted. Incorrect because evidence of malice aforethought is plentiful in the annals of corporate crime: the executives in Ford who calculated that it was cheaper to pay off burn victims and bereaved families than to fix Pinto cars designed so that they exploded in flames when hit from the rear (Cullen et al., 1987); the thrift owners in the Savings and Loan debacle who bought companies in order to loot their assets and rob those who had trusted their savings to these men (Calavita et al., 1997); the insurance companies that exploited Aboriginal religious beliefs on the need to return the dead to their ancestral lands to sell fraudulent burial policies (Braithwaite, 1995); the pharmaceutical companies that hid test results showing new drugs as unsafe, ineffective or dangerous (Braithwaite, 1984); the coal mine owners who tampered with coal dust samples (Braithwaite, 1985b); or the manufacturers of asbestos who knowingly exposed employees, their families and neighbourhoods to asbestosis and similar cancers, systematically hiding test results and scientific studies from them (Gunningham, 1984; for still other examples, see: Coleman, 1985; Green, 1994; Punch, 1996).

Looking historically, getting laws passed to proscribe the crimes of business has always required, in every country where this has occurred, decades of struggle. Resistance, publicity, political organization and public education were among the tactics used in the nineteenth century by a wide array of interests and groups. The business class fiercely resisted the notion that any of its profit-seeking activities could be considered immoral or criminal. It balked at the principle of state law overseeing business practice, seeing this as an abrogation of the near-sovereign rights of ownership then enshrined in English common law. Those who owned the workplace and the tools of production were assumed to have the right to determine everything that went on that workplace. So if the owner did not wish to pay more than ten cents a day, put guards on machinery, provide safety equipment, lunch breaks or clean, breathable air, the state had no right to interfere, the worker no right to protest (Paulus, 1974; Carson, 1970 and 1980). When reformers ("rabble rousers" and "communists," to the employer classes) began complaining about the number of workers losing arms, legs and lives to unsafe machinery, about employees dying before they were twenty of lung diseases brought on by fibre-filled air in unventilated workplaces, or about women too weakened by eighteen hour work-days in filthy factories to reproduce, discipline or supervise their children (Ursel, 1992; Marcus, 1974; Tucker, 1990), those in government were in a quandary. State policy throughout the nineteenth century was to ignore the costs of capitalism (which state legislators neither experienced nor saw, being mainly from privileged backgrounds themselves), celebrate its accomplishments, and use law to punish the feckless, inebriate and larcenous—in other words, the poor and powerless. (The use and abuse of opium or marijuana by "inferior" races, prostitution, delinquency and the genetic inferiority of "criminals" were all popular targets for criminalization.) But, by the latter half of the century, it was becoming politically dangerous for legislators to ignore the mounting evidence of corporate carnage, when (male) workers were getting the right to vote and socialist notions were gaining adherents. It is also true that many parliamentarians—and some employers as well—were sincerely concerned about the pace of social change and the suffering of the "deserving" poor.

In the province of Ontario, for example, industrialization grew rapidly from 1870 to 1900, bringing concomitant increases in the size of firms, the length of the work day and the demands placed on employees. As 60 hour work weeks became common, workers began to complain about the speed and intensity of production and the risks they were forced to take. Women and children workers became the focus of reform campaigns by upper-middle-class feminist and religious groups, because they endured the same conditions as men for even lower wages and were often subjected to sexual harassment as well (Ursel, 1992). (While sexual harassment was neither named nor criminalized at that time, it was nonetheless a fact of life for working women, who were shamed, blamed and fired if they dared to complain.) Injuries and deaths on the job were common, but employees had no redress except the common law right to sue their employers for damages. Since law suits required time, effort and money, and workers laboured sixteen hours a day for wages too low to cover their daily necessities, few cases were brought to court. The few that were launched were generally unsuccessful, because law at the time presumed that, by "voluntarily" accepting a job, workers had also accepted the working conditions attached to that job, thereby forfeiting their right to object to these conditions (Austin and Dietrich, 1990).

Changing this mind set and law took decades of demonstrations and government inquiries. A few muckraking media published pictures of mutilated workers and starving widows, a few crusading pastors wrote religious tracts and preached sermons on the human costs of industrialization, workers demonstrated and first wave feminists pointed out the toll on women's reproductive and social health. Ontario's first Factory Act was finally passed in 1884, two decades after the first Factory Acts became law in Great Britain (Carson, 1970 and 1980). The immediate stimulus was a Conservative Member of Parliament, who became concerned that the employment of working class women and children was causing a decline in their morals. Eventually, the solid and impenetrable opposition of employers crumpled. The most prosperous industrialists, members of the Canadian Manufacturers Association, came to see that the National Policy (the tariff imposed on all imported goods) meant that major producers like themselves would still be able to charge high prices and realize high profits. They began to see legislation as inevitable and switched from blanket resistance to compromise, with an emphasis on shaping the upcoming legislation in their own interests. This tactic resulted in a number of concessions to accommodate employer demands. Thus the initial Factory Act covered only factories, not shops or other workplaces; it provided a ten hour day and a six day week, and it set limits on compulsory overtime rather than forbidding it. Employers were directed to allow workers one hour per day for lunch, and were obliged to provide a room in which to eat it. Washrooms became mandatory, and women were to be provided with separate facilities from men. The employment of boys under twelve and girls under fourteen was banned, and fourteen to eighteen year-old girls were banned from jobs where their health was likely to suffer permanent injury. (Presumably it was fine for boys to be permanently injured, they were not seen as vehicles of reproduction.) Rudimentary ventilation and guards on certain types of machinery became mandatory (Tucker, 1990). Over time, these laws were strengthened and augmented, and conditions in the workplaces of Ontario gradually improved.[5]

This does not mean that most employers or major business organizations ever supported this kind of legislation. Small entrepreneurs and retailers were particularly vehement in their opposition because they, unlike the big guys, were often unable to pass increased costs on to customers or clients. In competitive markets, they either had to operate more efficiently or forego some of their profits, and the National Policy tariff just increased their costs, forcing them to purchase more expensive manufactured products made here. And sizeable segments of the business class continued to object to any and all government interference with their heretofore unchallenged right to determine the conditions and rewards of employment in "their" workshops. They accused politicians of selling out: "Employers felt that virtually the whole legislative programme put forward by organized labour and any favourable political response to it represented an attack on business interests" (Bliss, 1974: 123). And, "when Parliament began to make highly visible responses to labour pressure after 1900—establishing a Department of Labour, founding the "Labour Gazette," introducing fair wage provisions into federal work contracts, and giving a friendly hearing to Bills to institute the eight-hour day on Dominion public works— employers were outraged at how politicians had abandoned impartiality for fear of offending organized labour and in order to secure patronage" (Bliss, 1974: 120). (Note that government was deemed to be acting with "impartiality" when it supported the interests of business; it was "biased" or partial whenever it did not.) Every concession to employees or consumers was seen as a backward move, an act which threatened the productivity and competitive position of the capitalist class. And the continued prosperity of this class, then as now, was deemed synonymous with the prosperity of the nation.

It is therefore no surprise that the victories of employee classes were partial and fragile, or that failures to get laws passed were more common than successes. In the early days in Canada, spokesmen for the railroads argued against safety laws by telling the Royal Labour Commission that running along the tops of moving freight cars to apply brakes by hand was only dangerous when workers were careless or "not looking where they are going" (Bliss, 1974: 59). The railway companies also argued that, since the employees decide when to stop the train and the employees know that applying the brakes requires them to climb onto the roof of the cars, how can the railway companies be responsible if they fall off and get killed? It was their decision to put on the brakes in the first place! In addition, they "knew about the hazards when they took the job" (Bliss, 1974: 59). In the United States, "between 1879 and 1906, 140 pure food and drug bills were presented in [the U.S.] Congress and all failed because of the importance of the persons who would be affected" (Sutherland, 1977: 45). And dozens of attempts to pass laws to protect consumers or workers were simply abandoned because of the overwhelming size and power of the corporate lobby. Such failures to legislate have cost billions of dollars and hundreds, sometimes thousands, of lives (Coleman, 1985: 151-92).

But the point is that governments did not always cave in to business interests. Over the years, these struggles created a new consensus about permissible standards of exploitation, a consensus backed by state laws that spelled out the minimum conditions employers in Canada should provide, and the minimum standards Canadian employees should accept. These new standards did not come about automatically, or because employers suddenly decided to become "responsible employers." This does not mean all employers were unethical or lacked moral standards: their behaviour was not seen, by themselves or by mainstream political or religious authorities of the time, as irresponsible or unethical. Employing ten year olds in unhealthy workplaces for sixteen hours a day *was* ethical (as well as legal), because the ideological struggle which redefined the limits of ethical corporate behaviour was still in its infancy. This process of redefinition continued throughout the twentieth century, spurred by the growth of democratic socialism and the invention of the post-war welfare state. It resulted in a gradual improvement in the ethical and legal standards in the workplace and beyond—the progress now put at risk by the corporate counter-revolution.

The disappearance of corporate crime, then, matters because it has important ideological and symbolic effects. Criminalizing an act is a censure (Sumner, 1983). Decriminalizing conveys the opposite message: that monopolizing the banking business or owning all the newspapers in a province or failing to maintain safe workplaces or pay employees a "decent" wage is no longer seen as a social problem. The perpetrators of such acts are henceforth inappropriate targets for social censure. They are not expected to "make amends" or "be ashamed of themselves" because they have not done anything blameworthy. The ideological process which shapes the social distribution of blame has exonerated these kinds of harmful acts and, therefore, the actors responsible for them.

When the exploitative acts committed by employers against employees are no longer identified or named, let alone measured, monitored or sanctioned, they no longer "count" as crime. This is true literally as well as symbolically, and it has important implications. Making truth claims in modern society is contingent upon the ability to name a phenomenon and study it scientifically. This means that a school of knowledge claims can be developed around the phenomenon, it can be studied by "experts" with advanced training in a "discipline," and described in ways that generate a set of claims to create what counts as knowledge in modern society (Foucault, 1979; Ericson and Haggerty, 1997). The initial stage of the process though which sexual harassment gained credibility as a social problem, for example, involved naming and defining it. At this point, its frequency could be documented, its incidence and effects statistically described and analysed. Then state law was created, and calls were made to secure increased public resources. Media attention, "survivor" accounts and celebrity cases, important components of shaming, blaming and punishing this new class of offenders, appeared.

The exact opposite process is underway with corporate crime. Removing state law, decriminalizing and deregulating, makes a behaviour less visible, more elusive. With the disappearance of state law, the victims of these acts (no longer "offences") have no one to whom to complain, no state body from which to seek redress or justice. With no official body to validate complaints or record the frequency of occurrence, incidence data are no longer available to researchers or activists. Corporate crime loses the sharp edge of legal definition, the public resources and the social attribution of blame that accompany acts signified as crime.

Losing state definition directly affects the job of the researcher or scientist, the knowledge professionals responsible for affixing the stamp of legitimacy to social problems. For corporate crime, these are the criminologists, sociologists and law professors who originally "discovered" and named white collar crime, then classified corporate crime as an important dimension of it. For these researchers, data sources, always problematic, have become more so. Major studies of corporate crime have always been based on the records of regulatory agencies or state departments of criminal justice (Shapiro, 1985: 181; Edelhertz, 1970). Information on the number of enforcement actions, the sanctions imposed, the decisions of courts and regulatory commissions, or the sentences imposed by criminal or administrative courts have constituted the most affordable and socially legitimate evidence available (for example, Wheeler et al., 1982; Clinard and Yeager, 1980).[6] The only alternative to state data requires researchers to generate their own data, a Herculean task. Not only does it require a massive research budget, it requires access to information. The average researcher has no way of forcing busy, high status, socially important and politically powerful actors or corporate bodies to reveal practices and predilections they have every reason to hide. With government regulations gone, and self-regulation, market incentives and risk assessment replacing state officials and monitoring agencies, the amount and the availability of official, accredited data have dramatically declined. Determining the "dark figure" of corporate crime, assessing the "actual" number of offences which have occurred and documenting the harm they have done have all become more difficult.[7]

Securing the resources, access and data to study the offences by employees against employers, on the other hand, have all become easier. Private foundations and consultants are competing for funds to study and document "white-collar crimes" of this kind, the work of naming, blaming and punishing the crimes of employees is flourishing. A prime example would be the discovery of a new "crime" committed by employees against employers. The newly designated "Theft of Time" problematises unauthorized time spent away from the primary work task by employees. Advances in technology have made it possible to measure exactly how long employees spend in the washroom, whether they take twenty minutes for coffee instead of fifteen, or talk to customers longer they should (time-management experts have charts specifying how many seconds employees "should" spend to complete a sale or find a phone number). Thus, it is now possible to study and criminalize a new sub-category of employee-offenders, identify those most likely to commit this crime, and investigate the causes, incidence and effects of their delinquency.[8] Soon there will probably be a test employers can administer to weed out "high risk" employees, an addition to the plentiful array of screening tools presently employed (like those designed to test for drug use and "honesty"). Knowledge is also being created on other newly discovered employee offences. New computer crimes, for example, such as gaining "unauthorized entry" into corporate or government databases and "theft of software" (copying software "owned" by corporations onto one's own machine) are two that have been recently criminalized. Massive public resources are now expended in passing laws, training enforcement agents and educating scientists to create classification systems and categorize this new breed of criminal.[9]

The creation of new knowledge, then, is a *political* as well as a legal act. And corporate crime researchers are not the only group affected by the disappearance of state law on corporate crime. Environmental activists, consumer spokespeople, feminists and other counter-hegemonic social movements cannot call the state to account, nor can they provide numbers to back up their arguments without data and public access to it. If longitudinal data are no longer gathered, it becomes impossible to show that certain companies are long term offenders, recidivists, even career criminals and dangerous offenders. Labels such as these, derived from the master censure of criminal law, are particularly powerful. They attract media, state and public attention. But establishing such claims requires access to "official" statistics gathered by "scientific disciplines"—the very data no longer collected, the knowledge no longer created. The process of policy formation is also set back. If state officials are unable to monitor workplaces or take preventative action, life-threatening factories or mines will be discovered only after disasters have occurred. Crimes that produce "only" injuries, or ambiguous illnesses with many possible causes, or workplace and environmental conditions that cause cancers that take years to develop are unlikely to be detected at all, and they will certainly never be traced back to the corporate conditions that produced them. The harms caused by the antisocial acts of corporations, then, become once again, as in earlier centuries, the fault of careless individuals or unhealthy lifestyles.

Finally, the significance of the disappearance of corporate crime speaks volumes about the potential of state law to harness capital. The corporate counter-revolution illustrates how profoundly dependent the promulgation and enforcement of nation-state law is on the balance of powers operating within a society. Thus, where labour unions and/or social movements such as environmentalism or socialist feminism are strong (as in many western European and Scandinavian countries), laws controlling the destructive but profitable acts of capital will also be strong, downsizing and decriminalization will be resisted longer and more successfully. Where such groups and forces are weak, as in United States and Canada, laws will be reluctantly passed, little enforced, and ignored as soon the spotlight of public attention shifts. With labour unions throughout the world under serious attack, ideologically and financially, the burden of maintaining the pressure on corporate capital falls by default on progressive social movements. In general this means groups must use the individualizing, class-biased language of law and of rights discourse to press governments to provide broader rights for citizens, consumers and employees. With all its drawbacks, the discourse of resistance (if not necessarily empowerment) is now that of risk (Ericson and Haggerty, 1997). Citizen groups may get laws passed, or at least resist their dismemberment, by claiming legal rights to breathe clean air, drink pure water, and not be exposed to toxic materials and other dangers at home or work. Emphasizing government obligations to provide such "goods" provides a vehicle to resist deregulation in the short term, and to strengthen it in the long term. More counter-hegemonic strategies would include seeking broad-based rights to a fair wage, to job security, to high quality health care, day care and education. And certainly, in an era of global capitalism, international counter-hegemonic alliances are essential. The primary value of such struggles will be ideological, not legal—the goal is to challenge beliefs that employers can do anything they like to employees, communities and countries in the interests of increasing profits for corporate stockholders. Such struggles reinforce agency, they empower people to become part of a self-fulfilling, beneficent prophecy: by challenging the idea that resisting global corporate power is futile, the limits of nation-state and citizen power are inevitably explored and expanded.

State law, then, has little power to resist corporate capital in the absence of strong, counter-hegemonic citizens' groups. Law is in no sense a "magic bullet." But the strategic importance of law in the modern state, its immense power as a censure, its ability to grab media attention and mobilize opposition, as well as build the membership base of movements, all make law a tool much too important to be ignored.

ᛄ CONCLUSION

This essay has argued that the disappearance of corporate crime signalled by the abandonment of state law is an event with massive political, legal and ideological consequences. State law has not "kept pace" with the growth and development of corporate wealth and power (Wells, 1993); indeed, it has retreated, fled in ignominious defeat, ceded victory to corporate counter-revolutionary forces. For those who seek to create more equitable societies, this development represents a giant step backwards. It is one thing to argue that state law was inefficient—that governments seldom took effective action against corporations—and quite another to argue that they should jettison the capacity, and the legal obligation, to do so. As we have seen, abandoning state sanctions has far-reaching symbolic and practical consequences. State laws are public statements which convey important public messages about the obligations of the employer classes (Ayres and Braithwaite, 1992).[10] The situation is paradoxical indeed: while crimes of the powerful were never effectively sanctioned by state law, such laws are nonetheless essential to the operation of democratic societies.

𝔐 ENDNOTES

1   As noted above, the spoils of capitalism are very unevenly distributed from a worldwide perspective and the disparity is getting worse, not better (United Nations, 1996).

2   All the known perpetrators were men, although some women were peripherally involved (Calavita et al., 1997).

3   The most recent discourse switch has been the transformation of corporate criminals into "stakeholders" (Canada, 1998: 3).

4   In this context, one could cite virtually the entire corpus of literature on corporate crime. In the American literature this record has been documented in studies from Sutherland's (1949) classic *White Collar Crime* to Clinard and Yeager (1980), Shapiro (1984), Coleman (1985) and Green (1994); more international accounts are found in Box (1983), Clarke, (1990) and Punch (1996). Recent studies go beyond description to explanation and reform (see, for example: Braithwaite 1995; Yeager 1991; Tombs 1996; and articles in Pearce and Snider 1995).

5   In countries where such laws are absent, children are still being hired, and 60 hour work weeks in dangerous environments are commonplace. As illustrated by exposes of working conditions in *Nike* and *Nortel*, in the *maquiladeros* of Mexico and the rug manufacturing workshops of India, companies provide healthy, safe workplaces only where forced to do so (Pearce and Tombs 1998; Dobbin 1998; Fudge 1998). So what will happen in First World countries when all state laws and sanctions have been replaced by "voluntary" agreements?

6   This dependence on available (state-collected) data also explains why so many recent American studies of white collar crime have documented virtually no high level corporate crime. No analysis that uses as its data source FBI data on prosecutions, for example, will unearth many CEOs of major corporations in the lists of offenders. Their power, their legal departments and the insulating layers of bureaucracy in modern corporations all protect senior executives from becoming known to the FBI, much less charged. Thus such studies turn up the most powerless

individual white collar criminals, often black bank tellers who are assiduously pursued by law enforcement authorities for embezzling a few thousand dollars (see, for example: Weisburd et al., 1990).

7   Self-report data are not a satisfactory alternative in this area, because people are often not aware they have been the victims of negligence or fraud. Without state officials to investigate and publicize dishonest business practices, for example, victims identify "bad luck" or "accident" as causes. One of the few attempts to utilize this method is reported by Pearce (1990) in Islington (a suburb of London England), who found working class victimization from corporate crime many times higher than revealed in official statistics.

8   If trends follow the now standard route in traditional criminological literature today, some enterprising investigator will next suggest that some employees have a genetic predisposition to steal time. Scientific resources will then be focused on isolating the particular gene responsible.

9   Massive sums are also spent designing technical systems to make such offences more difficult. The preferred method, the one deemed most cost efficient, is to eliminate the human employee entirely.

10   It is surprising that the citizens in so many democratic countries have allowed this to happen. Abandoning regulation and de-criminalizing harmful acts was not achieved by state dictatorship in Canada. It was a public process, negotiated into existence. This does not mean everyone was consulted. It was largely a process of changing the minds of elites and of those citizens who vote. But, with the partial exception of environmental regulation (where active social movements were and are present), the disappearance of corporate crime never became a major news story, or election issue.

🏛 REFERENCES

Austin R. and S. Dietrich, 1990, "Employer Abuse of Low-Status Workers: The Possibility of Uncommon Relief from the Common Law," in D. Kairys (ed.), *The Politics of Law: A Progressive Critique*, New York: Pantheon.

Ayres, I. and J. Braithwaite, 1992, *Responsive Regulation: Transcending the Deregulation Debate*, New York: Oxford.

Bardach, E. and R. A. Kagan, 1982, *Going by the Book: The Problem of Regulatory Unreasonableness*, Philadelphia: Temple University Press.

Bell, D., 1996, "Regulators' Perspectives," in M. Mehta (ed.), *Regulatory Efficiency and the Role of Risk Assessment*, Kingston: Queen's University School of Policy Studies (Environmental Policy Unit).

Bliss, M., 1974, *A Living Profit: Studies in the Social Organization of Canadian Business*, Toronto: McClelland & Stewart.

Box, S., 1983, *Power, Crime and Mystification*, London: Tavistock Publications Ltd.

Braithwaite, J., 1995, "Corporate Crime and Republican Criminological Praxis," in F. Pearce and L. Snider (eds.), *Corporate Crime: Contemporary Debates*, Toronto: University of Toronto Press.

Braithwaite, J., 1985a, "White Collar Crime," *American Review of Sociology* II: 1–25.

Braithwaite, J., 1985b, *To Punish or Persuade: The Enforcement of Coal Mine Legislation*, Albany: State University of New York Press.

Braithwaite, J., 1984, *Corporate Crime in the Pharmaceutical Industry*, London: Routledge and Kegan Paul.

Calavita, K., H. Pontell and R. Tillman., 1997, *Big Money Crime*, Berkeley: University of California Press.

Canada, Industry Canada, 1998, Annual Report of the Director of Investigation and Research, Competition Act (for the year ending March 31, 1997), Ottawa.

Canada, Industry Canada, 1997, Annual Report of the Director of Investigation and Research, Competition Act (for the year ending March 31, 1996), Ottawa.

Canada, Environment Canada, 1995, *It's About Our Health: Towards Pollution Prevention*, Report of the House of Commons Standing Committee on the Environmental and Sustainable Development, Ottawa: House of Commons, #81 (a.k.a. CEPA Review).

Canada, Bureau of Competition Policy, 1989, *Competition Policy in Canada: The First Hundred Years*, Ottawa: Consumer and Corporate Affairs.

Carson, W., 1980, "The Institutionalization of Ambiguity: Early British Factory Acts," in G. Geis and E. Stotland (eds.), *White Collar Theory and Research*, Beverly Hills: Sage.

Carson, W., 1970, "White Collar Crime and the Enforcement of Factory Legislation,"*British Journal of Criminology* 10: 383–98.

Clarke, M., 1990, *Business Crime*, Cambridge: Polity Press.

Clinard, M.B. and P. Yeager, 1980, *Corporate Crime*, New York: Free Press.

Coleman, J.W., 1987, "Toward an Integrated Theory of White-Collar Crime," *American Journal of Sociology* 93: 406–439.

Coleman, J.W., 1985, *The Criminal Elite: The Sociology of White Collar Crime*, New York: St. Martin's Press (2nd ed., l989).

Comish, Shaun, 1993, *The Westray Tragedy: A Miner's Story*, Halifax: Fernwood Publishing.

Cressey, D., 1953, *Other People's Money: A Study in the Social Psychology of Embezzlement*, Glencoe, Illinois: Free Press.

Cullen, F., W. Maakestadt and G. Cavender, 1987, *Corporate Crime Under Attack: The Ford Pinto Case and Beyond*, Cincinnati: Anderson.

Dobbin, M., 1998, "Unfriendly Giants,"*Report on Business Magazine*, 15 (July): 73–80.

Edelhertz, H., 1970, *The Nature, Impact and Prosecution of White Collar Crime*, Washington, D.C.: National Institute for Law Enforcement and Criminal Justice, Department of Justice.

Ericson R. and K. Haggerty, 1997, *Policing the Risk Society*, Toronto: University of Toronto Press.

Foucault, M., 1979, "Governmentality," *Ideology & Consciousness* 6: 5–21.

Fudge, J., 1998, "Corporate Campaigns Against Labour Abuse: Consumers to the Rescue?" Paper presented at (Ab)Using Power: The Canadian Experience, Conference held at Simon Fraser University, Vancouver, B.C., May 7–9.

Gallon, G., 1996, "Ontario Government Backsliding on Environment," *Canadian Environmental Business Letter: The Gallon Report* 11, no. 46 (November 20).

Glasbeek, H., 1995, "Preliminary Observations on Strains of, and Strains in, Corporate Law Scholarship," in F. Pearce and L. Snider (eds.), *Corporate Crime: Contemporary Debates*, Toronto: University of Toronto Press.

Goldman, C., 1989, "The Impact of the Competition Act of 1986," Address given to the National Conference on Competition Law and Policy in Canada, Toronto, October 24–25.

Green, G., 1994, *Occupational Crime*, Chicago: Nelson-Hall.

Gunningham, N., 1984, *Safeguarding the Workers*, Sydney: Law Book Co. Ltd.

Jobb, Dean, 1998, "Westray: A Deadly Misuse of Power," Paper presented at (Ab)Using Power: The Canadian Experience, Conference held at Simon Fraser University, Vancouver, B.C., May 7–9.

Marcus, S., 1974, *Engels, Manchester and the Working Class*, New York: Random House.

McQuaig, L., 1997, *The Cult of Impotence: Selling the Myth of Powerlessness in the Global Economy*, Toronto: Viking Press.

Mehta, M., 1997, "Risk Assessment and Sustainable Development: Towards a Concept of 'Sustainable Risk,' " *Risk: Health Safety and Environment*, forthcoming.

Mehta, M. (ed.), 1995, *Regulatory Efficiency and the Role of Risk Assessment*, Kingston: School of Policy Studies, Queen's University.

Milner, B., 1998, "Competition Cops Flex Muscle," *Globe and Mail Report on Business*, March 30: B1, 3.

Miyoshi, M., 1993, "A Borderless World? From Colonialism to Transnationalism and the Decline of the Nation-State," *Critical Inquiry*, University of Chicago: 726–51.

Nikiforuk, A., 1997, *The Nasty Game: The Failure of Environmental Assessment in Canada*, Toronto: Walter & Duncan Gordon Foundation.

Noble, C., 1995, "Regulating Work in a Capitalist Society," in F. Pearce and L. Snider (eds.), *Corporate Crime: Contemporary Debates*, Toronto: University of Toronto Press.

Paulus, I., 1974, *The Search for Pure Food: A Sociology of Legislation in Britain*, London: Martin Robertson.

Pearce, F. and S. Tombs, 1998, *Toxic Capitalism: Corporate Crime and the Chemical Industry*, Aldershot: Ashgate/Dartmouth.

Pearce, F. and L. Snider, 1995, "Regulating Capitalism," in F. Pearce and L. Snider (eds.), *Corporate Crime: Contemporary Debates*, Toronto: University of Toronto Press.

Pearce, F., 1993, "Corporate Rationality as Corporate Crime," *Studies in Political Economy* 40 (Spring): 135–162.

Pearce, F., 1990, *The Second Islington Crime Survey*, Middlesex: Middlesex University Centre of Criminology.

Pearce, F., 1989, *The Radical Durkheim*, London: Unwin Hyman.

Punch, M., 1996, *Dirty Business: Exploring Corporate Misconduct*, London: Sage.

Regush, N., 1991, "Health and Welfare's National Disgrace," *Saturday Night* (April): 9–18; 62–3.

Reiman, J., 1994, *The Rich Get Richer and the Poor Get Prison* (4th ed.) Toronto: Allyn & Bacon.

Reiss, A., 1984, "Selecting Strategies of Social Control over Organizational Life," in K. Hawkins and J. Thomas (eds.), *Enforcing Regulation*, Boston: Kluwer-Nijoff.

Reiss, A., 1992, "The Institutionalization of Risk," in J. Short and L. Clarke (eds.), *Organizations, Uncertainties and Risk*, Boulder: Westview Press.

Richard, Justice K. Peter (Commissioner), 1997, *The Westray Story: A Predictable Path to Disaster*, Report of the Westray Mine Public Inquiry, Province of Nova Scotia.

Rothman, D., 1995, "More of the Same: American Criminal Justice Policies in the 1990s," in T. Blomberg and S. Cohen (eds.), *Punishment and Social Control*, New York: Aldine de Gruyter.

Shapiro, S., 1984, *Wayward Capitalists*, New Haven: Yale University Press.

Shapiro, S., 1990, "Collaring the Crime, not the Criminal: Considering the Concept of White Collar Crime," *American Sociological Review* 55 (June): 346–65.

Shapiro, S., 1985, "The Road Not Taken: The Elusive Path to Criminal Prosecution for White Collar Offenders," *Law and Society Review* 19 (2): 179–217.

Snider, L., 1998, "Towards Safer Societies," *British Journal of Criminology* 38 (1): 1–38.

Snider, L., 1998a, "Understanding the Second Great Confinement," *Queen's Quarterly* (Spring): 29–49.

Snider, L., 1997, "Nouvelle Donne Legislative et Causes de la Criminalite 'Corporative,' " *Criminologie* XXX (1): 9–34.

Snider, L., 1996, "Options for Public Accountability," in M. Mehta (ed.), *Regulatory Efficiency and the Role of Risk Assessment*, Kingston: School of Policy Studies, Queen's University.

Snider, L., 1993, *Bad Business: Corporate Crime in Canada*, Scarborough: ITP Nelson.

Snider, L., 1991, "The Regulatory Dance: Understanding Reform Processes in Corporate Crime," *International Journal of Sociology of Law* 19: 209–36.

Snider, L., 1987, "Towards a Political Economy of Reform, Regulation and Corporate Crime," *Law and Policy* 9 (1): 37–68.

Snider, L., 1978, "Corporate Crime in Canada: A Preliminary Report," *Canadian Journal of Criminology* 20: 142–68.

Stanbury, W., 1988, "A Review of Conspiracy Cases in Canada, 1965–66 to 1987–88," *Canadian Competition Policy Record* 10 (1): 33–49.

Stanbury, W., 1986–87, "The New Competition Act and Competition Tribunal Act: Not with a Bang but a Whimper?"*Canadian Business Law Journal* 12: 2–42.

Stanbury, W., 1977, *Business Interests and the Reform of Canadian Competition Policy 1971–75*, Toronto: Carswell/Methuen.

Stanbury, W., 1995, "Public Policy Towards Individuals Involved in Competition Law Offences in Canada," in F. Pearce and L. Snider (eds.), *Corporate Crime: Contemporary Debates*, Toronto: University of Toronto Press.

Statistics Canada, 1998, National Census, Ottawa: Supply and Services.

Statistics Canada, 1997, *Income Distributions by Size in Canada*, Ottawa: Ministry of Supply and Services.

Statistics Canada, 1996, *Death and Injury Rates on the Job: 75-001-XPE*, Ottawa: Ministry of Supply and Services, Summer.

Sumner, C., 1983, "Rethinking Deviance: Toward a Sociology of Censures," *Research in Law, Deviance and Social Control* 5: 187–204.

Sutherland, E., 1977, "White-Collar Criminality,"in G. Geis and R. Meier, (eds), *White Collar Crime*, New York: Free Press.

Sutherland, E., 1949, *White Collar Crime*, New York: Dryden.

Sutherland, E., 1940, "White-Collar Criminality," *American Sociological Review* 5 (February): 1–12.

Tombs, S., 1998, "Health and Safety Crimes: (In)Visibility and the Problems of Knowing," (forthcoming).

Tombs, S., 1996, "Injury, Death and the Deregulation Fetish: The Politics of Occupational Safety Regulation in United Kingdom Manufacturing Industries," *International Journal of Health Services* 26 (2): 309–29.

Tombs, S., 1995, "Corporate Crime and New Organizational Forms," in F. Pearce and L. Snider (eds.), *Corporate Crime: Contemporary Debates*, Toronto: University of Toronto Press.

Tucker, E., 1995a, "The Westray Mine Disaster and Its Aftermath," *Canadian Journal of Law and Society* 10 (1): 92–123.

Tucker, E., 1990, *Administering Danger in the Workplace: The Law and Politics of Occupational Health & Safety Regulation in Ontario, 1850–1914*, Toronto: University of Toronto Press.

Tucker, E., 1995, "And Defeat Goes On: An Assessment of Third Wave Health and Safety Regulation," in F. Pearce and L. Snider (eds.), *Corporate Crime: Contemporary Debates*, Toronto: University of Toronto Press.

United Nations, 1996, *Human Development Report*, New York: United Nations.

Ursel, J., 1992, *Private Lives, Public Policy: 100 Years of State Intervention in the Family*, Toronto: Women's Press.

Varrette, S.E., C. Meredith, P. Robinson and D. Huffman, ABT Association of Canada, 1985, *White Collar Crime: Exploring the Issues*, Ottawa: Ministry of Justice.

Walters, V., W. Lewchuk, J. Richardson, L. Moran, T. Haines and D. Verma, 1995, "Judgments of Legitimacy regarding Occupational Health and Safety," in F. Pearce and L. Snider (eds.), *Corporate Crime: Contemporary Debates*, Toronto: University of Toronto Press.

Weisburd, D., E.F. Chayet and E.J. Waring, 1990, "White Collar Crime and Criminal Careers: Some Preliminary Findings," *Crime and Delinquency* 36 (3): 342.

Wells, C., 1993, *Corporations and Criminal Responsibility*, Oxford: Oxford University Press.

Wheeler, S., D. Weisburd, and N. Bode, 1982, "Sentencing the White-Collar Offender: Rhetoric and Reality," *American Sociological Review* 47: 641–59.

Yeager, P., 1991, *The Limits of Law: The Public Regulation of Private Pollution*, Cambridge: Cambridge University Press.

Yeager, P., 1995, "Management, Morality, and Law: Organizational Forms and Ethical Deliberations," in F. Pearce and L. Snider (eds.), *Corporate Crime: Contemporary Debates*, Toronto: University of Toronto Press.

Zey, M., 1993, *Banking on Fraud: Drexel, Junk Bonds and Buyouts*, New York: Aldine de Gruyter.

PART 4

CRITIQUE AND HOPE:
NEW QUESTIONS,
NEW DIRECTIONS

13

International Conference on Penal Abolition: The Birth of ICOPA

Lisa Finateri and Viviane Saleh-Hanna

The movement toward penal abolition, while not explicit within mainstream ideology, nonetheless maintains a strong following. A world-wide commitment is evident through the birth and existence of the International Conference on Penal Abolition (ICOPA). Beginning in 1983, this conference has drawn together activists, academics and (ex)prisoners in solidarity. A better understanding of this position is achieved through a historical analysis of the trends and shifts occurring through the evolution in form and content of these conferences.

Following the 1981 official public declaration of support for prison abolition, the Canadian Quaker Committee on Jails and Justice in 1982 embraced the vision of ICOPA. In hopes of strengthening this movement, Canadian abolitionists Ruth Morris, Bob Melcombe, Jake Friesen and Jonathan Rudin began organizing ICOPA I in Toronto, Canada to be held at the University of Toronto in May 1983. Grassroots action focused on creating international unity among those already adhering to the prison abolitionist approach. "ICOPA conferences would not be like others talking about alternatives within the system, and providing a platform for governmental people to defend the indefensible." Every second year, the conference was to alternate between North America and Europe with hope of globally expanding throughout the years.

Structures were put into place and committees were formed establishing four primary defining principles. The first principle was to motivate the abolitionist community while increasing its solidarity. The second was to provide a forum for the flow and exchange of ideas advancing abolitionist goals. The third entails public sensitization and education on these issues while, fourth, addressing the question of viable alternatives (Morris 1994: 1). In short, answering why prisons exist, how to move towards their abolition, and what can be offered in their place (Morris 1985: 18).

ᛘ ICOPA: A JOURNEY THROUGHOUT THE WORLD

Following the above-mentioned mandate elected in 1983, ensuring the international dispersing of ICOPA, the second conference in 1985 was hosted by the Criminologisch Instituut in Amsterdam, Netherlands. Where ICOPA I had featured many grassroots representatives, the conference in Amsterdam followed an academic agenda. In fact, it was at this point that Claire Culhane, a leading Canadian anti-prison activist, felt she could no longer participate and support in essence an "all talk—no action" endeavour.

ICOPA III held in Montreal, Canada in 1987 was hosted by The Prisoners Rights Committee, L'Ecole de Criminologie, Universite de Montreal and the Department of Criminology, the University of Ottawa. In straying from its roots in Amsterdam, Montreal saw the rejuvenation of ICOPA's grassroots foundation. As stated by Ruth Morris (1997), "ICOPA I included more activists and (ex)prisoners, and Native people. ICOPA II included many European academics and had a strong base of academic presentations." Coupled with this, the second conference indicated a growing awareness of the role a punitive and retributive criminal justice system plays in erecting and maintaining prisons. As a result, a fundamental decision in the third conference was made: The International Conference on *Prison* Abolition was transformed into the International Conference on *Penal* Abolition. This change in title acknowledges the importance of language and widens the parameters of abolitionist issues. This shift is based on the notion that the dismantling of prison walls will not eliminate the state use of coercion and social control. The penal structures that allow and maintain the existence of the prison as a response to social troubles need to be dismantled in order for a truly healing and humanitarian "alternative" to thrive.

Continuing in the tradition, the next conference presented an ironic twist; "ICOPA IV, 1989 was held in Poland, organized by Monica Platek, and was historic because of its location in Eastern Europe in the days when that was very daring" (Morris, 1997). The irony endures in that ICOPA V, 1991 was held in Indiana, United States of America, the epic model of the never-ending trajectory of carceral control. This conference employed an equal mix of activists and academic representation.

₥ REFORM OR ABOLITION

Reflecting a change over time, ICOPA organizers began to acknowledge the fact that prison and penal reformers would be in attendance. This was taken as an opportunity to educate, whereby an introductory session into abolitionist argumentation is presented and explained. ICOPA VI, 1993 epitomizes this through the higher rates of attendance by Latin American justice and prison officials. In Costa Rica, there was "…a memorable opening day when Louk Hulsman, Monica Platek and Ruth Morris presented abolition and answered questions about it from these assembled participants… all day" (Morris 1997). It is important to note that this conference, organized under Elias Carranza, the director of the United Nations institute on crime, brought legitimacy to the abolitionist position in Latin America, as well as abroad. ICOPA VII, 1995 held in Barcelona, Spain worked to maintain this international network.

The essence of ICOPA may therefore, be captured through the metaphor of a rolling movie script as opposed to still life photographs. While each frame may be reminiscent of the context and content of each conference, it is perhaps more important to look at them as an evolution of the penal abolitionist movement over time. Although, on a cautionary note, it is erroneous to assume that ICOPA accurately represents and portrays the theoretical and/or activist abolitionist movement. From its beginnings in 1983, the unfolding of various trends is evident. Nonetheless, the patterns and changes throughout the decade are reflected in the shape and form ICOPA holds today.

ICOPA VIII: AOTEAROA 1997 – LIMITS AND FUTURE ASPIRATIONS

In it's eighth occurrence, ICOPA was held on the North Island of Aotearoa (New Zealand) in February 1997, once again venturing into new territory. A conscious effort was made to ensure the inclusion of the Maori, where higher rates of imprisonment are manifest. Direct ties between the struggles of Aboriginal peoples in all colonized countries became obvious. On the other hand, inadequacies of past conferences were again present.

An under-representation of activists, (ex)prisoners and their families was clear as was the over-representation of governmental and prison officials. Of all the keynote speakers present, very few could personally represent the voices of those imprisoned. It is of importance to remark that when these voices were heard, they came from the back of the room, making it evident "who was driving the bus." This theme resounded throughout the rest of the conference. Although there was a clear attempt at being sensitive toward Maori issues and culture, it may be seen as problematic that although on the Marae, hierarchy was still visible. As official hosts, it seemed that their participation throughout the day was perhaps not fully encouraged. It was remarked that some of the cultural aspects were not carried out according to traditional custom. The official welcoming ceremony, which is of great importance to the Maori, was simplified thereby losing its full meaning.

A parallel can be drawn within the lack or loss of penal abolitionist understanding among conference attendants. The rigid time limits restricted the amount of discussion allowed. This, coupled with the numerous workshops running concurrently, only exasperated the level of misunderstanding in regards to penal abolition. The structure of the workshops and lectures, where the speaker presents to an audience, aids in this misinterpretation through the inherent hierarchy of this style. Abolition is built on a fundamentally different ideological position, once advocating empowerment and equality.

Further embedded in the power structure was a lack of grassroots representation. Not only was there a lack of prisoners' voices, or those on behalf of prisoners, but prison and government officials were in abundance, thus posing a constant struggle against "reformer" ideology. This is clearly implicit within the disregard of opinions and comments presented by marginalized voices. Within the context of this conference, it is even more ironic that applause and continual recognition was bestowed upon a newly appointed "judgeship." Also, the individual welcoming of various highly ranked government officials during the opening session, seems to fall into contradiction with an abolitionist stance.

A main obstacle of ICOPA VIII's productivity was this lack of comprehension of abolitionist theory, despite the efforts of ICOPA organizers and veterans. There remains a lack of understanding as to the origin of prisons and their mandate. Some scholars claim that the use of prisons as a form of sanction evolved from attempts at eliminating the brutality of corporal punishment and public executions. Cohen (1985) asserts that while humanity has been the motivating force behind the birth of the prison system, it seems humanity has long been omitted from the end result. Reform under the rhetoric of "good intentions," becomes exposed.

Foucault (1977), would argue that prisons are designed to fail and therefore, succeed in their failure. At this point, it becomes reasonable to discuss prisons within the penal system as industry. Designated "dangerous classes" by the ruling elite are scapegoated and used as "raw- material" fuelling the machine of social control (Christie 1994). This is further exemplified by the growing trend towards privatization of prisons. While this issue was not formally addressed by designated speakers, it resounded from the floor as being of timely and grave concern. Unfortunately, "crime control as industry" in some ways went unrecognized throughout the conference.

Embedded within the industrialization of the criminal justice system, is the War on Drugs. One of the presenters emphasized the use of caution when applying mainstream assumptions concerning substances deemed illicit. While recognition of the problematic employment of the medical model was partially reflected in that workshop, another presenter embraced a "scientific" medical solution to drug "addiction." Many ICOPA VIII attendants proclaimed a strong stance against the illegality of drugs and were disappointed with the lean coverage this topic received. The lack of a better understanding of drug-related issues remained rooted in the dominant adherence to "scientism" and the insufficient, in-depth historical analysis of the origins of substances deemed illicit. As a result, the ceremonial and ritual use of drugs was not recognized, nor were the cultural aspects of various substances (Szasz 1985).

Cultural diversity within ICOPA VIII was not fully representative of the international field. Because of the remote location and other intervening variables, this criticism is not necessarily reflective of the organizers themselves.

Consequently, those in attendance could have been better utilized as guest speakers while further attempts at increasing the multicultural feel of ICOPA is greatly needed.

The United States of America was often looked upon as the epitome of failure and corruption in relation to its overuse of the criminal justice system but the unacceptable number of African American and Hispanic peoples warehoused there was seldom highlighted throughout this conference. Considering "four of every ten African American males between the ages of 19 and 29 are under some form of control by the criminal (in)justice system" (DiBenedetto & Seidenstein, 1997: 16) yields testimony to "...the fact that the criminal justice system in New York, as elsewhere, is the only institution that eagerly welcomes young Black and Latino males" (Morse 1995: 11). It seems problematic that no speaker or workshop fully addressed this phenomenon; responsibility was left to one of the conference attendants who spoke up and condemned the technological "genocide" and the "continuation of slavery in modern society."

The negative effects of oppression have been apparent through out history, but the striking parallel between negative consequences faced by Native peoples (Aboriginal, First Nations, Maori etc.) around the world through colonization is important to acknowledge. At the conference, recognition of the similarities was apparent, although this issue as a global concern was not addressed. The use of Aboriginal values within the criminal justice system, although appropriated, has been among the few productive methods dealing with social troubles. A well established comparison indicating the similarities and differences among Native communities, in regards to their cultural notion of "justice" and "wrongdoing" would yield beneficial results. In addition, a study between tribal and dominant European ideology could contribute to useful insight and discussion concerning the social construction and production of socially problematic situations.

ṁ NEW DEFINITIONS

Such a discussion can only evolve if a dramatically different approach regarding traditional notions of "crime," "victim," "offender," and "justice" is undertaken. In applying a new approach, Professor Louk Hulsman of the Netherlands, explained that a new language must be implemented, one that is completely separate from the vocabulary of the existing criminal justice system. This is necessary for the recognition of "Victims—Both Sides" (Allridge, 1995), or rather on *all* sides of the retributive and punitive criminal justice system. It seems to follow that those who victimize others, are then victimized by the state (if not before). Families, especially the children, on both sides are negatively effected. This universal suffering is best captured by Art Solomon (1989), a Native Spiritual Leader, in his poem entitled *The Wheels of Injustice:*

> *It seems like they grind*
> *Forever.*
> *And what they grind*
> *Is Human Beings,*
> *And how they grind.*
>
> *They grind away*
> *The Humanity*
> *Of the victims*
> *Who get caught*
> *In its jaws. (8)*

In the end, communities become victimized by fear, hatred and revenge, thereby propelling the cycle of violence.

The most visibly evident form of state victimization is directed towards the "criminal." "In prison a person learns just what it means to be oppressed, and how far-reaching that oppression is" (Senger 1987: 12). Deliberate and clear sanctions are executed upon these people while justified and legitimized through the ideals of deterrence, punishment and revenge. Stigmatization, alienation, isolation, the physical and emotional brutalizing of people, and other effects such as victimization are not calculated into the equation of the sentence handed down. As explained by McCormick (1993), "there are two kinds of prisons. One kind is built with concrete, steel, and razor wire. The other is built in the dungeons of our minds" (23). It seems that, in general, society holds a simplified and ignorant view of imprisonment and the impact it has on human beings.

When someone is sentenced to prison, the family is also sentenced to suffer; the children specifically are greatly affected. This familial problem imposed by the courts can be broken down into two main categories: the problems associated with the prison and those related to the social response of the community the child lives in. The prison separates the child from the parent and at the same time directs much negative influence and control into the child's life. Visits are privileges the parent must earn while phone calls are limited because of expense and availability. Many aspects of the child's life change for the worse, ranging from economic, social and environmental to emotional, behavioural and psychological. Prison not only separates children from their parents, it also stigmatizes all those connected to it (Breen 1995). During ICOPA VIII, these concerns resounded from the floor and are present in the 1997 resolutions; unfortunately, these issues of state victimization were not discussed.

Added victimization of traditionally defined "victims" by the state, while not as clearly explicit, nevertheless results in increased suffering. Generally, they are completely left out of the criminal justice process where the initial victimization is often used by the state to legitimize punishment-causing re-victimization. In the words of Robert Elias (1993), "victims are solicited to pursue policies that contradict their own best interests" (4). Despite discussion in regards to empowerment of the victim in Family Group Conferencing workshops, this issue of state re-victimization was not always made conscious throughout the conference. Although, a realization of the cyclical nature of violence and victimization in all these cases was apparent, a true change in language did not occur thereby allowing co-optation by the current system.

ṁ RESTORATIVE JUSTICE VS. PENAL ABOLITION

Appropriation of "good intentions" through the misuse of language has presented an obstacle to the goals of Restorative Justice initiatives. A main focus of ICOPA VIII was on Family Group Conferencing, deriving of Maori tradition, which has now been integrated within legal policy concerning young offenders. The procedure involves less legal intervention in determining sanctions, nonetheless remaining under state surveillance. The problematic nature of the concept of crime and all that it entails still endures. Clear distinctions as to guilt and innocence, of "victim" and "offender" have not changed. As put forth by one presenter, it is impressive and not to be discounted that five young offender prisons remain in New Zealand, where fourteen once existed. Yet "restoring" back to a situation in which injustices such as racism, elitism and other inequalities still predominate cannot yield humanitarian solutions. Pathways are no longer a means toward the goal of penal abolition but become in and of themselves the vision. In explication, advocating the move towards implementing Family Group Conferencing in adult court became a *goal*, not a *step* closer to abolition.

Family Group Conferencing does not present a "competing contradiction," for it operates within the current penal system. For abolition of the penal system to prevail, it is imperative that initiatives not be "based on the premises of the old system… [where it] does not belong to, is not integrated or woven into, the old system" (Mathiesen 1974: 13-14). Once again, while benefits seem apparent (i.e. decreased imprisonment rates) abolition as a final goal becomes obsolete.

Perhaps some of this confusion can be located within the misattribution of ICOPA as remaining a conference on prison abolition, not penal abolition. The abolitionist discourse was at times lost and may have been reflective of this restorative focus. Dr. Ruth Morris continually attempted to clarify this issue through persistent insistence on the use of the term "transformative" verses "restorative." As mentioned, restoring is not sufficient. A complete transformation of societal structure, values, morals and attitudes is essential. Without dismantling the structures which create and maintain the existing methods of social coercion and control, a more egalitarian and humanitarian community is an impossibility.

A critique of the present situation leads to future visions. ICOPA IX, 2000, to be held in Toronto, Canada will hopefully address some of the issues and concerns previously mentioned. The first step must involve getting back to ICOPA's abolitionist roots. A lack of understanding of this stance cannot be allowed to divert the focus away from penal abolition. Above all, a strict screening of papers to be presented must occur. This is not to discourage or prevent the participation and attendance of those not fluent in abolitionist theory and thought; it is however to ensure that all present become educated within this ideological position. In all fairness to the ICOPA VIII organizers, a filtering system was utilized, perhaps it was not strict enough in its criteria and controls.

Aiding in pursuing this objective, an introductory session during the commencement of the conference is needed, in hopes of versing attendants on the abolitionist stance. This would consist of various leading "experts" presenting this position with ample time allotted for questions and discussion. A solid understanding of the support and reasoning behind this thought would greatly aid in the general flow of the conference proceedings. A suggested panel would include: Nils Christie addressing the "crime control industry"; Stanley Cohen presenting victimization through "net widening"; Louk Hulsman illustrating the importance of language; Thomas Mathiesen explicating "the impossible dream" (and possibly the concept of "the unfinished"); Ruth Morris differentiating between the three modes of justice; Sebastein Scheerer highlighting the successful reality of past abolition movements; such a discussion should help in alleviating misconceptions concerning reform verses abolition and prison verses penal abolition.

A more balanced distribution of voices would follow in an increasingly realistic presentation of the concept of abolition and the need for this social transition. Contributions from the academic field are necessary, however their thoughts are generally well represented and therefore, concern should be on ensuring the expression of marginalized voices throughout ICOPA IX.

(Ex)prisoners have a direct insight as to the atrocities suffered at the hands of the penal system towards the human mind, body and spirit. In addition, a differentiation needs to be made between political and socially conscious prisoner's difficulties, as well as the problems faced by other prisoners in general. Contributions of different prisoners' experiences are essential because of the significance of this experiential knowledge and the contextualizing aspect their presence ensures. Such insight can help in identifying real issues and the shaping of healing solutions to social problems. Included here, would be the representation of the families of those imprisoned, since they too are punished and suffer alongside their loved ones.

It seems somewhat unrealistic to discuss penal abolition without hearing the concerns of traditional "victims" of "street crime" (including their families). Despite the increasingly conservative public and political climate, it is not necessarily impossible to locate "victims" who advocate healing as opposed to revenge. Some possible presenters could include: a "Murder Victims' Families for Reconciliation" representative (Allridge, 1995: 65); a Hollow Water Nation community speaker; or community activist Wilma Doerksen whose daughter Candace was murdered. This perspective would yield testimonial to the power of healing and the possibility of regaining a sense of societal balance.

Where inequalities exist, equilibrium cannot exist. Globally, women are marginalized and repressed. Such a situation is exasperated within the realm of the criminal justice system. The obstacles and problems women encounter are not totally parallel to those faced by men. This is not to say that either suffers more than the other does (for in fact, men experience far greater rates of imprisonment), but there are differences that are seemingly systemic of a sexist society. Therefore, these issues require conference attention.

The notion of empowerment is a necessary tool in overcoming all social hierarchies. Yet, empowerment cannot be effective without the recognition of diversity. Racism is often internationally reflected within penal policy and practice. Considering the American criminal justice system's influence upon other nations, it is imperative that the blatant discrimination against the African-American and Hispanic populations be exposed and combated at ICOPA IX. In addition, the destructive forces of colonization upon Aboriginal cultures internationally need to be highlighted; as does the fact that, in many countries a striking overrepresentation of these populations are found in prison. Recognition of the similarities and differences in the effects of colonization that exists between them, coupled with a study of their traditional cultures, may help in finding pathways to holistic and healing forms of "justice." Representatives and/or activists are needed to speak out on behalf of all marginalized groups, in order to ensure the viewing of social troubles in their entirety.

Substances deemed illicit are publicly viewed as one of the biggest problems society faces today. This is evident through the globally growing war on drugs. "Instead of searching for a realistic solution to the drug and alcohol related crimes, the government has chosen to throw millions upon millions of dollars into a failing system that serves to warehouse this growing segment of society" (Anonymous 1987: 4). Dealing with the "drug issue" is imperative in discussing the future of penal abolition. The origins of the very illegality of various substances, the use of scientism in this process (Szasz 1985), as well as the use of propaganda and fear in fuelling the war are all topics in need of discussion (Alexander 1993). The victimless nature of drug "offences" must also be included, especially in relation to "restorative" approaches; where the notion of guilt through wrong doing remains. To whom a drug user must apologize remains questionable. At this point, it becomes important to include people who have first hand experience with these substances, to share their stories, thereby dispelling existing myths and aiding in answering *why* people use certain substances—not *what* substance they use.

The war on drugs is not the only method of manipulation employed by the state. In fact, in many ways, the penal system is used to propel elitist ideals, whereby the "Rich Get Richer and the Poor Get Prison" (Reiman 1998). The criminal justice system's focus on "street" verses "suite crime" is yet another example of social inequality needing attention. This is not to advocate increased penal sanctions in this area (for this would contradict the abolitionist position), but to minimize public victimization and to reduce scapegoating of "street crime."

This pain for profit mentality is further reflected in today's trend toward the privatization of prisons. A decrease in accountability and information availability creates even greater obstacles in attaining the goal of penal abolition. Injustices will be expected to expand, as a prisoner's quality of life is in essence, correlational to profit margins. ICOPA IX therefore, must firmly reiterate that "prisoner's lives are not for sale" (Justice Alliance, 1996).

🏛 ICOPA IX: NEW STRUCTURE, MORE TALK

To ensure that the relevance of different issues and root causes of various social problems are properly dealt with and fully grasped, ICOPA IX must construct the necessary structures allowing ample time for discussion and debate. In facilitating this, workshops should employ a circle type format, although it is noted that this may pose problems for opening and closing sessions were all participants are in attendance. To deal with this dilemma, ample time needs to be allotted for group interaction in these contexts.

We feel it is important to include grassroots action and civil disobedience activism as this was a founding quality of ICOPA, and should remain an integral part. It is, "by bringing prisons into the public eye, we enlighten society as to the need for some serious changes in our basic values, thus taking out first step toward the abolition of prisons" (Brown 1987: 7). Some possible activities include protests, public education and fundraising initiatives that increase awareness of abolitionist issues (i.e. concerts, exhibits, poetry readings etc.). Such activism in Toronto would hopefully draw on the resources of the student body and the social justice activists, thus uniting all generations in the vision of penal abolition. In addition, it is important in this multicultural country to reflect and respect diversity in all possible ways.

From its birth, ICOPA's historical journey has experienced varying shapes and forms. With this growth, as with any change, both positive and negative consequences have emerged. Despite the critique, ICOPA VIII was a valuable learning experience both personally and academically. Hopefully, ICOPA IX is attempting to benefit from past inadequacies and (re)integrate the positive aspects of ICOPA tradition. ICOPA IX, by addressing these concerns poses a nourishing and intellectually stimulating endeavour for all who participate. Since penal abolition is generally considered a marginal or "radical" ideological position, these conferences are important in providing strength in numbers, gained through international solidarity.

𝔪 BIBLIOGRAPHY

Alexander K, Bruce (1993) *Peaceful Measures: Canada's Way Out of the War on Drugs,* Toronto: University of Toronto Press.

Allridge, James (1995) "Victims—Both Sides" in *Journal of Prisoners on Prisons,* Vol. 6, No. 1, 64-67.

Anonymous (1987) "An inside viewpoint" in *Journal of Prisoners on Prisons,* Vol. 1, No. 1, 4-5.

Breen, A. Peter (1995) Families in Peril: Corrections Today, *Bridging the Barriers,* 57, 98-99.

Brown, Ray (1987) "A Prisoner on Abolition" in *Journal of Prisoners on Prisons,* Vol. 1, No. 1, 6-8.

Christie, Nils (1993) *Crime Control as Industry: Towards Gulags Western Style,* Oslo: Scandinavian University Press.

Cohen, Stanley (1985) "Master Patterns," Chapter 1, pg. 13-39 in *Visions of Social Control,* Cambridge: Polity Press.

Di Benedetto, L & S. Seidenstein (1997) "Facts For Now" in *California Prison Focus*, Vol. 1, No. 1, pg. 16.

Foucault, Michel (1977) *Discipline and Punish: The Birth of the Prison,* Toronto: Random House of Canada.

Justice Alliance (1996) *Private Prisons Information Action Kit,* Collingwood: Justice Alliance.

Mathiesen, Thomas (1990) *Prison on Trial,* California: Newberry Press.

Mathiesen, Thomas (1974) *The Politics of Abolition,* New York: Wiley Press.

McCormick, Joseph (1993) "Two Kinds of Prisons" in *The Journal of Prisoners on Prisons,* Vol. 5, No. 1, pp. 21-25.

Morris, Ruth (1997) "History of ICOPA" justiceaction@breakout.nlc.net

Morris, Ruth (1995) *Penal Abolition: The Practical Choice,* Toronto: Canadian Scholars' Press Inc.

Morris, Ruth (1989) *Crumbling Walls: Why Prisons Fail,* Oakville: Moasic Press.

Reiman, J. (1990) *The Rich Get Richer and the Poor Get Prison,* New York: MacMillian Publishing Company.

Sebastien Scheerer (1986) "Towards Abolitionism," in *Contemporary Crisis* 10: 5-20,

Senger, W. (1987) "Abolition: Good/ Bad Approach" in *The Journal of Prisoners on Prison* Vol. 1, No. 1, pp. 12-14.

Solomon, A. (1989) "The Wheels of Injustice" in *Crumbling Walls: Why Prisons Fail*, Oakville: Mosaic Press, p. 8.

Szasz, T. (1985) *Ceremonial Chemistry*, Holmes Beach: Learning Publications Inc.

14

Empathy Works
Obedience Doesn't

Hal Pepinsky

🏛 ABSTRACT

This is an elaboration of a theory of how to make peace instead of making war on crime and personal violence. From a war-making perspective safety from crime and personal violence lies essentially in making individuals obedient to commands from the proper authorities. From a peacemaking perspective as proposed here, safety from personal violence lies essentially in building empathy rather than in commanding obedience. Signs of obedience, like remorse, are inherently unreliable indicators that people are safe company. When it comes to safety from personal violence, empathy works, obedience does not.

🏛 CRIMINOLOGY AS PEACEMAKING

It has been just over a decade since I turned to studying explicitly how to make peace instead of making war on crime and violence. Criminology and

---

Reprinted by permission from *Criminal Justice Policy Review*, Vol. 9 no. 2. Copyright © 1998 by Indiana University of Pennsylvania.

criminal justice are essentially negative enterprises, about what not to do, about why we do what we should not, about how to stop us from doing wrong. In studying peacemaking I sought to understand how we get the kind of human relations we DO want. Essentially, I seek to understand how we become safer in the face of violence. I want to find out what safety is and how we get more of it with one another. There are many other words we use for the opposite of being enmeshed in violence—security, community, compassion... I like "safety" because it is such a plain, blunt word.

I began my explicit inquiry into peacemaking by stating a theory that peace supplanted violence whenever interaction became "responsive" (Pepinsky 1988; expanded in Pepinsky 1991). While violence and the fear and pain it engenders came from people pursuing their own independent agendas and objectives regardless of how others were affected, responsiveness was interaction in which actors' personal agendas shifted constantly to accommodate others' feelings and needs. Responsiveness was how people acted in participatory democracy, which Paul Jesilow and I had earlier proposed as the way to "make people behave" instead of punishing criminality (Pepinsky and Jesilow 1992 [1984]: 127-38).

Thus enterprise would become safer and more honest if tax incentives and other subsidies supported worker/client-democratically-owned-and-operated businesses; prisons would become safer if democratically governed as Tom Murton (1968)—who became "Brubaker" in a movie—did in the mid-sixties in Arkansas; and responses to crime and violence like Victim Offender Reconciliation Programs (VORPs) built safety by encouraging victims and offenders to have community support in creating their own ways into secure community life or, as Christie (1977) had put it, to own their own disputes. In all our proposals, democratization was the path to peace.

In Montreal in 1987 at the Third International Conference on Penal Abolition (ICOPA III), I was also made aware of three parallel streams of thought in action: radical feminism as Kay Harris had propounded it at ICOPA II in 1985 (revised statement in Harris 1991), "abolitionism" as propounded by Knopp et al. in 1976 as represented in her Safer Society Program for victims of sexual violence and for offenders (Knopp 1991), and "restorative justice" beginning under Mennonite auspices with establishment of VORPs first in Kitchener, Ontario, in 1974, and in Elkhart, Indiana, in 1977 (Zehr 1990). At about this time, aboriginal alternatives to prosecution and punishment were beginning to gain recognition. In 1989, New Zealand adopted Maori ways, offering "family group councils" to all young people petitioned into juvenile court for delinquency—circles including family and friends of victims and offenders, sitting in a circle with officials and lawyers, convened by a social worker (Consedine 1995). All these strands focused on the harm done by crime and violence in tearing both victims and offenders from reciprocally trustworthy relations with others, on trying to repair the damage caused by violence rather than focusing on identifying, isolating, separating, and punishing the offender. This body of work has been summarized in a special issue on "The Phenomenon of Restorative Justice," inaugurating the journal *Contemporary Justice Review* (Sullivan 1998).

Richard Quinney, our contributors and I began drawing these strands of thought and action together into a field we labeled *Criminology as Peacemaking* (Pepinsky and Quinney 1991). I have since tried to gain understanding of basic mundane elements by which people make peace in place of violence.

I have found one set of accounts of how to make peace in place of violence, which to me precisely describe the basic structural elements of peacemaking. These accounts describe the Navajo worldview in which "peacemaking courts" have been constituted by the Navajo Supreme Court. Navajo Supreme Court Chief Justice Robert Yazzie (1998) has been joined by Zion (1985) and Gross (1996) in describing how the court functions. The peacemaker, recognized by community members as "someone who thinks well, speaks well, and shows by his or her behavior that the person's conduct is grounded in spirituality" (Yazzie 1998: 125), follows a mediation process which culminates in a circle, joined by individuals aggrieved and their clans, and individuals who have aggrieved and their clans. The peacemaker begins a conversation about violence, which simply moves around the circle, each individual free either to speak or to pass the floor to her or his left. Each time the conversation returns to the peacemaker, s/he summarizes what has been said, and may, and in all probability will, continue around the circle again and again. At any time the peacemaker may pass the floor to a particular member of the circle, who may then pass as asked. To the Navajo, violence is a matter of imbalances of power in interaction. All human interaction is viewed as a conversation. When any person or group in interaction monopolizes the conversation, the conversation—in Navajo terms—becomes imbalanced. Peace is restored by balancing the conversation henceforth. Everyone leaves a truly balanced conversation free to choose what s/he does next. To the Navajo as to me, it is a contradiction in terms to make someone responsible; rather, a peacemaking process liberates one's heart to be in tune with others and to continue taking turns in interaction. Participating in a balanced conversation stimulates one's assumption of responsibility.

Wagner-Pacifici (1993) has analyzed transcripts of negotiations between MOVE and the City of Philadelphia, confirming the hypothesis that violence escalated and eventually erupted as MOVE members' voices and concerns were taken out of officials' conversations in the negotiation process. As Fisher et al. (1992) depict peacemaking in international diplomacy, "getting to yes" entails "moving from position to interest." The quarrel over position is, to borrow Anglo legal terminology, over whether a party has "standing to be heard." Parties are able to move to inventing ways to accommodate one another's concerns once they take for granted that everyone's interests equally deserve airing and hearing. Again, balanced participation in conversations among those who live with the consequences is the essence of making peace.

My recent published work has been directed toward describing how balancing conversations in response to personal violence makes us safer and more secure, in everyday life (Pepinsky 1998a), in criminological research (Pepinsky 1998b), and where legal protection against personal violence fails (Pepinsky 1995). In this work, I focus on the basic substance of peacemaking— to what it is that happens as our conversations become more balanced, to what safe results are. Here I discuss what safety IS.

I propose from a peacemaking point of view that we become safe with others essentially when our relations become empathic, while from a war-making point of view safety lies in making individuals perfectly obedient to the commands of proper authorities. I am not a prophet, and so I don't propose whether at any moment we will do what makes us safer rather than threatening us with greater violence. I do propose what safe relations are when we manage to build them, that is, as we make peace. My thesis about what reduces the threat of violence and yields safety in its place is simply this: empathy works, obedience doesn't.

▥ REMORSE AND EMPATHY

We are born with the capacity to ask for help, and the capacity to offer a loving gaze or embrace. That much is undisputed. To the degree we regard child rearing as a warrior's duty to command a child's obedience, parental duty lies in suppressing inappropriate or intolerable expressions of feeling and commitment. We justify parental war on children on grounds that adults know better than children what children should feel, say, and do.

278

In my home culture parents speak with fear of handling "terrible twos" and adolescence. And from a warrior's point of view, in both cases, it is vital that the parent establish that s/he is in charge. Good children do as they are told. When children do bad, they need—in the current local cliché—to be "given consequences," as though hurting someone isn't consequence enough in itself to deal with. And when we are thus "disciplining" our children, what sign of having become trustworthy do we look for first and foremost? Remorse. "I'm sorry. I know it was stupid. I'll never do it again, promise."

Remorse is the widely known best chance of talking one's way out of a speeding ticket. Remorse is the primary objective of criminal prosecution. When, shortly after the death of Mao Zedong, criminal codes were enacted in China in 1978, Chinese legislators were berated by colleagues of mine in the U.S. for virtually requiring criminal defendants to confess guilt at trial or face dire consequences. I noted at the time how we in the U.S. do the same; woe to the criminal defendant who demands to go to trial and (as most do) loses (Pepinsky 1980).

I suffer watching defendants plead guilty in local courts. It is such a humiliating experience, assuring the judge count by count, "Yes, your honor, I have done it and know it was wrong and have no excuse for my behavior." Thus the judge leaves a clean record that the plea is "free and voluntary." We put a premium on obedience. We do so to our peril, I believe.

Alice Miller (1990 [1983]) calls commanding obedience "poisonous pedagogy." It is poisonous pedagogy, as her book title suggests, to make a child feel or do something for his or her own good. "Stop whining, you know this is good for you!" You learn that to please the parents you spontaneously love and want to please, to say nothing of to avoid pain and rejection, you smile when you are supposed to, you say the right thing, no matter how tempted you are to protest or show fear or pain. You learn, in other words, to lie. The poison in this pedagogy is that we teach ourselves as children to lie, to dissociate from our own feelings and inclinations, to bury them, to reject our own true selves.

Nothing is more fundamental to safe social relations than honesty. Insofar as we manage to bury our true feelings and respond—mechanically—as instructed, we are essentially what psychiatrists in my culture these days call sociopathic. We are essentially expedient. We are, as Miller argues using Hitler and a serial sadistic killer as case studies, in the dissociated frame of mind in which Milgram's (1973) research subjects demonstrated enough "obedience to authority" to try to give lethal shock to stooges who begged for their lives.

Short of being murdered or severely disabled, vaginal or anal rape is a fair candidate for being the form of criminal personal violence we fear most. Those who have raped, who talk about it, characteristically express surprise that those they have raped are complaining, thinking, "They asked for it," or, "They deserved it." While those being raped fear that their attacker is so out of control that "He could kill me!" those who are raping are oblivious to the pain and fear they cause. Or as a friend, Cynthia Ford, infers of her father's state of mind when he ritually tortured her during her childhood:

> *My sense is that abusers dissociate first, and that the part that arises isn't oblivious to the pain and terror inside themselves by harming another. They project their own helpless inner kid onto the victim, and then destroy the pain and terror inside themselves by harming another. Or that is one reason. My father for instance NEEDED my pain and terror in order to feel better. The sexual release was only a sort of artifact or perhaps a symbolic finishing or denouement.*

In either event violence begins in a state of dissociation or detachment from the feelings, needs and wishes of the person to be victimized. That dissociation permits violence to begin and to repeat itself.

At the other end of the spectrum from those who subordinate others wantonly to those who conform to our norms, how are you supposed to trust the yes-person who assures you that "I'll be there for you"? At one end of the spectrum, personal violence does not happen unless the assailant dissociates. At the other, you don't know whether you can count on anyone who has had to learn to turn her or his true feelings off and tell you what s/he thinks you want to hear. This is what Alice Miller tells us that poisonous pedagogy—doing and feeling as you're told—produces. When the conformist who tells you "I'll be there for you" feels the demand to shift allegiance to some other power figure at your expense, you lose. The promise is not really a promise. The promise is oriented toward an external set of rewards and punishments, which may shift with political winds, not toward your needs. The promise is an act of obedience, not of empathy. One common promise for obedience sake is to apologize for one's violence and promise never to do it again.

It is remarkable that we so venerate remorse. Remorse is in thorough disrepute among those who work with those victimized by so-called domestic violence. In the run-of-the-mill cycle of repeated assaults, each assault is followed by a "honeymoon period" in which the assailant expresses remorse, says he's sorry, tries to do anything to make it up. Those who work with those who most regularly are battered, including those who are routinely raped, regard remorse as worthless. Experience tells them so. I find it quite remarkable that we can find remorse in our subjects, such as criminal defendants and children, so reassuring.

Conversely, empathy may supplant violence with no remorse expressed. A friend recently described to me how she had found safety in the company of a mother who had chronically emotionally abused her. This friend, who, in my view, has done a heroic job of balancing compliance with court orders and protecting herself and her children from apparent violence, had stopped calling her mother because her mother would invariably combine two themes: "What is so wrong with you that all this trouble keeps happening?" and, "You're not showing me you love me."

My friend's father had told her that her mother has cancer, and that metastasis had set in. Her mother had started going shopping with her. One of the faults the mother had criticized my friend for was for compulsive shopping. That stopped. They don't talk about Lynnette's problems. They don't talk about the cancer either. Her mother doesn't complain to her daughter at all, bent instead on enjoying time together looking for bargains and such. Her mother's behavior is what I would call "responsive": she by her action demonstrates what hurts her daughter and responds instead to what her daughter enjoys. My friend and I agree that her mother is demonstrating a reliable commitment to saying goodbye on good terms. The mother's conduct combines a hard-nosed projection of how the mother herself wants to die with attentiveness to what truly makes her daughter feel safe in her mother's company.

Since having supposed that empathy might be a reliable ground upon which to build trust and become safe in others' company, I have noticed how hard it is for those who are at risk of continuing emotional or physical assaults to fake empathy. Remorseful violators can go on and on about how terrible THEY feel over how they hurt you, but until they become honest with themselves and you about getting what they want, they suffer emotional attention deficit disorder. If they do get forced to talk about how they think you feel and what they think you want, it just won't sound like you to you. I have learned to depend on empathy to decide whether I can afford to let down my guard with others. Empathy may come and go, of course, mine included. It is not that the world can be separated into empathic and sociopathic people. Rather, while it is being shown, empathy indicates that any of us can be depended upon to be responsive rather than untrustworthy. Empathy amounts to letting others' true selves into our conversations, and when we do so, we are literally there WITH others, in a frame of mind to notice others' fear and pain and offer validation and reassurance.

In recent years I have gotten to know a number of children and parents caught in struggles over evidence that the children are seriously assaulted by parents, to know large numbers of those who describe having been raised in horrendous violence, commonly known as ritual abuse, and to know a number of those who have treated people for the trauma such violence leaves behind. I have gotten to know these people in the context of offering a seminar on children's rights and safety and another class in which I introduce peacemaking. I invite a number of them to these classes. I seldom have money even to cover their travel expenses, but I do offer my home to those who stay overnight. Among these guests is a woman who I believe indeed was born in a prominent cult bloodline, and long after she thought that she had renounced the occult, still got "triggered" into an "alter" state to impose "discipline" on member groups in a multi-state region for twenty years thereafter. I asked my students how they felt about my inviting her, and several survivors of like violence that she has taken in, into my home. Some were outraged and dismayed that I could do so. I sent their comments to my friend, who wrote back a long letter.

The letter, which I have shared with my students and others, is not long on remorse. My friend says that she herself did hands-on "sacrificing" of people only until she rose high enough to let others do it instead, that she did it without feeling/knowing that she would be killed if she did not. She explicitly distinguishes herself from despicable serial killers like Ted Bundy.

She also describes going through books of pictures of missing children, looking to see whether she recognizes any of her victims. She offers assistance to law enforcement, including telling them about her past (which is unprosecutable because bodies would not be found). She takes in others trying to escape. She is in touch enough with what she now regards as an alien part of herself—the part that could be triggered and called out to cult activity—that she ensures that she is always in safe company, so that she has no chance to "lose time," as happens when people switch among multiple personalities. In so doing she is in touch with her real self, just as she pays attention to others. On her own initiative, she started visiting a prisoner with whom I have been corresponding for some years. She not only shows sensitivity and empathy for those in whose company I see her; ultimately she shows empathy for me. She is for instance scrupulous about honoring my request to come and go to suit my family schedule. She and her guests notice and express appreciation even for little demonstrations of hospitality. Noticing their empathy, I am confident that they will in no way hurt my family or me. Their displays of empathy are exercises in personal responsibility—in becoming different from the way they were when they tortured and killed others.

To become responsible and empathic, you have to have confidence in the value and legitimacy of your own feelings and needs. So my friend may show some remorse implicitly by having tried for instance to identify her victims, but my safety with her now in my judgment rests on her knowing that it was a part of her that she now considers alien, that she knows that basically she is better and more trustworthy than the part of her that formerly hurt others. You have to like and accept a part of yourself that you do not dissociate from in order to be honest with others about what you do feel and want, and it appears to me in this and other cases that one's empathy sets in only as one feels one can be oneself without being rejected for it. Trying to induce remorse and shame is therefore counterproductive, for success in shaming lies in making one loathe and reject and demean oneself. In shame, one may either choose a safe, loving, vulnerable target such as one's child and lash out in anger, just split off from attention to the subject's feelings and let the rage out. It is easy to imagine that when one is on the receiving end of such an outburst, it feels as though you're going to die. In the numbness and shame that follows victimization, shame may do more than bottle up rage for politically convenient outbursts. One may adapt by concluding that in this world such as it is, you don't deserve or cannot expect better than to hang onto one's abuser. The patterns protective mothers describe to me indicate that those who aim to prey on "their" children pick out women who have been beaten into feeling responsible for being violated, into feeling that it was their worldly, religious duty to serve men (generally) who degraded them, and then beat them.

In neither case does shame help one's affliction. When feeling ashamed one is oriented toward one's own prior conduct. When empathizing, one attends instead to feelings and sensibilities here and now—to the present rather than to one's past. Safety rests not on knowing one has done wrong or right, but on noticing and being moved by what others are feeling here and now.

While empathy attends to the present for its own sake, martyrdom and servitude—also unreliable indicators of safety—are instrumental. Empathy is neither self-recrimination nor selflessness but participation in social moments free of attachment to outside agendas. Empathy is an openness to new experience, a relaxing of preconceptions as to what is expected, in English metaphor, an opening of the heart. In Buddhist terms it is pure life(-giving) energy, compassion in action. As Quinney (1991) tells us, we end suffering by noticing it and responding openly. Elements of empathy are captured in this saying attributed to the Navajo, which I have posted in bold letters outside my office:

⋔ SHOW UP PAY ATTENTION TELL THE TRUTH DON'T BE ATTACHED TO OUTCOME

Attachment to outcome means that you know, before you hear from others, what needs to be done. If you already know what needs to be done, you have nothing to learn from listening to others before your next move, in terms of what most demands your attention. Your priorities are not up for discussion.

The energy in compassion or empathy lies in learning something new to do by listening to those who will be most affected by what you do next. Empathy is a suspension of one's agenda to "pay attention" to what they say, and to let their feelings soak into one's own conscious nervous energy. Empathy begins with unencumbered listening (Pepinsky 1998a). Of course, in order to pay attention you have to "show up"—or as I hear people in my daughter's generation say, "be there." Paying attention means showing interest in and drawing out the voices which are least heard in whatever setting or reference group you find yourself, in order to introduce balance into the conversation—the structural manifestation that peace is being made.

Our ultimate cultural barrier to substituting empathy for obedience is our presumption that adults know more than children. In a sense of course, that is true. But as children, we have some vital gifts of our own to add to conversations. Chief among these is our blatantly honest desire to please and be accepted by adults. We bring honesty to conversations, unless adults shut us down. We may be the first to cry when we are all frightened. We may be the first to relax and pay attention at school when the parents we so much want to please stop frightening each other. Adults who leave "their" children out of their conversations are prone to impose lessons gained from experience, including having to lie, as Alice Miller puts it for the children's "own good." How blind. How damaging to the very gift of empathy the child spontaneously offers to our conversations.

Norway is a second home to me. There at the dinner table in party company, children are almost ritually brought into conversations, to describe their worlds in their own terms, as adults pay attention.

As adults share among themselves what they hear as they pay attention to children, adults legitimize in safe company reliving traumas of their own childhoods. I have seen this happen time and again; as mothers trying to protect their children recognize ways in which, as children themselves, they too were sexually assaulted by someone they loved and trusted. Without magically fixing their children's problems, I have seen them and their children gain strength— as in the case of those with eating disorders literally gaining weight. These mothers have the greatest respect for the honesty, courage, and wisdom of their children. That is their primary solace. This, to me, is truly a break in an intergenerational cycle of violence and victimization.

I sense that as growing numbers of children and adult survivors share stories, validate one another, and speak out, we will overcome our ignorance of what our children, including the children buried in our adult selves, have to teach us. That will be the profoundest peacemaking of all.

In the mid-sixties in law school I learned that a minority of states were setting a national trend, permitting "no-fault" divorces. The common-law rule, in effect in New York State at the time, was that one could obtain a divorce only if one's spouse committed a statutory offense (adultery in New York), and if one had "clean hands." So if one spouse sued another for divorce proving adultery, and the other spouse proved that the plaintiff was also committing adultery, the law required that family to be reunified, unless perhaps they consented to separate for an extended period and then ask for a divorce together.

Women's shelters started opening up not long after. And in growing numbers, women do leave battering relations. From what I know of where custody disputes began (as from Children of the Underground founder Faye Yager in 1973; Carpenter and Dietrich 1997), children whose fathers were established in communities in the middle class or higher first began to feel safe enough to talk to mothers, who felt detached enough to believe what they heard rather than telling their children to stop telling lies. And in therapy, adults began to talk about the violence of their own childhoods and be heard, especially by women's advocates. (One sad void, for instance, is in support groups for male survivors of childhood incest.) Surveys were first conducted in the late eighties asking people how often they had been sexually assaulted by someone they knew. And so, I would say, out of the movement to allow women to leave men who beat, rape, and threaten them, we have liberated children's voices of victimization into public discourse.

The results are scary. What amounts to unrelenting torture of children once plainly described suddenly seems as though it might be happening all around us. As I see it, this is an awakening of our empathy for childhood, our own included. As we recognize that children have as much to offer in decisions that affect them as adults, our children will free themselves of violence more readily. All it takes, actually, is for a single adult whom the child manifestly likes and laughs with to offer the child sanctuary from any adult whose company scares the child, and for other adults to let sanctuary happen (Bianchi 1994). There you have the fundamental prerequisite of any child's safety. This may be hard to achieve in a warring world, but people do gain small bits of empathy, which provide remarkable measures of safety. One survivor of cult torture, led by her socially and politically prominent father, remembers a fifth-grade teacher looking at her as though she understood that something wrong was being done to her. That bit of empathic connection carried her forward until she broke from the cult, and she has attained safety and trust as in a very fulfilling and safe marriage. A small dose of sanctuary can be life sustaining.

The bad thing about scary news is that it makes you feel that you have to shut the problem down. I have testified in one case in which a judge actually ordered children NOT to be in counseling so that they would stop saying bad stuff about their father; I know of many others like it. All this is in the guise that children are causing trouble for themselves by threatening sacred family bonds. It is terrifying to think that if we probe enough in our very own families, we may discover that a valued relative was Jekyll and Hyde, or that a monster may lurk in our child's daycare center or school. As I hear individuals whom I know in other contexts talk about how violence in the home including violence by children is getting out of hand, I am struck that the tone and substance of the protest is like that of someone confronting any personal feeling or fear that s/he has denied. It is inherently scary to emerge from denial of a problem, all the more so when one's denial amounts to cultural blindness. And yet, I see that as progress toward safety, in which each of us learns to create families of choice rather than just doing our ancestral duties. As I see it, record numbers of children and adult survivors are sharing stories and being heard about problems that for millennia in our European ancestry at any rate were almost totally buried. As DeMause (1982) traces it, children in Europe and Euro-America were not legally and politically recognized as people to whom adults owed any duty until about a hundred years ago. So we have come a long way.

We can of course follow the same principles of making peace in any company, with or without children. Basically though, our defenses against forsaking duty for empathy lie embedded in the violence we suffer as children. We may join the mob in going after this or that public villain, but at root, in areas of our lives remote from police and legal surveillance, we are most likely to be trapped in violence or safe from it. Empathy and honesty pay off anywhere in daily or political life. By "showing up" and "paying attention" to the voices of our childhood, we most directly accomplish the safety which Karl Marx (1963 [1843]) called "human emancipation."

In the Navajo saying, "telling the truth" refers to honesty. If you want someone honestly to talk about his or her reaction to having committed a crime, you don't set up plea bargaining ceremonies of remorse in order to draw out how the offender honestly feels and believes. The condition for honesty is essentially acceptance of this principle: When I ask you for truth, I grant you the responsibility of how next what you tell me gets used.

This condition sets the principle behind "Incidents Teams" established by the dean of students office on my home campus of Indiana University. I am delighted to have representatives of the nearly decade-old Racial Incidents Team, and Gay/Lesbian/Bisexual Anti-Harassment Team make presentations in my classes on "social control." The Racial Incidents Team invites people to report harassment or crimes committed against them that appear based on race or ethnicity, or on religious beliefs. The GLB Anti-Harassment Team invites reports of gay bashing (whether or not the person victimized is gay). Among other things the teams annually publish summaries of every incident reported annually. Each is a team of professional staff who first invites each complainant to elaborate, and then brainstorm options as to what the complainant might do further. The options are diverse and imaginative, ranging from education to notification to invoking disciplinary or legal processes. It is up to the complainant to ask the Team to help her or him implement the package of the complainant's choice.

In most cases, complainants are satisfied to have the report on file, and want to go no further. Team members report occasional frustration when, for instance, a complainant declines to report a crime to police or the prosecutor. But the rule of confidentiality and abiding by complainant wishes is ironclad.

This is precisely the rule followed by therapists and rape or domestic violence crisis counselors. The one who has been victimized suffers a loss of control. Restoration of a sense of personal safety rests on the one who has been victimized resuming control of her social relations. Since s/he is the one at hand who has most been stripped of a voice in what happens to her or him, her or his voice is the one most urgently needing to be drawn into the ensuing conversation. If that voice matters, it will guide and be supported by what it says. Let the one who has most been traumatized by victimization be the primary guide to what comes next. This is the principle by which the Incidents Teams operate. It seems to me that incidents teams would be a useful independent adjunct to police, prosecutors and courts. Those who complained could have the support of the Team on their terms regardless of what police or prosecutors decided duty demanded of themselves. This would represent organizing to create empathy in the wake of violence, as a supplement to organizing to demand obedience of perpetrators. Time and again I have heard survivors of traumatic violence like incestuous rape say that the most healing, energizing response they received when they first told about the event was from those who sat, listened, said as little as "How terrible; I'm so sorry," and did nothing else to try to take over and fix it. Incidents team members at IU report much the same experience. Offering safe refuge from further violence is the next most crucial step to safety.

Martyrdom and servitude represent trying to do things for others on pain of social or heavenly rejection. Regardless of whether people who martyr themselves or serve others are forced by other people to do so or "choose" to subordinate their own needs to others', at a basic internal level they feel they have or deserve no choice. They must discern and obey the demands or fill the needs of the gods or people they serve; or else... they cut off their social and spiritual connections at the roots. As Weber (1999 [1904-5]) discerned, the difference lies in whether one is born in a state of grace, or has to earn grace. If one is born in a state of grace, one does not have to justify one's existence. If one must justify one's existence, one is trapped into meeting external standards to make one's life worthwhile.

When doing one's painful duty to abide by external needs or rules, one is literally just following orders. Regardless of whether this defense is accepted as a legal justification for violence, the honest truth is that obedient actors have forsaken personal responsibility for their actions, quite literally so. Responsibility is implied instead by the simple claim, "I did it because I wanted to." You can assume responsibility and expressly choose to enjoy the safety of empathic relations because you feel want to hear and respect the sensibilities of those whose turn it is to join the conversation, because it makes you feel connected. As Quinney would say, you have heard the suffering at hand and been moved by it. When you do that, by definition, your violence stops in its tracks.

I have been close to people who I believe to be repeatedly assaulting or harassing others. I have heard plenty of remorse. I have seen how hard it is for those who I find at risk of repeating their violence to empathize. They are too hung up on their own problems, and desperate to do whatever they feel they must to cling to others. I find that empathy, unlike a polygraph, is hard to fake. And when people like the houseguests whom I describe above show one another and me empathy, I find that I can afford to let down my guard and enjoy my safety in their company. I also notice that I receive ample warning as empathy shuts down before someone bursts into violence, which helps me relax and be able to empathize myself, rather than to be on guard for renewed attack.

At the individual level one's capacity for empathy with others remains in balance with what I consider empathy for oneself—"telling the truth" to oneself and others about what one feels and needs to feel validated and connected to others merely for being oneself, not denying one's own needs and feelings in martyrdom or self-sacrifice. In enjoying the safety of empathy one takes heart from watching those who have been victimized gain voice and assume responsibility for their lives, and one's satisfaction rests in being there to validate and honor the occasion. In martyrdom or self-sacrifice one becomes what Schaef (1992) and others call co-dependent, trying to decide and do for others what you think they need to do or have done. When enjoying empathic relations, one loses "attachment to outcome." Faith that balanced participation will yield proper results supplants conviction that results have to come out a certain way. From showing up to letting go of attachment to outcome, the Navajo saying summarizes the range of elements on which empathy rests.

Trying to make anyone else empathic or responsible rests on the fallacy of making empathy an act of obedience. The logic on which empathy rests determines that empathy and responsibility can only be invited by showing empathy and responsibility. This means listening down—drawing out voices most excluded from our conversations and being guided by them—rather than subordinating others, which literally is a refusal to grant empathy. It means listening down in balance with listening down into one's own self. It is by allowing one's sharing of one's own feelings and self with others to emerge that one can feel at all, truly feel, and hence feel what others are expressing in the event. It is as one turns off one's own feelings and denies one's own sensibilities that one turns instead to connecting with others in the manner of one of

Milgram's obedient subjects. This includes feeling too ashamed and inadequate to deserve to have one's feelings and sensibilities count, or have them enter the conversation. Ultimately, shame deprives not other offenders but oneself of one's capacity to enjoy empathy with others in concert with empathy with oneself. One bears responsibility as one dares to bare oneself and let outcomes fall where they may. Insofar as one bears oneself, one cares and dares to listen to others' pain and fears without having to fix or solve them either. Letting go of attachment to outcome allows one to attend and respond to one's present. It is, as Ernest Becker (1968: 327-46) concludes, our self-esteem rather than our shame that allows us to connect safely and honestly with others. That is no less true of one's worst enemy than it is of oneself. One cannot dictate whether anyone gives empathy, but safety lies only where feelings of the moment are noticed and recognized, and acted upon. Empathy rests on embracing a part of one's own inner self as a foundation for rejecting what has been wrong with oneself.

I work in many cases of apparent violence against children these days. Contrary to war-making expectations, I find that children facing violence are much more compassionate and reasonable than adults around them are. One child advocate I know who had to fight off her own stepfather's regular demands for oral sex just wanted him out of the home while the police wanted her to either seek prosecution of her stepfather or stop complaining. Quite typically, children who are "molested" by a parent want to work out some safe form of contact, while adults around them fight over whether that parent deserves to own the child's company on the parent's unilateral terms or not at all. The mission of Adult Children of Alcoholics recognizes how out of loving duty children go out of their way to feel, be, and do what their parents need rather than the reverse. As children learn languages readily so as to communicate as circumstances allow, so when as children we are in war-making perspective most ignorant and out of control, we are in fact more responsible than we generally dare grow up to be. We grow up learning agendas we must perform, learning to bury our own feelings. In the process of learning what agendas we ourselves must follow, we also learn how we must treat others and what we must make them do, all empathy aside.

Ironically, then, age and experience seem to harden our propensity to lie or deny even our own feelings and experience. Age and experience are liable to ingrain defenses and prejudices in us that a child's fresh eyes can see through more readily. In any command structure, it is fallacious to presume that superiors know and do better than their subordinates. Power over others preaches and embeds in our psyches its own false justification—that power holders are wiser, truer and kinder than subordinates. Balancing conversations is the only way out of thralldom in this falsehood.

🏛 OBEDIENCE IS INHERENTLY UNFAIR

Obedience is a matter of choosing whose voices get to be heard as against others'. The very definition of who offends and who gets victimized becomes a matter of who is entitled to define who the offenders and victims are. This is a power trip. The logic of a system run by mobilizing power over others is inescapable: Those who enjoy most power to dictate definitions of others' situations are by virtue of power alone odds on to—as Jeffrey Reiman (1997) puts it, "get richer [while] the poor get prison." It doesn't take long growing up in the game of obedience to learn that in cases of difference, the one who is highest in the power configuration gets to decide that in case of dispute, what I say goes. The realities of subordination manifest themselves repeatedly. Nowhere recently have these realities more clearly manifested themselves to me than in contests between children who say that a custodian is sexually assaulting them, and the caretakers accused. It appears as though the more corroborative evidence there is, like a child's having a sexually transmitted disease or torn anus or vaginal opening, and the more serious the assault would be if the fact of it were recognized, the greater the odds that officials will rule evidence of the caretaker's assaults inadequate to find fault, and hence that the child should be taken from the presence of any parent or therapist to whom the child complains (Rosen and Etlin 1996).

In the face of the rule that those who hold more power are more likely to win power games, as we continue to seek safety via subordination of miscreants, we find ourselves in ever more jeopardy, caught in a world where "inequalities" and "injustice" harden and grow. From the peacemaker view, I am safer the more readily those who are obedient find relations in which they share attending to one another's will and needs. Extend the boundaries within which those whom I mistrust and I share empathy, and I become safer. Raise the number of those whose fates I separate from mine via subordination, and I become endangered, not only from those authoritatively subordinated as by being labeled "offender," but from all those who empathize and share destinies with them. Thus, justice is something that happens to me and my fellow creatures together, one way or the other. The gods who render justice don't appear to care who started violence. It is simply that the more firmly separated enemy fates become, the more endangered we are. The justice we face is that we all ultimately become safer or more endangered together. This is what Hindus call karma. In terms of how stressed out or relaxed I am while I survive, and indeed in terms of how likely some friend will feed, shelter, and hold me in need, insofar as we enjoy empathy, we enjoy safety. Insofar as we resort to violence, we fear and hurt from violence. That is not a prophecy. That is simply how justice gets done one way or the other.

Within the microlimits of our individual lives, just having friends with whom we can safely, honestly share fear and pain is the essence of being safe from personal violence. Personal investment in empathy pays off in personal security and self-esteem. Personal investment in empathy means not letting one's own feelings and sensibilities be subordinated, balanced with hearing first and foremost the most subdued voices in one's own here and now. One proposition I have put to students is that it is safer to invest in friendship than in Wall Street. When the market crashes, I rest my survival on having friends who will take me in and feed me from their own stocks. That is my primary social security. The more heavily others follow my lead in investing in this market of peace, the more readily we all will free ourselves from violence, regardless of how quickly or steadily the personal safety we build close around ourselves with friends translates into global safety. Within the peacemaking frame, the broader the divergence in background, class, status, power among those who empathize, the brighter and broader the halo of empathy around that accommodation. But empathy pays off in the personal safety of the one who invests in it regardless of how slowly culture follows.

It is presumptuous of anyone to suppose that s/he knows how to accomplish justice. It is practical to invest empathy for safety's sake, where safety lies in treating one another fairly and with balance.

Until as recently as my "peacemaking primer" (Pepinsky 1995), I looked on "dumping up" as a means to making peace. I recant. Any form of dumping is a bid for obedience. I know from growing up and circulating among rich and powerful people that people up there tend to suspect that no one really loves them for themselves and feel mighty scared, vulnerable, driven to defend their claim to a social stake. I know they are as wary as are street-people I have met.

Fitness to survive unrelenting struggles over power and obedience entails becoming ever more vigilant against betrayal by those whose obedience one has enforced. Like other addictions, maintenance of obedience requires bigger and bigger fixes. Those who find the legitimacy of their power positions drawn into question naturally focus more on establishing who remains in charge, and in justifying the system to which one belongs, than to noticing how subordinates feel and see and hear things. We can by empathy and refuge free people from subordination far more readily than we can beat power holders into empathy.

A little listening means a lot, especially to those like women and children who are structurally situated to be silenced and ignored. Those who are trapped in recurrent victimization offer large doses of personal appreciation to anyone who just stops and listens to them. Rather than depending on dumping up, the logic of balancing conversations by spreading empathy dictates that I instead help amplify the left-out voices, to let them speak for themselves rather than seeking to speak for them. In the practice of mediating imbalances in conversation, the floor oscillates back and forth between concerns of those at the poles of each interest in conflict, so that once those who are weakest are aired and heard, the floor passes upward, so that those who have offended and those who hold power may enjoy their turn at being heard, honestly heard. Peacemaking entails taking turns in conversation about oneself and one's own feelings and interests, up and down the power structure like a child's seesaw or teeter-totter. Insofar as one offers empathy rather than a demand for obedience, one offers a gift rather than imposing an obligation. Whatever the response, it is responsible and trustworthy only insofar as it is not commanded, or more implicitly, expected. What matters is whether concern for others' interests manifestly redirects the response. Empathy may be reciprocated and hence create safety; a command will never do so. The peacemaker's faith is that the co-generation of empathy will create responses that will accommodate everyone's needs more readily than any other response. The karmic promise, the promise of justice, is that social security and equity in having needs accommodated will resonate outward from individual increases in safety against personal violence, from taking turns listening in dyadic conversations, to allowing workers and customers fair shares of ownership in corporate decisions and losses or profits to, to mediating conversations between those we designate victims and offenders... wherever, at whatever social level one wants to measure equity of participation in conversations. That's the starting point and the way regardless of how far apart people start.

When we are truly responsible, we are responsible for our own choices and for responding to the consequences, not oxymoronically responsible for making others do anything. Insofar as we become conscious of the role our empathy alone plays in creating the results, I propose that we will feel safer, and by any number of measures of violence and inequality will become safer.

Balancing voices in our conversations requires that we individually feel secure enough to dampen our narcissism, including letting go of getting our own points across, relaxing our determination to reach some objective we have set for ourselves or for others in advance. Implicit in a concern for doing justice, rather than making sure others too have a balanced say in what happens, is a need to justify a result rather than attention to the process by which results are achieved. Gaining safety makes a simple but unyielding demand—that we pay attention to the sensibilities of the people we live with rather than to performing some higher social agenda.

CONSEQUENCES

There has been a lot of talk for over twenty years about "widening the net" of criminal justice (Cohen 1979, Pepinsky 1973). When programs are introduced which are supposed to offer alternatives to incarceration, the odds shift toward using the alternatives on those who otherwise would have had less done to them, with potential for creating records of failure of alternatives which justify and thus increase use of incarceration. I have noticed over the years an impasse between academicians who recognize this dynamic and practitioners who protest that they use alternatives and are not widening the net. Recently, an official who works with youth explained how those who seek to mitigate punishment widen nets.

She was speaking of the need for a local juvenile detention center. She said that since it was so expensive to have juveniles transported several counties away to be detained, the judge could only really afford to send juveniles for a minimum stay of six days. Meanwhile, there were youths at risk who had had the benefit of all the alternatives the system had to offer, and who might be turned around from getting into further trouble by just being given 24 hours in detention to teach them that wrongdoing "has consequences." So if the local detention center is built, new classes of youths will be given this "shock." And what is to be done if they for instance fail the routine urinalysis (given by that juvenile probation office regardless of offense charged) in the aftermath? Finckenauer (1982) found that those who had been "scared straight" in confrontations with lifers in a maximum security prison afterwards got arrested more than a matched control group of those who had not undergone the program. In the game of demanding obedience, the need for sterner measures spreads inexorably.

It is like what a parent faces who has spanked a child hard and yet had a recurrence of disobedience. A sterner measure is called for in the logic of commanding obedience.

The same official who illustrated to me how people think as they widen nets also was giving reassurance to volunteers in a new Victim Offender Reconciliation Program. She noted that after 13 years of work she had taken heart from some people who had come back to her years later and had told her that because she had cared when other adults had not, she had turned their lives around. I expect that these were moments of empathy that tend not to be shared or even remembered because they don't count in the game of imposing consequences. Empathy matters nonetheless.

No matter what our formal or official exteriors, we show empathy in some measure, almost all of us. It is indeed what makes the doing of any of our jobs socially worthwhile. It is just too bad when we feel obliged to attribute what our empathy has achieved to doing our duty to command obedience.

The popular criminal legal jargon these days around me is that since we know the system is out of hand and don't really favor punishment, we "give consequences" instead. It occurs to me as I begin service as a VORP mediator that my preoccupation is with focusing attention on consequences—first and foremost harm to those victimized—which have already occurred. Why demand that people attend instead to consequences others or I have devised? I seek to have those most affected by the crimes referred to us tell one another what they have done and what has already happened, and then assume responsibility for devising responses to the consequences at hand. Results of that process may feel safe. Introducing consequences means that I assume responsibility and make decisions for others, taking away their room for exercise of responsibility. I don't even give myself a chance to learn how they might respond if I did not impose my own consequences. And as by urine testing, I who impose consequences will want to ensure accountability not to my subject's personal responsibility, but to me. I will find myself driven to imposing closer and closer scrutiny of my subjects. How unsafe to be on guard so.

Anyone with a problem of violence in or out of the criminal justice system enjoys a measure of discretion whether next to listen or pass on what someone says, or to execute or follow an order. That is the only remedy I see for an escalation in incarceration in my home United States since the Vietnam War ended in 1975, which otherwise could be diverted only by sending a mass of young U.S. soldiers abroad into open combat with a foreign enemy (Pepinsky 1996, 1991: 34-61).

A year after I moved to my current town, in 1977, my county whose population has since climbed from ninety to a hundred and twenty thousand hired a not-for-profit consultant who told us that our county jail could be gutted and made into 40 cells which would last us until well into the next millennium. That consultant then formed a for-profit firm, so that by 1983 he had forecast that we would need 95-110 cells to last us into the next millennium. I joined a friend suing to void county council approval of a leasing arrangement for a jail which—to round off corners on the top of a new "justice building"— would have 124 cells. We lost. That jail was opened in 1986, and episodically spilled to over capacity within six months of its opening. Now we appear destined to approve building a jail truly sufficient to meet our needs as we enter the new millennium—with 400 to 500 cells.

I was talking with a friend who inspired my failed lawsuit, and we agreed that—karmically—our efforts to tell people that the new jail would be filled had helped create the monster we now face. A burst of official effort went into organizing and using defendant- or offender-subsidized "alternative" "consequences" for offenders, which apparently generated records of failure of "lenient" measures, and widened the net far faster than I might have imagined.

As I begin learning how to serve as a VORP mediator, I have no illusions that VORP or any other restorative justice program will empty the jail. Nor do I think that officials are more to blame for placing obedience before empathy than the will in all of us to rely on official action for our safety.

I have fantasized about a bumper sticker: "Safer to Carry a Friend than a Gun." There is remarkable, significant safety in each empathic connection we make. All structural safety, all signs of the withering away of oppression and inequality, rest on attending to empathy, which in turn requires letting go of obedience. The science and art of achieving safety in the face of personal violence is that of empathy, which I call making peace instead of making war. Empathy can start anywhere, on any job. Empathy is the only mechanism that protects us against personal violence. The personal violence recorded by criminologists and police is but a shadow of the violence and terror of isolation (and attendant worthlessness) that threatens us routinely in our daily lives, where outsiders, including police and child protection workers, fear to intrude. Whether we humans achieve greater violence or safety, justice will prevail, where the just results of our efforts to become safer in one another's company will show that for us all, empathy works, obedience does not.

𝄢 ENDNOTES

Many thanks for helpful ideas and criticism go to Bill DuBois, Cynthia Ford, Shirley Julich, Nanci Koser-Wilson, Joe Maizlish, Natti Ronel, and Dennis Sullivan.

𝄢 REFERENCES

Becker, E. (1968), *The Structure of Evil: An Essay on the Unification of the Science of Man,* New York: George Braziller.

Bianchi, H. (1994), *Justice as Sanctuary: Toward a New System of Crime Control,* Bloomington, Ind.: Indiana University Press.

Carpenter, M. (reporter), and Dietrich, A. (photographer) (1997) "Children of the Underground," *Pittsburgh Post-Gazette* (Dec. 14-18; five-part series)

Christie, N. (1977), "Conflicts as Property," *British Journal of Criminology*, 17. 1-19.

Cohen, S. (1979), "The Punitive City: Notes on the Dispersal of Justice," *Contemporary Crises, 3.* 339-63.

Consedine, J. (1995), *Restorative justice: Healing the Effects of Crime,* Lyttleton, N.Z.: Ploughshares Publications.

DeMause, L. (1982), *Foundations of Psychohistory,* New York 10024-0401: Creative Roots, Inc.

Finckenauer, J.O. (1982), *Scared Straight and the Panacea Phenomenon,* Englewood Cliffs, N.J.: Prentice-Hall.

Fisher, R., Ury, W., and Patton, B. (1992), *Getting to Yes,* New York: Houghton Mifflin.

Gross, E.K. (1996), "A Preliminary Evaluation of the Navajo Peacemaker Court." Paper presented at the annual meeting of the American Society of Criminology, Chicago.

Harris, M.K. (1991), "Moving into the New Millenium: Toward a Feminist Vision of Justice," in Pepinsky, H.E. and Quinney, R., eds. *Criminology as Peacemaking,* Bloomington, Ind.: Indiana University Press.

Knopp, F.H. (1991,) "Community Solutions to Sexual Violence: Feminist/Abolitionist Perspectives," in Pepinsky, H.E. and Quinney, R., eds. *Criminology as Peacemaking,* Bloomington, Ind.: Indiana University Press.

Knopp, F.H., et al. (1976), *Instead of Prisons: A Handbook for Abolitionists,* Orwell, Vt.: Safer Society Press.

Marx, K. (1963 [1843]), "Bruno Bauer: *die Judenfrage,*" in . Bottomore, T.B., ed. and trans., *Karl Marx: Early Writings,* New York: McGraw-Hill.

Milgram, S. (1973), *Obedience to Authority: An Experimental View,* New York: Harper and Row.

Miller, A. (1990 [1983]), *For Your Own Good: Hidden Cruelty in Child-Rearing and the Roots of Violence,* New York: Noonday Press.

Pepinsky, H. (1998a), "Safety from Personal Violence,"*Humanity and Society,* 22. 238-52.

Pepinsky, H. (1998b), 'Transcending Literatyrrany," *Contemporary Justice Review,* 1. 189-212.

Pepinsky, H. (1997), "Geometric Forms of Violence," in Milovanovic, D., ed., *Chaos,Crime, and Social Justice,* Westport, Conn.: Greenwood Publishing Co.

Pepinsky, H. (1995), "Peacemaking Primer," *Peace and Conflict Studies,* 2 *(Dec.)* 32-53.

Pepinsky, H.E. (1991), *The Geometry of Violence and Democracy,* Bloomington, Ind.: Indiana University Press.

Pepinsky, H.E. (1988), "Violence as Unresponsiveness Toward a New Conception of Crime," *Justice Quarterly,* 5: 539-563.

Pepinsky, H.E. (1980), "On Handling Contradictions Between Dynastic Tradition and Marxist Humanism: The New Criminal Law in Communist China as an Effort to Legitimizemize the Post-Mao State," in Tsai W., ed., *Struggling for Change in Mainland China: Challenges and Implications,* Taipei, Taiwan: Institute of International Relations.

Pepinsky, H.E. (1973), "Toward Diversion from Diversion from the Criminal Justice System, with a Written Reply by Robert Maynard Hutchins. Paper presented at a conference on diversion from the criminal justice, Center for the Study of Democratic Institutions, Santa Barbara.

Pepinsky, H.E. and Jesilow, P.D. (1992), *Myths That Cause Crime, 3rd Edition,* Santa Ana, Calif: Seven Locks Press.

Pepinsky, H.E., & Quinney, R. (1991*), Criminology as Peacemaking,* Bloomington, Ind.: Indiana University Press.

Quinney, R. (1991), "The Way of Peace: On Crime, Suffering, and Service," in Pepinsky, H.E. and Quinney, R., eds., *Criminology as Peacemaking,* Bloomington, Ind.: Indiana University Press.

Reiman, J. (1997), *The Rich GetRricher and the Poor Get Prison: Ideology, Class, and Criminal Justice, 5th Edition,* Needham Hts., Mass.: Allyn and Bacon.

Rosen, L., & Etlin, M. (1996), *The Hostage Child: Sex Abuse Allegations in Custody Disputes,* Bloomington, Ind.: Indiana University Press.

Schaef, A.W. (1992), *Co-Dependence: Misunderstood, Mistreated,* San Francisco: Harper Publishing.

Sullivan, D. (Ed.) (1998), "The Phenomenon of Restorative Justice," Special Issue of *Contemporary Justice Review,* 1: 1-174.

Wagner-Pacifici, R. (1993), *Discourse and Destruction: The City of Philadelphia Versus MOVE,* Chicago: University of Chicago Press.

Weber, M.M. (1999 [1904/5]), *TheProtestant Ethic and the Spirit of Capitalism,* Parsons, Talcott, trans., New York: Routledge, Chapman and Hill.

Yazzie, R. (1998), "Navajo Peacemaking: Implications for Adjudication-Based Systems of Justice," *Contemporary Justice Review,* 1: 123-131.

Zehr, H. (1990), *Changing Lenses: A New Focus on Crime and Justice,* Scottsdale, Pa.: Herald Press.

Zion, J.W. (1985), "The Navajo Peacemaker: Deference to the Old and Accommodation to the New," *American Indian Law Review, 11.* 89-109.88

15

Towards a Theology of Transformative Justice

Jim Consedine

"I have come to believe fervently that forgiveness is not just a spiritual and ethereal thing, unrelated to the real world, the harsh world out there. I have come to believe very fervently that without forgiveness, there is no future."

Archbishop Desmond Tutu

🏛 INTRODUCTION

I sometimes wonder whether western culture is obsessed with street crime and its effects. Practically every night we are inundated with television "news" stories of crime committed in our localities and around the world. The first television news bulletin I saw when I arrived in the United States commenced with four "street crime" crime stories. One was a murder arrest, while the other three were stories of assaults. Only then the bulletin moved onto other world issues. We need to reassess our understanding of crime and ask why it is that corporate crime and governmental crime advance virtually unhindered, while localised "street crime" has become so central to so many. The answer lies somewhere in the mixed realm of our own hidden fears and our sense of powerlessness in the face of crime, and the immense power of corporate vested interests who gain so much from the current situation and control so much of what we view and read.

Corporate crime is endemic the world over. It hits us in so many ways: from the added-on costs in our supermarkets to the pollutants in the air we breathe, from the hidden cost of our banking and financial systems to the costs of medicines we take for our illnesses. The tentacles of corporate crime touch all these areas and many more. For example, through false and misleading advertising, just one tobacco company arguably kills and injures more people than all the street thugs put together. The *New York Times* claimed in an editorial "that 400,000 Americans die annually from tobacco" (23 September 1999). We can assume that Third World tobacco deaths would more than double that figure. This is more than one million deaths per year. Is this not huge global crime? Are not many of these deaths preventable homicide? Will anyone go to prison for them? Not likely.

In Canada that same week, five companies in a world bulk vitamin cartel pleaded guilty to rigging Canadian markets over a period of years. They artificially inflated by up to 30% the price of bread, cereals, milk and other products. This theft cost every Canadian an average of $10. After a plea bargain, the companies pled guilty and were fined $88 million. This is probably about one fifth of the profits accrued in that time. No one went to prison yet they stole from several million people.

The World Bank estimates that over one billion workers in Third World countries live on an income of less than one dollar per day (World Bank Development Report, 1995). We are all complicit in this sin because we know that such starvation wages enable you and me to benefit and buy their products for ridiculously low prices, at the same time as we put huge profits into corporate coffers. This is huge criminal offending against one sixth of the world's population. Does anyone ever get charged with criminal offending for stealing from such workers? Never. Does anyone ever go to prison? Never. Am I truly my brother and sister's keeper? Not really, it seems.

The Iraqi people continue to be punished by the US Government and its allies for a war that was not of their making. The sanctions, which inflict malnutrition, disease and death on tens of thousands of children and poor families every year, may be legal, but they are highly immoral. Will any government officials ever be charged over such genocidal criminal behaviour? Of course not.

Many of these cases of corporate and governmental crime are perfectly legal but fail every test of morality that seeks to promote justice and protect the Common Good. Too often ever increasing profit is the sole criteria for corporate policies. The rights of workers, their families and the needs of the wider community for gainful employment are ignored. As corporations focus on cheap labour markets and build-in economic tax-free zones, there is no sense of solidarity, little protection of human rights and the poor are the disposable fodder used to make even more money for an already rich elite. Such reprehensible behaviour is not just spiritually bankrupt but totally immoral according to God's law and Church social teaching. It is sinful. It clearly constitutes massive crime and exploitation against hundreds of thousands of workers. But most of it is perfectly legal. Such is the gap so often between law and morality.

The point I am making is that crime is far bigger and more pervasive than we normally perceive. There is huge crime committed at governmental, corporate, as well as street level. It is only the street level crime that the media and the wider public focus upon. It is for street level crime that prisons are built. With exceptions, it is for street level crime that the vast apparatus of the criminal justice system is primarily employed. It is time we started asking why this is so. Is the corporate agenda and the power of money so strong that even the justice system, one of the most sacred of societal structures, now primarily a puppet in their hands? More and more are now saying "yes" to this understanding. They are seeing that it is usually only the poor who are going to prison and it is for the poor that new prisons are being built.

At the heart of the problem modern society faces are the questions of how to deal with criminal offending and what to do about punishment. Punishment has become an obsession in many countries. A criminal justice system built primarily on a philosophy of vengeance and punishment does not produce fairness, either to victims or the offenders. We need to ask some fundamental questions about these matters. Given the incredible failure rate of the current retributive system, with between a 60-80 percent recidivist rate within two years of release, should punishment remain the primary focus of the criminal justice structure? Are we wasting millions of dollars on a self defeating system which hits minorities unfairly, dehumanises those caught, and simply guarantees more crime?

Prisons are the dinosaurs of the modern age. They fail on practically every front. They fail to rehabilitate. Nearly eighty percent of inmates re-offend again within a short time. They are extremely expensive. Basically it is money wasted. They undermine family life and leave children minus a parent. They are spiritually bankrupt in that they suppress the growth and freedom of people. They help create more crime by bonding similarly minded rejected members of society. They upskill their graduates in further anti-social techniques, which makes prisons the most successful tertiary institutions in any country. They breed violence and are the principal recruitment locations for gangs. They guarantee continued high rates of re-offending. They punish the innocent, especially partners and children. They fail in practically every positive human indicator scale. As a 1993 *Time* magazine front cover boldly proclaimed, "Each year jails take large numbers of hopeless people and turn them into bitter hopeless people." Yet we keep building more. In terms of community usefulness and the promotion of the Common Good, they are a systemic failure. The penal system stands condemned by its own violence and unfairness. Indeed by its own inhumanity.

There are unquestionably a "dangerous few" who need to be kept out of circulation for the safety of both themselves and the community. But these would need to be only a small portion to those currently incarcerated. They should be kept in humane containment and encouraged to make constructive use of their time. Otherwise, non-violent constructive alternatives should be used.

𝔪 CHURCH RESPONSE

In dealing with issues of crime and law and order, the Church has to proclaim the age old message that Jesus came to bring the world: "Good news to the poor, liberty to captives, new sight to the blind, healing for the sick, freedom for the oppressed." That is our mandate. The teachings of Jesus can bring new light to bear on the difficult issues of conflict and crime in the community. They offer grounding principles to deal with them. These will involve promoting processes based on justice, equity, fairness and accountability. But such an approach must always be guided by wisdom, tempered by mercy, and allow for the possibility of healing, forgiveness and reconciliation for both victims and offenders.

In his 1988 social encyclical, Pope John Paul II wrote of the conditions which prevail to produce what he called "structures of sin." He was referring to social systems which enslave or oppress people and attack the Common Good.

These "structures of sin" are found where people are crushed, marginalised or oppressed and are denied the opportunity to develop their God given gifts. It is clear that the development of the modern prison industrial complex is such a "structure of sin." How can Christians and people of good will stand in solidarity with the poor and their victims, speaking justice, development and peace, when so many are being crushed by such structures?

Do we need to question the very legitimacy of prisons themselves? Locking grown adults into a 4m x 3m cell for up to 22 hours a day for months or even years on end should be abhorrent to any thinking person. It should be particularly abhorrent to Christians. It runs contrary to practically everything that the Church teaches. Only the twisted could regard such a procedure as acceptable. Or those with a vested interest. Sadly, there are many groups in the community with a vested interest in maintaining the status quo regardless of how destructive the system might be. We need to recognise that these vested interests do exist, that they have extremely effective propaganda machines, that there is huge money involved and that the message of Christ will not always be a popular one. The Church clearly though should maintain its clearly defined role, and not allow itself to be compromised by such vested interests.

🏛 A QUESTION OF MORALITY

Justice and the Law

Given this starting point, what then should be the relationship between justice and the law? It is appropriate to start by quickly looking at what justice is since it is the basis from which we should act. In a recent widely praised pastoral letter, the Catholic bishops of England and Wales taught, "In essence justice is an active and life giving virtue which defends and promotes the dignity of every living person and is concerned for the Common Good insofar as it is the guardian of relations between individuals and peoples. Justice is at the same time a moral and a legal concept in that it fosters an equitable sharing of burdens and benefits. It makes whole and leads, not to division, but reconciliation. At its deepest level it is rooted in love and is tempered by mercy."[1]

From justice flows the law which also has two dimensions, moral and legal. Law is built on morality and is never neutral, always reflecting a system of values. Fairness, truth, honesty, compassion and respect for people are the basic tenets of an acceptable morality that flows from justice and seeks to protect and enhance the Common Good.

Law and justice are not synonymous terms. The law is not sacrosanct and does not stand alone. What is sacrosanct is justice. In a secular society, for law and justice to meet, they have to be grounded in the principle of the Common Good. There is no other way. The law is the mechanism by which either the Common Good or sectional interests are achieved. Injustice occurs when the law is written by powerful groups with sectional interests. This is the basis for unjust law. Much of the legislation in the past that discriminated against indigenous peoples was defined by sectional interests. The laws relating to apartheid in South Africa were an obvious case. Just law and just government should define, defend and protect the Common Good. This is precisely what government in a true democracy should be about.

Justice and the Common Good

The Common Good is the principle that has attempted to hold the fabric of society together on some form of just basis for centuries. It is based on the notion that each person is a social being and reaches his or her potential in relationship with others. Collectively, they form a society. The bishops' pastoral defined the Common Good as being the whole network of social conditions which enable human individuals and groups to flourish and live a fully genuine human life. Far from each being primarily for him or herself, all are responsible for all.[2]

They expanded the concept in order to meet the particular needs of the modern world. They said that the Common Good cannot exist today without the presence of four other principles that are essential to its realisation. The first is the principle of subsidiarity supports a dispersal of authority as close to the grass roots as good government allows. It prefers local over central decision-making. It has everyone working at the level of their capacity.

The second is the principle of solidarity implies the interconnectedness of all human beings, one with the other, regardless of race, gender, culture, age or religion. We form one family. Solidarity teaches us to stand with one another, particularly when either of the final two principles are threatened—that of human rights or an option for the poor.

The third is the protection of human rights, our understanding of which has been accelerating this century. No longer are we able to dehumanise various groupings of people because of their differences to us. Each person now has certain legislated protection under charters from the United Nations which help protect the fabric of the Common Good.

The fourth is an option for the poor. By that is meant that the most vulnerable, the poorest economically, the most handicapped must be protected and respected if the Common Good is to be achieved.[3]

▥ BIBLICAL JUSTICE

For at least the past 800 years, Western civilisation has been built on underlying Christian moral principles which have guided the way we live. In their simplest form they were summed up by the ten commandments of the ancient Hebrew Scriptures and the central command of Christ that we were to love God and our neighbour.

The Bible speaks often about crime and punishment. Naturally it deals with what flows from violations of law, and in particular with what flows from violations of its most sacred law, the Torah, which contains the commandments of God. But all law was not of equal status in biblical times. Consequently, how one dealt with offenders varied depending on a wide variety of circumstances. There was no centralised code of law or criminal justice system such as we have now. A Jewish understanding of Hebrew law has often been quite different from a Western understanding of the same law. So when Jesus is accused of breaking the law on the Sabbath, rather than being arrested and charged, he merely has an argument with his accusers about the ruling itself and the nature of law, and he is left to move on.

Surely the scriptural quote most abused and taken out of context has been that of "an eye for an eye." Public perception of its meaning is usually the opposite of what is intended. The concept of lex talionis, the law of proportionality, simply says that you should never claim more than the value of what is damaged. If property worth 100 gold coins is stolen, then you cannot claim 200 coins in return. If you took more than what was just, then you in turn could be punished. Jewish scholar Martin Buber in his German translation of the Scriptures, translates "an eye for an eye and a tooth for a tooth" as "an eye for the value of an eye, a tooth for the value of a tooth." It is a concept that occurs only three times in Scripture, whereas mercy appears several hundred times.[4] The emphasis in Scripture was usually on restitution and restoration, not vengeance and punishment. Restitution was seen as a way of setting things right. If property was stolen, then the property should be returned; if damage was done to someone's house or field, then the person responsible for the damage should repair it.

The focus on crime in biblical times was not so much on individuals as on the community. Corporate responsibility was central to the Hebrew understanding of crime. The Scriptures renounced any scapegoating that claimed that crime was only the responsibility of a few evil individuals within the society. When the law was broken, there was corporate responsibility. Violence and breach of law pointed to a crisis in the very fabric of the society.

The central feature of biblical law is a constant calling forth of the people to a future promise. The emphasis is on the future health and well being of the community, and not on the immediate transgressions of the law. The covenants agreed to by the people with Yahweh always emphasises this future direction.

Shalom, Social Justice and the Covenant

The three most central concepts of biblical law and justice relate to shalom, social justice and the covenant. Crime was a violation of shalom, of social justice and of the covenant. Repairing the damage was the key, not punishment. In his seminal book on restorative justice, *Changing Lenses*, Howard Zehr points out that shalom is not just a peripheral theme of Scripture but a basic core belief from which God's vision and plan for creation and the development of the human family flow. Hence notions of salvation, atonement, forgiveness and justice have their roots in shalom. In English shalom is usually translated to mean peace, but that is a very inadequate translation.[5] Perry Yoder describes three basic dimensions to its meaning. They are physical well being, including adequate food, clothing, shelter and wealth; a right relationship between and among people; and the acquisition of virtue, especially honesty and moral integrity. The absence of shalom means the absence of one or other of these features.[6] There is a flow-on of this concept in the New Testament where Christ's life and teachings and eventually his death and resurrection transform relationships between and among people, thus inaugurating the New Creation, wherein shalom is lived by believers.

The prophetic voices of Jeremiah, Amos, Micah, Isaiah, Zephaniah and Ezekiel remind the people that to remained blessed required they practise social justice. These ancient prophets crystallise the centrality of social justice as a pre-requisite for God's continuing blessing. Time and again they remind their listeners that God will not continue to uphold the people if they refuse to practice justice, especially to the poor, the needy, the oppressed, the marginalised. It is from this understanding that the prophets are able to warn that the entire nation is doomed because some widows have been mistreated or because the hungry have not been allowed to glean the fields. Not only all the people but the land itself is caught up in sin and all its consequences, for the meadows lie barren and the mountains quake and the trees bear no fruit. For Israel, the fullest response to crime was not the isolated punishment of an individual law-breaker, but the repentance of the entire nation. It is the voice of prophets down through the centuries to our own day. Without freedom and justice, there can be no salvation.

The third major concept that has a direct relationship with law and justice is that of covenant. A covenant is a binding agreement between parties. There were several in the Scriptures, starting with God and creation, God with Abraham, Sarah and the newly created People of God, God with Moses representing the people on Mount Sinai when the Ten Commandments were given. The culminating covenant came with Jesus and the whole of humanity at the Last Supper. This new covenant opened up for humanity a new way of viewing things, of relating, of recognising the dignity of each person within the context of their community. Crime was a violation of the covenant. It needed to be repaired.

The test of justice in the biblical view is not whether the right rules are applied in the right way. Justice is tested by the outcome. The tree is tested by its fruit. It is the substance, not the procedure, that defines justice. And how should things come out? The litmus test is how the poor and oppressed are affected.

In biblical times such justice was enacted on an everyday basis in Jewish settlements. Citizens went to the city gates to seek justice from the judges or elders who presided there for this purpose. The whole focus for this "court" setting was to find a solution for the aggrieved person. The judge was not primarily the one who rewarded some (distributive justice). He was the one who created order and restored what had been destroyed. Restoration, then, was the keynote, not retribution. The words in Hebrew for "paying back" and "recompense," *shillum* and *shillem*, have the same root words as *shalom*. Restoring *shalom* was what such courts were all about. Helping people re-establish their covenant with God and one another was at the heart of this justice. When punishment was meted out, and on occasion this included execution, it was always seen as a necessary element to the restoration of the covenant and the re-establishment of *shalom*.[7]

The New Testament and Justice

In the New Testament Jesus clearly states that justice should be based on principles of forgiveness and reconciliation; that retaliation plays no part. He forgave the Genasene maniac, the prostitute, the adulteress, the tax gatherer who was an extortionist, the robber. He charged us both to place distinctions between wrongdoers and the virtuous, yet to see ourselves as all in the same camp—brothers and sisters with varying strengths and weaknesses.

Jesus specifically rejects "an eye for an eye," that proportional response so abused by popular usage. "If anyone hits you on the right cheek, offer him the other one as well. Give him your coat and your tunic, walk two miles not one." (Matthew 5:38) This is radical stuff—and quite practical today if properly understood. Jesus is asking for a generous response from those who have been victimised by crime. He knows—indeed God teaches—that unless people take such an attitude, they will usually end up becoming doubly victimised. The first time will be with the actual crime. The second will be through the hurt, bitterness and feelings of vengeance that can so easily poison a person's spirit if allowed to germinate. These are wise teachings indeed.

Jesus teaches generosity of spirit when it comes to dealing with crime. To the woman facing the death penalty, he said simply "go and sin no more." He rejected any notion of "just desserts" in the story of the prodigal son and loving parent (Luke 15:11-32) and in the vineyard workers parable (Matthew 20:1-16). In the latter, the day workers give us another reminder as to how God's justice works. Each got paid at the end of the day what they needed to feed their families, even though they had worked uneven hours. Its a parable of restorative justice. Provide what is needed. Forgive seventy-seven time seven. Surely too hard? Not so, says Jesus. Its not easy but it can be done. In effect he teaches that if we don't attempt these very difficult matters then we run the grave risk being damaged spiritually.

Imprisonment is condemned by New Testament teachings where it represents a power of death that is separate from and opposed to God. Death is also present in other forms, including illness, hunger, injustice and opulence. The proclamation of liberty to captives does not relate simply to a notion of spiritual freedom. Such an interpretation helps make sense of the miraculous nature of the deliverance of the apostles from prison in two instances, Acts 5 and 12. The releases are an assertion of divine authority over the state and over the fallen principalities and powers.

A final word on justice at the time of Jesus concerns the notion of sanctuary. It is a further illustration that Jewish law valued life over property, and valued people over punishment. Several mentions are made in the ancient Scriptures to cities of refuge (Deuteronomy 4:41-3, 19:1-3, Numbers 35:6-34). Both Israel and its neighbours recognised the right of a person needing protection from revenge to go to the altar in the temple, where the person was to be kept from harm until the matter could be decided through formal judicial process (Exodus 21:12-14). But the altar might be far away, and the wrongly accused person might be caught before reaching the protection of the sanctuary. So the law provided for six cities of refuge, which were to be centrally located and reached by well-built roads, so that someone suspected of murder could get to protection easily. Mercy and fairness lie at the heart of sanctuary. People were more important than punishment and, as a result, procedural safeguards were built into the law so that the rights of the offender could be protected while the case was being considered by the judicial authorities.

Respect, Mercy, Forgiveness and Pardon

A reflection on justice and a fully developed morality must include a consideration on the place of respect, mercy, forgiveness and pardon. These are among the most mature and demanding of virtues. True justice and the common good cannot be achieved without employing them. A sound morality starts with a respect for the dignity of all. The current criminal justice system displays a lack of respect to all involved. We demand respect towards people and property in our law, yet show little in our systems dealing with law breakers. Any one who has worked in a prison or even visited one will know exactly what I mean. Depersonalisation is built into the very fabric of the system itself. The only thing missing is the numbering on inmates' chests. It all reflects a lack of respect for inherent human dignity. We should not be surprised that such lack of respect carries on in the wider community because our policing, court and penal systems pay such little attention to it.

The notion of a loving and merciful God is one that fills the pages of Scripture. Here mercy is portrayed as an intrinsic dimension to the very being of God. We have only to skim through the pages to see God portrayed as a protective presence, a helper who offers hope, one whose power is merciful and benevolent, one who makes faithful and enduring commitments. Mercy is the foundation of God's covenant love. Jesus is portrayed in the New Testament as the merciful one. We hear about his responses to the poor and oppressed, widows and single women, social outcasts, sinners, the sick, the wayward. He feeds the five thousand, heals the blind, the lame, lepers. "Have mercy on us, Son of David," they cry (Matthew 9:27). They had faith in God's mercy.[8]

Forgiveness is the toughest of the four to practise. It is not the glib "forgive and forget" call of the simplistic. It is a tough but essential quality of human growth which can often benefit the person who forgives more than the offender. Kim Phuc, the running, screaming nine-year-old girl etched in the memory of the world through that amazing 1972 photo, suffered massive burns when US supplied napalm was dropped on her village in Vietnam. Now nearing 40 years of age, she has forgiven those who attacked her and has grown through her pain to become a leader who tours frequently on behalf of UNICEF asking the question, "why war?" and demanding "war, never again." Despite having a deeply scarred body, her spirit has healed and is whole again—because she has forgiven. She is fully human, fully alive, because she has learnt mercy and forgiveness.

Archbishop Desmond Tutu, who chaired the Truth and Reconciliation Commission in South Africa and heard literally thousands of testimonies from victims and offenders, speaks eloquently about forgiveness as an essential component of healing.

> *I have been bowled over by the incredible humility one has experienced from the victims, both black and white, who have suffered as much as they have. By rights they should have been hate-ridden by lust for revenge. They have exhilarated me by how ready they are to forgive. I have come to see that. Yes, of course you have to have an acknowledgment by the wrongdoer that they have done something that was very wrong, that they owe to us confession so that the victim, the survivor, be enabled, be willing to forgive. But I have come to believe fervently that forgiveness is not just a spiritual and ethereal thing unrelated to the real world, the harsh world out there. I have come to believe very fervently that without forgiveness, there is no future.*

The ultimate expression of forgiveness lies in pardon and amnesty. Pardon is an essential characteristic of the Christian community. It is a virtue that the Church rarely preaches these days, especially in the area of criminal justice. Yet its importance cannot be over estimated. It has a central place in Christian tradition. If God has pardoned us through Christ, then we need to be able to pardon one another. To pardon means not to fixate on past grievances but to create the opportunities for people to put the past behind them and move forward in new and constructive ways. To pardon is to cancel out the past, to allow the past to be the past no matter how horrific and unjust it may have been, and to reach for a new future.

We should not fear the reaction of sections of society through our preaching of the huge potential of pardon. Pardon lies at the heart of compassion and sits at the centre of the theology of the Cross. It is only when pardon is able to be exercised that we can confidently build Christian community with one another.

Towards the New Millennium

What then are some of the real alternatives based on the justice and mercy of God as revealed in Christian tradition? There are six that readily come to mind which, if expanded and properly resourced, would reduce re-offending, help offenders take responsibility for their behaviour, produce better more healing results for victims, offenders and the community, make our communities healthier and safer, and be much more affordable.

1 DIVERSION. The price of criminalising so many is something that needs to be looked at seriously. Even when people have broken the law, why do they usually have to be prosecuted and criminalised? What positive purpose does it serve? In Japan, two thirds of all arrested people are diverted. They never come to court. Other options involving apology and restitution are taken. Diversion is a sign of maturity, of wisdom, of imagination.

2 WELLNESS CENTRES. Following a government inquiry which reported in 1989, the New Zealand Government established a series of wellness or habilitation centres. Named from the Latin root word *habilitare*—meaning "to empower," "to enable"; the concept is based on the premise that the vast majority of offenders need to deal with their aggression, their sexual aberration, their drug, gambling or alcohol addictions, if they are going to make useful crime-free futures for themselves. The concept recognises that many have had little opportunity in the past for such development.

The recommendation from the Commission of Inquiry was that as soon as an offender had been sentenced to a custodial term, that person be given the option of going to prison or a wellness centre to face their problems and deal to them during their actual sentence. It was recognised that most inmates needed an incentive to change. Engaging in habilitative processes during their sentences away from the harsh prison culture was regarded as the best way forward.

3   VICTIM/OFFENDER FACILITATION and COMMUNITY PANELS. The former is a well-tried process on both sides of the Atlantic and involves a facilitated conference between the immediate victim and the offender. It has its limitations but can be very effective in some moderate and minor cases of offending. Community panels using a restorative approach can also be very useful.

4   RESTORATIVE CONFERENCING. New Zealand for the past ten years has had mandatory conferencing for its juvenile offenders. This process involves a meeting convened by a skilled facilitator to which the victims and the offenders are invited. Both are encouraged to bring family and friends in support. At the conference, apology is given, explanations made as to why the offence occurred and reparation discussed. The victims are encouraged to express how it has been for them and have any questions answered. It is important for them to be acknowledged, to be offered apology, to receive restitution, to experience justice, to have basic fears allayed and questions answered. Usually consensus is reached as to what to recommend to the judge. The offender signs the contract. Judges accept 93 percent of such contracts and most are fulfilled. No conviction is entered. In the ten years 1989 until 1998, the number of young offenders appearing before the courts has dropped from 8193 to 4210, a decrease of 49 percent. It is amazing how contrite and shamed most young offenders are after hearing of the effects on their actions on their victims. Most youth prisons and detention centres have closed.

The secret of the New Zealand success lies in the "carrot and stick" approach, which forms part of restorative philosophy. The key to this is that all participants work out a recommended conference plan to which all must agree if at all possible. This is the incentive, the carrot, which encourages offenders to front up and take responsibility for what they have done. They get the chance to participate in a reparative outcome. The principle incentive for victims lies in the recognition and acknowledgement of the pain they have experienced. They get to hear an apology and to get answers to such questions as "Why me?" "Will it happen again?" Under the current retributive system, victims get virtually nothing.

5 TRANSFORMATIVE JUSTICE PROCESSES. These include much of what is recommended in restorative conferencing, but take into account wider background issues. These also recognise that crime is far wider than usually imagined and that corporate and governmental crime is endemic across the world. For all that, it recognises "street crime" as important and that the transformative conference creates an opportunity to address it and wider related issues. These might include inter-generational abuse, violence, addiction and poverty. They may look at the resources available or otherwise in the community to help people, the opportunities for employment and constructive living, the need for the wider community to take some responsibility for its health and wellbeing. For example, if a town has three bars and no sports teams, no recreation centre and no employment opportunities, it is likely to have more alcohol-related crime than if it did have these facilities. The transformative process can be a vehicle for community growth and development in ways that will bring out the best qualities of many in the community. The offending can be a trigger to convene such a gathering.

The key to successful conferences and change involves participation and encounter between the parties. It is the dynamics of the group which provide the energy for the whole process. Anything which impedes this basic movement reduces the chances of real responsibility being taken by offenders, which in turn inhibits the possibilities for real change and future accountability. Within the actual conference itself and the dynamics of it lie the greatest potential for real change and real growth. This is why professionals other than the facilitator need to take a back seat.

6 AMNESTY. With the celebration of a Christian Year of Jubilee in the year 2000, it is appropriate to speak of the biblical injunction

that Jubilee be celebrated by "proclaiming liberty throughout the land." (Leviticus 25) While there has been a wonderful concentration on the abolition of Third World debt, the idea of Jubilee was that people be given a fresh start. Amnesty or pardon is a concept that should sit at the heart of every Christian's life, since we have all been pardoned through Christ. It is something the Church needs to proclaim clearly as being part of its teaching. Jubilee recognised that from time to time we need to step outside the usual laws governing society and think laterally, so that compassion, justice and generosity could be better practised.

To celebrate the year of Jubilee and honour 2000 years since the birth of Jesus, delegates to the 1999 World Congress of the International Commission of Catholic Prison Pastoral Care held in Mexico City called for an amnesty for as many prisoners as possible by releasing them or shortening their sentences. This was to include all prison inmates serving a sentence of twelve months or less, women inmates who have dependent children, detainees seeking asylum and under-aged persons. Jesus has warned us that if we do not forgive and pardon one another, we can hardly expect pardon from God. This was a timely reminder that the grace of Jubilee should be extended also to people in prison.

🏛 CONCLUSION

The nations of the world desperately need enlightenment and fresh direction in their dealings with crime and lawlessness. They desperately need a system that gives a better deal to victims, that promotes apology, healing, understanding, accountability, personal and collective responsibility, forgiveness, even reconciliation. We all need to re-learn how to practise compassion and mercy in our dealings with one another. We need a system that reduces imprisonment and only uses it as a final resort for the most dangerous offenders. Transformative and restorative processes provide opportunities for these to happen. The current criminal justice system doesn't.

Prisons victimise the poor, they do not provide justice, they offend against the Common Good, and they are a direct contradiction to the teachings of Scripture. On a global scale they have become huge profit-making foundations, centres for a unhealthy focus on vengeance and punishment, "structures of sin." Christian tradition and the Scriptures offer constructive and positive insights, values and guidelines for conducting just and fair processes to help deal with criminal offending. We must challenge any criminal justice process or prison system that dehumanises people and fails to treat them with dignity and respect. We are promised the grace to bring light to the dark shadows of the criminal justice and prison worlds.

If we take such a message seriously, the Common Good of all would be enhanced, better social justice delivered and safer communities built.

⋔ ENDNOTES

1   Pastoral letter, "The Common Good and the Catholic Church's Social Teachings," Catholic Bishops of England and Wales, 1996.

2   Pastoral letter, ibid.

3   Pastoral letter, ibid.

4   Exodus 21:23-25; Leviticus 24:19-20; Deuteronomy 19:21.

5   Howard Zehr, *Changing Lenses*, Herald Press, Scottdale, Pennsylvania, 1990, p. 133.

6   Perry Yoder, *Shalom: the Bible's Word for Salvation, Justice and Peace*, Faith and Life Press, Newton, Kansas, 1987, p. 130.

7   Zehr, op cit. p. 144.

8   Alice Sinnot RSM, "Mercy—Ever Ancient, Ever New," *Listen Magazine*, 1999.

16

Community Conferencing: A Supply Side Contribution to Prison Abolition

David B. Moore

🏛 INTRODUCTION: STRATEGIES OF ABOLITION

The International Conferences on Penal Abolition challenge the philosophy of retribution. The movement challenges punitive imprisonment as the primary realisation of that retributive philosophy. Opposition to the philosophy of retribution and the practice of imprisonment takes several forms. At the level of theory, abolitionists develop alternative philosophies such as "restorative" or "transformative" justice. And they seek to shift the focus of attention, by engaging in the debate about the relative harmfulness of crime in the streets and crime in the suites.

At the level of practice, abolitionists may work to improve general social circumstances outside the prison system. They may lobby against the further expansion of the prison industry (Christie 1995). And they may lobby for improvements to circumstances inside prisons.

This looks like a very broad strategy. Yet the statistical evidence would suggest it has been unsuccessful through the 1980s and 1990s. The United States, in particular, experienced an unprecedented increase in the prison population and in new prisons during those decades.

A significant factor in the growth of the prison industry has been the use of correctional monies in declining regional economies. Economists call this pump-priming; political analysts call it pork-barrelling. Either way, the trend is particularly clear in rural areas. Old rail towns become new jail towns. The system then takes on its own inexorable logic. Once a jail is built, it will tend to fill.

This nexus between social fragmentation in the inner-city and the economic decline in the countryside has been strengthened by mandatory sentencing laws and by the "war on drugs." Similar tendencies can be seen, if less strongly, in the criminal law of other industrialised democracies: (i) the discretion of the judiciary is diminished, and (ii) the distribution of some narcotics and stimulants continues to be defined as a primarily military and criminal matter, rather than a social and medical one. So to the list of abolitionist strategies can be added the restoration of judicial discretion, and pressure for drug laws consistent with a philosophy of harm minimisation.

In all these cases, abolitionists are focusing on the proximate mechanisms by which the prison industry is expanded, and clients are fed into it. To rail against that industry is to focus on the demand side of the equation. But what of the supply side? Traditionally, we focus on the supply side of the equation by asking criminology's core question: why do some people sometimes engage in criminal behaviour? Or we can reverse the question: why do most people, most of the time, not engage in behaviour that can be defined as criminal? If there are plausible answers, they raise a practical political challenge: how to establish a system that, in response to behaviour defined as criminal, does not ask:

- who has done it? and
- what is to be done to them?

but instead asks:

- what happened?
- what has happened since? and
- what do we need to do now?

The process known as community conferencing asks this tripartite set of questions. Most radically, it shifts the focus of an intervention from a single individual to a *network of relationships*. Community conferencing avoids the individualist error of focussing simply on present or potential clients of the prison industry. Nor does it just additionally focus on people who have been directly harmed as a result of the actions of those clients.

But community conferencing also avoids the collectivist extreme of trying to focus on something as nebulous as *society* (otherwise known as *the* community). Its focus is, instead, on a group located at a mid-range between the isolated individual and the impersonal collective. The focus of each community conference is a community defined by a particular conflict. By definition, all the members of that community have been affected by the conflict in question. They all have a vested interest in making things right.

The generic community conference process is a practical realisation of a theory of "transformative justice," a term popularised by writers and activists such as Ruth Morris (Morris 1992). My colleagues and I adopted that terminology when naming TJA, a company we established in Sydney 1995 to promote conferencing and related practices. As we have worked with the theory and practice, it has become clearer that the "justice" component is both a *design principle* of conferencing, and an *outcome* of community conference interventions. The actual dynamic at work is perhaps more accurately described as "*conflict transformation.*"

This transformation of conflict works within people, between people, and between communities of people. In essence, those involved experience the transformation of the negative emotions associated with conflict into the positive emotions associated with cooperation.

When used in criminal justice settings, community conferencing appears to:

- minimise the likelihood of the harmful behaviour being repeated;
- maximise the sense among all participants that justice was done; and
- maximise the number of relationships either created or improved as a result of the intervention.

In short, the process appears to build social capital (Moore with Forsythe 1995; Sherman and Strang 1996-9, Chatterjee 1998).

So community conferencing offers a significant promise to prison abolitionists: If we can build programs of conflict transformation into neighbourhoods and other communities, we should be able to reduce the supply of people to the prison industry.

In fact, this may already be an effect of programs in Australasia, North America and Western Europe. Full scale comparative evaluation of neighbourhood-based community conferencing programs lies further down the track. For now, let us consider the theory behind conferencing practice, and thus the reasons why this "supply-side" component of an abolitionist strategy might indeed work.

ṁ THE COMMUNITY CONFERENCE DESCRIBED

Consider first the generic *process* of community conferencing (see Moore and McDonald 2000a). This process can be applied under the aegis of many different *programs*. The social and political rationale of those programs may vary. But the generic process is essentially the same. A community conference facilitator:

- **identifies sources of conflict in a system of relationships;**
  A system of relationships, a community, may be marked by conflict in circumstances where there is
  - no specific dispute between members of that community,
  - a single specific dispute, or
  - many disputes.

  More will be made of this crucial distinction between disputes and conflict in the next section. The key point to note here is that most interventions in the criminal justice system deal with an incident of harmful behaviour. Where those most affected all agree the incident occurred, and where those most responsible for the harm admit their involvement, then the most immediate cause of conflict in that community is an incident of *undisputed harm*. Alternatively, in cases where all those affected have known each other for some time, because they live and/or work together, conflict may have caused and been caused by many *poorly resolved disputes in the past and/or the present*.

- **brings the people in that system of relationships together in a circle;**
  The circle is a standard format for a democratic conversation. Again, more will be made of this in the next section. The key point

to note here is that the circle allows each participant to communicate with every other participant while surrounded by supporters. There is no differentiated or privileged position. The format emphasises that the process is not for or about *anyone* in particular. It is about *everyone*.

- **asks questions of participants in a scripted sequence;**

  The questions asked by a community conference facilitator are designed to help the participants collectively to paint a picture of what happened, and what has happened since. Consistently, the most effective sequence in which to ask these questions has been:
  - the person/people most directly responsible for the harm;
  - the person/people most directly harmed;
  - supporters of the people most directly harmed;
  - supporters of the people most directly responsible for the harm;
  - any other affected parties (onlookers, participants known to all, state officials).

- **begins with open questions about incidents and/or issues that contributed to the conflict;**

  The people most directly responsible for the harm are asked to describe what happened, what they were thinking at the time, how they felt when they met with an official response, what has happened since, who they feel has been affected, and how.

- **moves to questions that foster acknowledgment and greater understanding of the conflict;**

  Other participants in the circle are prompted to add their experience of what happened, and what has happened since, to the expanding picture of the past and the present.

- **moves to questions about how the community might move from conflict to cooperation;**

  When a community has experienced the deeply felt insight that they are all affected by the conflict among them, and that it is in the interest of each and every one to seek a cooperative solution, the role of the facilitator can change. Up to that point, the facilitator must use a range of techniques in order to referee the process in a minimalist manner. In other words, once the dialogue has been catalysed, the facilitator continues to safeguard the *form* of the dialogue, but seeks to become invisible to participants. This "melting into the background is achieved by a range of techniques all designed to overcome two tendencies: (i) the reluctance of some professionals to relinquish responsibility for the *content* of the dialogue and (ii) the reluctance of some community members to accept that responsibility.

- **referees the process as participants play out the transformation of conflict through all stages of the conference.**

    Once a collective picture of past and present has been painted, and participants have reflected on that picture of the causes and consequences of their conflict, the style of the facilitation changes. The facilitator's role now becomes that of assistant to a negotiation. Participants are helped to negotiate a plan of action, which will include very specific answers to the questions of what is to be done and why, how, by whom, where and when.

The "what" and "why" questions are answered with plans to repair physical and emotional damage, with support for those who most need support, with acknowledgment of the lessons to be learned, and with plans to ensure that the harmful behaviour is least likely to be repeated.

🏛 GENERAL PRINCIPLES

The design of the community conference is informed by a set core concepts: justice, conflict, and democracy (Moore and McDonald 2000b).

When asked what they understand by justice, participants in our community conference facilitators' workshops have routinely rephrased questions of "justice" as questions of "fairness." And fairness is then most readily defined by its absence. People provide examples of social interactions or situations which are "unfair." These situations can be distilled to some very simple principles. It seems that, for an experience to be judged as just or fair, those affected need to feel that:

- the *rules* of the intervention are acceptable to the participants;
- participants have *played by the rules*, usually with the help of a third party referee;
- the *outcome* was reached by acceptable rules, adequately refereed, and meets general objective criteria that were understood before the intervention.

If any of these three aspects of an interaction between people is judged unfair—rules, play, or outcomes—the entire experience will *feel* unfair.

From a very young age, we are sensitive to questions of fairness. Indeed, this is one of the first abstract concepts about which young children converse (and argue). Generally, we are sensitive not only to unfairness to ourselves, but also to unfairness to others. And most of us, most of the time, try to treat others fairly. The question of why this should be so has long fascinated science (Sober and Wilson 1997).

When the same question is put to a group of workshop participants a long list of reasons is given. We have had the opportunity to ask this question across a wide range of diverse communities and cultures. The answers tend to be much the same. Why do most of us, most of the time, try to treat others fairly? Some answers would be: upbringing, morality, a sense of reciprocity or social contract, to minimise trouble and make life easier, out of respect for oneself and for others, to seek "right relationships," and so on.

All of these factors, and any more one might care to add, can be placed in one or both of two simple categories:

- minimising conflict *within* oneself;
- minimising conflict *between* oneself and others.

But this insight raises further questions about first principles: what is conflict, and how does it differ from a dispute? Again, in many different community and cultural contexts, people arrive at similar answers: the difference between a dispute and a conflict is a difference in *quality*, not just quantity. It is a difference in *kind*, not just degree. A disagreement or dispute is primarily:

- a contest over a specific set of *facts*,

and should be distinguished from more general conflict,

- a state in which the affected parties experience generally negative *feelings* about one other.

This experience of negative feelings in the presence of others is not uncommon in social life. Indeed, conflict can never be fully removed from social life and is no more to be "solved" than is gravity, energy or housework. The negative feelings associated with conflict motivate us to act in particular ways, as do positive feelings. Nevertheless, with an understanding of the nature of conflict, we are more likely to be motivated to constructive behaviours. And the distinction between disputes and conflict is an essential diagnostic tool to this end.

For example, in cases where two parties are faced with a *pure* dispute about facts, they may seek assistance from a third party offering (interest-based) mediation to help the two disputants "get to yes." Mediation might limit the emergence of any destructive conflict while the disputants seek an optimal outcome

But this approach proves problematic in cases where a dispute is actually a symptom of underlying conflict. In such cases, a process that focuses on "clarifying the facts" will create stronger fuel for the existing fire of conflict. The facts of any particular *symptomatic* dispute are not the real cause of ill-feeling and poor communication between parties. A symptomatic dispute is simply fuel for self-perpetuating conflict. Conflict creates the conditions for the emergence of new disputes which fuel further conflict. Parties in conflict are no longer open to hearing the other—if they ever were.

- Community conflict may be generated by acts of *undisputed harm*.
- Neighbourhoods, workplaces and other communities experiencing conflict will often have a history of poorly resolved disputes. A community with a history of poorly resolved disputes is also likely to have a series of unresolved disputes at the present time. In short: *multiple past disputes and/or multiple present disputes*.
- Community conflict may also be generated in cases where there is neither an act of undisputed harm, nor any apparent unresolved disputes, either in the past or the present. Instead, conflict may arise from basic differences, in personality, style, ethnic or national

origins, or any other factor that distances people. In such cases, people can be in conflict even when they appear to have *no specific dispute*.

Once conflict has developed, that conflict may in turn generate:

- multiple further disputes; and/or
- acts of undisputed harm.

In our experience, *dispute resolution* processes such as mediation are simply "the wrong medicine" and inappropriate in cases where there is no dispute, and in cases where there are many disputes. In both sets of cases, the dispute is not the main problem. The main problem is the conflict.

Processes that focus on *disputes* can be placed on a spectrum running from discussion, through negotiation, assisted negotiation, mediation, conciliation, and arbitration, to adjudication. At one end of the spectrum, processes seek to *minimise conflict* so as to maximise the likelihood of rationally determining the optimal outcome.

At the other end of this spectrum, processes seek to *maximise conflict*. In cases where disputants have given up hope of a win-win outcome, both parties may take their chances with the possibility of a win-lose outcome imposed by an arbitrator or adjudicator. A common result in such cases is actually a lose-lose result. Neither party feels the process or the imposed decision have been just.

In addition to conflict maximisation and conflict minimisation, we recognise a third general approach to disputes and conflicts: *conflict transformation*. In those situations where general conflict between people has become more significant than the specific facts of any associated dispute(s), the most constructive approach is likely to be one in which the conflict is acknowledged, then transformed.

In our experience, if a process is to help participants acknowledge and transform conflict, it will need to fulfil all four precepts for democratic decision-making in small groups (Fishkin 1995). A goal of such decision-making is to improve on the *unilateral* decision-making of a tyrant, the *polling* system of a representative democracy, and the *compromise* of group bargaining. The goal is to reach decisions by consensus. Several basic principles are required to make consensus possible. In essence, these principles are very simple:

- everyone affected should be encouraged to attend (*participation*):

- everyone in attendance should be given the opportunity to contribute (*equity*);
- each contribution should be listened to and then given adequate consideration—"talked through" (*deliberation*).

A fourth and final principle is that there must be a mechanism for ensuring this all happens. In other words, a process of deliberative democracy needs to be safeguarded. There must be a policing mechanism, to ensure that:

- no one is stopped from attending, or speaking, or having an issue they have raised being adequately addressed (*non-tyranny*).

To be judged genuinely democratic, a decision-making process must satisfy these four principles of *participation*, *equity*, *deliberation*, and *non-tyranny*.

ᨇ PROGRAMS

The generic community conference process offers justice to communities in conflict by rigorous adherence to these precepts of participatory democracy. The adoption of community conferencing process by government and community sector agencies constitutes a revolution. It is likely to be a sustainable revolution, since it appears as a step-by-step evolution. But in essence, a single shift is happening as the net result of these step by step changes: systems that relied on conflict minimisation and maximisation are introducing the third approach of conflict transformation or, as it applies in justice systems, "transformative justice." To date, there has been a standard pattern of adoption. Since the renowned New Zealand legislation of 1989 (Hudson et al. 1996), community conferencing has been adopted first in juvenile justice, with parallel programs in child protection/welfare. The process has then been adopted in education, first in secondary schools, then in elementary schools.

The Australian state of New South Wales (NSW) provides some suggestions as to what is likely to happen next. By 1999, New South Wales was using or planning to use community conferencing. Here are their suggestions.

In the State School System

A pilot program of community conferencing began in 1997 in three districts (one inner city, one coastal suburban, and one remote rural). The pilot appears significantly to have reduced rates of suspension and exclusion in those districts. On the strength of these results, the program is now spreading from one district to another across the state, as a (decentralised) initiative of local District Offices (roughly the equivalent of Area Boards). The system of private and Catholic schools is beginning to follow suit. A predictable systematic effect should be to reduce the flow of clients to the juvenile justice system.

In the Juvenile Justice System

Legislation passed in 1997 sought to incorporate systemic lessons from New Zealand, South Australia, the Australian Capital Territory and an earlier pilot program in New South Wales. The legislation provides for a system of one administrator in each district responsible for a pool of trained conference convenors who sub-contract to the NSW Department of Juvenile Justice on a case by case basis, and are paid at a standard hourly rate. The guiding philosophy is to maintain quality control while avoiding over-professionalisation of the process by having each community conference convened by a member of the local (geographic) community whose vocation is something other than juvenile justice administration. A predictable systematic effect of this program should be to reduce the flow of clients to the adult justice system

In the Adult Justice System

The Department of the Attorney General in 1999 established a board with the task of expanding community conferencing into adult justice. As in education and juvenile justice, one effect should be to shift the focus of each intervention away from individuals towards social networks. The effect should be *diversionary* in many cases. But here, too, there is a shift in emphasis. The emphasis is not so much on diverting *from* the punitive prison system as it is on diverting *to* strengthened communities.

In Corrections

The NSW Department of Corrections in 1999 established a Restorative Justice Unit. The Unit is looking to use conferencing in at least three ways: (i) as a service that might be initiated by any member(s) of a community affected by an incident that has led to probation, parole or a custodial sentence, (ii) as a mechanism of social reintegration at the end of a custodial sentence, (iii) as a process for experiential learning among groups of people under a custodial sentence. The long-term systemic effects of this reform are likely to be significant and positive.

In Industrial Relations and Family Law

The work of TJA is being recognised by organisations such as labour unions, employer's groups, and the Law Society of NSW. The idea that conflict transformation represents a third way beyond conflict minimisation and conflict maximisation is beginning to enter the legal culture. A key artistic phenomenon is now contributing to that. Early in 1999, Australia's foremost playwright, David Williamson, met with critical acclaim for his play based on a series of case studies of TJA workplace conferences. In the early months of 2000, the play, *Face to Face,* was taken on an Australian tour while other productions played in Melbourne and Darwin.

At the time of writing, David Williamson was preparing the second play in his transformative justice trilogy. The case in the second play is one in which the key protagonists have been involved in an incident that involved a death through culpable behaviour and thus also a prison sentence.

A cultural event likes this confronts us directly with questions about culpability, free will, individual and collective responsibility and justice. It shows that, when we seek to achieve justice, the questions we ask determine the answers we provide. When we ask not "Who did it and what is to be done to them?" but "What happened, how have people been affected, and what do we need to do now?" we get a very different sort of justice. We get a justice process that involves the acknowledgment of conflict, then the transformation of conflict into cooperation. That is the general result form the process, regardless of the program that employs it.

Structured programs offering community conferencing at the neighbourhood level are developing at key sites across Canada, and at a smaller number of sites in the United States. In Baltimore, for instance, a coordinated network of neighbourhood groups has begun offering community conferencing. They are doing so with the imprimatur and oversight of justice system officials, but in a way that leaves responsibility in the hands of democratically constituted local groups. Their emphasis is not on the weaknesses of criminal justice theory and practice. It is on the often untapped strengths of neighbourhoods. But if programs such as this succeed, we may begin to see real decreases in the supply of clients to the prison industry.

⋔ REFERENCES

Chatterjee, J., 1998, *Evaluation of the RCMP Restorative Justice Initiative*, Ottawa: RCMP Community, Contract and Aboriginal Policing Services.

Christie, N., 1995, *Crime Control as Industry: Towards Gulags, Western Style?* London: Routledge.

Fishkin, J.S., 1995, *The Voice of the People: Public Opinion and Democracy*, New Haven: Yale University Press.

Hudson, J., Morris, A., Maxwell, G., and Galaway, B. (eds), 1996, *Family Group Conferences: Perspectives on Policy and Practice*, Monsey, NY: The Willowtree Press.

McDonald, J.M. and Moore, D.B., 1998, *Community Conference Facilitator's Kit*, Sydney, TJA.

McDonald, J.M. and Moore, D.B., 2000, "Community Conferencing as a Special Case of Conflict Transformation," in J. Braithwaite and H. Strang (eds) *Restorative Justice and Civil Society*, Cambridge: Cambridge University Press.

Moore, D.B. with Forsythe, L., 1995, *A New Approach to Juvenile Justice: Family Conferencing in Wagga Wagga*, (Report to the Criminology Research Council) Wagga Wagga: Centre for Rural Social Research.

Moore, D.B and McDonald, J.M., 2000a, "Guiding Principles of the Conferencing Process," in G. Burford and J. Hudson (eds) *Family Group Conferences: Perspectives on Policy, Practice and Research*, Monsey, NY: Willow Tree Press.

Moore, D.B and McDonald, J.M., 2000b, *Transforming Workplace Conflict: A Guide to Preparing and Convening Workplace Conferences*, Sydney: TJA.

Morris, R., 1992, "A Practical Path to Transformative Justice", (unpublished pamphlet), Toronto.

Sherman and Strang, H., 1996–1999, *RISE Papers*, Canberra, ANU. Available at <www.aic.gov.au/rjustice/progress/index.html#contents>.

Sober, E. and Wilson, D.S., 1998, *Unto Others: The Evolution and Psychology of Unselfish Behavior*, Cambridge, MA: Harvard University Press.

17

Towards the 21st Century: Abolition—An Impossible Dream?

Thomas Mathiesen

🏛 INTRODUCTION: IMPOSSIBLE DREAM?

Many years ago I flew from Oslo via London to Strasbourg, where I was, at the time, engaged in some research work. It was in the good old days when the planes flew lower, so you could see something on the way. I saw the hills, the plains, and the contours of the large cities and even some of the small towns of Europe. The sun was bright and shiny and the sky was blue. And I remember I thought that I, in my lifetime, would experience a Europe without prisons, or at least virtually without prisons.

It did not go that way. In the 1960s and 1970s a complex set of political factors created a favourable context for a radical critique of prisons. Abolition of prisons—indeed, abolition of the criminal control system as we know it today—seemed to be possible goals, at least to some of us. And during the first part of the 1970s, the prison population of several Western countries in fact went down, a trend that seemed to substantiate our view. But towards the end of the 1970s, and in the 1980s, the tide turned. The downward trend in the prison population during the first part of the 1970s ended as a "U-shaped curve": By the end of the decade, the decrease had been cancelled out. And during the 1980s, the figures rocketed. They continued to do so in the 1990s, giving the Western world an all time high record in terms of prison population. Between 1979 and 1993 US figures increased from 230 to 532 per 100 000, Canadian figures from 100 to 125, British figures from 85 to 95, Norwegian figures from 44 to 62, Dutch figures from 23 to 52, and so on (Christie, 1994). In addition, the figures have increased steadily since 1993. The only two Western exceptions from the pattern that I know of, are earlier West Germany and Finland. What was originally West Germany showed a substantial drop during the 1980s. But the drop was cancelled out by a renewed equally substantial increase in the early 1990s. Finland has shown a downward trend, but then the Finnish figures were extremely high at the outset (106 per 100 000 in 1979), and the Finnish situation is very special. On the whole, prisons are on the march. And they march fast.

Should we, then, conclude that abolition of prisons is "an impossible dream"? On the face of it, it seems that way. The present and immediate future appear dark, to say the least. The political climate strongly favours prison; indeed, the political climate favours a revival of something as medieval as the death sentence. The politician in the US, who today goes out against the death sentence, is finished. "Three strikes, and you're out" is the order of the day.

Yet, I think the conclusion of "impossible dream" is too hasty. In a thought-provoking piece on the memories of abolitionist victories of the past, the German criminologist Sebastian Scheerer reminds us that "there has never been a major social transformation in the history of mankind that had not been looked upon as unrealistic, idiotic, or utopian by the large majority of experts even a few years before the unthinkable became reality" (Scheerer, 1986: 7). As examples, Scheerer mentions the fall of the Roman Empire and the abolition of modern slavery. Slavery, he argues, had succeeded in looking extremely stable almost until the day it collapsed, and the abolitionists who were around were regarded as awkward customers, to say the least, almost until it happened. Similarly, to most of the observers at the time, the total collapse of the Roman Empire was unthinkable almost until it happened. Other examples on the same scale may be added. A major example, perhaps the most important political example of the 1900s, are the political transformations which took place in central and eastern Europe during 1989 and 1990. Think back ten or fifteen years. Who would have dared to predict those transformations in 1987, two to three years before the they took place, let alone in 1982, seven to eight years before? In 1982, Soviet rule was solidly planted throughout Eastern Europe, and unrest in Poland had resolutely been met, the year before, by martial law. In 1987, Gorbachov's Glastnost was on the way, to be sure, but would you have predicted a total dissolution of the Soviet Union, and a complete dismantling of the Iron Curtain within three years? At least I would not, and did not. And who, for that matter, would have dared to predict, in 1989 and 1990, the disillusionment with the subsequent political and economic developments which came a little later, in the early 1990s? Developments like these are easy to "predict" in retrospect, when we know the answers. But that is actually postdiction rather than prediction.

⍜ THE STORY OF THE SPANISH WITCH HUNTS

This is all very well, you might say, but it deals with the downfall of whole empires, like the Roman and Soviet, or with vast economic institutions like slavery. Do experiences from such contexts apply to specific penal systems, with their lawmakers, judges and numerous dedicated well-paid administrators?

I will tell you a story. The story is a bit long, but I hope you will bear with me. I have not made it up; it is from real life. It is the story of how a whole penal system, on a world wide scale, seemingly solid and ever lasting, with its law makers, judges and thousands of administrators, crumbled and vanished within the period of four years.

The example is historical, going almost four hundred years back. Therefore, I am not suggesting that it can be used as a complete model for us today. Conditions today are different, partly very different; among other things, we have the modern mass media and their influence to think about. I will return to them later. But the example at least shows that it is possible, under given conditions, to have penal systems crumble, and crumble extremely fast. This is important to realize at a time when the chips are down, disenchantment reigns and the notion of "impossible dream" is spreading as far as modern prisons goes. And it is important at a time when we need to take a close look at past abolitions to learn more about the conditions of abolition. We know so much about the conditions sustaining systems; far less about those fostering radical change.

The story is that of the abolition of the Spanish witch hunts—a hundred years before the abolition of the hunts in other regions. The witch-hunts across the Spanish territories ended in 1614. Think first back about 150 years from 1614, and place yourself in that context. Who would have believed, in 1487, when Heinrich Institor Krämer and Jakob Spränger published their major theological and legal dogmatic work on witches, *Malleus Maleficarum*—"The Witch Hammer"—that the institution of witch hunts would some day disappear, as in fact would the Inquisition itself? We know the story of the two inquisitors, who turned to Rome, where Pope Innocent VIII resided, to complain of the resistance against the persecution of witches, and of how Pope Innocent on 5 December 1484 issued his papal bull on witches, *Summis Desiderantes Affectibus*, which provided the decisive churchly sanction to the witch hunts. And we know the rest of the story—of how Krämer and Spränger with the bull as basic authority went on to write *Malleus Maleficarum*—a work which was printed in fourteen editions within a period of thirty years, the second edition including a reprint of the Pope's bull—and of how that book became profoundly important as a theological-legal basis for the subsequent witch hunts in Europe. Who would have thought, at the time, that all of this would one day wither and be gone?

As I have said, this was 150 years before the hunts withered and went in the Spanish territories. Not an excessively long time in the life of a penal system, but a fairly long, and perhaps it can not be expected of people to predict much over such a period. Conditions in the late 1400s were in many ways very different from those in the early 1600s. But who would have believed, in Spain in 1610, that the witch hunts were to be history throughout the Spanish empire within four years—in 1614?

The early 1600s saw extensive witch crazes—frenzied waves of persecution of witches—for example in Northern Spain. French witches were presumably crossing the border in great numbers, creating a lot of trouble in the Spanish regions. In 1610, a solemn auto-da-fé was held in Logrōno, where eleven witches were burnt—some in effigy because they had been tortured to death—during the presence of some 30,000 spectators. Imagine the crowd; imagine the symbols of power and authority. The times were certainly against the witches, and for the hunts. The Logrōno auto-da-fé was one of the greatest manifestations of the witch-hunts for years. To all sane contemporaries, the institution of the hunts appeared to be unchangeable, solid and stable.

But there were doubts. Deep inside the Inquisition itself, hidden from public observation. What was the Inquisition? To use a metaphor, a huge spider of a surveillance and police force, first established in the 1200s as a special force to combat heresy, organized in Spain during the late 1400s, with thousands of employees and a wide net of intelligence services, secret police forces, sentencing authorities and arrests; during the early 1600s organized in nineteen—later twenty-one—tribunals of inquisitors throughout the enormous Spanish empire.

And after the auto-da-fé in Logrōno in the Basque province in 1610, doubts among some were growing. The Danish historian Gustav Henningsen has described in detail how the doubts developed (Henningsen, 1981; see also Henningsen, 1984), but they have also been described earlier, notably by the historian Henry Charles Lea in his great four volume work from 1906 on the history of the Spanish Inquisition (Lea, 1906/1966).

Central in the sequence of events was a particular inquisitor, Alonso de Salazar Frías, in the Logrōno tribunal. Salazar had set his name and agreed to the auto-da-fé in 1610. But he was worried over proof. When grace was given denouncements and confessions were withdrawn. On what grounds could greater authority be given to confessions than to withdrawals? When there was a great deal of talk about witches, witches would appear in great numbers, and when there was less talk, they would disappear. Couldn't the cause-effect relationship just as well be from talk to appearance of witches as from appearance of witches to talk about them? And couldn't confessions contain delusions? Mind you, this could—for the individual—imply a development from bad to worse, because it could imply that the correct legal categorization—and Salazar was an excellent lawyer—would be heresy rather than witchcraft, and heresy, not folksy witchcraft, was the primary business of the Inquisition. But at least, the individual would not be taken as a witch.

Organizationally, when members of the local tribunal agreed, la Suprema— the central authority of the Holy Office in Madrid—rarely intervened. But when there was disagreement, extensive communication with the central authority would ensue. And Henningen and Lea describe how Salazar in fact began to disagree in his tribunal. In those days, communication was slow, disagreements took time, and doubts grew also in other quarters of the vast institution. In my words, a major battle of a normative, cultural kind now took place within parts of the Inquisition.

Finally, la Suprema in Madrid cut through. The following is an important point: La Suprema had a long tradition of restraint in sentencing witches—as did in fact the Italian Inquisition: The major European persecutions predominantly came in areas outside the jurisdiction of the Inquisition. In fact, la Suprema had a practice of frequently pardoning those sentenced to the stake by the local tribunals. Liberal views thus had a sounding board in la Suprema. In other words, two levels—the supreme authority that gave support and the executive level that initiated the change—were involved. We recognize this pattern from partial abolitions in our own time, such as Jerome Miller's famous closing of the training schools and Massachusetts in the 1970s. His revolt found support from the Governor of the state, who functioned as a protective shield as he triggered the closure (Rutherford, 1974).

There is also another similarity: In both cases, the case of the witches in the early 1600s and that of the training schools of the 1970s, the point was not reform, but outright, quick abolition, a little bit like a coup. To make a long story short, la Suprema authorized Salazar and his aides to undertake what we today would call a major empirical investigation of Basque witches—in their words, an extensive Visitation with an Edict of Grace to all members of the sect of the devil—interviewing over 1800 individuals in the region and resulting in 11,200 pages of interrogation notes. The first major empirical study of witches, I believe! The major finding of the study was no proof whatsoever of witchcraft.

Let me be precise here: Salazar appears to have believed that witches existed; the point for him was the intellectual question of decisive proof. And he found that the best weapon against the appearance of a large number of witches was in fact silence: "I deduce," he said, in Lea's translation, "the importance of silence and reserve from the experience that there were neither witches nor bewitched until they were talked and written about" (Lea, 1906/1966, Vol. IV: 234). In the end, la Suprema decided to follow Salazar's recommendation to suspend the witch cases. It was done as lawyers would do it: La Suprema asked him to prepare a new set of regulations for the handling of witches. In practice, the new regulations would, if adopted, put an end to the cases, and they were in fact adopted, with almost no changes, by la Suprema in 1614.

A liberal inquisitor with support from above thus became instrumental in the subsequent abolition of witch burning and hunts, in a way interestingly reminiscent of the professionals involved in the prison reductions and abolitions of more modern times. The top level as well as the practitioners' level were involved. And my interpretation is that a major cultural change took place within and permeated through the Inquisition—for which there was a certain cultural preparation in the first place, a kind of "cultural restraint" against at least the most widespread kinds of hunts. That "cultural restraint," you could say, became the authorized definition of the situation, and was followed by abolition despite the fact that in the environment, there were what we today would call major moral panics about the witches.

🏛 THE IRRATIONALITY OF PRISON

The example is heartening to an abolitionist. It goes to show that abolition of whole penal systems is in fact possible. But as I have said, conditions are admittedly different today. If the Inquisition wanted to, it could go completely against the people. And completely against the mass media, which were not there—except for the printed book. The cultural change within the Inquisition, victory on the part of an alternative culture and understanding within the system was therefore a sufficient condition for abolition. Today, a cultural change within the penal system, and a change towards a sense of personal responsibility on the part of those who work there, is just as necessary. But it would not be a fully sufficient condition because the present penal system, carved out as it is by politicians, is far more dependent on the broader context of what we call "public opinion" and mass media.

I will return to this important point later. My starting point is this: Prison, which I confine my analysis to, is a "giant standing on clay soil." The expression is translated from the Norwegian, connoting a seemingly solid system with very poor underpinnings, much like slavery, the Roman Empire in its final stage, and the Soviet rule in it final stage.

The Achilles heel, the clay soil, of the prison is its total irrationality in terms of its own stated goals, a bit like the witch-hunts without proof. In terms of its own stated goals, the prison contributes nothing to our society and way of life. Report after report, study after study, by the dozens, by the hundreds, by the thousands, clearly show this.

As you very well know, prison has five stated goals that are or have been used as arguments for prison. First, there is the argument of rehabilitation. Over the past decades, however, criminology and sociology have produced a very large number of solid empirical studies showing, quite clearly, that the use of imprisonment does not rehabilitate the incarcerated law-breaker. The studies I am thinking of, include experimental and quasi-experimental studies of a wide range of rehabilitation programs, as well as a number of studies of prison organization and culture, the latter showing that prison in fact is counter-productive as far as rehabilitation goes. Time prevents me from detailing these studies. Let me just briefly quote to you a telling statement made over forty years ago, by Lloyd W. McCorkle, an experienced warden of the New Jersey State Prison at Trenton in the United States, and Richard R. Korn, director of education and counselling in the same prison. They said, in an article from 1954 (McCorkle and Korn, 1954: 88):

> *In many ways, the inmate social system may be viewed as providing a way of life which enables the inmate to avoid the devastating psychological effects of internalizing and converting social rejection into self-rejection. In effect, it permits the inmate to reject his rejecters rather than himself.*

The statement summarizes well the results of the thousands of studies and hundreds of meta-studies of rehabilitation that in fact followed the article they wrote, in the 1960, 1970s, and 1980s.

Second, there is the argument of individual deterrence—the notion that the offender who is brought to prison will be scared away from crime by being brought there. I can be brief here. To a very considerable degree the same arguments and studies go against the notion of individual deterrence of the offender. The inmate social system and subculture is especially important.

Third, there is the argument of general prevention, that is, of the deterrent, educative or habit-forming effects in the wider society—on others who have not been punished, or are not undergoing punishment at the moment. Mind you, I am here talking of the preventive effect of prison. The hypothesis of general prevention is less amenable to empirical research. But a very conservative statement would be that the effect is at least uncertain and certainly far less significant in determining the development of crime in society than are features of economic and social policy. A somewhat bolder—but not very bold— statement would be to say that we have a large number of studies suggesting that the preventive effect of prison is very modest or even minimal in population groups where we might want the effect to be strong—groups predisposed to crime, groups of intensive law-breakers—while it is perhaps somewhat more of a force in groups which for other reasons are law-abiding anyway. This is a way of summarizing econometric studies, historical studies before and after legal changes, cross-sectional studies of various legal systems, interview and questionnaire studies of effects of expected sanctions, and so on. Notably, and most important in connection with the use of prison, it is also a way of summarizing the effect of the expected severity of punishment over against the expected probability of punishment. While the expected probability of punishment—expected detection risk—appears to show a very modest effect in some contexts, the expected severity of punishment, which strikes at the core of the prison issue, in fact shows no effect. This result runs through a large number of studies. Let me specifically mention one of them—the German criminologist Karl Schumann and collaborators' large study of general prevention among German youth (Schumann et al., 1987). This was primarily a study of expected severity of punishment. Its effect on registered as well as self-reported criminal behaviour was studied. The study showed that the expected severity of punishment in fact had no effect on youthful criminal activity. Neither, incidentally, had the expectation of youth prison. What the researchers did find, was that the subjective experience of detection risk had a certain effect. But not on the performance of serious crimes, not even on the performance of all types of trifling crimes, but only on some types of trifling crimes—shop-lifting, trivial physical assault, using the subway without paying, and the like. And even here, the effect as measured through multivariate analysis, was—in German—characterized as "rechts bescheiden," quite modest. Let me add to this that youths who are most likely to be detected, rarely commit such crimes anyway. They tend to commit the types of crime that showed no preventive effect (Schumann et al., 1987).

You may ask, "Why these results?" Let me briefly suggest that the preventive inefficiency of prison constitutes a communication problem. Punishment is, in this context, a way in which the State tries to communicate a message, especially to particularly vulnerable groups in society. As a method of communication, it is extremely crude. The message itself is difficult to get across because of the incommensurability of act and reaction, the message is filtered and skewed during the process, and it is met by a cultural response in the groups concerned which is not at all taken into account in the communication process, and which neutralizes the message. Add to this the deep moral problem embedded in the punishing of some people with the goal of preventing others from acting likewise—a moral problem which is not lost on important target groups—and you have the lot. What is surprising, is not the minimal effect of, but rather the persistent political belief in, such a crude method of communication.

Fourth, there is the argument of incapacitation of offenders. Traditionally, the argument has taken two forms—that of collective and of selective incapacitation.

Collective incapacitation implies the use of prison against whole categories of likely recidivists. You simply get rid of them by locking them up and throwing away the key. This is largely the present policy in the United States. The point in the US today is not to rehabilitate offenders, and not to prevent others from committing similar acts, but simply to bring offenders out of social circulation. Collective incapacitation has been intensely studied in Scandinavia as well as in the US. Even if we accepted the morality of it, the results are, to put it mildly, very modest. Let me again mention one report among a very large number. The Panel on Research on Criminal Careers, sponsored by the National Institute of Justice, published its major two-volume report in 1986 (Blumstein et al., 1986). The panel paid close attention to collective incapacitation. Between 1973 and 1982 the number of state and federal prisons in the US almost doubled. During the same period, the crime rate did not decrease. It increased by 29 percent, certainly a dismal result. Estimates available to the panel suggested that depending on the assumed individual offending frequency, the rate would have been only 10 to 20 percent higher if the almost 100 percent increase in prison figures had not occurred. This may be viewed as a modest gain, but it contains three basic flaws. For one thing, it is certainly an extremely costly gain in view of the dramatic increase in the prison population. Furthermore, you very quickly reach a point of diminishing return. Further reductions would, and I quote from the report, "require at least 10 to 20 percent increases in inmate populations for each one percent reduction in crime." (Blumstein et al., Vol. 1: 128).

Finally, and most importantly, the present generation of delinquents is not the last one. New generations will appear in the streets. This means that the reduction in the crime rate, if any, will soon fade. Of course, collective incapacitation could be renewed for new generations. But you would never catch up, because of the ever-present input of new generations. At the same time, those already incarcerated would have to be locked up for very long periods, because of their presumed persistence. In short, you would end up with huge numbers of prisoners and negligible effect. Exactly this has happened in the United States, and in other countries—such a Poland in the recent past.

Then you have selective incapacitation—the individual prediction of high-risk violent offenders on the basis of specified background criteria. A number of studies have shown that prediction of this kind is extremely difficult, and that the so-called false-positive as well as the false-negative rates—that is, the errors of prediction—are very high. As some of the proponents of selective incapacitation—participants in the large scale Rand studies of selective incapacitation during the 1980s—have formulated it: "Nevertheless, we cannot now recommend basing sentencing policy on these conclusions" (Chaiken and Chaiken, 1982: 26).

Fifth and lastly, add to this balanced justice—the neo-classical response to crime through prison, and the list is complete. Though it is admitted that prison cannot prevent anything, it can presumably balance off the reprehensible act, equalizing the weights of justice. But can it? To put the matter briefly: It cannot in any precise way balance off the act, because the criminal offence on the one hand and time on the other are incommensurable entities, and above all because the scale of punishment cannot be securely "anchored" (von Hirsch, 1986; von Hirsch, 1993; for a critique, see Mathiesen, 1990; Mathiesen, 1996). For these reasons, the punishment scale builds on sand, and changes rapidly with the political wind. We see this happening today. For the same reasons, the punishment scale gives the victim little satisfaction. It is the political wind rather than his or her quest for justice that is decisive.

ᏤᎢ THE SECRET OF PRISON IRRATIONALITY

So, then, prison is a deeply irrational system in terms of its own stated goals. The difficulty, however, is that this knowledge to a large extent is a secret.

If people really knew how poorly prison, as well as other parts of the criminal control system, protected them—indeed, if they knew how prison only creates a more dangerous society by producing more dangerous people, a climate for dismantling the prisons would necessarily get under way. Because people, in contrast to prisons, are rational in this matter. But dry information would clearly not be enough; the failure of prisons would have to be "known" in the sense of felt on a deeper emotional level, and thus be a part of our cultural definition of the situation.

The direction of that new climate is of course hard to predict, but most likely it would imply a renewed emphasis on real support to the victims as well resources and social services on the offender side, since the highly repressive solution had failed so completely. The politicians, who have created and maintained, indeed expanded the present system, would have to follow suit in order not to lose voters—their prime preoccupation.

I envisage—and this is just a short hand list—support to the victims in a number of ways: Economic compensation (from the state) when that is in order, a simplified insurance system, symbolic support in situations of grief and sorrow, shielded places where victims who need protection can get it, support centres for battered women, conflict resolution where that is natural, and so on. The victims get nothing out of the present system, and get nothing out of enlarging and accelerating the present system, and could get so much out of changing the direction of the system in the way I have suggested. A fundamental idea and principle would be to change the system 180 degrees: Rather than increasing punishment of the offender with the gravity of the offence, which is basic to the present system, I would propose increased support to the victim with the gravity of the offence. In other words, not a punishment scale for offenders, but a support scale for victims. This would admittedly be a dramatic shift, but one which would be rational from the point of view of the victims, and probably also helpful in overcoming resistance to the dismantling the present system.

I envisage resources on the offender side in the form of a whole string of measures. In general terms, the war on crime should become a war on poverty. Again, I am just giving you a short hand list; many details would have to be sorted out: Decent living quarters, work programs, school programs, treatment programs, but not programs based on force, and—most importantly—a change of our drug policy. Legalizing drugs, and making drugs as well as methadone available under sanitary and supervised conditions, would neutralize the illegal drug market and reduce the amount drug-related crime drastically. It would in itself go a long way towards emptying our prisons. A change of our drug policy would at the same time strike at the core of organized drug crime, dependent as it is on market forces. It would, in other words, effectively threaten and undermine the power of the big fish who do not end up in prison today, because prison today is systematically reserved for the poor.

You may ask, "Who should pay for this?" The answer is that the prisons should pay for it: The dismantling of the prisons would give us extremely large sums of money, billions and billions of US dollars, which we could spend generously on the victims and the offenders.

Admittedly, perhaps a possibility to hold a few individuals would remain. Our handling of them would have to be very different from what goes on in our prisons today. One way of ensuring against an increase in their numbers due to a change of criteria would be to set an absolute ceiling on the number of closed cells to be accepted in our society for such people.

The call for a ceiling on prison space could also be a useful weapon in our present struggle against prison. In a time of dramatic acceleration it should be carefully be considered as a strategy. But, excepting the call for a ceiling, I have for the last few minutes expressly talked about the future. Let us return to the present, and to where we are—in the difficult first stage: People do not know how irrational our prisons are. People are made to believe that prison works. The true irrationality of prison is one of the best-guarded secrets in our society.

If the secret got out, it would strike at the roots of the present system, and imply the beginning of its fall. Three "layers" function as protective shields for prison, keeping the irrationality of prison a secret.

★

The first and innermost layer consists of the administrators, in a wide sense of the word, of the criminal control system.

The administrators largely know about the dismal state and total failure of the prisons, but are silent. Three processes make for silence.

For one thing, the administrators are silent because they have become co-opted by the system; they have become part and parcel of it. Co-optation takes place through a subtle process by which evidence going against the system—abundant as it is in the prison context—is selectively weeded out, relegated to the background, and not taken into account. When reminded of it, those representing the evidence rather than the evidence itself become the target of attack: Those representing the evidence are defined and labelled as theoreticians, dreamers, revolutionaries, while the evidence per se is not focused, let alone challenged.

Furthermore, the administrators are silent out of loyalty with the system. There is a culture of loyalty, just as there was a culture of loyalty to the German leaders among the rank and file during the latter part of World War II. Besides, the system is considered legal, which adds to the spirit of loyalty.

Finally, the administrators are silenced by being disciplined. The processes of social discipline, which vary along a continuum from very subtle hidden measures to blunt open measures, are continuously operating within the prison and penal context. The subtle, hidden measures for example include the many meetings where the means and goals have the authority of the taken-for-granted, thus inculcating increased pulse, insecurity and silence among would-be opponents. The blunt, open measures include reprimand and perhaps the threat of loss of job.

★

The second layer, in a sense along the edge or border of the prison system, consists of intellectuals and researchers—social scientists in a broad sense of the word. Also they are silent, or at best whispering their protests.

The position of the numerous researchers may be seen within a particular context. The French sociologist Pierre Bourdieu has used the Greek phrase *doxa* to connote that which is unquestionable and taken for granted within a culture. *Doxa* is something you do not discuss or debate, because it is inherently good and therefore undebatable. Every culture has its *doxa*. Around *doxa*, there are two spheres of debate: The orthodox and the heterodox debate. In the orthodox debate, details are discussed, but the basic premises of the system in question remain undiscussed, and remain doxic. In the heterodox debate, fundamental questions about the basic premises of the system are raised. *Doxa* attempts to limit the heterodox debate, and if possible to silence it completely. If this is not attained, attempts are made to convert the heterodox debate into an orthodox debate, a debate about surface details. If opponents stubbornly insist on being heteroxical, and if the political system is undemocratic, they are exterminated as heretics. In democratic societies they are not exterminated, but largely relegated to peripheral meetings, organizations, journals and other similar contexts. Only occasionally are they allowed to enter the central meetings and media, often as radical alibis for the system.

The broad category of intellectuals and researchers, well acquainted with the dire results of prison research, are today on the move from heterodoxy to orthodoxy, and even into *doxa* itself. In the climate of the 1970s, with radical critique of institutions in general and prisons in particular, the researchers who conducted research on rehabilitation were largely heterodoxical: They saw and defined the research and findings as devastating to the prison system. Today, those researching for example selective incapacitation and prediction of violence, subtly change standards. The correlation between social indices and future violence are admittedly low, they say, and the percentages of false-negative and the false-positives are high. But then, they go on to say, so are all correlations in medical, psychological and social science. Correlations of .35 can now, with new and improved measures, be increased to .37, or perhaps even approach .40. That, presumably, makes the results acceptable. Thus, the researchers of the present, in contrast to those of the 1970s, have moved into an orthodox debate or even into support of the system, into *doxa*. Again, the change of view on the part of the researchers is contextually produced: The general public debate today is drastically different from what it was like in the 1970s. The researchers have followed suit (for more details, see Mathiesen, forthcoming in *Law and Human Behaviour*).

★

This brings us to the third layer. The third, and—for reasons I will outline in a minute—the most important layer, exists over the edge or border of the prison system: The mass media as the all embracing public sphere or space in modern Westernized society.

The information that comes out of the prison system is systematically filtered and skewed by the mass media. This has occurred increasingly through our century. But a significant qualitative jump took place with the advent of television after World War II. A further tremendous qualitative jump took place roughly from the mid-1970s on, with the many ingenious technological advances which occurred in the late 1900s, making television instantaneously reach all of the corners of the world.

The point is that with the advent and accelerating development of television, we have entered something that is equivalent to a new religion. When the automobile arrived around the turn of the century, many people believed it was a horse and buggy, only without the horse. Reminiscent of that, we still speak of "horse power." But it was not a horse and buggy without a horse, it was something entirely new, which contained the seeds of an entirely different society. So with television. When television arrived, some people believed that it was just a newspaper in pictures. But it was not just that, it was an entirely new medium creating a completely new society, and, it might be added, a new medium which fundamentally influenced the shape and content of the old media.

The question of the influence of television on specific attitudes and behaviour pattern is much discussed and studied but relatively unimportant. The important point is the total "paradigm" or "Gestalt" which emanates from the medium. The American media researcher George Gerbner has put it succinctly, as follows (Gerbner and Gross 1976, p. 180):

> *[The point is a concept of] broad enculturation rather than of narrow changes in opinion or behaviour. Instead of asking what communication "variables" might propagate what kinds of individual behaviour changes, we want to know what types of common consciousness whole systems of messages might cultivate. This is less like asking about preconceived fears and hopes and more like asking about the "effects" of Christianity on one's views of the world...*

The parallel drawn to religion should be taken as more than a metaphor. Our relationship to television has several of the characteristics of the relationship of the faithful to the Church. The British media researcher James Curran has put it this way, in functional terms (Curran 1982, p. 227):

347

The modern mass media in Britain now perform many of the integrative functions of the Church in the middle ages. Like the medieval Church, the media link together different groups and provide a shared experience that promotes social solidarity. The media also emphasize collective values that bind people closer together, in a way that is comparable to the influence of the medieval Church: the communality of the Christian faith celebrated by Christian rites is now replaced by the communalities of consumerism and nationalism celebrated in the media "rites" such as international sporting contests (that affirm national identities) and consumer features (that celebrate a collective identity of consumers). Indeed, the two institutions have engaged in some ways in very similar ideological "work" despite the difference in time that separate them. ... The modern mass media have given, at different times, massive and disproportionate attention to a series of "outsiders" ... comparable to the hunting down and parading of witches allegedly possessed by the devil by the medieval and early modern Church....

The transformation may be described in more precise terms. As Neil Postman (1985) has emphasized in his important analysis of modern television, in terms of media form we are in the midst of a crucial transformation from an emphasis on the written message towards an emphasis on the picture. The emphasis on the picture, and on the picture as that which defines what is true and false, as that which defines what actually happened as if staging did not exist, implies a fundamental cultural change in the West. The change also includes the modern press, for example through the "tabloidization" of the newspapers, with large "on the scene" pictures, large punchy headlines and brief texts. Foucault's notion of a "panoptical" development, in which the few see and survey the many, is paralleled by an enormous contrasting but functionally related "synoptical" development, in which the many see, survey and admire the few—the media stars on the media sky. In a double sense of the word we are, as I have tried to formulate it in a book I have written on the topic, living in a "viewer society" (Mathiesen, 1987; Mathiesen, forthcoming in *Theoretical Criminology*).

In terms of media content, we are in the midst of a parallel change towards entertainment. We need not agree with an implication on the part of Postman, that the transformation in terms of form to the picture necessarily changes the content into entertainment, to agree with him that we are, in fact, "amusing ourselves to death." Even the most serious news and even the most violent of reported events are defined as "shows," and are given an "entertaining slant." Information and entertainment are fused into "infotainment." Writing is still with us, to be sure, as are serious analyses. But in terms of tendency, public news space is predominantly filled with pictures and tabloids which "entertain." Time forbids an analysis of the forces that in turn shape these tendencies. Suffice it to say that a new technological era, witnessing entirely new production systems as well as communication systems in the mass media area, with countless satellites filling the sky, has enabled market forces to enter public space in a way unthinkable three or four decades ago.

🏛 ALTERNATIVE PUBLIC SPHERE

My basic point is this: Of the three "layers" which protect the prison and keep the irrationality of prison a secret—the administrators in a wide sense of the word, the researchers and the media—the media are most fundamental.

If the media, especially television, changed content from superficial entertainment to critical knowledge, it would create a basic cultural change, a change in the cultural climate, which would have repercussions throughout the ranks of researchers and intellectuals as well as administrators. As I have alluded to already, the administrators and the researchers, inside and along the edge of the system, generally "follow suit": When the cultural climate surrounding the prison becomes tougher, they become tougher. When the cultural climate softens, they soften. They are not independent heroes; rather, their antennae are basically directed outwards, toward the cultural climate, mediated as it is through the mass media. A shift in the external cultural climate, in the opinion about what is the "correct line," would create a parallel shift among the researchers close to system and the administrators inside it. To be sure, there would still be long drawn-out struggles along the edge of as well as inside the prison, perhaps the basic cultural change in along the edge and inside would partly have to wait for the next generation, but it would follow over time.

From this we may conclude that much of our struggle to reach, rip open, lay bare and thus strike at the Achilles heel of the prison system—its fundamental and total irrationality—must be geared towards television and the mass media in general as its most protective shield. This would make the other shields fall, and let the secret out. In view of the great economic interests in show business and the enormous technological advances involved, this is a formidable task.

Frankly, I don't foresee an easy struggle. Let me briefly mention one line of action.

The key word is, in Norwegian, "alternativ offentlighet," in German "Alternative …ffentlichkeit," in English the much more cumbersome phrase "alternative public space." The point is to contribute to the creation of an alternative public space in penal policy, where argumentation and truthful principled thinking rather than entertainment represent the dominant values. I envisage the development of an alternative public space in the area of penal policy as containing three ingredients.

The first ingredient is liberation from what I would call the absorbent power of the mass media; liberation from the definition of the situation implying that one's very existence is dependent on media coverage and media interest. Without media coverage, with silence in the media, I presumably do not exist, my organization does not exist, the meeting has not taken place. In Westernized society, it is probably impossible and inadvisable to refrain completely from media participation. But it is certainly possible to say "no!" to the many talk shows and entertainment-like "debates" referred to earlier which flood our various television channels, and, most importantly, it is certainly possible not to let the definition of our success be dependent on coverage in the media. Coverage in the media regularly converts and perverts our message completely.

The second ingredient is a restoration of the self esteem and feeling of worth on the part of the grass roots movements. It is not true that the grass roots movements, emphasizing network organization and solidarity at the bottom, have died out. What has happened is that with the development of the mass media that I have outlined, these movements have lost faith in themselves. An important example from recent Norwegian history of the actual vitality of grass roots movements: In 1993, thousands of ordinary Norwegians participated in a widespread movement to give refugees from Kosovo-Albania long-term refuge in Norwegian churches throughout the country. The movement ended in a partial victory, in that all of the cases concerning Kosovo-Albanian refugees were reviewed again by the Ministry of Justice. The example suggests that grass roots solidarity even with "distant" groups like refugees did not die out with the Vietnam war.

The third ingredient is a restoration of the feeling of responsibility on the part of intellectuals in a wide sense of the word. I am not thinking of all of the orthodox researchers along the edge of the system. They can not be relied on as initiators of change; they can only be expected to follow suit. I am thinking of the independent researchers who still are around, and, most importantly, the whole range artists, writers, actors, musicians, in addition to a very wide variety of researchers and scientists for example in the humanities and the liberal arts. The prison issue is not an issue for a segment, but for all of us. Their refusal to participate in the mass media show business would be important. They have a bargaining power in relation to the media. A revitalization of research taking the interests of common people as point of departure is equally important. This point is not new, but goes, of course, several decades back in Western intellectual history. The area is full of conflicts and problems, but they are not unsolvable.

You may ask how the three ingredients I have mentioned are to be triggered and developed. The task is of course very long-range. Let me give you a small example: We have tried to do some of this in Norway, in the organization KROM, The Norwegian Association for Penal Reform, a strange hybrid of an organization, with intellectuals and many prisoners, with a common cause (Mathiesen, 1974; Mathiesen, 1995). We have organized large conferences on penal policy every year. We have so far organized 25 of them, and to create a tradition, we have organized them in the same place, a mountain resort outside Oslo. To begin with, in the late 1960s, participation was narrow; over the years it has become much broader, and to day participation is defined as a "must" in very wide professional circles. A whole range of professions and agencies relevant to penal policy, and many prisoners, are there. We also organize regular seminars as well as other activities. In a sum, we try to create a network of opinion and information crossing the formal and informal borders between segments of the relevant administrative and political systems. The point is precisely that of trying to create an alternative public space where argumentation and principled thinking are dominant values, a public space with a different culture that in the end may compete with the superficial public space of the mass media.

This kind of attempt has the advantage, over against what goes on in the mass media, of being based on actual and organized relationships between people. The public space of the mass media is in that sense weak: It is a public space which is unorganized, segmented, splintered into millions of unconnected individuals—this is its truly mass character—and equally segmented into thousands of individual media stars on the media sky. I have spoken of the Achilles' heel of prison. This is the Achilles' heel of the public space of the media, which we try to turn to our advantage.

This is one line of thinking and working. There are obviously others. Much of our time should be spent finding them. The task of getting the irrationality of prison out to the people, which would make the system crumble much like the Spanish witch hunts 400 years ago, requires them all.

ṁ ENDNOTES

Paper read at the VIII International Conference on Penal Abolition, Auckland, New Zealand, 18-21 February 1997; to be published by the Association for Humanist Sociology. Published in Portuguese in Edson Passetti and Roberto B. Dias da Silva (eds.): *Conversações abolicionistas. Uma Crítica do sistema penal e da sociedade punitiva* 1997.

ṁ REFERENCES

Blumstein, Alfred et al. (eds.), *Criminal Careers and "Career Criminals,"* Washington, DC: National Academy Press, 1986.

Bourdieu, Pierre, *Outline of a Theory of Practice*, Eng. ed. Cambridge: Cambridge University Press, 1977.

Chaiken, Jan M. and Marcia R. Chaiken, *Varieties of Criminal Behavior—Summary and Policy Implications*, Santa Monica: Rand Corporation, 1982.

Christie, Nils, *Crime Control as Industry: Towards Gulags, Western Style?* London: Routledge, 1994.

Curran, James, "Communications, Power and Social Order," In Michael Gurevitsch et al. (eds.) *Culture, Society and the Media*, London: Methuen, 1982.

Gerbner, George and Larry Gross, "Living with Television: The Violence Profile," *Journal of Communication*, Spring 1976, pp. 173-198.

Henningsen, Gustav, *Heksenes advokat* (The Witches' Advocate), Copenhagen: Delta, 1981.

von Hirsch, Andrew, *Past or Future Crimes: Deservedness and Dangerousness in the Sentencing of Criminals*, Manchester: Manchester University Press, 1986.

von Hirsch, Andrew, *Censure and Sanctions*, London: Clarendon Press, 1993.

Lea, Henry Charles, *A History of the Inquisition of Spain*, New York: AMS Press, Inc. 1906, 2nd ed., 1966.

Mathiesen, Thomas, *The Politics of Abolition: Essays in Political Action Theory*, London: Martin Robertson, 1974.

Mathiesen, Thomas, *Seersamfundet: Om medier og kontroll i det moderne samfund* (The Viewer Society: On Media and Control in Modern Society), Copenhagen: Socpol, 1987.

Mathiesen, Thomas, *Prison on Trial: A Critical Assessment*, London: Sage Publications, 1990.

Mathiesen, Thomas, "About KROM: Past—Present—Future," Institute for Sociology of Law, Oslo 1995.

Mathiesen, Thomas, *Perché il carcere?* Torino: Edizioni Gruppo Abele 1996 (Italian translation of *Prison on Trial*, with a new postscript).

Mathiesen, Thomas, "Selective Incapacitation Revisited," *Law and Human Behaviour*, forthcoming.

Mathiesen, Thomas, "The Viewer Society: Michel Foucault's 'Panopticon' Revisited," *Theoretical Criminology*, forthcoming.

McCorkle, Lloyd W. and Richard R. Korn, "Resocialization within Walls," *Annals of American Academy of Political and Social Science*, 1954, pp. 88-98.

Postman, Neil, *Amusing Ourselves to Death: Public Discourse in the Age of Show Business*, London: Heinemann, 1985.

Rutherford, Andrew, *The Dissolution of the Training Schools in Massachusetts*, Columbus: Academy for Contemporary Problems, 1974.

Scheerer, Sebastian, "Towards Abolitionism," *Contemporary Crises*, 1986, pp. 5-20.

Schumann, Karl F. et al. *Jugendkriminalität und die Grenzen der Generalprävention (Juvenile Delinquency and the Limits of General Prevention)*, Cologne: Luchterhand, 1987.

PART 5

AFTERWORD

18

Jubilee in 2000?

Ruth Morris and W. Gordon West

As we noted in the introduction, the modern day penal abolition movement has many very deep roots: some religiously-based faith convictions, some very politically pragmatic convictions, some intelligently social science based conclusions, and some more radically critical of our conceptualizing of *penality*.

Throughout this collection, authors of various articles, coming from each and all of these roots, have drawn on these various roots of penal abolition.

But as Jim Consedine and others have eloquently pointed out through their papers, the Year 2000 has a special significance for Christians (and other faith-based opponents of our contemporary systems of penality):

> *With the advent of a Year of Jubilee in the year 2000, it is appropriate at this time to speak of the Biblical injunction that Jubilee be celebrated by "proclaiming liberty throughout the land" (Leviticus 25). Jubilee should be extended also to people in prison (J. Consedine, 1999).*

ICOPA will discuss aspects of key connections between the penal system and the "new" corporate agendas, between corporate crime and incarceration rates pathologically growing around the world, locking up more and more of the unemployed, unhoused, uncared for, and marginalized. No previous conference and no previous group at a major international conference has focussed so explicitly on how the penal system and this corporate system serve each other, while violating community, justice, and reconciliation. In so doing we hope to widen the reach of ICOPA and strengthen the alliance between those interested in both issues, in the on-going struggle against various forces which are threatening the future of our lives, our communities, and our world.

About the Contributors

John Clarke was born in England and has always been involved in labour and social justice work. Out of an effort to form a union of unemployed workers, John emerged with the Ontario Coalition Against Poverty, whose creative and courageous efforts to empower the poor have challenged the right-wing agenda in many humorous as well as delightful ways. John can quote the history of oppression as eloquently as he can speak about the eviction of a family or the persecution of a homeless man.

Jim Consedine has been a prison chaplain for over 20 years and national co-ordinator of the Restorative Justice Network in New Zealand, Jim is known to most legislators in New Zealand for his active lobbying for healing justice. He travels around the world promoting healing justice and disseminating his books, which provide an overview of our failing retributive justice systems worldwide. A Catholic Worker priest, Jim lives simply and witnesses mightily. He has an inspiring knowledge of the structural basis of inequality in the world and its relationship to incarceration. His books include *A Poison in the Blood Stream* and *Restorative Justice: Healing the Effects of Crime*; he also co-edited *Restorative Justice: Contemporary Themes and Practices (1999)*.

Lisa Finateri has an MA in Criminology from the University of Ottawa. She is involved in the penal abolitionist movement both academically and as an activist; currently she works as a prison advocate and researcher with the John Howard Society of Kingston, Canada.

John McMurtry is Professor of Philosophy at University of Guelph, Canada. He is the author of five books, the two most recent books of which are *Unequal Freedoms: the Global Market as an Ethical System* and *The Cancer Stage of Capitalism*. His articles have appeared in many academic journals, and he has been a regular columnist and magazine contributor. Over 300 of his letters to editors have been published around the world, and his documentaries have appeared on CBC and NBC television. His writings appear in over 50 textbooks, and he has travelled to over 80 countries. John has keynoted many conferences on issues of corporate rule and other topics.

Thomas Mathiesen is Professor, Institutt for Rettssosiologi, University of Oslo, Norway. His writings on criminology and abolitionism are among the best known in the world. His latest works challenge the view that abolitionism cannot move forward in these conservative times. Some of his major publications include: *The Politics of Abolition: Essays in Political Action Theory*; *Seersamfundet: Om medier og kontroll i det moderne samfund* (The Viewer Society. On Media and Control in Modern Society); and *Prison on Trial: A Critical Assessment*. He works from Oslo Norway.

Marc Mauer, Assistant Director of The Sentencing Project in Washington, D.C., has authored some of the most widely cited reports in the field of criminal justice, including "Young Black Men and the Criminal Justice System," and a series on "Americans Behind Bars." His new book, *Race to Incarcerate*, has been described as a "meticulously researched rejoinder to the 'war on crime.'" He is frequently interviewed by leading newspapers and media and has received awards for his outstanding contributions to criminal justice research.

Ruth Morris is a Quaker activist, networker, advocate, writer, and speaker for transformative justice and penal abolition. Born in the USA, and the mother of four children, she began her activist work in the fight against the Vietnam War, racism and poverty. Her move to Canada in 1968 led her soon into penal justice issues, as she soon saw that the penal system is the most perfect incarnation of racism and classism in our culture. The author of eight books, on such topics as penal abolition, street people, and faith topics, she has done speaking tours in Latin America and New Zealand, as well as many keynote addresses in North America. Ruth has appeared on over 300 call-in shows on penal abolition, alternatives to prisons, and social justice topics.

David B. Moore studied in Australia and Germany and holds degrees in languages, political science and political economy, with a doctorate in social theory (Griffith University). He taught politics and history at the University of Melbourne and Charles Stuart University, where he coordinated the Justice Studies Program. David subsequently worked in legal and administrative policy with the Queensland Department of Premier and Cabinet. He co-founded TJA (www.tja.com.au) in 1995 with John and Mark McDonald. He has published extensively in justice and related fields.

Frank Pearce has taught and researched on international corporate crime in England, India, and Canada. He grew up in a working class family in England, with a Catholic Irish mother and a Protestant English father, a situation that exposed him to both class and ethnic prejudice and to the strength of working class culture. Currently a Professor of Sociology at Queen's University, his books include *Crimes of the Powerful, Global Crime Connections* (with Laureen Snider), and *Toxic Capitalism: Corporate Crime in the Chemical Industry* (with Steve Tombs). He has worked with the Permanent People's Tribunal on Industrial Hazards and Human Rights, especially in regard to the Bhopal chemical disaster.

Hal Pepinsky is Professor of Criminal Justice at Indiana University; during the 1999-2000 academic year, he has been a visiting Professor of Sociology at Iowa State University. During a long and distinguished career, Hal has been a major contributor to both peacemaking criminology and the international movement for penal abolition; he has held several visiting professorships both in the US and abroad. He organized ICOPA V in Indiana, the only ICOPA yet to be held in the USA. The author of numerous books and articles, Hal corresponds equally with prisoners in many places and with leading academics in the field.

Viviane Saleh-Hanna is a Masters student at the School of Criminology at Simon Fraser University, Vancouver, Canada. She has a Bachelor of Arts in Criminology with a concentration in Psychology from the University of Ottawa. She has been involved in work with prisoners serving life sentences in Ontario for many years. on a national level, she has advocated for the enforcement of human rights to those serving federal sentences in Canada through the office of MP Peter Mancini, NDP Justice Critic and Critic to the Solicitor General.

Laureen Snider is Professor of Sociology, Queen's University, Kingston, Ontario, Canada. Laureen has written and published widely on corporate crime, linking this with issues of concern to women, and the implications of mass media. She has been a pioneer in developing critical criminology in Canada, a regular contributor to national commissions concerning the regulation of corporate crime, and an invited scholar at numerous international conventions and visiting lectureships. Among other publications, she co-authored *Global Crime Connections* with Frank Pearce.

Steve Tombs is a Professor of Sociology in the Centre for Criminal Justice, Liverpool John Moores University. He has worked for a number years in the critical academic left in Britain and has a long-standing interest in the incidence, nature and regulation of corporate crime. His recent publications include *Corporate Crime* (Longman, 1999), with Gary Slapper and *Toxic Capitalism: Corporate Crime and the Chemical Industry,* (Ashgate, 1998, Canadian Scholars' Press, 1999), with Frank Pearce; he has recently completed co-editing a text, *Risk, Management and Society* (Kluwer-Nijhoff, 2000), with Eve Coles and Denis Smith. He is Chair of the Centre for Corporate Accountability.

Gordon West has taught and done research at a number of universities and has held various positions in political and community organizing in Toronto and Chicago. He has been a visiting lecturer, researcher and professor throughout Europe, the Americas, and the Pacific Rim. Some of his major publications include: *Childrens' Rights: Legal and Educational Issues, Young Offenders and the State: A Canadian Perspective on Delinquency,* and *Modernizacion: Un Desafio para la Educacion.* Gord works as a Research Associate at Rittenhouse and is presently editor of *Justritt News* (http://www.interlog.com/~ritten) for ICOPA and Rittenhouse.

Also of Interest from Canadian Scholars' Press

Test of Faith: Hope, Courage and the Prison Experience
By Eva Evelyn Hanks

Test of Faith is one in the series of Canadian Scholar's Press Justice books. It offers a unique perspective on prison life seen predominantly from the view of the wife of an inmate—but also from the views of her husband, other inmates and guards, as well as mainstream society. In this startling insider's view Eva Evelyn Hanks walks us through the difficult years between her husband's incarceration for bank robbery to his release from prison. Through her eyes we learn about the arbitrary and cruel nature of the penitentiary system.

$19.95   Paperback   6x9   ISBN 1-55130-176-8   Published May 2000

Stories of Transformative Justice
By Ruth Morris

Ruth Morris is one of the world's leading spokespersons on penal abolition and transformative justice. In this book, she outlines why the current adversarial system of justice fails victims, offenders, their families and ultimately society as a whole. Citing stories from Canada, the U.S., New Zealand, Australia, and around the world, Morris demonstrates that there is another path to follow that would transform misery victimization and punishment into new opportunities for healing and understanding. This is an inspirational work that proves that turning the other cheek unleashes the power of transformation.

$19.95   Paperback   6x9   ISBN 1-55130-174-1   Published May 2000

Penal Abolition: The Practical Choice
By Ruth Morris

Most people would agree that the criminal justice system does not satisfy our society's growing needs. Despite this dissatisfaction, the criminal justice system continues to grow into what is universally recognized as a failure. Morris believes that if society is to find its way out of this predicament, we must focus on these key questions: What's wrong with the system we have? Why is it still in place? What do we want instead? How do we get there? In a concise style this text answers these questions citing evidence and giving examples. This book is an excellent addition to the criminologist's library.

$14.95   Paperback   6x9   ISBN 1-55130-078-8   Published 1995